The American Surveillance State

"Few writers have done more than David Price to drag the secret history of America out of the shadows and into the clarifying light of public scrutiny. In a nation obsessed with secrets, the biggest and darkest secret of all is the one Price exposes here: the deviously surreptitious—and often illegal—lengths our own government has gone to surveil and disrupt the daily lives of its own citizens."
—Jeffrey St. Clair, editor at *CounterPunch* and author of
Born Under a Bad Sky

"Wielding a finely-honed anthropological perspective and armed only with the Freedom of Information Act, David Price has spent decades of meticulous research in uncovering the sordid and often absurd history of American political surveillance. Rather than Orwell's fictional tales of Big Brother, his book makes extensive use of the files compiled by the FBI and its legions of informers to show how the realities of governmental monitoring and harassment impacted on the lives of law-abiding women and men whose words and deeds were deemed to threaten dominant power structures in American society."
—Michael Seltzer, Professor Emeritus at Oslo
Metropolitan University, Norway

"U.S. intelligence agencies have expanded their grip to the point that now, as never before, millions of Americans accept surveillance as a normal part of everyday life. In this meticulously-researched book, David H. Price relentlessly dissects the history of the American surveillance state, from the Palmer Raids to the Snowden Files and beyond. Price's razor-sharp analysis exposes the malignant tissue connecting America's spy agencies to the forces of capital. Citizen-scholarship at its finest!"
—Roberto J. González, Professor and Chair of the
Anthropology Department at San José State University

T0015237

The American Surveillance State

How the U.S. Spies on Dissent

David H. Price

First published 2022 by Pluto Press
New Wing, Somerset House, Strand, London WC2R 1LA
and Pluto Press Inc.
1930 Village Center Circle, Ste. 3-384, Las Vegas, NV 89134

www.plutobooks.com

British Library Cataloguing in Publication Data
A catalogue record for this book is available from the British Library

ISBN 978 0 7453 4602 1   Hardback
ISBN 978 0 7453 4601 4   Paperback
ISBN 978 0 7453 4604 5   PDF
ISBN 978 0 7453 4603 8   EPUB

This book is printed on paper suitable for recycling and made from fully
managed and sustained forest sources. Logging, pulping and manufacturing processes are expected to conform to the environmental standards of the
country of origin.

Typeset by Stanford DTP Services, Northampton, England

Simultaneously printed in the United Kingdom and United States of America

Contents

Preface

This book documents the workings of the American surveillance state while examining how new forms of surveillance fit into a long history of American political surveillance. The U.S. government has long monitored and interfered with the freedom of thought and dissent—this history shows a great continuity that connects themes of political surveillance and oppression from the 1930s to the present. These forms of political oppression have always been a significantly underacknowledged function of the FBI.

Each chapter draws on government documents from the FBI and other agencies, released to me under the Freedom of Information Act, to examine impacts and trajectories of government surveillance on American society. The chapters in the book's four parts examine the form, functions, and outcomes of surveillance of individuals struggling to live free lives in a society whose secret police judged them and their ideas as threatening the public good; judgments rarely based on evidence of specific laws being violated, and frequently tied to the perceived threats these dissidents presented to the rich and powerful. In many instances, this "public good" the FBI claimed was threatened were the private economic interests of elites profiting from the stratified system threatened by these individuals. *The American Surveillance State* explores how the FBI, NSA, and CIA's political judgments have limited intellectual debates in American society. I use an anthropological lens to connect these surveillance campaigns with the latent and manifest features of the larger culture in which they were embedded, while critically examining how these select uses of state power reveal connections between these manifestations of America's secret surveillance apparatus and larger forces of political economy.

The book's parts explore four elements of contemporary state surveillance systems. The first part provides an historical and theoretical context for understanding the development of centralized surveillance systems in the United States, with special focus on the public's long resistance to these intrusive developments, and on efforts to socialize this public into accepting previously unthinkable levels of surveillance. I consider both individuals (like J. Edgar Hoover) and agencies (CIA, FBI, NSA, etc.) birthing and supporting the surveillance state, but my primary focus remains the political economic structures within the American capitalist military industrial economy that nurture and profit from these limitations to freedom.

The second part analyzes a series of Cold War era FBI files documenting the FBI's routine spying on law-abiding citizens and organizations who threatened the institutions supporting American social, racial, and economic inequality. As a law enforcement agency disproportionately representing the interests of American elites, one of the FBI's historical functions has been to monitor, harass, and police deviant individuals who, while breaking no laws, publicly argue against social formations that empower a small group of elites and victimize the many who have little access to power. When these FBI investigations become publicly known, sometimes the stigma causes the subjects of these investigations to be lanted, or marked in ways making them less desirable to others.[1]

The book's third part uses the investigatory files of several outspoken divergent individuals to consider the forms of surveillance undertaken against them. These individuals include prominent public intellectuals, a journalist, a phone phreak, and a community organizer. While the political projects of these individuals were significantly different, the similarities of the FBI's campaigns of surveillance and harassment reveal common tactics in which the FBI's surveillance is shown to be state efforts to alter or suppress political activities of individuals threatening the status quo. That such campaigns were routine but hidden features of twentieth century American political life prefigures many of the themes now present in post-9/11 America and this continuity should heighten concerns with current expanded uses of surveillance.

The final part examines the FBI's files on two important twentieth century economists, Walt Rostow and André Gunder Frank, whose explanations of the distribution of global wealth and poverty dramatically clashed with each other. Rostow's Modernization Theory claimed that development programs from the North would transform the global South into rich nations, while Gunder Frank's Dependency Theory showed how programs such as those advocated by Rostow did not improve the economic fate of recipients, and increased debt and dependence. Yet, despite the differences in these political projects, their FBI files show Hoover's rampant paranoia drove intrusive investigations of both these intellectuals. Other chapters in this section document the FBI taking on roles policing global inequality, as it monitored anthropologist Angel Palerm at the Organization of American States, and Saul Landau's work in Cuba and Latin America.

The concluding chapter considers what these case studies reveal about the deep contours of the American surveillance state, and it reflects on how these contours connect with rapidly changing new developments in means of electronic surveillance capabilities within America's changing political landscape. The details of these past examples of the American surveillance state's targeting progressive activists and public intellectuals for surveillance operations provide the historical depth necessary to contextualize past, present, and future surveillance operations.

Acknowledgments

Shorter versions of some of the chapters in this book were previously published. In most instances I have added newly released FOIA materials as well as expanded analysis. The initial versions of these chapters are listed as follows: Chapter 2, "Memory's Half-Life," *CounterPunch* 2013, 20(6): 10–14, and "Quand le peuple américain refusait qu'on espionne Al Capone: Avec l'affaire Snoden, les Estats-Unis accentuent leur derive sécuritaire," *Le Monde diplomatique* August 2013: 10–11; Chapter 3, "The New Surveillance Normal," *Monthly Review* 2014, 66(3): 43–53; a Spanish language version of the essay appearing in Chapter 4 was published as "El FBI y las ciencias sociales," *Historia anthropología y Fuentes Orales* 2005, 34(3): 29–46; Chapter 5 appeared as "Tribal Communism under Fire," *Journal of Northwest Anthropology* 2004, 38(1): 21–32; one section of Chapter 6 appeared in "Mark Zborowski in a World of Pain," *CounterPunch* July 1–31, 2011; Chapter 7, "Ruth First and the FBI's Historical Role of Enforcing Inequality," *CounterPunch* December 2015, 22(9): 10–14; Chapter 8, "Seymour Melman and the FBI's Monitoring of the Demilitarization Movement," *CounterPunch* June 1–15, 2009: 1–4; Chapter 9, "How the FBI Spied on Edward Said," *CounterPunch* December 1–15, 2005, 12(21): 1, 4–5; Chapter 10, "Inside Cockburn's FBI File: Snoops, Snitches and Secrets," *CounterPunch* January 2013, 20(1): 9–12; Chapter 12, "Blind Whistling Phreaks," *CounterPunch* March 16–31, 2008, 15(6): 1–3; Chapter 15, "Biosocial Factions of American Capitalism," *CounterPunch* September 2014, 21(8): 9–11; Chapter 17, "André Gunder Frank, the FBI, and the Bureaucratic Exile of a Critical Mind," *CounterPunch* 1 June 16–30, 2007, 4(12): 1–4; Chapter 19, "Portrait of the Radical as a Young Man," *CounterPunch* January 2016, 22(10): 11–15.

Much of the writing and organizing of the book occurred during the Covid-19 pandemic, in Copalis Beach, on Washington's rainy Olympic Peninsula. This work benefited from the input of many people during the last three decades. Among those who assisted this work were: David Aberle, Perry Anderson, Thomas Anson, Julian Assange, Jeff Birkenstein, Robin Blackburn, Noam Chomsky, Alexander Cockburn, Andrew Cockburn, Patrick Cockburn, Eric Corley, Dale Depweg, Sigmund Diamond, André Gunder Frank, Irina Gendelman, Henry Giroux, Aaron Goings, Usama Goldsmith, Roberto Gonzalez, Becky Grant, Heather Grob, Marvin Harris, Bob Harvie, Janice Harper, Nora Jeffries, Andrea Kueter, Saul Landau, Herb Legg, Robert Lawless, Stephen X. Mead, Sidney Mintz, Laura Nader, Shawn Newman, Steve Niva, Valerie Park, David Patton, Bill Peace, Milo Price, Midge Price, Lisa Queen, Eric Ross, James Ridgeway, Mariam Said, Wadie Said, Jeffrey St. Clair, Eric Ross, Roger Snider, John Thorne, Cathy Wilson, and Dustin Zemel. Chapter 3's title "The New Surveillance Normal" is adapted from Catherine Lutz's excellent essay, "The Military Normal."

Abbreviations and Codenames

AAA	American Anthropological Association
AAAUG	Association of Arab-American University Graduates
ACLU	American Civil Liberties Union
ADEX	Administrative Index. Security Index (began in 1971) maintained by the FBI
ANC	African National Congress
BIA	Bureau of Indian Affairs
BOSS	South African Bureau for State Security
CIA	Central Intelligence Agency
COINTELPRO	Codename for the FBI's 1956–71 program attacking domestic leftist political groups and individuals.
CP	Communist Party
FBI	Federal Bureau of Investigation
FISA	Foreign Intelligence Surveillance Act
FOIA	Freedom of Information Act
HUAC	House Committee on Un-American Activities
ICE	U.S. Immigration and Customs Enforcement
INS	Immigration and Naturalization Service
IRA	Irish Republican Army
IRS	Internal Revenue Service
ISP	Internet Service Provider
IUEF	International University Exchange Fund
KGB	Soviet, Committee for State Security
KKK	Ku Klux Klan
LHM	Letterhead Memorandum, memo identified as coming from the FBI
LYL	Labor Youth League
MPTB	U.S. Motion Picture and Theatrical Branch
NAA	National Anthropological Archives, Smithsonian Institution

NAACP	National Association for the Advancement of Colored People
NARA	National Archives and Records Administration
NCASP	National Council of Arts Sciences and Professions
NLG	National Lawyers Guild
NSA	National Security Agency
NSC	National Security Council
OAS	Organization of American States
OWI	Office of War Information
PAC	Palestine American Congress
PAU	Pan American Union
PETA	People for the Ethical Treatment of Animals
PFLP	Popular Front for the Liberation of Palestine
PLO	Palestinian Liberation Organization
PRISM	Codename for NSA program collecting internet information from internet service providers
SAC	Special Agent in Charge (FBI)
SADEX	South Africa Development Information/ Documentation Exchange
SANE	Committee for the Sane Nuclear Policy
SBT&T	Southern Bell Telephone and Telegraph Company
SDS	Students for a Democratic Society
SWP	Socialist Workers Party
UNESCO	United Nations Educational, Scientific and Cultural Organization
USA PATRIOT Act	Uniting and Strengthening America by Providing Appropriate Tools Required to Intercept and Obstruct Terrorism
USAID	United States Agency for International Development
USDS	United States Department of State
USSR	Union of Soviet Socialist Republics
WEA	Washington Education Association

Introduction: Contextualizing Old Patterns and New Shifts in American Surveillance

Throughout the last quarter century, I have used the Freedom of Information Act (FOIA) to declassify tens of thousands of pages of government documents held by the U.S. Federal Bureau of Investigation (FBI), Central Intelligence Agency (CIA), National Security Agency (NSA), State Department, Office of Strategic Services and other government agencies. When I began this research, I was trying to learn more about anthropologists' contributions to the Second World War and Cold War, but as records were slowly released I became increasingly interested in other aspects of these agencies' surveillance of other Americans. This research led to the release of several hundreds of FOIA documents on interactions between anthropologists and intelligence agencies, on the impacts of McCarthyism on the development of American anthropology, on anthropological contributions to the Second World War, and anthropological Cold War and terror war collaborations with the CIA and Pentagon.[1] Over time, my interest broadened to studying the impacts of FBI surveillance of public intellectuals and others challenging the circumscription of free thought in American society at large. FOIA was an invaluable tool in pursing these endeavors, and *The American Surveillance State* uses FOIA released documents to examine how surveillance culture has shaped and limited American discourse and democratic movements challenging American power structures.

Florian Henckel von Donnersmarck's 2006 film, *The Lives of Others*, explores how the process of surveillance impacts the watchers, as Stasi agents' lives are transformed by their spent time spying on East German dissidents. The act of entering the private spheres of these dissidents transforms these watchers as they come to understand their political positions from others' perspectives. During my decades of FOIA work, I looked for clues in FBI files suggesting similar transformations among the FBI or CIA's watchers, but found few relics indicating such transformations, yet my own engagement with this historical research changed me; it changed my understanding of state surveillance systems, of the citizenry subjected to this scrutiny, and heightened my understanding of how limited American freedoms are. In some ways reading these declassified files radicalized me. Anthropologists have long recognized a natural tendency for researchers to come to identify with those they study. When we spend extended periods of time in towns, cities, villages, and communities, anthropologists frequently come to empathetically appreciate the hopes, dreams, and values of the people we live with. Two and a half decades of historical research on FBI surveillance of dissident anthropologists and public intellectuals of the mid-twentieth century changed my reactions to these invasive surveillance campaigns, most generally in ways increasing my own sympathetic alignments with those subjected to these state intrusions. This work gave me a sober appreciation of the dangers Americans faced with the Bush administration's terror war and the Obama, Trump, and Biden administrations expansions of secrecy and dogged persecution of whistleblowers. What I learned from studying the FBI's attacks on anthropologist activists for racial equality during the 1940s and 1950s, and the other later activist scholars whose files are examined here, radicalized my analysis and my own politics; and it taught me the dangers of silence. What I learned about the workings of the National Security State elevated my concerns of the threats this apparatus presents to the privacy necessary for the fostering of democratic ways of life.

THE STATE OF SURVEILLANCE IN THE AMERICAN SURVEILLANCE STATE

Anthropologists studying states have at times focused on cultural notions of surveillance, whether in classical models of cultural evolutionary theory focusing on taxation systems needed for monitoring and control, or more postmodern approaches drawing on notions of panopticons and biopower. Elements of state surveillance are as old as the state itself because states are built not on some imagined Hobbesian bargain of shared gains, but upon the coercion and threats of armed bullies wielding force on the masses they subsume. In the 1950s, Karl Wittfogel's work on despotic, ancient central state irrigation systems directed anthropological attentions to the totalitarian tendencies of state systems capable of monitoring, corralling, and controlling circumscribed populations to construct and manage massive irrigation works. James Scott explored how states demand legibility, and modern states incorporate surveillance as tools of control. State legibility measures are linked to schemes of taxation, regulating commerce, and quelling resistance.[2] Nation states try to socialize citizens to accept forms of surveillance and identity standardization as necessary components of the socially constructed notions of "freedom," as these measures reduce the freedoms these states claim to preserve.

As social formations, all national intelligence agencies share some basic characteristics. Modern states share similar needs they hope surveillance can fulfill. While states' divergent ideological commitments to markets or collectivism, or professed values of individual liberties and privacy may vary in deeply significant ways between nations, there are shared commonalities of state surveillance systems when monitoring identified "enemy" or "potential threats" within a domestic population. The intelligence needs of Stasi, FBI, CIA, KGB, Mossad, M15, M16, NSA, CONTROL, or SAVAK share similar patterns, as do the basic means of electronic and human intelligence. While the size, scale, and informer base of Stasi sets it apart from the tactics of the FBI during the Red Scare of the 1950s, in some anthropological sense these differences in tactics or scale, while rendering them unique specimens of surveillance culture, do not mark them as being wholly unique.

I have toured the KGB's official museum in Moscow and the FBI's museum at their headquarters in Washington, DC and found each presented sanitized Disneyfied historical accounts of their operations and glories. Each intelligence agency presented differing narratives, and each misled their audience in unique and similar ways—ways that erased references to their own atrocities, while gloating about successful missions performed against enemies, complete with captured trophies taken from enemy spies and ridiculously elaborate gear that seemed to come out of a Bond film or a *Mad Magazine* Spy vs Spy cartoon panel. While differences of scale and atrocity exist, these agencies' institutional approaches to problems of individual and mass surveillance shared similarities. Of course, the Soviet excesses, from Pavlik Morozov, denunciations, public mood reports, and disappearances were of another order of magnitude of betrayal than those practiced in the United States,[3] the motifs, ploys, and theatrics shared many familiar properties with American Cold War practices. McCarthy's show trials may not have led their victims to a vast geography of gulags, but they shattered lives and isolated victims in other ways.

All states face tremendous bureaucratic problems when monitoring and tracking ideologies of dissent. The problems associated with creating post hoc cross-indexes for massive databases in the pre-computer age vexed military and intelligence agencies around the world. Devising ways of quickly retrieving and analyzing data in meaningful ways shaped the functioning of various civilian and military intelligence agencies. During the Cold War, America developed different cataloging systems in their internal (FBI) and external (CIA, NSA) intelligence agencies, though both achieved similar ends. The Soviet Union's KGB, and East German Stasi developed complex cross-referenced indexing systems linking individual files and reports from different agencies. In her book *Stasiland*, Anna Funder's interviews with former Stasi agents compiles stories of ruthless state surveillance, where the state went to absurd lengths gathering information and artifacts (underwear stolen and stored in jars so tracking dogs could follow the scent if needed at some future date).[4] Such blind collecting for unknown future possible uses is a practice commonly fetichized by surveillance states. During the early Cold War, under the CIA secret "Graphic Register" program, the Agency curated a massive collection of somewhat random photographs collected by Agency employees during vacations and other travels, collected for unknown imagined future use.[5] Such desire to collect objects and information for unknown future uses runs deep within all state intelligence agencies; and these collections forced innovations in the development of organizing the retrieval systems. During the Cold War, the British intelligence service MI5 made impressions of, then meticulously catalogued and kept copies of every residential and office key its agents encountered, just in case at some unknown future date they might need to surreptitiously enter a building.[6] In the United States, during the 1930s FBI Director J. Edgar Hoover invented an ingenious cross-indexed record system allowing the Bureau to index individuals and organizations mentioned in FBI files, and to connect these references to information in files held in cabinets in field offices across the country. Hoover's filing system had roots in his years spent working his way through law school at the U.S. Library of Congress.[7]

These intelligence agencies' obsessive-blind-collection-drives reveal traces of a seldom bluntly stated "duty" these agencies apparently feel to try and become—as Norman Mailer claimed, the "mind of America."[8] As if the massive collection of unconnected objects itself could provide answers to questions that no one had yet asked, or even more absurd, that this "mind" could emerge through a nearly aimless process of this particularist collecting project. Such blind conceits helped rationalize outrageous invasions of privacy from the early twentieth century to the more contemporary invasive NSA and CIA monitoring programs revealed by Edward Snowden.

It was the compilation and collection of information, co-mixing truth and rumor to form dossiers that empowered Hoover and FBI in mid-twentieth century America. These dossiers mixed hearsay with Better Business Bureau credit reports, employment records and interviews to concoct narratives that took on lives of their own. As Don DeLillo observed of these emerging dossiers,

in the endless estuarial mingling of paranoia and control, the dossier was an essential device ... The dossier was a deeper form of truth, transcending facts and actuality. The second you placed an item in the file, a fuzzy photograph, and unfounded rumor, it became promiscuously true. It was a truth without authority and therefore incontestable.[9]

Through such processes, the "truth" of the file became a powerful force. It mattered little that this "truth" was frequently based on lies and agents' sloppy work, it became a force changing lives simply because of the power of the dossier. Insofar as things like FBI files exist as secret, classified, objects, there is little chance that the errors and half-truths within these files will be corrected. In most cases a process of reification passing as verification occurs as file details are recirculated in new file entries even though a recirculated detail may have no basis in fact; yet this detail's reality seems to be confirmed though endless processes of recirculation in new reports.

It is important to understand that the reason why surveillance is so problematic isn't because it doesn't work. Surveillance often does work, but it is so reprehensible because it works by violating basic trusts. It can be a very effective way to find out what people are really thinking, especially in guarded situations. In public settings where observers are obvious, people are more guarded in what they say, doubly so if they know their remarks are being recorded. There is a profound moment illustrating this in Peter Jackson's 2021 documentary *Get Back*, where viewers have watched hours of footage showing the Beatles' dysfunctional dynamics, aggressive, passive aggressive, and unacknowledged hostility recorded by the ever-present documentary crew. At one point Lennon and McCartney forbid the film crew to follow them to a cafeteria, where unbeknownst to them their conversation was secretly recorded by a microphone hidden in a flower arrangement. In just a few minutes of dialogue, the audience hears a frank exchange between John Lennon and Paul McCartney laying bare dynamics hidden from view. These two minutes of surveillance tape shed more light on what's happening than the previous three hours of film. And while the film does not explore the costs of such invasions of privacy, and we the viewers are seduced by access to this private moment of a certain type of truth, there is a prurient sickness in such spying—albeit, an attractive sickness, and it is this attractiveness that exposes the dangerous alure of surveillance. This alure is the common currency of state surveillance systems.[10]

George Orwell's vision of totalitarian states' oppressive centralized governments correctly described but one part of the coming modes of surveillance. Orwell's postwar historical vantage point revealed a coming rise of oppressive state power, but he missed concurrent developments in the ascendency of corporate power that would develop similar modes of panoptical monitoring and profiling. Orwell did not foresee the central roles that corporations would play, as they would be vested with human rights, and once harnessed to the power of computers these corporations would be given full access to our private reading habits, political discourse, consumption patterns, physical movements, online lives and even our private electronic communications. Our world became one where the public is monitored to gain assurances that we live and think within parameters of a certain, yet shifting, matrix of orthodoxy.

Growing up in the United States during the 1960s, I learned Cold War horror stories focusing on the oppressive nature of Soviet life. These stories often focused on features of daily Soviet routines, illustrating the totalitarian nature of life under centralized communist rule in very effective ways, making me and classmates thankful we did not live in a world where both parents worked at jobs requiring them to leave their children during the workday at (state-subsidized) childcare centers where, we were told, an army of Grandmothers watched them, or state surveillance systems monitored the phone conversations and tracked the networks of associations used by its citizens. We were told of Soviet dissidents monitored by the centralized state, reporters arrested for documenting state abuses, intellectuals espousing unpopular views faced difficulties finding proper employment or were fired from teaching positions. Dissidents' names appeared on lists maintained by secretive policing agencies that limited their abilities to easily travel; there were secret prisons, and those detained were denied forms of due process common in Western law since the Magna Carta. Forms of torture and punishment produced confessions from enemies of the state.

The many convergences between what was once comfortably identified as totalitarian monitoring and controlling of citizens, and the now routine practices by corporations and the American government are striking. There are obviously important differences between the Soviet's state surveillance apparatus and America's post-9/11 surveillance methods, yet it is striking not only to find some general parallel developments, but also how rapidly the American public so easily adapted to accept new forms of surveillance and denial of due process. While accepting some basic forms of monitoring and surveillance, Americans also have deep cultural roots fostering attitudes of suspicion of state or federal systems monitoring American citizens. A generation ago, significant numbers of Americans resisted basic efforts to use Social Security Numbers as universal markers for federal, state, or corporate databases. But with dogged efforts by governmental and corporate forces, the American public was coaxed to accept ongoing surveillance and monitoring at a level that would have been unthinkable two decades earlier. Technological enticements coupled with the fear campaigns of post-9/11 America ushered in new levels of surveillance acceptance. One result of this is that I now routinely encounter smart, well-adapted college students in my classes who comfortably embrace Orwellian arguments, claiming that if the government didn't undertake massive surveillance under programs such as the NSA's PRISM program, their own rights to safety and privacy would be violated by those opposing these programs. The surveillance state feeds on itself. Its hunger knows no limits, and assumptions that this hunger serves the public good become an unstated premise of contemporary electronic life in America.

But even while the American surveillance state appears to now be growing at exponential rates, increasing surveillance need not necessarily be our future. History provides examples of surveillance states being dismantled or curtailed, and their collected materials made public. One example is found in the 600 million pages of Stasi files made public (albeit, these documents were released in a largely disarticulated, unindexed difficult to use form) after the collapse of the German Democratic Republic. In postwar Europe, some regions that had been occupied by the Nazis, such as the Netherlands, revised their telephone billing systems so that specific numbers dialed could no long be identified in the billing process. Though such events are historically rare and tend to mark the end of regimes. Twentieth century America had its own short-lived but real revolutionary moments of relative transparency and accounting marking brief regime shifts. One such moment occurred during the mid-1970s as the world glimpsed a brief post-Watergate view inside the machinations of CIA and FBI secrecy as the Church and Pike Committees revealed shocking FBI and CIA practices.[11] During this period the Freedom of Information Act had a moment of forceful power before the Reagan administration again weakened FOIA's power, as did most of the presidents who followed. As Otto Kirchheimer observed over half a century ago, "one might nearly be tempted to define a revolution by the willingness of the regime to open the archives of its predecessor's political police. Measured by this yard-stick, few revolutions have taken place in modern history."[12]

While technologies of surveillance and the American public's acceptance of surveillance significantly changed during the last several decades, there are thematic continuities connecting governmental campaigns targeting activists and other deviants challenging features of American capital that connect past and present.[13] During recent years, the FBI investigated members of the Occupy Movement, at times searching homes or harassing protestors and organizers.[14] This followed the old established pattern of American political surveillance: with increased domestic critiques of capitalism's failures came increased domestic surveillance under absurd claims of terrorist investigations, with broad reductions of civil rights as the FBI reprises its role from the days of J. Edgar Hoover: monitoring, infiltrating, and harassing legal, domestic, democratic movements threatening the economic interests of American elites.

HOOVER'S FBI AND THE INSTITUTIONALIZATION OF SURVEILLANCE

The creation of something like J. Edgar Hoover's FBI, and the abusive history of surveillance that he spawned, was an inevitable development of twentieth century capitalism; regardless of whether Hoover, very much the architect of the system, ever existed. Anthropologist Leslie White's (1900–75) determinist theory of culture described culture as something external to our wills and power to control. White's version of cultural determinism all but eliminated the possibility of individual agency; essentially relegating the possibility of individual's impacting change to issues of timing. He identified cultural forces and external conditions setting the stage on which individuals performed roles provided to them by historical forces. White rejected notions that history was the product of Great [wo]Men, insisting that history's prominent individuals merely embodied the nexus of converging historical forces.[15] If we play with White's deterministic vision of culture, we can see J. Edgar Hoover's rise to unchecked power at the FBI not simply as the obsessive persecutions of a solitary man directing a powerful government agency with little oversight, but as structural responses to the needs of an invasive bureaucratic capitalist system—a system devoted to protecting the inherent inequalities of Capital and the American political economic system on which it rested.

While it might be tempting to blame the development of much of the FBI's long history of violations of civil liberties, anti-communist hysteria, racist practices, and suppression of democratic peoples' movements simply on the many personal shortcomings of longtime FBI director, J. Edgar Hoover, following a Whiteian view of culture we can see Hoover as effectively fulfilling a significant predetermined need of American capitalism. While Hoover's personal shortcomings made him comfortable with using the FBI for such tasks, the structural forces favoring the creation of the surveillance network he established at the FBI had a greater significance on the establishment of these practices than his personal quirks. Certainly, Hoover's personality and unchecked power aligned in ways that made him an ideal person for the job. It seems fair to assume that a less ruthless and less megalomaniacal individual, or one more concerned with civil liberties, would not have maintained the Directorship for nearly half a century, but if we consider the cultural forces at work during this period of capitalism's Cold War America, I can easily imagine that the system itself would have evolved in much the same way had Hoover never been born. While Hoover planted and nurtured the roots of the modern American surveillance state, I assume it would have developed in some form had he never directed the FBI. To be sure, Hoover had unusual dark talents that made him well suited for this job, but the nature of this job was shaped by the political economy in which it was embedded and whose interests the Bureau served, far more than it was shaped by the oppressive habits of this unusual man.

Right or wrong, such a pseudo-essentialist vision of the FBI's history, insisting the Bureau's dark history flowed as it did for reasons beyond the will of Hoover or any other individuals, can help us consider the Bureau functioning as a particular sort of arm (and ear) of American capital. After his years running agents abroad as a CIA officer, Philip Agee came to understand that his own role in the Agency had been something like this when he declared that the CIA functioned as the "secret police of American capitalism, plugging up leaks in the political dam night and day so that shareholders of U.S. companies operating in poor countries can continue enjoying the rip-off."[16] While the CIA polices American capital interests abroad, the FBI's jurisdiction remains primarily domestic, both serving the same shareholders.

Just as the FBI's penchant for policing the private political beliefs and practices of others cannot be reduced to Hoover-the-man, the last two decades' expansion of America's domestic surveillance apparatus cannot be reduced to the attacks of 9/11. The PATRIOT Act did not so much bring wholly new forms of monitoring the private lives of Americans as it brought bold new methods and approaches to the old sort of deviant hunting techniques preferred by J. Edgar Hoover in the mid-twentieth century. We can find historical continuity of themes if we substitute the word "terrorist" for "communist" and update the technology of surveillance to the computer age. There are continuities of basic themes of the propagation of fear, and acquiescence to the state's desires to monitor, assess, and control reemerged after 9/11, with not only the FBI, but the CIA (which was suddenly authorized by the PATRIOT Act to engage in domestic surveillance and to infiltrate legal domestic political groups) Homeland Security, and other intelligence agencies.

Forty-five days after the 9/11 terror attacks, Congress adopted Public Law 107-56, titled the United and Strengthening America by Providing Appropriate Tools Required to Intercept and Obstruct Terrorism Act, better known under the acronym: USA PATRIOT Act. As America's leaders panicked, there was no public discussion of who the authors were of this complex 132-page legislative passkey for intelligence agencies; and there were no real debates over its impact on expectations of privacy in America. The USA PATRIOT Act removed limitations on the FBI and police departments' abilities to conduct surveillance operations on domestic political groups, and it expanded the abilities of the CIA to work with domestic investigatory operations. The USA PATRIOT Act opened the door for broad forms of domestic electronic surveillance of American citizens. It invited the FBI back into American libraries, and librarians and their professional associations did little to directly obstruct the FBI's access to patron's private records. The USA PATRIOT Act's Section 215 required American bookstores and libraries to surrender to the FBI lists of books or other materials that customers or patrons accessed. Libraries were soon instructed under order of law to not disclose the FBI's presence or interest in the reading habits of particular patrons. Alerting patrons, or the public of the occurrence of an FBI library visit brought threats of arrest. Some libraries initially adopted a policy of hanging signs in library entry ways declaring "The FBI has not visited here today," with assumptions that these signs would be removed upon an FBI visit. But the socialization processes desensitizing Americans to the new normalities of surveillance culture were ongoing, and with time these warning signs disappeared from protesting libraries as Americans became absorbed into the new surveillance normal; these removals marked American public libraries' acquiescence to our new world where we are always half-aware of any transaction that might be monitored as part of the new surveillance normal.

This underacknowledged omnipresence of government and corporate surveillance, or sometimes even just the *possibility* of being monitored has become a background feature of our lives today. That this remains largely underacknowledged on a daily basis even after Edward Snowden's revelations, or the daily bombardments of highly personalized ads greeting us as we log onto the web, is a monument to how normalized our surrender has become. It now goes without saying that anything we say, do, purchase, search for, contemplate, or aspire to become *could* be tracked and added to some record in the clouds—a status of profane phenomena that just a few generations ago could only be interpreted within the context of the sacred.

While the presence of such monitoring technologies is well known, even assumed, today, what is missing from popular understanding of this world is how governmental agencies have recurrently used surveillance data to monitor, harass, and criminalize

American radicals and progressives advocating for economic or social changes challenging core features of American capitalism. This book provides some historical context for understanding the growth and trajectory of the American surveillance state, and the case studies that follow provide historical context to understand how the FBI, CIA, and other U.S. agencies have historically viewed progressives as dangerous threats to society.

Because those who try to predict the future are generally doomed to failure, I don't pretend to know exactly what developments come next with American surveillance; but I do know it is vital to understand how we got to the present and what this past suggests about our current and coming predicaments. The long trajectory of political surveillance of progressive activists deserves our attention if we are at least going to make sense of how we got here, who is watching, why they watched in the past, and what they did with their catch. While the particulars of a future yet to be woven are necessarily unknown, so long as America's future is embedded in capitalism—even with unimaginable forms of yet to be realized surveillance—I assume the critics of this system will be targeted in ways that thematically connect to those discussed in these pages.

PART I

The Long View: Historical Perspectives of American Surveillance

The evils of Stalinism did not guarantee a corresponding virtue in one's own country.

—Jason Epstein (1967: 18)

1

J. Edgar Hoover and the FBI's Institutionalization of Surveillance[1]

J. Edgar Hoover was a uniquely American creature at the heart of the development of the American state surveillance system. That someone *like* J. Edgar Hoover came to dominate the American state for so much of the twentieth century was no accident. The power of state systems releases monstrous potentials within humans, and state concentrations of power allow some individuals to grow in power and impact. The managerial requirements of states allow for the development of a certain centralized ruthlessness and "order" is maintained only through violence, threats of violence and hegemonic control over the populous' values. States evolve bureaucracies of control with varying degrees of brutality, but the evolution of a sprawling nation state the size and scope of the twentieth century United States, with such disparities between the rich and poor necessitated the creation of some*thing* like an FBI to maintain these inequities. Given the economic, demographic, and technological realities of twentieth century American capitalism, a creature like J. Edgar Hoover was an inevitable creation.

Hoover's selective incompetence as a lawman was remarkable. One need look no further than his inability to identify and convict significant numbers of actual Soviet spies working in the United States during the Cold War—even as thousands of progressive American activists were monitored and harassed by Hoover's FBI because they fought mid-century American racial, economic, and gender discrimination. Hoover refused to acknowledge the existence of the Mafia until the 1960s, and throughout much of his career he turned a blind eye to endemic levels of corporate-based organized crime, anti-labor racketeering, unchecked police corruption and violence, price fixing operations, Sherman law anti-trust violations, and lynchings. For Hoover, these and other issues not adversely affecting America's corporate ruling class were not of an importance worthy of FBI investigations.

Someone more psychologically inclined might search for the roots of Hoover's trajectory in his childhood (and no doubt his sycophantic relationship with his domineering mother would reveal many valuable pearls) but as an anthropologist, I find much more interesting his genesis in the cultural institutions which birthed him. Hoover's first flickers of monstrosity developed as he persecuted the foreign born during his First World War service on the Alien Enemy Bureau, but after the war he came of age assisting Attorney General A. Mitchell Palmer.[2] When Theodore Roosevelt's Attorney General Charles Bonaparte created the Bureau of Investigation in 1908, it was originally only empowered to investigate violations of interstate commerce and anti-trust laws, but the First World War transformed the Bureau into a covert arm of the presidency that persecuted political radicals opposing the war. This sort of expansion of surveillance powers claimed necessary during wartime, then never fully relinquished after armistice, would become a familiar dance step of the American surveillance state, connecting the past to our present age. After the war Attorney General Mitchell "the Fighting Quaker" Palmer and his Special Assistant at the Bureau of Investigation, 24-year-old John Edgar Hoover demonstrated the true potential of the FBI as a tool of political oppression by combing the stacks at the Library of Congress (where Hoover had worked from 1913–17) to compile a massive index of left-wing political subversives—in this massive effort to detect thought crimes, Hoover oversaw the indexing of half a million names of American radicals.[3] Hoover understood the power of lists, and his talents in tracking and indexing growing numbers of individuals formed the needed skeleton of America's growing surveillance state.

Between 1918 and 1921 Palmer and Hoover orchestrated an aggressive campaign to demolish American socialist, communist, and anarchist movements. In November 1919, Palmer and Hoover oversaw the arrest of 10,000 domestic and foreign-born radicals in a campaign culminating in the deportation of Emma Goldman and 247 other radicals. The January 2nd, 1920 Palmer Raids led to the arrest of another 6,000 individuals, held for extended periods under vague national security claims. Palmer's tutelage of Hoover during this period established the direction of J. Edgar's life work. From Palmer he learned techniques of thought-crime investigations, and he learned that state-directed political attacks could effectively subvert popular political and labor movements threatening the interests of elites.

With time the Bureau strayed from the easy pickings of terrorizing individuals and groups with little power, and after it was caught illegally spying on President Harding's Congressional critics (who had roasted Harding with the Teapot Dome Scandal) the Bureau needed a bureaucratic facelift. In 1924 the Federal Bureau of Investigation was born, Palmer was purged and his minion, Hoover, was installed as Director—a post he maintained until his death almost half a century later. Congress was assured that it would have oversight over this new branch of the secretive federal police and Hoover cultivated a straight-arrow clean-cut image that testified to the goodness of the Bureau's men and purpose.

The private Hoover hid behind a secret identity—he underwent transformations whenever he stepped beyond the carefully cropped public view and was transformed from the straight, smiling, firm, upholder of law and order into a vindictive blackmailing thug who was judge, jury, and moral standard while closeting his own gambling addiction and sexual identity. This hidden, purulent Hoover was a vindictive bureaucrat who used others as tools to wreak havoc on the lives of those who threatened *his* America.[4]

Hoover fed on secrecy. He fetishized this hunger with the endless creation of lists and secret files filled with private details to be scurrilously used as needed at some later date. Hoover created the world's most comprehensive pre-computer era cross-listed filing system profiling millions of Americans. The FBI pooled information from informers ranging from criminals-in-a-pinch, to ideologue members of the American Legion and other reactionary citizen groups who mailed-in informer-reports based on their suspicions of coworkers, neighbors, or fellow citizens, clipped letters to the editors of local newspapers or reported free-floating suspicions of local citizens who did not fit a Legionnaire's right-wing notions of political propriety. Yet even though this FBI program was widespread, its value was less in the actual information it produced than in the extension of fear, paranoia, and surveillance that allowed the FBI to spread beyond its institutional limits. As Athan Theoharis observed, "by nonbureaucratic standards, the American Legion Contact Program was never cost effective, and it detracted from the ability of FBI field offices to fulfill their law enforcement responsibilities. Yet law enforcement had never been as high a priority to FBI officials as extending the surveillance of dissident activities nationwide."[5]

When conducting routine government employee background investigations, Hoover's agents collected and catalogued whatever gossip that came to its attention for possible future use. Sometimes Hoover shared this information with U.S. presidents who could use these tidbits for their own purposes; at other times he used his files to protect himself against presidents trying to limit his power. For years, Hoover worked with Ruth Shipley, perhaps the most powerful American woman of the mid-twentieth century, who directed the U.S. Department of State's Passport Division between 1928 and 1955, at times personally deciding which Americans would or would not be issued passports and tracking the international activities of certain Americans abroad.

When it came to suspicions of secret communists, the institutional paranoia of Hoover's FBI had few limits. In 1942, the FBI suspected that American poet William Carlos Williams might be a communist using his poetry as a means of passing on encrypted messages to fellow communists at unknown locations. One FBI memo

recommended that William Carlos Williams be temporarily watched because an informant had turned in "seventeen sheets bearing typewriting of a suspicious nature." An agent believed that some of William's poems might be a clandestine code, commenting that "they appear to have been written by a person who is very queer or possibly a mental case." In ordering an investigation of the poet, the Bureau advised that it should be "conducted in such a manner as to avoid embarrassment for the informant," probably an employee in Dr. William's medical offices.[6]

After five months of spying on Dr. Williams at work and elsewhere, the FBI concluded that he was nothing more than a poet writing in a voice that the FBI found difficult to comprehend; as if America's national security might somehow depend on the color of Williams' wheel barrow glazed with rain water.

Hoover was an enshrined protector of the status quo, and in stratified mid-twentieth century America, this meant that he worked to protect industry and state, at least as much as he did for the American people. Pick a trait representing the inequalities of twentieth century American life and in most cases, Hoover's FBI was protecting those representing this trait against the actions of "deviant" individuals or groups seeking social change favoring greater equality. Those struggling for wage, housing, banking, educational, or racial equality routinely became FBI surveillance and harassment targets.

Hoover exploited American fears of communism with great skill. He was a gifted spin doctor, running the most sophisticated secretive intelligence agency on earth with no meaningful oversight. He bolstered public narratives insisting that individual Americans joining the Communist Party, regardless of personal actions and motivations, were part of larger global conspiracy undermining both capitalism and *democracy*—as if economic systems and political systems were one and the same.

Hoover was a showman with pretty good timing. He knew how to exploit public fears and how to spin a bit of luck into a tale of a well-laid plan. Early on he established the FBI's famous "Most Wanted" list as a way of cooking the books by moving names to the top of the list right before agents made arrests. He staged the arrests of celebrity criminals, like Louis "Lepke" Buchalter of "Murder Incorporated." With the help of journalists like Walter Winchell he publicly played out these captures as if they were circus parades.[7] He took credit (and royalties) for the writings of others. The public was impressed by his book *Masters of Deceit*, but those inside the FBI knew he never wrote the articles and books bearing his name—as William Sullivan remarked, he and his fellow agents within the Bureau "used to joke in the bureau, '*Masters of Deceit*, written by the Master of Deceit who never even read it.'"[8] Agents were forced to hawk his books, and those with good sales received pay bonuses. FBI Agent M. Wesley Swearingen later wrote that he "was mad as hell that Hoover had taken all the credit and that he received royalties on the book, which was a violation of federal law, while I had written parts on Claude Lightfoot and Alfred Wagenknecht."[9] Hoover carefully controlled his public image by limiting the photographs of him appearing in print—preferring serious crime fighting no-nonsense shots and rumor squelching shots with beautiful celebrity women like Dorothy Lamour, while prohibiting the publication of pictures showing him gambling or drinking.[10] He controlled public access to his own secrets just as he collected the secrets of others.

Some historians like Athan Theoharis insist that Hoover's homosexuality or cross-dressing remains an open question, while many of J. Edgar's acquaintances were certain he was gay. Hoover's sexual orientation is open to speculation, though his decades of secretly living with his longtime devoted companion Clyde Tolson establishes a life of same sex companionship.[11] Hoover's possible homosexuality has significance because Hoover the blackmailer long plied proof of the closeted homosexuality of others for his own ends. As FBI Director, Hoover compiled an "investigatory" pornography collection rivaled only by the Vatican. William Sullivan reported that an agent once rummaging through Hoover's desk found a stash of "lurid literature of the most filthy kind ... that dealt with all sorts of abnormal sexual activities."[12] While Hoover collected smut for his office files, his agents dutifully produced obsessively surreal reports on things like Adali Stevenson's visit to a Peruvian archaeological exhibit of pornographic Inca pottery in the national museum in Lima.[13]

In 2015, Christopher Elias published an essay on a strange 1933 article by Ray Tucker published in *Collier's* magazine, attacking the Bureau of Investigation, and mocking Hoover. In the article, Tucker wrote, "In appearance, Mr. Hoover looks utterly unlike the story-book sleuth. He is short, fat, businesslike, and walks with a mincing step ... He dresses fastidiously, with Eleanor blue as the favorite color for the matched shades of tie, handkerchief and socks."[14] *Collier's* focus on Hoover's "mincing step" and "Eleanor blue" (which, Elias explains "was actually more of a lavender, a shade which by 1933 had already become a euphemism for male homosexuals") wardrobe were unusual public references to his femininity. Such descriptions in the press would be unthinkable in later years as his personal abuse of power and vindictive tendencies became well known. Stories claiming Hoover dressed in women's clothing, or that Clyde Tolson was his gay lover have been broadly reported. Broadway star Ethel Merman knew Hoover and Tolson socially since 1936, and remained friends with them for decades. Anthony Summers wrote that

> in 1978, when a reporter asked [Ethel Merman] to comment on Anita Bryant, the anti-homosexual campaigner, Merman had an interesting reply. "Some of my best friends," "are homosexual. Everybody knew about J. Edgar Hoover, but he was the best chief the FBI ever had. A lot of people have always been homosexual. To each his own. They don't bother me."[15]

Regardless of the particulars of Hoover's sexuality, the institutional homophobia at Hoover's FBI was remarkable. Former FBI assistant director, William Sullivan wrote of a sensitive operation designed to protect a Soviet defector by renting an upper-middle-class home in a New York suburb. After a month of 24-hour FBI protection in this safe house, the neighbors in surrounding houses began to act oddly. One day, a neighbors beckoned for one of the agents to come over to an adjoining fence—the neighbor then pointed to another house and said, "see that house over there ... that man bought a rifle to protect his children." The FBI agent asked the neighbor what he was protecting his children from. The man replied, "From you three men ... from you homosexuals ... You live together, eat together, walk together. None of you is with anyone else. Not one of you this past month has had a date with a woman." The strains of FBI homophobia were so severe that Agent O'Toole blew his cover and showed the neighbor his FBI badge and told him all about the operation—national security concerns were secondary to maintaining a straight reputation.[16]

Because American democracy failed to limit Hoover's unchecked reign of the Bureau, Hoover's personal failures became national failures. Hoover's oversight of and involvement in the day-to-day activities of FBI agents was remarkable. After 1942, he instituted a policy requiring that he be consulted before agents performed black-bag operations. Theoharis noted that Hoover conceded that although

> break-ins were "clearly illegal," [he] was unwilling to "obtain any legal sanctions," and insisted on not seeking the approval of the attorney general or the president for these activities. Instead, Hoover simply required FBI agents to obtain his (or a designated FBI official's) advanced authorization beforehand, outlining the safeguards they would adopt to prevent discovery.[17]

Hoover's disregard for the law was mitigated by his and his agents' delusions that he and the FBI were above the law.

Hoover instituted bigoted hiring policies at the FBI that assured no Blacks, Jews, Catholics, or Hispanics were hired until the 1940s. William Sullivan noted that Hoover liked to brag that "there will never be a Negro Special Agent as long as I am Director of the FBI." For his luxurious Miami Beach vacations with his companion Clyde Tolson, he sought out hotels with signs declaring "No Jews, No Dogs." Even in the 1960s when Hoover begrudgingly allowed the FBI to hire some Jews, an attitude of anti-Semitism prevailed at the Bureau. Agent Jack Levine was shocked to learn in the 1960s that one of his FBI supervisors said that he saw "nothing subversive about the American Nazi Party, because 'all they are against is Jews.'"[18]

Hoover despised civil rights organizations and was convinced that campaigns championing racial equality were part of a grand communist conspiracy, and any group garnering his suspicions was targeted for surveillance. When Ralph Bunche became the first African-American to be awarded the Nobel Peace Prize, Hoover's FBI intensified their surveillance of him and his associates. Hoover's hatred of American civil rights leaders led him to use the FBI to conduct surveillance on prominent Black leaders like Malcolm X, Fred Hampton, Bobby Seale, and Martin Luther King. Under COINTELPRO Hoover moved from surveillance to harassment of these and other Civil Rights leaders. On November 21, 1964, soon after the announcement of his coming Nobel Peace

Prize, the FBI sent Martin Luther King an anonymous threatening letter in which they wrote,

> King, look into your heart. You know you are a complete fraud and a great liability to all of us Negroes. White people in this country have enough frauds of their own but I am sure they don't have one at this time that is anywhere near your equal. You are no clergyman and you know it. I repeat you are a colossal fraud and an evil, vicious one at that. You could not believe in God and act as you do. Clearly you don't believe in any personal moral principles.[19]

The FBI enclosed portions of a surveillance transcript indicating King's involvement in extramarital sexual affairs, and the letter closed with threats to King telling him his "filthy, abnormal fraudulent self [would be] bared to the nation" if he didn't withdraw from accepting the Nobel Peace Prize.

COINTELPRO's mission of spying on and undermining various leftist political organizations during the 1950s, 1960s, and 1970s damaged American democracy. It was America's most aggressive counterinsurgency program devoted to maintaining American inequality, and Hoover's use of illegal governmental intimidation championed right-wing racist ideology while weakening radical and progressive political movements. Between 1956 and 1971, the FBI conducted 2,370 COINTELPRO operations against Americans. These operations ranged from anonymous poison pen letters, surveillance and harassment operations, threatening letters and phone calls, interrupting public meetings and other disruptions of legal political processes.[20]

Hoover became such an important part of America's power structure that many were unprepared for the new landscape that emerged after his death in 1972. Reportedly, upon learning from H.R. Haldeman that J. Edgar Hoover had died, President Nixon preserved the solemn dignity of this moment by ejaculating: "Jesus Christ! That old cocksucker!"[21] Later that day, Nixon wrote in his diary that he was relieved Hover had died before he was forced to fire him later that year—a move that Hoover would have no doubt fought with his own files on Nixon. Two days later, Nixon politely eulogized Hoover at his funeral saying he'd been an "invincible and incorruptible defender of every American's precious right to be free from fear."[22] Nixon's relief at Hoover's death must have been reduced in the weeks and months to follow as the Watergate burglars bungled their break-in, and Nixon's White House botched the cover-up—this was just the sort of disaster that Hoover excelled at cleaning-up. It seems likely that had Hoover still been the FBI Director as the Watergate cancer enveloped Nixon's White House he would have preempted the investigation that took down Nixon. This seems especially likely when we consider that Woodward and Bernstein's primary source, Deep Throat, turned out to be former FBI Agent Mark Felt, who so resented being passed over for Hoover's job that he leaked details of Nixon's crimes not out of a sense of justice, but as classic Hooverian payback for not gaining the FBI promotion he believed he deserved.[23]

Hoover would never have allowed the public inspection of FBI agents like Alfred C. Baldwin and G. Gordon Liddy's involvement in Watergate. Hoover's death made it possible for one of his own rogue FBI agents to take down the Nixon White House by providing the press with the sort of leaks Hoover would never have tolerated. Watergate was just the sort of crisis that empowered Hoover over the decades and such crises were the cornerstone of his historical relationships with American presidents wherein he alternately threatened, bailed out and was then rewarded by presidents from Roosevelt to Nixon. Potty-mouth Nixon could have really used this old man he referred to as "that old cocksucker."

* * *

Hoover's legacy is impressive, far-reaching, and difficult to encapsulate—for my money, he was the most powerful American of the twentieth century. Perhaps Hoover's most vital power was his ability to quell upheaval, and to keep American capitalism on a course of wanton profiteering with power-holding for a select few. This was his cultural role, and he excelled at it. He used the FBI and illegal domestic covert counterinsurgency programs like COINTELPRO to undermine democratic movements not of his liking—infiltrating and attacking not just socialist and communist democratic organizations, but the American Indian Movement, environmental organizations, groups advocating for political prisoners, women's rights and pacifism.[24] Hoover acted as if he owned America and he repeatedly demonstrated disdain for the Bill of Rights. When it served his own political purposes, he freely leaked classified documents to people like Joseph McCarthy.[25] Without fear of arrest, he wiretapped journalists, Supreme Court justices, poets, environmental visionaries, and even comic geniuses.[26] He spied on JFK's sexual trysts with Danish beauty queen and suspected Nazi spy Inga Arvad, and on the anti-racist lectures of anthropologists Franz Boas, Ruth Benedict, and Margaret Mead.[27] He was an unchecked power who used surveillance to maintain the status quo of inequity that the FBI so frequently sought to protect.

Hoover did not accomplish such feats alone, there were plenty on the political left and right who lent a hand. The legions on the right were multiple and mostly obvious, but many contemporaries might be surprised at how many liberal organizations functioned as Hoover-enablers. Hoover maintained a friendly, secretive correspondence with ACLU board member and Lead General Council (1929–55), Morris Ernst. Decades later, journalist Harrison Salisbury established that Ernst betrayed individuals seeking aid from the ACLU during the McCarthy period and Ernst "sent Hoover and Nichols scores of confidential letters written to him by friends and associates."[28] This friendship perhaps explains how the ACLU came to present an award to Hoover for his opposition to the detention of Japanese-Americans during the Second World War; whereas another interpretation of Hoover's wartime stance was simply one based on administrative in-fighting over which agency would be allowed to commit such abuses of civil rights and Hoover was a sore loser.

For many on the political right, J. Edgar Hoover has become a symbol of some imagined lost age of law and order, most usually brought out by those seeking to revoke civil liberties in new ways. As the screws of centralized surveillance and increased forms of control were retightened in the post-9/11 era, Ann Coulter became a shrill voice calling for a retro-Hooverian-rehabilitation undertaking rites of fictional renewal designed to resurrect Hoover's spirit to once again haunt America. Coulter considered Hoover to be a misunderstood progressive civil libertarian who protected

Americans from what she claimed was an actual, effective vast communist conspiracy.[29]

But despite Coulter and others' failures to resurrect Hoover, there are reasons to worry. As with all classic monsters, we can't be sure that just because he died in the last scene that he won't come back. In fact, his post-mortem cameos and sequeled returns have been multiple—though admittedly played by a series of other hack actors like Ed Meese, John Poindexter, William Barr, and John Ashcroft. The trick to keeping Hoover in his grave (a grave located in the Congressional Cemetery just meters from his lifelong companion, Clyde Tolson) isn't garlic, silver bullets, wooden stakes, or holy water: but light and memory. Hoover's monstrous reincarnations could never flourish in a world of transparency, memory of past atrocities, oversight, and a functioning Bill of Rights—but these are the features of American society that are now under attack at levels not seen since Hoover's Golden Age.

In the end, history matters. And the institutional and personal roots of the American surveillance state matter for all sorts of reasons, but they matter most significantly because of the continuities connecting the past to present, especially in what this history reveals about the strong ties connecting far-reaching rogue surveillance operations with illegal campaigns of political suppression of the sort that J. Edgar Hoover nurtured as he launched the FBI on its institutional trajectory.

2

Memory's Half-life:
Notes on a Social History of
Wiretapping in America

Back in 2013, when Edward Snowden's revelations of massive NSA electronic surveillance and metadata mining of domestic telephone and internet activities first became public, there was a short-lived wave of renewed scrutiny of American intelligence agencies' intrusions into the lives of Americans and people around the globe.[1] But along with this news of NSA, CIA, and outsourced surveillance came disturbing measures of Americans embracing governmental monitoring of our private electronic communications. A *Pew/Washington Post* poll conducted days after Snowden's disclosures showed 56 percent of U.S. respondents found the NSA PRISM program's collection of domestic metadata was "acceptable," and 45 percent believed that the government should "be able to monitor everyone's email to prevent possible terrorism."[2] Media and pundits spun largely unchallenged narratives of NSA surveillance as a harmless, necessary, and effective tool in network-centric borderless warfare, and for a variety of reasons, the initial public shock over the extent of NSA surveillance subsided with little pushback or legislative oversight. Even now, in the years past the Snowden revelations, passive public acceptance for ubiquitous surveillance operations remains as a new generation of Americans are further socialized to accept invisible omnipresent intrusions as necessary, and non-threatening, and normal.

But it has not always been this way. American attitudes about the acceptability of governmental surveillance have historically dramatically shifted in waves linked to political forces—forces that have been sometimes manipulated by the U.S. government, which itself has consistently desired to monitor the public at the highest level it can get away with.

The post-9/11 shift in Americans accepting and internalizing new levels of state surveillance marked a significant departure from American's century-long distrust of electronic surveillance that was a long time in the making. Historical memory is fragile, and even deep cultural values can shift and be managed by elites; yet our best defense against these memory-wipes begins with historical considerations of how we got to the post-9/11 years, in which a large portion of the American population expressed not necessarily liking but accepting a world of perpetual tracking and surveillance.

Yet two decades after the 9/11 attacks on the United States and the long failed wars in Afghanistan and Iraq, and with increasing homeland surveillance, the American public is beginning to again express what have historically been long-held anti-surveillance views. While the coordinated fear campaign following 9/11 was powerful and resulted in increased American support for a broad range of surveillance activities, two decades later Americans again express concerns over state surveillance. With a decade-long half-life, Americans' approval for governmental monitoring of phone calls between people within and outside the United States fell from 49 percent approval in 2011 to 28 percent approval in 2021, and monitoring of domestic phone calls fell from 23 percent in 2011 to 14 percent in 2021.[3] These dramatic drops appear to indicate a return to pre-9/11 levels of distaste for ongoing government surveillance, and they raise questions about how easily future events can be managed to resurrect popular support for invasive surveillance operations, which remain with us today.

The key moment for understanding shifts in American surveillance attitudes away from what had been a long history of skepticism occurred in the immediate aftermath of the 9/11 terror attacks. This was a point in time when the American public hastily abandoned a century of fairly consistent opposition to government surveillance. Survey data indicates that just months before the 9/11 attacks, distrust of the FBI was at one of its highest historical levels, as the June 20, 2001 *USA Today* headline proclaimed "Poll: 4 in 10 Americans Don't Trust FBI."[4] The fear spread by the 9/11 attacks and Bush's terror wars brought uncertainties that helped cloud memories of intelligence agencies' historical abuses.

Decades of longitudinal survey data collected by the Justice Department records deeply rooted American opposition to governmental wiretaps with disapproval levels fluctuating between 70–80 percent during the 30 years preceding 2001.[5] But on December 12, 2001, the *New York Times* published a poll indicating that only 44 percent of respondents believed widespread governmental wiretaps "would violate American's rights."[6] Post-9/11 fears flushed previous civil liberties concerns down the memory hole. As Noam Chomsky wrote just hours after the World Trade Center towers fell, these terrorist attacks were "a gift to the hard jingoist right, those who hope to use force to control their domains."[7] While public opinion shifts to favor increased surveillance powers were fed by the 9/11 attacks, these shifts were also the result of long-standing efforts by intelligence agencies to persuade the courts and public that expanded electronic surveillance was necessary for the social good.

As with any cultural trait, American views on wiretapping are complex, shifting, varied and at times contradictory. While American culture has long traditions of distrusting government, there are concurrent themes of patriotic zealousness as well as a quiet subservience to the militarization of the federal budget. Distrust of government surveillance is shared by members of the far left and right. But even with such contradictions, it is clear that for the better part of a century most Americans consistently opposed governmental wiretaps—even wiretaps of criminals. Americans had to be coerced into accepting these limits on privacy, freedom of association and expression, and the history of American wiretapping finds consistent ongoing efforts by governmental agencies to increase surveillance capabilities.

The particulars of American wiretapping should be viewed in light of what is known of larger developmental processes extending beyond the particulars of American society and are rooted in the political economic and technological developmental elements of state systems. Anthropologists understand that beneath nationalistic claims to the contrary, as evolutionary forms nation states share common modes of social management—though individual cultures have developed various means to limit the state's encroachment on the private spaces of individuals. Anthropologically speaking, as cultural forms the differences between the FBI, CIA, Homeland Security, Stasi, KGB, MI5, or Mossad and other secret police agencies are differences of degree not of kind. States have interests in monitoring and controlling individuals and groups opposing the interests of the state or its elites, and wiretaps are but an extreme manifestation of state desire to make their populous legible.[8]

In this context wiretapping is a recurrent component of various societies maintaining order through the means of police states. While all states manage and monitor their populations, state wiretaps or other forms of broad electronic surveillance undermine democracy. People living under threats of ongoing state monitoring and tracking are not free to develop requisite critiques. Self-censorship spreads under such conditions and limits dissent.

Electronic surveillance violates boundaries between individuals and the state. State eavesdropping and metadata mining threaten notions of private and public spheres, these practices dislodge public understandings of freedom, and expose the naked scaffolding of police states. It matters little whether these violations occur with the approval of courts or as illegal state operations: wiretaps and electronic monitoring are primal social violations not easily repaired by legal sanctions or oversight, and their damage is systemic and contagious. U.S. Supreme Court Justice Brandeis clearly saw that "as a means of espionage, writs of assistance and general warrants are but puny instruments of tyranny and oppression when compared with wire-tapping."[9]

Though you would not know it from the surveillance-friendly attitudes of American citizenry that have dominated for much of the last two decades, when the possibility of wiretapping first became known to Americans they were outraged that the police would be able to listen in to private conversations of any sort, even those of criminals. Through a century of persistent conditioning the American public has been educated to lose this sense of outrage. Even before the 9/11 attacks, Americans were becoming comfortable with increasing numbers of court authorized wiretaps, and uncounted unauthorized taps—and it is these changes in attitudes and forgotten oppositions that must be understood if we are to counter the current movement to increase the ease of state surveillance.

EARLY WIRETAPS

All technologies evolve within the context of specific social relations, and new technologies often generate new uses not always apparent to their inventors. The contested credit for inventing the telephone by Antonio Meucci, Elisha Gray, and Alexander Graham Bell in 1876 was decades removed from the adoption of the phone as a common component of American social life. In 1877 the world only had a single telephone line spanning any significant distance, with 778 phones operating on one line connecting Boston and Salem, Massachusetts. At the beginning of the twentieth century, about one in a thousand Americans had telephones, but by the 1920s one in a hundred Americans had telephones, and at mid-century about one in three homes had them. Today, the United States has more phones than people; surprisingly, Americans own more phones than guns. By the early 1990s there were over one billion land-based telephone lines on earth, and an estimated six billion cellphones, and today, the spread of cell or even satellite technology expands the phone's reach to most of the planet's inhabited surface.[10]

Until the late-twentieth century's disbursement of fiber-optic lines and cellphones, wiretaps required little technical equipment or assistance from the phone company. All one needed to tap a traditional copper-wire phone line was access to the phone-wire and alligator clips to attach to the red and green wires, a speaker or tape recorder. Tapping a traditional telephone was always a physically simple feat to accomplish without the assistance or knowledge of the phone company, and for about as long as there have been people connected by telephones, there have been people tapping them. Digital conversations and data transmissions over fiber-optic lines are still vulnerable to tapping at telephone company switches (using high-tech access ports), and at end destinations (using low-tech copper wire and clips as most residential and office lines still use copper wire for phone lines). Both analogue and digital cellular phones, and wireless computer communications are also susceptible to electronic eavesdropping using both simple and complex means.

During the early decades of the twentieth century, Americans were outraged when they first learned of law enforcement's use of wiretaps. During the First World War, wiretapping became so commonplace that Congress outlawed the practice despite the obvious threats to national security posed by spies and saboteurs; threats to privacy and freedom were viewed as clearly outweighing threats to national security. Because of the rise of wartime surveillance, after the war dozens of states enacted state law further limiting the electronic surveillance powers of local police.[11]

During Prohibition, bootleggers used telephones to establish lines of communication between producers, distributors, and buyers. Local and federal police agencies ignored laws prohibiting wiretaps and routinely eavesdropped on bootleggers' phone calls. As local police increasingly used wiretaps, the federal government took actions to limit law enforcement agents' uses of wiretaps. With support from the public, in 1924, U.S. Attorney General Harlan Friske Stone forbade the Justice Department from conducting wiretaps. The Treasury Department, and the Bureau of Investigation resented Stone's policy and both agencies continued to secretly employ wiretaps.

A 1926 Seattle rum-smuggling case, in which federal agents used wiretaps to prosecute former police lieutenant and bootlegger Roy Olmstead, established important legal rulings regarding the constitutionality of wiretaps. Though federal agents had illegally wiretapped Olmstead, the trial judge ruled that violations of state wiretapping law were immaterial, and Olmstead was found guilty of several Prohibition violations.[12] In the dissent to the 1927 Ninth Circuit Court appeal Judge Frank Rudkin found that despite criminals' threats to the greater public good, when law enforcement officials tapped phones they violated a basic social contract and threatened the foundations of privacy and freedom. Rudkin argued that

a person using the telegraph or telephone is not broadcasting to the world. His conversation is sealed from the public as completely as the nature of the instrumentalities employed will permit, and no federal officer or federal agent has a right to take his message from the wires, in order that it may be used against him. Such a situation would be deplorable and intolerable, to say the least ... If ills such as these must be borne, our forefathers failed in their desire to ordain and establish a government to secure the blessings of liberty to themselves and their posterity.[13]

While some in the judiciary understood the threats of wiretaps to the development of a free society, it was a captain of capitalism who would later rail the hardest against the police's invasion of their *customer's* privacy. When *Olmstead* made its way before the U.S. Supreme Court in 1928,[14] Seattle's Pacific Telephone and Telegraph Company's brief supported the right of illegal smugglers to not have their conversations monitored by the police, arguing:

when the lines of "two parties" are connected with the central office, they are intended to be devoted to their exclusive use, and in that sense to be turned over to the exclusive possession of the parties. A third person who taps the lines violates the property rights of both persons then using the telephone, and of the telephone company as well.[15]

It is difficult to imagine a communication company today advocating for the privacy rights of their customers employing such a constitutionally based argument; indeed, the communication industry's initial opposition to Congressional mandates that all fiber-optic switches be accessible to law enforcement personnel with wiretap warrants was easily overcome with the aid of funds to facilitate this invasion of customers' privacy. Snowden's revelations of Facebook, MSN, Google and other corporations' compliance with NSA surveillance requests revealed industry working hand in hand with state surveillance in seamless ways.

Though the U.S. Supreme Court found against Olmstead in a five to four decision, in his dissent Justice Brandeis wrote that

Decency, security, and liberty alike demand that government officials shall be subjected to the same rules of conduct that are commands to the citizen. In a government of laws, existence of the government will be imperiled if it fails to observe the law scrupulously. Our Government is the potent, the omnipresent teacher. For good or for ill, it teaches the whole people by its example. Crime is contagious. If the Government becomes a lawbreaker, it breeds contempt for law; it invites every man to become a law unto himself; it invites anarchy. To declare that in the administration of the criminal law the end justifies the means—to declare that the Government may commit crimes in order to secure the conviction of a private criminal—would bring terrible retribution. Against that pernicious doctrine this Court should resolutely set its face.[16]

Most Americans were outraged by the court's blatant disregard of Fourth and Fifth Amendment protections. Walter Murphy observed that across the country "the majority of editorials disapproved of what the court had done" in the *Olmstead* case.[17] The *New York Times* critically assailed the Court's decision to so narrowly interpret the Fourth Amendment,[18] and even conservative newspapers in Washington communities criticized the ruling. In the thriving coastal lumber town of Hoquiam, the conservative *Washingtonian* wrote,

Better for everyone if enforcement officers recognize wire tapping as highly unethical. The Supreme Court called it that even while it said that the practice does not violate constitutional guarantees. The public will not stand for it in ordinary police work. But there are times when the end justifies means. Olmstead's operation was one of these. If wire tapping is not abused, it can remain as a club of the head of those who, like Olmstead, are known to be violating the law on a wholesale scale and yet make it difficult to prove a case in court on evidence obtained by the ordinary methods.

The decision may have very far-reaching effects. It will go far beyond the Olmstead case, perhaps dangerously far. Perhaps it will be necessary for Congress to enact a law which will protect the secrecy of telephone messages by making them inadmissible in evidence in federal trials. It will be if federal agents abuse the decision of the court, and it is open to grave abuse.[19]

These sentiments were not those of some left-leaning protector of civil liberties, as labor historian Aaron Goings notes, the *Washingtonian* "at times used its pages to advocate vigilante action against labor activists."[20] In Everett, the *Herald* commended the Prohibition Department for stating it would only use wiretaps in "extreme situations," but then added that "Telephone wire tapping may be 100 percent legal, and yet there isn't one of us who doesn't rebel at the thought of it ... when a man is in his own home conversing with a friend in his own home that conversation should be fairly immune from official snooping."[21] Public outrage over the Supreme Court's approval of wiretaps bridged party lines. At the 1928 Republican Convention, Nicholas Murray Butler was jeered for his defense of the *Olmstead* decision.[22] There was a broad feeling that there was something innately un-American about wiretapping, even wiretapping criminals.

Because of broad public disapproval of wiretaps, the FBI adopted a fake public posture regarding electronic surveillance. The FBI's 1928 operations manual maintained that wiretapping was not allowed and that it was "improper, illegal ... and unethical," and J. Edgar Hoover "assured Congress that any agent caught wiretapping would be fired," meanwhile, the FBI conducted secret wiretaps.[23] Hoover consistently exploited high publicity crimes and public fears to push for greater wiretapping powers. After the 1932 Lindberg baby kidnapping, Hoover expanded the FBI's reach to include a new class of crimes, and Hoover argued for increased FBI surveillance powers, though the courts were reluctant to grant such intrusive powers. Sensationalist press coverage of the Lindberg baby kidnapping spread awareness of police wiretapping into popular culture, and fictional super cop Dick Tracy used wiretaps to catch super villains.[24]

Section 605 of the 1934 Communications Act federally criminalized the tapping of telephones, and in 1939 *Nardone v. the United States* (302 U.S. 379), the U.S. Supreme Court upheld Congress's ability to federally outlaw the use of wiretaps.[25] Yet the FBI and other law enforcement agencies continued illegal wiretapping operations, gathering information not presented in court.[26] But the *Nardone* decision stopped short of repairing the damage inflicted by the *Olmstead* decision, and wiretaps gained new life as the Second World War years strengthened America's intelligence agencies while weakening civil liberties. The lessons of using national security fears to extend surveillance were not lost on Hoover's FBI.

FEEDING HOT AND COLD WAR FEARS

American attitudes towards wiretapping significantly shifted during the 1940s, as the war and changes in the class distribution of telephones helped shift judicial acceptance of wiretaps. In 1940 J. Edgar Hoover attempted to secure new wiretapping powers from Congress but was defeated by FCC Chairman James L. Fly. But President Roosevelt issued a secret executive order authorizing widespread Justice Department wiretaps of "subversives" and suspected spies.[27] Hoover used these vague new powers to investigate not just Nazis but anyone he thought subversive. Hoover's assistant, William Sullivan, later recalled that during the war, the FBI routinely conducted warrantless wiretaps, under the logic that "with the country's future at stake, getting approval from Washington seemed like an unnecessary legal technicality. Years later, the FBI was still listening in on other people's conversations without the authorization of the attorney general."[28] The social history of wiretaps is a history of mission creep, where FBI agents initially hunting for wartime Nazi white supremacist spies soon monitored progressive activists fighting American white supremacists' racial segregation.

During the 1940s, the telephone became an increasingly ubiquitous feature of American households—not merely the communication instrument of the elites with whom the Judicial Class consorted and protected. As the phone became a communication conduit not primarily for the rich, but also for the poor, the judiciary began to reconsider past wiretap opposition.

The FBI used the communist fears of the McCarthy period to expand illegal wiretaps: targeting not only suspected communists, but a wide range of progressives struggling for civil rights, union leaders, social workers, and progressive religious groups. But even during the McCarthy period, the courts did not sanction most FBI wiretapping. When the FBI disclosed it had illegally wiretapped conversations between accused Soviet agent Judith Coplon and her lawyer, the appeals court overturned her conviction.[29] Local police departments expanded wiretapping operations in the 1950s. New York police routinely wiretapped public phone booths during the early 1950s, and in 1953 and 1954, they launched an estimated 3,500 wiretaps.[30]

In 1959, Philadelphia District Attorney and future Senate Watergate Committee Chief of Counsel, Sam Dash, published a detailed examination of telephone surveillance practices, both legal and illegal, called *The Eavesdroppers*, which documented a surge in workplace and police surveillance practices.[31] As Brian Hochman notes, Dash's criticisms of police wiretapping practices in this study was a reversal from his previous work just a few years earlier arguing that the police would essentially be helpless without such surveillance powers.[32] The publicity that followed the release of *The Eavesdroppers* with its stories of widespread wiretapping abuses by local, state, and federal law enforcement agencies—and a hodgepodge of state laws that legalized, prohibited, or ignored wiretaps in various states—alarmed the American public and caught the attention of legislators concerned about wiretaps violating privacy.

Local police departments continued to conduct unauthorized wiretaps during the 1960s, even though *Benanti v. United States* (355 U.S. 96) clarified these wiretaps were criminal violations of Section 605 of the Communications Act. During this period, federal and local law enforcement conducted wiretaps in spite of the disapproval of the public and courts. In 1967's *Katz v. United States* (389 U.S. 347), the Supreme Court again ruled that the Fourth Amendment protections against unreasonable searches extended to telephone conversations. The following year Congress added provision in Title III of the 1968 Omnibus Crime Bill circumventing the *Katz* decision by identifying specific crimes (such as kidnapping, or elements of organized crime) meriting wiretaps. In intervening years, the list of crimes permitting wiretaps grew with bipartisan support.

The years following Hoover's 1972 death brought scandalous revelations about the FBI and CIA's illegal intrusions into Americans' private lives. The Church and Pike Committee investigations revealed extensive surveillance campaigns directed at Americans engaging in lawful political activities. Many Americans were outraged at the extent of the CIA and FBI's illegal activities, but an initial wave of shock gave way to complacency, and Congress failed to enact meaningful oversight of domestic and foreign intelligence agencies.

During the 1970s, as the Rockefeller Commission investigated CIA wrongdoing it found that in 1952 the CIA began secretly tracking mail between the Soviet Union and the United States, and in 1953 it began secretly opening and reading this mail. A string of CIA directors, U.S. Postmaster Generals, and Attorney General Mitchell knew about the program and the Commission found that "since 1958, the FBI was aware of this program and received 57,000 items from it."[33] Before the program ended in 1973 2,300,000 pieces of mail were monitored by the CIA, with 8,700 pieces of mail secretly opened.[34] The CIA's Soviet mail monitoring program claimed to focus on foreign individuals operating or trying to gain influence within the United States, but the CIA's secret Operation CHAOS could not sustain credible claims that it was directed at foreign operatives. Under Operation CHAOS the CIA indexed seven million individual names, including 115,000 American citizens. Over the course of six years CHAOS compiled 7,200 files on U.S. citizens, and issued reports to the FBI, White House, and other governmental officials.[35] This was a new era of CIA revelations when decades of silence were broken, and many Americans were shocked at the details of a lawless Agency operating in their name.

In 1978, former CIA telecommunications engineer, David Watters, testified before the Senate Intelligence Subcommittee about NSA monitoring and taping thousands of domestic and international phone conversations.[36] These revelations brought public disapproval and empty promises of Congressional oversight followed. With ECHELON and Carnivore, the NSA and FBI's capacities for telecommunications surveillance capacities grew unchecked.

One trophy in intelligence agencies' campaigns for America's acceptance of circum-constitutional procedures was the 1978 establishment of the Foreign Intelligence Surveillance Act (FISA), establishing a secret judicial system charged with authorizing wiretaps and other means of electronic surveillance relating to issues of "National Security." The FISA Courts conduct their work in total secrecy. A 2002 court ruling removed requirements of establishing probable cause before allowing FISA authorized electronic surveillance, and between 1978 and 2004 the FISA's kangaroo court rejected 5 of 18,761 warrant requests, and some years they have authorized every received request.[37] Such a record indicates there is no meaningful firewall preventing large-scale abuses. In the 1970s the NSA used trickery to "legally" simultaneously wiretap thousands of phones at a given instance. The NSA received a waiver of the wiretap laws permitting it to conduct wiretaps without warrants for a 90-day period.[38] Prior to the USA PATRIOT Act, the NSA sidestepped legal restrictions limiting domestic surveillance by getting its international partners in project ECHELON to conduct such operations for them.[39]

President Carter's Attorney General Levi limited FBI abilities to investigate alleged "domestic security" violations, requiring external examination of ongoing investigations. President Reagan evoked fears of "terrorism" as an effective passkey for bypassing civil liberties and judicial procedures. But first the Reagan administration had to roll back the surveillance limits established by Attorney General Edward Levi, because

Levi's aim of ending FBI surveillance of dissident political activities was not shared by the Reagan administration. To encourage the FBI to monitor these (renamed) "terrorist" activities, Ronald Reagan's attorney general, William French Smith, on March 7, 1983, rescinded the Levi guidelines. Under new and more permissive standards, FBI, "domestic security/ terrorist" investigations were authorized "when the facts or circumstances reasonably indicate that two or more persons are engaged in an enterprise [to further] political or social goals wholly or in part through activities that involve force or violence and the violation of the criminal law of the United States. Smith directed FBI officials to "anticipate or prevent crime."[40]

This notion of anticipating and preventing crimes through invasive surveillance is at the heart of Philip K. Dick's opiated vision of "pre-crimes" to be anticipated, terminated, and punished even before they ever occurred.[41] Such visions of pre-crimes during the Reagan years fed off the FBI's fears of terrorism, and helped the FBI regain its largely unchecked powers of surveillance and arrest they held during most of Hoover's reign—but the FBI could only go so far without a dramatic event on which to hang the public fear needed to obliterate concerns of civil liberties and blind vigilance.

Though the internet was in its infancy, first used primarily by military personnel and on university campuses, until the passage of the 1986 Electronic Communications Privacy Act it was legal to intercept email messages traveling through phone lines. This Act required that all electronic communications have the same legal protections as phone communications—though conversations made on cordless phones were not protected. As new technologies emerged, law enforcement found new ways to expand surveillance powers, even as new legislation tried to keep track with developments, and in many instances the American public struggled to keep track of the rapidly changing landscape.

Many Americans opposed the 1994 Digital Telephony Act, which required all fiber-optic-based switches be equipped to facilitate court approved wiretaps.[42] The ACLU and Electronic Privacy Information Center organized widespread opposition to the bill, and across the country letters to editors and editorials criticized the bill's obtrusive features. This was new territory as communication infrastructure was being built from the ground-up to include surveillance capabilities as a front-end design feature. There was a stark contrast between the communication industry's embrace of this bill and the industry's stance in the 1927 *Olmstead* appeal which opposed *all* efforts by law enforcement to tap phone lines.[43] The 1994 Communications Assistance for Law Enforcement Act mandated that all fiber-optic-based switches be equipped to facilitate law enforcement wiretaps. Any initial objections within the telecommunications industry were pacified with federal funds to pay any extra expense for these features.[44]

With little public notice the Reagan, Bush, and Clinton administrations each increased the use of federal wiretaps, and the conservative federal judiciary appointed during the 1980s brought little judicial opposition to wiretaps. Throughout the 1980s and 1990s there was a steady increase in wiretaps undertaken by federal authorities, but given the secrecy surrounding FISA approved wiretaps, these numbers only tell a small part of the story.[45] According to investigative journalist and longtime NSA chronicler, James Bamford, offshore surveillance networks such as ECHELON skirted pre-USA PATRIOT Act limitations on domestic surveillance by using third-party countries to monitor U.S. citizens' phones and email.[46]

It is remarkable how much technical information about surveillance practices and capacities of American intelligence agencies has long been openly knowable, but one impact of this available knowledge seems to be that of a general anesthetic to public concerns. Over the past decade numerous books, articles, and news stories have established how the NSA monitors, records, and analyzes phone conversations and uses computer programs to scan for keywords, but with increased knowledge of these operations there seems to also be an accompanying numbing helplessness of facing this reality.[47] Assurances that unspecified others (terrorists, etc.) are the targets of these intrusive investigations seem to set aside the concerns of increasing numbers of Americans, while those with different historical memories amplify their concern.

During the 1980s, corporations increasingly collected data on Americans in ways that post-Watergate governmental agencies were prohibited to do. After initial resistance, during a brief period, American attitudes shifted from resistance to acceptance. News reports in the late 1980s that the Lotus 123 Corporation would be compiling and publishing a set of CD-ROM platters containing basic information on the names and addresses of most Americans show Americans seriously outraged over the prospect of such centralized record keeping. But decades later the internet makes such intrusions invisible, voluntary, and inevitable, in ways documenting our national numbing and processes socializing us to accept our loss of privacy expectations.

Revelations during the late 1990s disclosed that the NSA monitored "international" telephone traffic, using computers to scan for keywords. New encryption technologies for personal computers and other communication technologies led Congress and Clinton to limit communication encryption schemes that would interfere with governmental electronic eavesdropping. Truly private telephonic or electronic communications threatened intelligence agencies' abilities to eavesdrop, and limits were placed on the distribution of RSA encryption, PGP freeware, the Clipper Chip and other programs that were required to include implanted backdoors and escrowed keys for law enforcement personnel.[48]

In the early and mid-1990s the American public's protections from electronic surveillance were further eroded by a series of court cases involving questions of whether workplace email had the same privacy protections as a letter or a phone call. Many of the judges establishing this case law were functionally internet illiterate and needed even the most basic features of email explained to them in court because they had never used it. Judges made important decisions in realms of social life of which they had no first-hand knowledge and they did not seem to understand arguments that they were abolishing the same expectations of privacy one had when using the telephone or mail in the workplace. As employers gained new powers of workplace surveillance, the working public was trained to accept an erosion of privacy and reduced expectations of electronic privacy rights. In 2000, Congressman Bob Barr and Senator Charles Schumer failed to garner enough support for a bill to limit employer workplace surveillance of employees; and without such legislation the later invasive surveillance of workers at places like Amazon "fulfilment centers" has sprawled out of control to a point where workers are now penalized or fired if robotic processes determine they have used the bathroom too much, or rested, during a shift. But the deprivations average workers can experience in the workplace are different from those experienced by the judiciary, as the U.S. Supreme Court in 2001 ruled to provide the judiciary with privileged workplace email privacy.[49] The dynamic of courts protecting privacy rights in situations they understand from first-hand experience, while violating privacies in unfamiliar situations runs deep in American jurisprudence. When the U.S. Supreme Court (*Kyllo v. United States*, 533 U.S. 27) limited law enforcement's ability to scan and search people's homes using thermal-imaging technology without warrants, they were concerned that if the government prevailed the police would need no warrant to learn "at what hour each night the lady of the house takes her daily sauna and bath—a detail that many would consider 'intimate.'"[50] In *Kyllo*, Scalia and the majority were worried about how non-warranted thermal intrusions into households could affect not just lower-class Americans, but themselves and their peers. We are left to wonder about the significance of the "and" (rather than "or") in Scalia's phrase "sauna and bath," and what details this sentence reveals about the luxurious bathing habits at the Scalia household that the majority protects. Scalia and the majority's phrasing marks class in ways different from a sentence that might have expressed concern over the government's ability to electronically monitor the activities in the public restrooms frequented by homeless people.

Had the judiciary in the early 1990s considered the nature of email communications as being little more than an electronic envelope, America might be a very different country today. The roots of such legal arguments for privacy were made by Justice Brandeis in his dissent to the *Olmstead* case when he anchored his reasoning for protecting the privacy of telephonic communications in *Ex parte Jackson*'s recognition "that a sealed letter entrusted to the mail is protected by the Amendment. The mail is a public service furnished by the Government. The telephone is a public service furnished by its authority. There is, in essence, no difference between the sealed letter and the private telephone message."[51] Yet, this remained a legal road not taken, and the post 9/11 world finds little hope that such reasoning will soon protect our emails or other online presence.

The USA PATRIOT Act, passed 45 days after the 9/11 attacks, removed post-Church Committee layers of judicial oversight of federal wiretaps and pen/trap orders (recording numbers dialed); it revoked restrictions prohibiting U.S. intelligence agencies like the CIA from spying on American citizens; enacted roving wiretaps that follow the subjects of investigation; and allowed for heavy online monitoring of email and web traffic. With the creation of the office of Homeland Security the state gained a centralized agency to coordinate domestic intelligence operations in ways only dreamed of by J. Edgar Hoover. The USA PATRIOT Act extended the powers and reach of the FBI and CIA not in a new direction, but along the same continuum long sought by Hoover and others without past legal hindrances or public opposition. The speed at which the 342-page USA PATRIOT Act was passed pushed aside consideration of the long history of the sorts of FBI and police surveillance abuses considered in this book.

A month after Edward Snowden's 2013 revelations of massive NSA and CIA surveillance programs, the New York Times reported that it wasn't just email, phone calls, and web activities being monitored by the government: the Postal Service is now scanning images recording the mailed envelopes of millions of Americans.[52] A broad resistance from Americans on the left and right arose in 2003 on learning of the Bush administration's secretive Total Information Awareness (TIA) program. Under the directorship of Admiral John Poindexter, TIA had originally planned to collect metadata on millions of Americans, tracking movements, emails, and economic transactions for use in predictive modeling software with hopes of anticipating terror attacks, and other illegal acts, before they occurred. Congress and the public were outraged at the prospect of such invasive surveillance without warrants or meaningful judicial oversight. These concerns led to TIA's termination, though as the Snowden NSA documents clarify, the NSA now routinely engages in the very activities envisioned by TIA. Bush overreached with Poindexter's failed TIA program, as public outcry rose opposing a federal agency empowered to mine metadata, but where Bush failed, Snowden's disclosures inform us, Obama and Trump prevailed with little public opposition beyond initial outcries at the time of Snowden's revelations.

But after 9/11 federal agencies like the FBI, CIA, and Homeland Security weren't the only ones who gained new surveillance powers. The New York Police Department had twice the number of personnel as the FBI, and after 9/11 it revived a political investigatory unit that was disbanded as the result of a 1985 legal settlement (known as the Handschu agreement); and this unit began collecting information and compiling political dossiers on individuals across the country and around the world.[53] New York viewed itself as a primary target for terrorist attacks, and New York police used the internet and telephone surveillance to compile dossiers on activists and dissidents. State legislatures across the country granted increased local police wiretap powers, and local police increasingly hired retired CIA and FBI personnel to advise them on monitoring "suspected terrorists."[54] But as is shown in the chapters of this book, we know from past surveillance campaigns during the 1940s, 1950s, and 1960s that the targets of surveillance will always include significant numbers of leftist activists challenging a wide range of social problems, people who are not terrorists, as the state increasingly sees all who threaten the status quo as being potential foreign agents.[55] These shifts connect the present with past surveillance campaigns of the 1940s, 1950s, and 1960s as new targets again include activists challenging the status quo approach to a wide range of social problems.[56] Anti-war protestors, the Occupy Movement, Greens, and others from the left and right opposing governmental policies became surveillance targets with these new post-9/11 surveillance tools.

So much of this new surveillance has become mundane to a point that it no longer shocks most people. It is becoming increasingly common for individuals in the United States selling their homes to place cameras and audio listening devices around the home to conduct surveillance on potential buyers touring their homes; with hopes of using information overheard in conversations to drive up the price, or to reject buyers who disparage decorating schemes. While the legality of this practice is questionable in many states requiring both parties' knowledge of recorded conversations, there seems to be growing acceptance of such spying. A 2018 Harris Poll found that 67 percent of Americans surveyed said they would use home security cameras and microphones for these activities if they were already present in the home—and over 7 percent of U.S. residences are already equipped with such surveillance equipment.[57]

But one of the most important shifts in American attitudes is how the American public is learning to surrender their rights to electronic privacy. Fewer and fewer Americans remember the long historical resistance to empowering our secret political police with such unchecked abilities and resources. In the months following Trump's followers' failed January 2021 insurrection at the Capitol building in Washington, DC, members of the American left further repressed any memory of the consistent ways that such surveillance has historically targeted leftist American activists, with calls for increased surveillance power to monitor right-wing political extremists.

COVID-19 PANDEMIC AND PUBLIC HEALTH SURVEILLANCE

Variations in national responses to the Covid-19 pandemic revealed differences in cultural and political attitudes towards surveillance as well as significant differences in technological surveillance capabilities and enforcement. Some countries, like South Korea and Taiwan, rapidly deployed cellphone-based monitoring systems. In tandem with widespread testing and access to well-functioning universal public health systems these countries initially controlled the viral spread in ways that allowed economies to continue functioning without massive shutdowns. Other countries, including the United States—already hampered by a fragmented dysfunctional public health system—stumbled through serial surges without any national tracking or disease surveillance system of the sorts deployed in South Korea and Taiwan.

One factor contributing to the U.S. failures to limit the rapid spread of Covid-19 was the politicization of attitudes opposing basic public health measures needed to track and isolate Covid positive individuals, and much of the langue of this opposition was routinely expressed in terms opposing government surveillance. Not without some historical basis, both right-wing conversative groups and left-wing civil libertarian groups voiced concerns that "temporary" emergency surveillance technologies introduced during the pandemic, once in place could easily become permanent surveillance fixtures in American culture. As the Covid-19 pandemic globally spread, within the United States attitudes about government control over masking, vaccines, and surveillance significantly shaped the country's failure to effectively curtail the virus' spread.

Even as President Trump displayed a complete inability to develop a national plan for the pandemic, American distrust of government control over bodily freedoms (framed as freedom of movement, to engage in commerce, freedom to not mask, freedom to not be monitored or tracked) took on a central significance. Tropes of resisting government control of free market capitalism and masks were fanned by the Trump presidency. Trump had not only years earlier dismantled significant parts of the U.S. Centers for Disease Control's ability to monitor and cope with a pandemic, but he refused to assert its national authority during the emergency; leaving states to set masking or lockdown policies and standards, and to battle against each other for protective gear, medical supplies and equipment, and tests. Within this chaos, there were localized and national expressions of surveillance fears appearing on blogs, talk radio, national TV shows and in countless discussion.

But other nations had very different experiences. Taiwan's successful 2020 response to the Covid-19 pandemic relied on heavy government surveillance and threats of serious fines; with police doing in-person and electronic monitoring of quarantined individuals, and electronically tracking individual contacts and networks.[58] Because a reliance on tracking, masking, and enforcing quarantines allowed countries like Taiwan and South Korea to reduce and contain Covid-19 spread in ways that allowed their economies to remain open, such technologies have been embraced by some (though not those, like Amazon, who financially benefited from the pandemic) U.S. corporate economic interests.

While it was predictable that the U.S. political response to the pandemic would give primary concern to keeping the capitalist economy afloat, the Trump administration's anti-science, anti-masking, anti-shutdown approach to the pandemic was not the only, or even most logical, pro-capitalist response to the crisis. Other capitalist nations, for example South Korea and Taiwan, developed responses that protected their economies by limited spread of the disease and protecting their populations; the most significant of these responses involved forms of surveillance and tracking that were abhorrent to many in the United States, though the levels of surveillance were not significantly more invasive than the daily tracking that most cellphone users surrender to on a daily basis. Meanwhile, in the United States, capitalist's booster cults like the Chamber of Commerce waffled with ambivalence for six months before endorsing adherence to scientific recommendations requiring masks in capitalism's marketplaces, a miscalculation that dearly cost the businesses they sought to represent.

Among scholars studying Covid-19 pandemic surveillance, there quickly developed shared acceptance that in times of crisis, acceptable standards of monitoring will shift; some scholars (such as Vitak and Zimmer) even made explicit comparisons to the shifts in surveillance that rapidly followed the 9/11 terrorist attacks:

> When considering surveillance and monitoring in response to COVID-19, we recognize that, in times of crisis, the norms around acceptable data flows may shift. At the same time, there is a risk that temporary measures established during a crisis become permanent and unnecessarily reduce citizens' privacy, which was the case in the United States following the September 11 terrorist attack.[59]

While not dismissing concerns about the dangers of increased surveillance, many U.S. scholars writing during the pandemic's first two years saw the growth of public health monitoring apps as necessary, while raising long-term potential privacy concerns.

We know from historical crises ranging from world wars to the 9/11 terror attacks, that periods of crisis can loosen restrictions on surveillance powers that once surrendered are not easily regained. Yet, the American failure to significantly monitor Covid cases and Republican politicians' inability to acknowledge the economic damage that would come from following basic public health guidelines to mask and social distance added to U.S. resistance to monitor and track people testing positive for Covid-19, much less those with whom they had contact.

The Social Science Research Council (SSRC) formed a new "Public Health, Surveillance, Human Rights Network" (PHSHR) to consider policies and implications of pandemic-related surveillance projects.[60] Their report identified one of the fundamental threats presented by the pandemic which was that urgent medical needs would push aside ongoing surveillance concerns in the interest of very real public health needs, and that once these surveillance practices became normalized during a time of crisis, they would later be very difficult to remove. As the PHSHR report observed, "moments of crisis often recast the roles of governments and the rights of individuals."[61] They acknowledged that while apps tracking people in the interest of preventing the spread of Covid-19 generated

> data that is valuable for public health but may also be commodified and used in an unintended fashion. Major data-gathering initiatives typically require partnerships between governments and private companies to create new digital infrastructure, develop software, and manage data collection. In many jurisdictions, government-corporate partnerships unfold with little accountability or transparency, raising questions about who ultimately owns the data and how it will eventually be used. The dramatic expansion of data gathering in response to Covid-19 has intensified many concerns about the threat of surveillance to individual freedoms.[62]

To many critics of government surveillance keenly aware of the dangers presented by the introduction of any surveillance mechanism, these epidemiological forms of surveillance appeared as reasonable *temporary* public health measures. While understanding that once present they become normalized and difficult to remove, during a global pandemic many argue that the public health good to be achieved by such surveillance mitigates the long-term threats presented by technologies such as phone apps.[63]

MEMORY AS DEFENSE

It took two decades, but Americans are now again showing signs of increased objections to state surveillance, objections that are approaching pre-9/11 levels. These shifts in attitude are profound, and while they indicate a return to long-standing skepticism of state surveillance, they have not led to the dismantling of the invasive surveillance systems that have taken hold during the last two decades.

Even while there are detectible trends in this history of American surveillance attitudes, including deep-rooted skepticism and resistance towards state surveillance, most Americans lack an awareness of this history, which leaves them unprepared to resist the increased surveillance regimes that seem to inevitably be coming, no doubt ushered in with waves of fear and claims of necessity. With little public debate, the USA PATRIOT Act rapidly removed judicial controls limiting America's domestic surveillance and persecutions. The restoration of old, and the granting of new, surveillance powers brought new levels of oppressive surveillance for all Americans, but we know that historically such powers have been used to monitor those challenging American domestic or foreign policies. Perpetuated fears of terror encourage Americans to forget a past they barely knew, and vague assurances that the rights of the "innocent" will be protected brush aside memories of well-documented historical violations of privacy and civil liberties as if these were not structured outcomes. As this review of past governmental efforts to increase surveillance shows, sustained public fear and a lack of collective memory can help perpetuate increased surveillance.

Much as the Smith and Hatch Acts undermined the civil rights of individuals and groups vaguely defined as "subversives" or "communistic," the USA PATRIOT Act undermined the rights of similarly ill-defined "suspect terrorists." It took the judiciary decades to dismantle the unconstitutional features of the Smith and Hatch Acts and today's courts have yet to overrule similar features of the USA PATRIOT Act.

As cultural beings we are all susceptible to the numbing and routinizing impacts of recurrent events. Time normalizes what were once obvious atrocities. Sustaining shock is always difficult, outrage's half-life is short and the toll of cognitive dissonance weighs heavy. With time the outrageous and offensive can be seen as the "unfortunately necessary," the potency of shock is short-lived as once current events become historicized.

The key to understanding the opinion shifts supporting the rise of domestic surveillance is that these developments are less something new than they are part of a long parade of legitimization validating the American intelligence agencies' campaign to erode constitutional protections against rampant wiretaps. Five years before the 9/11 attacks Richard J. Barnett argued that President Clinton's use of terrorism fears for political ends had dangerous consequences as the Clinton era Terrorism Prevention Act diminished civil liberties while expanding domestic wiretapping, "all in the name of making us feel safe."[64] The USA PATRIOT Act dismantled the firewall separating domestic criminal investigations from espionage investigations and empowered Homeland Security, FBI, and NSA to oversee roving wiretap and surveillance operations without public oversight.

The Snowden leaks confirmed what many scholars of American intelligence agencies had long suspected: the Bush and Obama administrations gave the NSA unprecedented surveillance authority to monitor domestic electronic communications. The public's acceptance of post-9/11 panoptical-surveillance necessitated learning to forget past abuses. While fear nurtures forgetfulness, fear alone is not enough: fear needs to be managed. Government and media-framed analysis help keep much of the nation from remembering a past scarred with constitutional abuses. Television-enforced amnesia coaxes Americans to coalesce with the needs of the intelligence-industrial complex. David Altheide describes these processes of managed fear as ones where we become "accustomed to giving up civil liberties to surveillance and enforcement efforts by formal agents of social control."[65] Issuing elevated Homeland Security terror alerts became a win/win situation for the presidency. Republican and Democrat administrations learned they could reap the gains of patriotic solidarity regardless of the outcomes: when no attacks occur the administration claims this shows how well the war on terrorism is working, and should actual attacks occur the administration benefits from the swelling of presidential approval ratings of the type seen after the 9/11 attacks. The public fears accompanying terror alert elevations are also used as wedges to pressure groups (Congress, industry, etc.) to undertake actions they would not otherwise. For example, the most significant outcome of Homeland Security's Orange Alert of the 2003 Christmas season was for U.S. and European airlines to abandon their opposition to invasive passenger background investigation programs advocated by Homeland Security.[66]

Sociologist Sigmund Diamond spent decades chronicling the intrusions of intelligence agencies into American academic life and the resulting threats to academic freedom. For Diamond the collective memory loss of past governmental abuses was an important weapon of the present. Diamond argued that "since historical memory is one of the weapons against abuse and power, there is no question why those who have power create a 'desert of organized forgetting.' But why should those who have been the victims sometimes act as if they, too, had forgotten?"[67] America's historical memory is the crucial battleground in the struggle to regain lost privacy and civil liberties, and those who would engage in this struggle must combat the "desert of organized forgetting" in ways that reawaken America's battered public memories. But in a nation where education reform relegates the teaching of history as less important than teaching students how to curtail thought in ways that fit within the narrow confines of standardized tests, these historical gaps loom large, and the recapturing of lost historical territory remains a daunting task.[68]

In the world of the novel *Underworld*, Don DeLillo asks whether "the state had taken on the paranoia of the individual or was it the other way around"; in our world we know the source of this paranoia.[69] America is now so lost in an environment of ever-present surveillance that our only choice is between memory loss and embracing paranoia.

3

The New Surveillance Normal: Government and Corporate Surveillance in the Age of Global Capitalism

The past two decades brought accelerated independent growth of corporate and governmental electronic surveillance programs tracking metadata and compiling electronic dossiers on individuals. The National Security Agency (NSA), FBI, Department of Defense, and CIA's metadata programs developed independently from, and with differing goals from, the consumer surveillance systems that now use cookies and consumer discount cards, sniffing Gmail content, compiling consumer profiles, and other means of tracking individual internet behaviors for marketing purposes. In the United States, public acceptance of electronic monitoring and metadata collection transpired incrementally, with increasing acceptance of corporate-based consumer monitoring programs, and reduced resistance to governmental surveillance.

These two surveillance tracks developed from separate motivations, one for security and the other for commerce, but both make individuals and groups legible for reasons of anticipation and control.[1] The collection and use of this metadata finds a synchronic convergence of intrusions, as consumer capitalism and the national security state leaves Americans vulnerable, and a world open to the probing and control by agents of commerce and security. As Bruce Schneier observed, "surveillance is still the business model of the Internet, and every one of those companies wants to access your communications and your metadata," yet surveillance capitalism is only half the story, as intelligence agencies, themselves dedicated to protecting this economic system, also harvest this growing body of data.[2]

The seductions of the internet are obvious, ominous, and apparently irresistible for most all socialized in its web. Questions, both trivial and vital, that once took hours in libraries to answer now take seconds. But this truth does not seem poised to set us free. As Thomas Pynchon argues, while we might "call it freedom, it's based on control. Everybody connected together, impossible anybody should get lost, ever again. Take the next step, connect it to these cell phones, you've got a total Web of surveillance, inescapable."[3]

But this convergence carries its own contradictions. Public trust in (and the economic value of) cloud servers, telecommunications providers, email, and search engine services suffered following revelations that the public statements of Verizon, Google, and others had long known that the NSA was monitoring their customers. A March 2014 *USA Today* survey found 38 percent of respondents believed the NSA violates their privacy, with distrust of Facebook (26 percent) surpassing even the IRS (18 percent) or Google (12 percent)—the significance of these results is that the Snowden NSA revelations damaged the reputations and financial standing of a broad range of technology-based industries.[4] With the assistance of private ISPs, various corporations, and the NSA, our metadata is accessed under a shell game of four distinct sets of legal authorizations. These allow spokespersons from corporate ISPs and the NSA to make misleading statements to the press about not conducting surveillance operations under a particular program such as FISA, when one of the other authorizations is being used—these other authorizations include: the 1978 FISA Act, Executive Order 12333, 2001 USA PATRIOT Act, Section 215, and Section 702 of the 2008 FISA Amendment Act.[5]

Edward Snowden's revelations revealed a world where the NSA is dependent on private corporate services for the outsourced collection of data, and where the NSA is increasingly reliant on corporate-owned data farms where the storage and analysis of the data occurs. In the neoliberal United States, Amazon and other private firms lease massive cloud server space to the CIA, under an arrangement where it becomes a sharecropper on these scattered data farms. These arrangements present nebulous security relationships raising questions of role confusion in shifting patron–client relationships; and whatever resistance corporations like Amazon might have had to assisting NSA, CIA, or intelligence agencies is further compromised by relations of commerce. This creates relationships of culpability, as Norman Solomon observed back in 2014, because Amazon hosted a $600 million CIA data farm contract, this raised questions about "if Obama orders the CIA to kill a U.S. Citizen, Amazon will be a partner in assassination?"[6] Such arrangements diffuse complicity in ways seldom considered by consumers focused on Amazon Prime's ability to speedily deliver a My Little Pony play set for a brony nephew's birthday party, not on the company's links to drone attacks on a wedding party in rural Afghanistan.

The internet developed first as a military communication system; only later evolving the commercial and recreational uses distant from the initial intent of its Pentagon landlords. Snowden revealed how the internet's architecture, a compromised judiciary, and duplexed desires of capitalism and the national security state converged to track our purchases, queries, movements, associations, allegiances, and desires. The rise of e-commerce, and the soft addictive allure of social media, rapidly transformed economic and social formations. Shifts in the base are followed by shifts in the superstructure, and new generations of e-consumers are socialized to accept phones that track movements, and game or exercise systems that bring cameras or GPS tracking into the formerly private refuges of our homes, as part of a "new surveillance normal."

We need to develop critical frameworks to understand how NSA and CIA surveillance programs articulate not only with the U.S. domestic and international security apparatus, but with current international capitalist formations. While secrecy shrouds our understanding of these relationships, CIA history provides examples of some ways that intelligence operations have supported and informed past U.S. economic ventures; likewise, the history of how surveillance has focused on progressive activists must be acknowledged. When these historical patterns are combined with details from Snowden's disclosures we find continuities of means, motive, and opportunity for neoliberal abuses of state intelligence for private gains.

THE NSA AND THE PROMISE OF INDUSTRIAL ESPIONAGE

Following Snowden's 2013 revelations of widespread NSA surveillance operations, several foreign leaders expressed outrage and displeasure upon learning that the NSA had spied on their governments and corporations, yet there remains little consideration of the meaning of the NSA's industrial spying.

The NSA is not the only government-based international hacking unit spying on global competitors. In China, the Shanghai Chinese People's Liberation Army's Unit 61398 purportedly targets U.S. corporate and government computers, with hacking campaigns supposedly seeking data providing economic or strategic advantage to the Chinese government or private businesses. Israel's Cyber Intelligence Unit (known as ISNU, or Unit 8200) has been linked to several political and economic hacking operations, including the Stuxnet worm and a 2012 attack on the Élysée Palace. While the extent of the Russian 2020 Solar Winds hack remains unknown, it is clear massive amounts of government and corporate data were compromised.[7] While many Western analysts take for granted that such economic espionage networks exist elsewhere, there is little analysis of the possibility that the NSA's surveillance will be, or has been, used by rogue individuals or agencies seeking economic advantages. Yet the leveraging of such information is a fundamental feature of market capitalism.

In January 2014, Snowden told the German ARD television network that there is "no question that the U.S. is engaged in economic spying." He explained that, for example, "if there is information at Siemens that they think would be beneficial to the national interests, not the national security, of the United States, they will go after that information and they'll take it."[8] Snowden did not elaborate on what is done with such economic intelligence, and there has been little effort by reporters or scholars to examine this claim.

In 2013, Edward Snowden released documents establishing that the NSA targeted French "politicians, business people and members

of the administration under a programme codenamed US-985D"
with French political and financial interests being "targeted on a
daily basis."[9] Other NSA documents show the Agency spying on
Mexican and Brazilian politicians, and the White House authorized
an NSA list of surveillance priorities including "international trade
relations" designated as a higher priority than counterespionage
investigations.[10] Leaked NSA documents include materials from a
May 2012 top secret presentation "used by the NSA to train new
agents step-by-step how to access and spy upon private computer
networks—the internal networks of companies, governments,
financial institutions—networks designed precisely to protect
information."[11] One leaked NSA PowerPoint slide mentions the
US$120 billion a year giant Brazilian petroleum company Petro-
bras with a caption that "many targets use private networks," and
as the Brazilian press analysis pointed out, "Petrobras computers
contain information ranging from details on upcoming commercial bidding operations—which if infiltrated would give a definite
advantage to anyone backing a rival bidder—to datasets with
details on technological developments, exploration information."[12]

In response to Snowden's disclosures, then Director of National
Intelligence James Clapper admitted the NSA collects financial intelligence, but claimed it was limited to searches for terrorist financial
networks and "early warning of international financial crises which
could negatively impact the global economy."[13] In March 2013
Clapper lied to Congress, claiming that the NSA was not collecting
"data on millions or hundreds of millions of Americans."[14] He later
claimed the NSA does not "use our foreign intelligence capabilities
to steal the trade secrets of foreign companies on behalf of—or give
intelligence we collect to—U.S. companies to enhance their international competitiveness or increase their bottom line."[15]

Over the course of several years, the NSA's Operation Shotgiant
hacked into the servers of Chinese telecommunications giant
Huawei. Shotgiant initially sought to learn about the People's Liberation Army's ability to monitor Huawei client's communications, but the NSA later installed hidden "back doors" in Huawei's
routers and digital switches—the exact activities that the U.S. government had long warned U.S. businesses that Huawei had done.
Such operations raise the possibility of the NSA gaining knowledge

to be used for economic gain by the CIA, NSA employees, or U.S. corporations. When pressed on these issues, a White House spokesperson claimed "we do not give intelligence we collect to U.S. companies to enhance their international competitiveness or increase their bottom line. Many countries cannot say the same." After this NSA operation was revealed, Huawei senior executive William Plummer noted that "the irony is that exactly what they are doing to us is what they have always charged that the Chinese are doing through us."[16]

There are many historical examples of intelligence personnel using information acquired through the course of their work for personal gain, such as selling intelligence information to another power. But what needs to be studied is a qualitatively different phenomenon: the use of such information for corporate profit or market speculation. The extent of such activities by U.S. intelligence agencies remains poorly documented, but there are some known instances.

In 1972, while investigating Nixon's presidential campaign finance irregularities, the Senate Foreign Relations subcommittee discovered documents indicating that Northrop had made a $450,000 bribe to Saudi Arabian air force generals to help secure a $700 million Northrop F-E5 jet contract. Retired CIA agent Kim Roosevelt (then running a multinational consulting firm operating in Saudi Arabia) denied any involvement in these bribes, but the investigation uncovered documents establishing that Roosevelt used his CIA connections for financial gain. The Senate subcommittee had identified private letters from Kim Roosevelt and Northrop officials with "repeated references to 'my friends in the CIA' who were keeping him posted about the moves of commercial rivals." Further, Wells wrote that

> there is no doubt that Roosevelt's inside track was of enormous value to Northrop. In the ringing prose of T.V. Jones, the Northrop president, unearthed by Senate investigator, Roosevelt was "... perhaps the key figure in ... contract values in this [Middle East] area in the past seven to eight years running close to a billion dollars." Roosevelt, when asked, grins and remarks, "By God, he's probably right."[17]

In the end, this embarrassing episode faded from public view with no legal consequences for the American prince; his use of public resources for his private looting was easily forgotten as the larger investigations of CIA impropriety disclosed other CIA abuses of public trust. The selfish filling of one man's pockets with unguarded loot paled in comparison to news of CIA assassinations, kidnappings, coups, corrupted elections, and broad illegal domestic surveillance and harassment campaigns. As the subcommittee focused its attentions on other more significant instances of CIA illegal activities, Roosevelt faced no legal consequences for these activities.[18]

The most rigorous study to date documenting intelligence data being used for economic gains in stock market trading was published in 2011 by economists Arindrajit Dube, Ethan Kaplan, and Suresh Naidu. The authors developed empirical measures to determine whether classified knowledge of impending CIA operations was historically used to generate profits in this manner.[19]

Dube, Kaplan, and Naidu recognized that most regimes historically overthrown by CIA coups had nationalized industries that were once privately held by international corporations; post-coup these industries returned to the previous corporate owners. Therefore, foreknowledge of upcoming coups had a significant financial value in the stock market. The authors developed a series of measures to detect whether, during past CIA coups, there were detectible patterns of stock trading taking advantage of classified intelligence directives, which were known only to the CIA and president.

Their study selected only CIA coups with now declassified planning documents, which attempted to install new regimes, and in which the targeted pre-coup governments had nationalized once-private multinational industries. They sampled five of 24 identified covert CIA coups meeting these three criteria: Iran (1953), Guatemala (1954), Congo (1960–61), Cuba (failed Bay of Pigs coup, 1961), and Chile (1973). Daily stock returns of companies that had been nationalized by the governments targeted by CIA coups were used to compare financial returns before presidential coup authorizations and after the coups. Dube, Kaplan, and Naidu found that four days after the authorization of coups their sample of stocks rapidly rose (before public awareness of these coming secret coups): for Congo there was a 16.7 percent increase on the day of the authorization, and a 22.7 percent return from the baseline four days later. The Guatemalan stocks showed a 4.9 percent increase upon coup authorization, a 16.1 percent increase four days later, and 20.5 percent seven days later; the Iranian stocks rose 7.4 percent four days after authorization, 10.3 percent seven days later, and 20.2 percent 16 days later. They found evidence of significant economic gains occurring in the stock market, with "the relative percentage benefit of the coup attributable to ex ante authorization events, which amount to 55.0% in Chile, 66.1% in Guatemala, 72.4% in Congo, and 86.9% in Iran."[20]

Dube, Kaplan, and Naidu concluded that "private information regarding coup authorizations and planning increased the stock prices of expropriated multinationals that stood to benefit from regime change. The presence of these abnormal returns suggests that there were leaks of classified information to asset traders."[21] By focusing on trading occurring at the point of the top secret presidential authorizations, they found that gains made from stock buys at the time of authorizations "were three times larger in magnitude than price changes from the coups themselves."[22] It remains unknown whether those profiting were lone individuals (either CIA employees or their proxies), or whether these investments were conducted by the CIA to generate funds for its black ops.

We do not know how such past measures of intelligence-insider profiteering do or do not relate to the NSA or CIA's present global surveillance operations. While Snowden released documents indicating NSA surveillance of corporations around the world, we do not understand how the NSA puts to use this collected intelligence. Even with these leaks the NSA largely remains a black box, and our knowledge of its specific activities is limited. Yet, the ease with which a middle-level functionary like Snowden accessed a wealth of valuable intelligence data necessarily raises questions about how the NSA's massive data collections may be used for self-serving economic interests. Dube, Kaplan, and Naidu establish past insider exploitations of intelligence data, and with the growth of insider-cheater capitalism of the type documented in Michael Lewis's Flash Boys, and expensive private inside-the-beltway newsletters, there are tangible markets for the industrial espionage collected and analyzed by the NSA and CIA under these programs. Snowden, after all, was just one of tens of thousands of people with access to the sort of data with extraordinary value on the floor of global capitalism's casinos.

THEORIZING CAPITALISM'S PERVASIVE SURVEILLANCE CULTURE

Notions of privacy and surveillance are always culturally constructed and are embedded within economic and social formations of the larger society. Some centralized state-socialist systems, such as the USSR or East Germany, developed intrusive surveillance systems, an incessant and effective theme of anti-Soviet propaganda. The democratic-socialist formations, such as those of contemporary Northern Europe, have laws that significantly limit the forms of electronic surveillance and the collection of metadata, compared to U.S. practice. Despite the significant limitations hindering analysis of the intentionally secret activities of intelligence agencies operating outside of public accountability and systems of legal accountability, the documents made available by whistleblowers like Snowden and WikiLeaks, and knowledge of past intelligence agencies' activities, provide information that can help us develop a useful framework for considering the uses to which these new invasive electronic surveillance technologies can be put.

We need theories of surveillance that incorporate the political economy of the U.S. national security state and the corporate interests which it serves and protects. Such analysis needs an economic foundation and views looking beyond cultural categories separating commerce and state security systems designed to protect capital. The metadata, valuable private corporate data, and fruits of industrial espionage gathered under PRISM and other NSA programs all produce information of such a high value that it seems unimaginable some of it will not be used for profiteering in global markets. It matters little what legal restrictions are in place; in a global, high-tech, capitalist economy such information is invariably commodified. It is likely to be used to: facilitate industrial or corporate sabotage operations of the sort inflicted by the Stuxnet worm; steal either corporate secrets for NSA use or foreign corporate secrets for U.S. corporate use; make investments by intelligence agencies financing their own operations; or secure personal financial gain by individuals working in the intelligence sector.

The rise of new invasive technologies coincides with the decline of ideological resistance to surveillance and the compilation of metadata. The speed of Americans' adoption of ideologies embracing previously unthinkable levels of corporate and state surveillance suggests a continued public acceptance of a new surveillance normal will continue to develop with little resistance. In a world where the CIA can hack the computers of Senator Feinstein—a leader of one of the three branches of government—with impunity or lack of public outcry, it is difficult to anticipate a deceleration in the pace at which NSA and CIA expand their surveillance reach. To live a well-adjusted life in contemporary U.S. society requires the development of rapid memory adjustments and shifting acceptance of corporate and state intrusions into what were once protective spheres of private life. Like all things in our society, we can expect these intrusions will themselves be increasingly stratified, as electronic privacy, or illegibility, may increasingly become a commodity available only to elites.

While the U.S. current state of surveillance acceptance offers little immediate hope of a social movement limiting corporate or government spying, there are enough historical instances of post-crises limits being imposed on government surveillance to offer some hope. Following the Second World War, many European nations reconfigured long-distance billing systems to not record specific numbers called, instead only recording billing zones—because the Nazis used phone billing records as metadata useful for identifying members of resistance movements. Following the Arab Spring, Tunisia reconfigured its internet with a new info-packet system known as mesh networks that hinder governmental monitoring—though USAID support for this project naturally undermines trust in this system.[23] Following the Church and Pike committees' Congressional investigations of CIA and FBI wrongdoing in the 1970s, the Hughes-Ryan Act brought significant oversight and limits on these groups, limits which decayed over time and whose remaining restraints were undone with the USA PATRIOT Act. Some future crisis may well provide similar opportunities to regain now lost contours of privacies.

Yet hope for immediate change remains limited. It will be difficult for social reform movements striving to protect individual privacy to limit state and corporate surveillance. Today's surveillance complex aligned with an economic base enthralled with the prospects of metadata appears too strong for meaningful reforms without significant shifts in larger economic formations. Whatever inherent contradictions exist within the present surveillance system, and regardless of the objections of privacy advocates of the liberal left and libertarian right, meaningful restrictions appear presently unlikely with surveillance formations so closely tied to the current iteration of global capitalism.

PART II

Lanting Those with a Communist Taint

Lant *n. Stale Urine.* It was preserved in a tank, and having been mixed with lime, used for dressing wheat before it was sown to prevent birds from picking up the seeds.

—Sidney Addy's 1888, *Glossary of Sheffield Words*

4

The Dangers of Promoting Peace during Times of [Cold] War: Gene Weltfish, the FBI, and the 1949 Waldorf Astoria's Cultural and Scientific Conference for World Peace

It should surprise no one that in a society championing military spending and maintaining ongoing wars and war preparation, those advocating for peace will be seen as dangerous individuals requiring monitoring and surveillance. During the Cold War, peace activists who maintained that peace could not occur without global-economic social justice were frequently marginalized, placed under surveillance and harassed by the FBI and other organs of social control.

This chapter considers the consequences for American anthropologist Gene Weltfish that followed her mid-twentieth century peace activism and academic peace research. As Weltfish's experiences, and many of her cohort demonstrate, during the Cold War, scholars pursuing radical critiques of the underlying nature of conflict and peace were often marginalized and targeted for FBI surveillance and harassment by repressive academic administrators. Weltfish took the problem of world peace very seriously and her efforts to advocate for solutions to mid-twentieth century wars led to clashes with Senator Joseph McCarthy and the FBI.

Gene Weltfish understood that it was impossible to speak of world peace without addressing the history of global colonialism and addressing where the wealth of Western nations came from.

But there were consequences for voicing such critical views. As Weltfish radically critiqued the possibility of establishing global peace under conditions of marked global inequality, she found herself at the margins of academia for choosing to confront rather than coalesce, and these views increasingly brought her under the surveillance of the FBI.

WELTFISH'S POLITICS AND FBI SURVEILLANCE

Gene Weltfish was born in New York's lower east side in 1902. She was an undergraduate at Barnard College in the 1920s, later studying anthropology with Franz Boas and Ruth Benedict at Columbia University. She conducted fieldwork with Pawnee Indians and completed her dissertation in 1929. She began teaching as a lecturer at Columbia in 1935 and was unable to advance beyond this rank due to the department's unusually burdensome requirement that all students must publish their doctoral dissertation.

Weltfish first came to the FBI's attention in the late 1930s because of her membership in several "popular front" groups advocating for racial equality, as these groups were assumed to be linked to the Communist Party. During the 1940s the FBI intensified their scrutiny of her. The 1940s were a time of increasing discomfort for Weltfish at Columbia, as university president Nicholas Murray Butler took steps "to tighten academic freedom of speech."[1] While many of Weltfish's colleagues tempered their speech and actions under these restrictive conditions, she continued to speak out and publish academic research on controversial subjects such as racial intolerance in America. In 1943 Ruth Benedict and Weltfish coauthored *The Races of Mankind* which critically examined the physical and social complexities of race.[2] The Public Affairs Council funded *The Races of Mankind* as a pamphlet designed to popularize anthropological views and critiques of American racial views. Its progressive critique of American racism led it to being withdrawn from military United Service Organization centers after "the chair of the House Military Affairs Committee, Congressman Andrew J. May, prohibited its distribution in the Army."[3] This anti-racist book would later be the focus of Senator Joseph

McCarthy and his aid Roy Cohn's interrogation of Weltfish before McCarthy's committee.

In 1944, anthropologist Ralph Linton told the FBI he considered Weltfish to be "on the fringe," that she was "almost fanatical" and that she was a fellow traveler with communists and other radicals.[4] Linton's role as an FBI informer extended to identifying Weltfish's ex-husband, anthropologist Alexander Lesser, as a communist, but he told the FBI that he

> was not certain that Gene Weltfish was ever a member of the Communist Party. However, he believed it likely that she may have been a member during Boas' regime in the Anthropology Department. He was of the opinion that it would definitely have been to her advantage to have become a member of the Communist Party at that time. Since the subject received favorable attention during that period, Linton drew the inference that Gene Weltfish had been a member of the Communist Party or at least a fellow traveler.[5]

FBI agents monitored Weltfish's mail, her public talks, and political statements to the press, and recorded her address and schedule in ways suggesting they might have illegally entered and searched her apartment as an FBI black-bag operation. But released records do not establish this.

The FBI reported on Weltfish's January 1945 protest of the American Red Cross' segregation of the blood of African American donors. One FBI informer who had attended a Weltfish lecture on myths of race and blood told the FBI that her talk, "made a deep impression on her and indicated it had impaired her faith in the Red Cross program."[6] This criticism of the Red Cross during the Second World War increased FBI concerns.[7] The FBI monitored her remarks at Henry Wallace's October 1946 Fight For Peace Rally in New York Madison Square Park where he advocated "that the American people demand of the United States Government that it stop those driving the United States towards war, and advocate instead a policy of peace with Russia."[8]

Four months prior to Gene Weltfish's participation at the Waldorf Conference for World Peace, Yale anthropologist George P.

Murdock had identified her and eleven other prominent members of the American Anthropological Association as dangerous communists in a four-page report submitted to FBI Director J. Edgar Hoover. Murdock was a reckless FBI informer whose choice of supposed communists (some of those identified as communists were, some weren't) betrayed a predilection towards anti-Semitism, but the FBI took Murdock's suspicions seriously and they intensified their investigations of the anthropologists named by him, causing serious personal and professional hardships for these colleagues.[9]

Murdock's accusations prompted the FBI's New York Field Office to reexamine its files on Weltfish. This spawned new investigations at Columbia University, where an FBI informant specializing in spying on suspected campus communists reported that "two organizations, 'Marxist Society' and the 'Progressive Student Organization,' are the instruments for spreading Communist Party doctrine within the university. Gene Weltfish, a professor, conducts the majority of the Marxist Society activities, according to this informant."[10] The FBI's intensified investigation of Weltfish following Murdock's accusations culminated in Columbia University firing Weltfish four years later. The timing of Murdock's FBI letter was particularly harmful to Weltfish because it focused the FBI's attention on her just as she was preparing to address the Waldorf Conference for World Peace.

THE WALDORF ASTORIA CULTURAL AND SCIENTIFIC CONFERENCE FOR WORLD PEACE

In March 1949, the National Council of the Arts, Sciences and Professions sponsored the "Cultural and Scientific Conference for World Peace" at the Waldorf Astoria Hotel. The National Council of Arts Sciences and Professions (NCASP) was an organization formed by supporters of Henry Wallace's presidential campaign. The Council's membership was characterized by Freda Kirchwey (publisher at *The Nation*) as being "made up of people of about the same range of opinion as the membership of the Wallace Party—Communists, near-Communists, and assorted liberals who believe peace requires a policy of conciliation with Russia."[11] The NCASP was never a large or powerful organization and its existence only spanned the years from 1947 to 1954, but membership in the Council brought FBI surveillance and political problems for members in the years to follow.

During McCarthyistic security and loyalty hearings of the 1950s, Council membership was touted as a sign of communist loyalties. Playwright Arthur Miller years later referred to the conference as "a hairpin curve in the road of history," as his conference participation marked him for life-altering harassment during the McCarthy period.[12] FBI agents infiltrated the conference, and the Bureau opened files on participants and collected information on their conference activities. Francis Saunders found that shortly after Howard Fast attended the Waldorf Conference,

> an FBI agent paid a visit to the publishing firm of Little, Brown, and told them that J. Edgar Hoover did not want to see Howard Fast's new novel, *Spartacus*, on the bookshelves. Little, Brown returned the manuscript to its author, who was then rejected by seven other publishers. Alfred Knopf sent the manuscript back unopened, saying he wouldn't even look at the work of a traitor. The book finally came out in 1950, published by Howard Fast himself.[13]

While some American communists belonged to the National Council, the conference was not the platform for party dictated communist indoctrination that its critics claimed. In fact, vocal intellectual critics—some of whom were supported by the CIA— were allowed to participate in some conference events and discussions.[14] Among the conference sponsors were well-known American and international intellectuals including Albert Einstein, Ben Shahn, Aaron Copeland, Studs Terkel, Isaac Stern, Dorothy Parker, Langston Hughes, Frank Lloyd Wright, Lillian Hellman, Dashiell Hammett, Leonard Bernstein, Linus Pauling, Charlie Chaplin, Henry Wallace, and Rockwell Kent.[15] Sociologist Bernhard Stern was a conference sponsor, and Franz Boas' son Ernst presented a paper advocating for a socialized government-managed health care system. Anthropologist and Ghanaian poet R.E.G. Armattoe spoke on racism in the postwar world.

The U.S. State Department issued visas to Soviet and Eastern Bloc delegates, but withheld visas from participants from Latin America (except for Cuba), France, Australia, Italy, Rumania, Hungary, and from all but a few invited participants from England.[16] The State Department made a strategic decision to not allow many of the more moderate foreign participants (from England, France, etc.) to attend the conference as a way to intensify the representation of radical, and therefore more easy to dismiss, critiques while eliminating voices from Allied nations that might have been more easily received in the American press. This censorship opened the U.S. government to international criticism. Freda Kirchwey wrote in *The Nation* just days following the conference that

> the behavior of the State Department betrayed a pathetic inability to distinguish reality from red tape and a lack of confidence in the capacity of America to survive without damage the brief visit, and not so brief oratory, of a handful of assorted European leftists. That such an attitude should be regarded as reasonable by a good many Americans only provides another illustration of the confusion of mind under which we suffer.[17]

The mainstream American press generally portrayed participants as communist invaders invited by American nitwit intellectuals trying to subvert democracy from the inner sanctum of freedom itself. Popular newspapers and magazines portrayed caricatures of propagandizing Soviet zealots and "superdupes"—as *Life* magazine designated American participants in a spread featuring a photograph of Gene Weltfish.[18] Less than two weeks before the conference, "Perry Brown, national commander of the American Legion said he feared that the conference 'may be a center for the exchange of important military information.'"[19] *The New Yorker* added some comical perspective, playfully depicting interactions between protestors, pedestrians, and police outside the conference in their "Talk of the Town" section.[20]

In the weeks leading up to the conference several sponsors, succumbing to pressures and death threats, withdrew conference sponsorships, with about a dozen of the over 500 sponsors withdrawing support.[21] Some troubled participants didn't withdraw, but used the conference to criticize organizers or other participants. Norman Cousins used his conference paper to attack conference organizers for not providing equal time to anti-Soviet intellectuals like Sidney Hook. After Cousin's paper Lillian Hellman dryly quipped that "I would recommend, Mr. Cousins, that when you are invited out to dinner you wait until you get home before you talk about your hosts."[22]

Over 2,800 individuals registered for the conference, and even with the State Department's efforts to intimidate participants the individual sessions were packed.[23] Some intellectuals participated with hopes that this extra-governmental exchange between American and Soviet intellectuals could repair the unraveled wartime alliance between these superpowers; others were more interested in using the conference to develop radical critiques of American domestic and foreign policies. Gene Weltfish pursued both these goals.

American Legion members, Hungarian-American activists, Catholic War Veterans and other conservative organizations picketed on the sidewalks and doorways outside the conference.[24] Arthur Miller later wrote that "it was big news in the press that every entrance of the Waldorf Astoria would be blocked by a line of nuns praying for the souls of the participants, who had been deranged by Satanic seduction."[25] In an effort to disrupt the conference the CIA covertly sponsored the presence of anti-Soviet or anti-Marxist intellectuals who harassed and jeered participants they believed were too pro-Soviet.[26] Chief among these intellectual-agitators was former communist and NYU philosopher Sydney Hook. The CIA secured a bridal suite at the Waldorf where Hook and other anti-Soviet intellectuals Mary McCarthy, Robert Lowell, Arthur Schlesinger, and Nicholas Nabokov planned their in-hotel disruptions of the conference.[27] This group engaged in "dirty-tricks," including intercepting "mail addressed to the conference's organizers, and sabotage[ing] their attempts to win over the press by doctoring official statements and releases."[28] At one conference session Nabokov aggressively confronted Shostakovich and demanded that he comment on *Pravda*'s recent denunciation of Hindemith, Schoenberg, and Stravinsky.

In the press, these anti-Soviet anti-communists publicly complained about the conference's narrow range of views. Sydney Hook protested that "not one well-known critic of Soviet totalitarianism was invited to participate" in the conference's main program.[29] Some on the American left saw Hook and his group of "professional anti-Communists [as being] as unprincipled and, [acting] in a ham manner, as Machiavellian as the party-liners or, for that matter the lobbyists for the power trust (who incidentally, dote on the Hook line—and sinker)."[30] Others on the left were disappointed by a lack of "free expression and exchange of ideas," as the Soviet participants were obviously monitored and constrained by silent watchful officials apparently from the Ministry for Internal Affairs (which became the KGB in 1953).[31]

The Soviets' heavy-handed efforts to control conference participants contrasted with Americans' more sophisticated strategies for monitoring and suppressing dissidents. These differences in approach and scope represented fundamental aspects of each state's apparatus for controlling dissent. The Soviet system rewarded intellectuals willing to think in ways aligned with state ideology and they harshly punished social critics with banishment, imprisonment, torture, and death; while the American system likewise rewarded scholars aligned with governmental policies, its punishments for dissident scholars existed (as Weltfish's career trajectory indicates), but were generally less severe in scope and scale.[32] While twentieth century America never experienced episodes of killings comparable to that directed by Stalin against Soviet dissidents, the American Red Hunts of the early and mid-century also relied on show trials and FBI harassment campaigns to intimidate American dissidents—acts that frequently led to dissidents (like Weltfish) losing their livelihood and becoming outcasts.

The Cultural and Scientific Conference for World Peace, played out on a stage set for high Cold War drama and a cast of characters from both sides of East-West polemics, seized the occasion to ridicule opponents; but for most participants the conference had been envisioned as an opportunity to consider the prospect of peace in the postwar world outside of the filters of the Soviet and American governments. Such hopes appear somewhat naive from an historical distance—but naive or not, the actions and consequences of a participant such as Weltfish inform us of the power of state surveillance, and of the consequences for scholars discussing the political and economic contingencies prohibiting peace even as her own state was working to maintain these very conditions of oppression.

WELTFISH'S WALDORF PAPER

On March 26, 1949, Gene Weltfish presented a paper on "Racism, Colonialism and World Peace," to the Waldorf Conference's panel on Economic and Social Sciences. The reason we know exactly what she said is because her FBI file includes a copy of her paper.[33]

When reading the published conference papers of some of Weltfish's co-panelists over 70 years later it is apparent that some of these authors' dire predictions and hopeful visions fell short of what has come to pass. For example, Paul Sweezy mistakenly predicted that the Marshall Plan would lead America to extract profits and create neo-colonial relations of dependency, wealth extraction, and domination under which Western Europe's economy would be reduced to the likes of those found in underdeveloped African nations. However, the observations, predictions, and analysis of other contributors to this session weathered better than Sweezy's. Colson Warne's paper on the "Economic Consequences of the Cold War in the United States" brilliantly characterized the emerging economic strategy in which the military-industrial complex took on much of the role of the pre-Depression business cycle. Warne compared America's domestic economic strategy with that he claimed had been characterized by "an able economist now high in the government" who'd imagined that the

American business cycles might be cured by maintaining a smoldering war with a mythical country. When business slumped, government expenditures for armaments would expand, and the army of unemployed would quickly be absorbed in ammunition making and in setting forth to conquer Atlantis. Such a drain on manpower would eliminate relief rolls, stimulate steel output, and, by expanding payrolls, hasten the day when the army might once more return to peacetime pursuits. Then, with business brisk, labor would be channeled into the production of consumer goods until the next decline again called forth another military exploit.[34]

While Warne's analysis is in line with many contemporary analyses of Cold War economics,[35] such views in 1949 were generally seen through a lens of jingoistic patriotism that cast Warne as disloyal and suspect. But for most Americans in 1949, it was not a time when being right was more important than being safe, and most played it safe.

Weltfish's paper examined the role of neo-colonialism in preventing peace in the postwar underdeveloped world. Her views have weathered well over the years. In fact, her analysis of neo-colonialism anticipates many of the critiques of imperialism and neo-colonialism developed decades later by such scholars as Kathleen Gough or Talad Asad.[36]

Thanks to FBI's surveillance, a single-spaced 14-page copy of her paper—entitled "Racism, Colonialism and World Peace"—survives in Weltfish's FBI file.[37] This appears to be a duplicate copy of her complete paper, and the FBI's copy contains about 25 percent of the material edited out of the later published version.[38] Her paper opened by arguing that the hope of peace is directly linked to reducing neo-colonial economic exploitation in Africa, Asia, and South America, stating that "the road to peace lies along the path of the ever greater improvement in the lot of mankind. The basic idea that production is more important than people which largely underlies our present way of life is antithetical to this objective."[39]

Weltfish described how international economic markets thrive on racism. She identified the neo-colonialist economic conditions prevailing in the postwar world and examined the role played by public and private American interests in the emerging conditions of the postwar period.[40] She analyzed the flow of wealth and the expropriation of raw materials in Africa, and in a section titled "thought control" she documented how indigenous journalists challenging these exploitive economic relations were imprisoned and eliminated as a means of quelling dissent among the exploited. But Weltfish believed these efforts to suppress indigenous journalistic critiques were doomed to fail and her paper issued a call for indigenous rights and a greater equity of economic and social justice, arguing that

> In all this is the underlying viewpoint that production is an end in itself and that raw materials are the means to its achievement, but the most essential part of the equation is left out— the people who work the raw materials—their wants, their rights, their needs and their power. If the racist-tainted mind in the U.S. and in the colonial countries believes that the colonial peoples do not see this error, he is mistaken. There is in some colonial peoples a certain refinement of mind that is foreign to our Western civilization.[41]

Weltfish argued that there can be no peace while international economic markets thrive on conditions of racism and economic exploitation. She identified the neo-colonialist economic conditions prevailing in the postwar world and described the role that the economic interests of profiteers played in these emerging conditions. In interpreting the economic policies of Great Britain, the United States, and other countries she focused on how these are designed to maintain the conditions of neo-colonialism, and she argued that until such economic systems of exploitation were dismantled there could be no peace.

Weltfish maintained that the former and then-present colonial powers of Europe owed the continents of Africa, Asia, and South America a portion of the wealth they extracted over the centuries. She argued that just as Europe was being rebuilt from the ravages of war with the Marshall Plan, so too must Africa be stabilized and compensated for the past taking of wealth. In considering the wealth of Africa she wrote that this

> vast continent gives us only the assurance of a great mineral and soil wealth, but [it] offers a challenge to the explorer for new and more bountiful wealth ... England and France with centuries of knowledge in colonization, the nations which will share largely in this experiment, control the major portion of the *exploitable* areas. Together with Belgium and Portugal, they can be *prevailed upon* to contribute to pro rata from their holdings ... It remains

our prime purpose to advocate merely the acceptance of Africa as the guinea pig ground for a world experiment of exploitation.[42]

She then proposed that the U.S. Congress "earmark 5 percent of all future appropriations for the Marshal Plan for the development of Central Africa."

Weltfish's paper concluded by outlining how a proposed African Development Company could work with the United Nations to help allocate repatriated funds throughout Africa. Weltfish's optimism for the UN typifies the attitudes of American progressive internationalists during this era. This was a time when liberals and radicals hoped the UN could function as a vital force opposing colonialism and neo-colonialism around the globe, and many of Weltfish's hopes were contingent on the UN acting to mitigate the inequities of the Underdeveloped World.

AFTER WALDORF: THE CONSEQUENCES OF CRITICISM

To contemporary eyes Weltfish may appear dreamy-eyed in closing her paper with specific recommendations for the return of some African wealth taken under colonialism. While Weltfish's critique and solutions *were* radical, her insistence that peace and stability in the underdeveloped world were inevitably linked to issues of economic justice should not be dismissed simply because of the difficulties involved in breaking such patterns of inequality between the developed and underdeveloped worlds. Whether or not such positions made Weltfish dreamy-eyed, they certainly made the FBI view her as a subversive whose views threatened American political policies.

After the Waldorf Conference, the FBI increased its surveillance on Weltfish, operations that included getting a student at Columbia University to spy on her, telephone surveillance, mail monitoring, spot checks, and interviews of acquaintances. In 1950, famed ex-communist professional witness (with an established record of lying to the FBI) Louis Budenz told the FBI that Weltfish was a "concealed Communist," a party member who kept her membership secret,[43] though my interviews with anthropologist-former-Communist-Party-members and family members revealed conflicting views regarding the possibility of her status as a party member.

Gene Weltfish's years of activism for peace and equality, her controversial statements regarding U.S. actions in the Korean War, as well as her subpoenaed April 1953 testimony before Senator McCarthy's Government Operations, Permanent Subcommittee on Investigations Committee angered Columbia's administration and created serious problems for her at the university.[44] Her ongoing contract at Columbia was suddenly terminated in 1953, ostensibly due to changes in university policies regarding lecturers, but the timing of her termination neatly coincided with her subpoena to appear before Senator McCarthy's Governmental Operations Committee, and followed soon after her controversial statements widely reported in the press suggesting that the United States may have used biological weapons in the Korean War.[45]

The American Anthropological Association (AAA) remained mute as Weltfish was hauled before local, state, and national loyalty and security hearings, and her rights to academic freedom were assaulted. Years of McCarthyistic attacks on anthropologists (such as Melville Jacobs, Richard Morgan, Bernhard Stern, Morris Swadesh, etc.) had whipped the AAA into a position of contrition and it learned to silently endure the bullying from these committees, and Weltfish was left to struggle on her own.

But the AAA's decision to ignore Weltfish as she came under attack did not mean that the lessons of her treatment were unnoticed by individual anthropologists who silently observed. Those who watched learned the values of doublethink and self-censorship. The fear that such episodes of punishment and humiliation generated was more important than the number of anthropologists who lost their jobs under McCarthyism's tribunals. McCarthyism's impact on academics and other public figures is not only measured in the numbers of individuals who lost their jobs—it is best measured in the extent it broadcast messages of fear and self-censorship to those who might otherwise have generated radical critiques or taken action for causes of peace or social justice.

These public humiliation rituals were the core of McCarthyism, and regardless of the guilt or innocence of Weltfish, the goal was to mark certain critical views as off limits to Americans, socially *lanting* and isolating these individuals.[46] After Columbia fired Weltfish, she spent much of the next decade continuing her Pawnee research, unemployed and underemployed until being hired at Fairleigh Dickinson University in 1961, where she taught until her death in 1980. But even though she later reentered academia she remained marked by her experiences and her discipline's abandonment of her and her right to dissent. McCarthyism was a successful tactic of oppression. It sent clear messages that it was dangerous to study and work to change domestic and international systems of inequality.

THE DANGERS OF TALKING PEACE DURING TIMES OF WAR

Weltfish's critique had unstated epistemological links to Marxist-Leninist global economic models. Her position that peace could not be achieved while Western capitalism continued to economically feed off of the hardships of the underdeveloped world was consistent with Lenin's analysis of imperialism.[47] Without untangling the conflicting information regarding questions of Weltfish's possible Communist Party membership,[48] it needs to be recognized that as far as the FBI was concerned it was irrelevant that Weltfish was likely not a member of the Communist Party: her analysis was opposed to U.S. policy, and thus her views were seen to be linked with real and imagined enemies of America's Cold War interests.

The Cold War created its own madness where logical arguments were easily overridden by the passions of volatile polemics. You get a sense of this in the transcripts of one Waldorf Conference session when a young Norman Mailer argued that both the imperialist West and Soviet East were responsible for the un-peaceful state of the world. Mailer insisted that "so long as there is capitalism, there is going to be war … [but] until you have a decent, equitable socialism, you can't have peace … [and] all a writer can do is tell the truth as he sees it, and to keep on writing."[49] As soon as Mailer said this, the room reportedly went wild. Mailer the provocateur was boo-ed by almost everyone present: pro-capitalists, pro-communists, anti-capitalists, and anti-communists alike. Mailer had "told the truth as he saw it" to an audience supercharged by the prime dialectic of the Cold War and they would not tolerate unaligned Mailer's efforts to have his cake and eat it too. The 1949 Cold War climate simply did not allow critiques to be seen outside of this great East-West divide—and Weltfish's position along this divide brought her years of hardship and alienation.

Weltfish's troubles with the FBI and Columbia are not simply episodes from a distant historical past. America's post-9/11 political developments clarify that academics contributing dissenting views to public policy debates still face similar threats. Just as Weltfish was seen as a threatening figure for publicly insisting that peace was not possible under conditions of neo-imperialist capitalist relations, contemporary scholars making the rather obvious but anti-jingoistic point that oppressive U.S. foreign policies contribute to global terrorism have been attacked and monitored in ways reminiscent of the McCarthy era.[50] In many ways, even two decades after 9/11, American academia remains stifled by the event's radiating impact on academic freedom.

But there is some small hope to be found in the words of journalist Izzy Stone who surmised that "all the official animosity" directed against the Waldorf Conference was based on the fear "that even a handful of Leftist intellectuals may somehow break through to the American people and interfere with the process of mobilizing them emotionally for war."[51] This is a good charge for intellectuals today: to somehow break through the media and political blockade and to challenge not only the perpetual state of warfare, but to also examine—as Gene Weltfish argued—the impossibility of achieving peace under a political economy that uses force and exploitation to garner wealth, power, and hegemony for nation.

5

Tribal Communism under Fire: Archie Phinney and the FBI

The FBI's surveillance and harassment of Native American activists during the 1960s and 1970s have been well documented by writers such as Ward Churchill, Jim Vander Wall, and Peter Mathiessen, while less research has been undertaken to document the FBI's intrusion into Indian activist movements of earlier periods.[1] Numerous documents released under the Freedom of Information Act (FOIA) establish that the FBI had both a visible and unseen presence on Indian reservations since the 1930s, and during the 1960s the Bureau became more actively involved in monitoring and provoking reservation political situations.[2] In the late 1950s, 1960s, and 1970s, the FBI launched a series of Counterintelligence Programs (known in Bureau-Speak as "COINTELPRO") designed to monitor and disrupt native people's efforts to find justice and increase their self-determination and self-rule.

The FBI's unofficial view of Indians' place in American society was crudely articulated by FBI Assistant Special Agent in Charge, Norman Zigrossi, in 1977 when he claimed Indians "are a conquered nation, and when you are conquered, the people you are conquered by dictate your future. This is a basic philosophy of mine. If I'm part of a conquered nation, I've got to yield to authority ... [The FBI must function as] a colonial police force."[3] While FBI personnel have rarely issued such statements publicly, the FBI's long-standing efforts to monitor and constrain native power movements over the decades seem to sustain the Bureau's widespread support for such unofficial sentiments. This history of FBI antipathy towards Indian autonomy appears clear in the released FOIA records from the FBI's investigation of anthropologist Archie Phinney's efforts to strengthen tribal managerial systems during the 1940s.

The FBI's interest in Phinney's political activism during the 1930s and 1940s, and the surviving FBI records establish a continuity of FBI surveillance and harassment linking the FBI's investigations of Phinney and the FBI's future COINTELPRO campaigns, as the FBI tried to monitor and undermine native individuals and groups seeking increased rights. I filed my first FOIA request for Archie Phinney's FBI records in 1996 after coming across some of the Bureau of Indian Affair's archival holding on Phinney at the Sand Point National Archives-Pacific Northwest Federal Repository. Knowing little about Phinney or his politics, I assumed that anyone who traveled to, or lived in the Soviet Union during the 1930s was likely a target of some sort of FBI investigation given FBI Director, J. Edgar Hoover's well-known paranoia. Four years after filing a FOIA request for Phinney's FBI records, the FBI sent me a photocopy of 109 pages of his 111-page FBI file.

PHINNEY AND THE FBI

Archie Phinney was born under the native name of Kaplatsilpilp, on the Nez Percé Reservation in Idaho in 1903. His mother was a Nez Percé tribal member, while his father was of Euro-American descent. One of Phinney's acquaintances from the Bureau of Indian Affairs provided the FBI with a summary of Phinney's early years:

Mr. Phinney was born and raised on the Nez Perce reservation. He attended Indian schools, finishing high school at an Indian boarding school, Haskell Institute, at Lawrence, Kansas. Being an outstanding student, he attended the University of Kansas while still boarding at Haskell. Apparently, he showed marked ability in the social sciences. His full-blooded Indian ancestry, knowledge of his native tongue, customs and traditions of his tribe, incurred the interest of several anthropologists interested in Indians. This, I believe, was the entrée through which he became acquainted with the late Franz Boas, eminent anthropologist, associated with Columbia University. Mr. Phinney continued his researches at Columbia under Boas and published the results of his study in a book on Indian mythology. This study I believe, was the springboard upon which he later became the recipient of some scholarship that permitted him to study abroad.[4]

Phinney earned his BA from the University of Kansas in 1926, then moved to New York to study anthropology under Franz Boas at Columbia University until 1931. Boas helped Phinney organize and publish his monograph, *Nez Percé Texts* with Columbia University Press.[5] Phinney received a fellowship from the Leningrad Academy of Sciences that allowed him to live and study at the Academy in the Soviet Union from 1932 to 1937, where he studied the native peoples of northern Russia and Siberia.[6]

While living in the Soviet Union, Phinney reported to the American Embassy in Moscow in December 1933 that his passport was stolen. After receiving assistance from ACLU Director Roger Baldwin, he was issued a new passport,[7] but the U.S. Department of State launched an investigation into whether the numbers of Phinney's passport had been altered or improperly recorded. In 1933 Phinney wrote Boas that he hoped to find a Soviet system in place that the United States could emulate to improve the rights and conditions of native peoples—though he wrote that he was aware some of the overall conditions in the USSR were not as developed as those found in the United States. He wrote Boas that

I am not optimistic about the value of the Russian method as a thing applicable to the U.S. Indian reservations. My study so far has been somewhat limited to those larger groups that were already in a good position to accept full autonomy. The Russian policy is sound enough and effective here but devised to operate within the range of a new set of economic relationships— economic relationships which on one hand the Indian Bureau isn't likely to consider for Indian tribes and on the other are not at once attainable by a moribund reservation group. I will find out, however, what if anything has actually been done to deal with natives who live under the least favorable circumstances. I get from what I read and from what is constantly told to me, too many facts about phenomenal development of native groups that were from the beginning rather well constituted socially and economically and not enough facts about the social rehabilitation or regeneration of tribes that haven't achieved an economic status consistent with the soviet industrialization plans.[8]

While still living in the Soviet Union, Phinney later corresponded with BIA Commissioner John Collier about matters relating to conditions on U.S. Indian reservations, and he eventually made arrangements for employment at the Bureau of Indian Affairs upon his return.[9]

PHINNEY'S RETURN FROM THE USSR

After returning to the United States in 1938, Phinney went to work for the Bureau of Indian Affairs (BIA) as a Field Agent in the Indian Service's Indian Organization Division. Later, in his capacity as a Superintendent at the Bureau of Indian Affairs, Phinney advocated that the Nez Percé Tribe adopt strong self-rule policies. He used his BIA position to promote the adoption of a Nez Percé tribal constitution which increased the collective role and power of the tribe while weakening individual property rights. The FBI interpreted this as a radical proposal, likely influenced by his time spent in the Soviet Union. The FBI failed to consider the traditional precedent for such a collective approach to a tribal political economy, and instead of viewing this as being based on what might have been thought of as derived from Native American traditions of collective stewardship, they viewed it as suspiciously anti-American. The FBI continued to monitor Phinney and eventually reported on his great disappointment when the Nez Percé Tribe did not adopt a self-rule constitution.

According to ██████ one of the provisions of the rejected constitution would have resulted in the tribe members being unable to will their property to anyone outside the tribe. If some tribe member died and did not have relatives in the tribe or willed it out, the land would revert to the Nez Perce Tribe itself. Any gain from such acquired land by the tribe would be shared by the members of the tribe.

████████████ said that perhaps some thought this Communistic. Many he thought opposed it for reasons such as having married outside the tribe and would under such an arrangement be unable to will the land to their wives or other relatives. ████████████ pointed out that under Federal legislation under the Wheeler-Howard Act the Indian tribes were given the opportunity of accepting or declining to come under the Act, which act has as one of its provisions the same method or similar method of handling Indian lands. He said therefore the idea was nothing new and was not originated by Mr. Phinney. He thought the proposed constitution was just an effort on the part of Phinney to get the tribe under a similar provision as provided in the Wheeler-Howard Act.[10]

The Wheeler-Howard Act of 1934 transferred significant governmental responsibility for the management of reservations from the U.S. government to local tribes. Part of Phinney's job as an agent of the BIA was to explain the meaning of this act to the Indians of Northern Minnesota and Wisconsin. The FBI kept Phinney under surveillance and monitored him as he undertook this task. One unidentified individual later interviewed by the FBI reported that Phinney

made about six trips to [the] Fond du lac [Reservation] and the meetings lasted from two hours to a half a day. [The informer] advised that Phinney at one of these meetings, had advocated that the Fond du lac reservation, which consisted of an area of 24 by 25 miles, consolidate into one group and have community holdings and all share the proceeds equally. [The informer] could not recall the exact words used, but from the words used ████████████ got the opinion Phinney was advocating that the Fond du lac agency establish an economy like that of Russia. [The informer] stated that he had, himself, read extensively on Communism and had talked to several people he believed to be Communists from Kettle River, Minnesota, and after hearing Phinney, he firmly believed him to be advocating the practice of Communism, on the reservation, although he could recall no specific statements.[11]

This individual told the FBI that after these meetings he wrote a letter to a member of Congress and requested that Phinney be investigated for holding communist beliefs. A March 16, 1948 memo from the Washington, DC field office established that

> Mr. William D. Savage, Chairman of Chippewa Indian Farmer-Labor Union, Calquit, Minn. in April, 1940, sent a letter to Hon. Henrik Shipstead, U.S. Senator, Minn. This letter advised that the Chippewa Farm-Labor Party at Calquit, Minn. had been informed and believes that one, Archie Phinney, Organization Field Agent, is a believer in and influenced by Communistic doctrines, having spent an extended period of time in Russia.[12]

This same unidentified informant (who could possibly have been Savage) told the FBI that his Congressman replied with a letter noting that Phinney was educated in Russia. This letter was read aloud at the next tribal meeting, at which Phinney was absent. Phinney was, however, present at the following meeting where the minutes recording the letter reading and discussion were read. Phinney confirmed that he had been educated in Russia, and "after his acknowledgment … the council told Phinney that his services were no longer needed and that the Fond du lac Chippewa Indians could get along without his services or instructions." Phinney reportedly did not return to the Fond du lac Reservation.[13] It is unknown how this Congressman knew of Phinney's years in Russia, but it seems likely that the FBI had a hand in the dissemination of this information, though no records establishing this were located within Phinney's released FBI file.

An FBI agent recorded a similar story from a member of the Nez Percé Tribe. In 1947 plans had been made to replace the tribe's system of leasing reservation lands to non-Indians using the federal government's "Lease-Clerk" system whereby a clerk handled all the details of the arrangement with the tacit understanding that the "Indians themselves are incapable of handling" such matters.[14] At a Coeur d'Alene Tribal Council meeting Phinney proposed that the old "Lease-Clerk" system be abolished and replaced with a plan he'd developed called "Enterprise Leasing." Under this proposed plan the management of these leased lands would shift from federal management to local, tribal control. The tribal member interviewed by the FBI the reported that

> This plan was twice rejected by the Tribal Council. About February 14, 1948 this plan was brought before the Coeur d'Alene Tribal Council for the third time by Phinney and was adopted. The only signatures necessary on the plan for its adoption were those of the President and Secretary of the Tribal Council. ███████████ charges that Phinney obtained these signatures by telling the Secretary of the Tribal Council that the President had signed the document and then in turn telling the President of the Tribal Council that the Secretary had signed; thus, both signed simply because each believed the other had signed first. ████████ said this plan did not represent the will or intent of the Secretary and President of the Tribal Council. According to ████████████████ he obtained this information concerning the signatures through personal conversation with the Secretary of the Tribal Council.[15]

The FBI reported that the following month the council rescinded their agreement to this plan, despite Phinney's threats that such action would lead to the loss of productive farmlands.

Rather than seeing Phinney's enterprise leasing plan as a means of increasing the tribe's autonomy from the Department of Interior, or as a way to increase tribal revenues, this individual reporting to the FBI said they believed Phinney's motivation behind this plan was to "increase his prestige as an efficient superintendent"—due to the reduction of federal funds and administrative costs.[16]

On April 17, 1947 the Butte, Montana FBI's Special Agent in Charge reported that on a recent trip to Portland, Phinney had said, "the capitalists must be done away with, that the government must own everything, and that revolution will come in time."[17] FBI Director J. Edgar Hoover advised the Butte Special Agent in Charge on July 22, 1947 that Phinney was reported to be "pro-Russian" and that he was "apparently exerting a great deal of influence on the Indians" of the Lapiway Indian Reservation.[18] An internal FBI report established a check of the records of the House Committee on Un-American Activities "reflect no information regarding" Phinney.[19]

The FBI's surveillance of Phinney increased with suspicions that he was using his position to help tribes collectivize. His FBI file records interviews with dozens of individuals involved with the Nez Percé Reservation (whites, Indians, BIA officials) with reports both praising and condemning Phinney, his work, and his character. Some individuals claimed he was a good, competent leader who'd significantly improved life on the reservation, while others blamed declining reservation health care and increased drunkenness on Phinney. One way that the FBI undermined Phinney was by repeatedly asking tribal members if they noticed any communistic tendencies in his actions or beliefs. Most said they had seen no such actions, though some said Phinney's views on the tribal constitution seemed somewhat communistic. Some tribal members said that they knew Phinney had lived in the Soviet Union, but he did not talk about his experiences there. One tribal member believed that "the Indians are a bit more antagonistic or perhaps more aggressive in dealing with 'Whites' than they were before Phinney took over the agency ... this attitude is not shown in the surface by acts and deeds but is more 'felt' than observed."[20] Another tribal member told the FBI that Phinney had not even been involved in the drafting of the proposed tribal constitution, but instead he (the interviewee) and two other tribal members had written it, and "Mr. Phinney only approved it."[21] One "Confidential Informant" reported that after Phinney returned from the Soviet Union he had told him that "he admired the Russians for their treatment of minorities and poor people and that he believed that Russia was doing a better job than the United States."[22]

In an effort to gather more information concerning his loyalty and links to communism, the FBI interviewed BIA employees who had worked with Phinney at Window Rock, the United Pueblo Indian Agency at Albuquerque, and in St. Paul, Minnesota. One person told the FBI that when he asked Phinney why he didn't stay in Russia he had answered that it was "because I am fed up with the Russian way of living and I must again see the hills of Idaho."[23] This same person told the FBI that Phinney struck him as a loyal American and reasoned that "if Phinney favored the Russian way of life and system of government, he would have remained in Russia instead of coming back to the United States."[24]

A December 6, 1947 investigation of Phinney undertaken by the Butte, Montana FBI Field Office provided the following investigative summary of Phinney:

██████████████████ North Idaho Indian Agency, Lapwai, Idaho, has been closely associated with ARCHIE PHINNEY through business and personal contact. ████████ as a member of the Nez Perce Indian Tribe. He states that Mr. PHINNEY is very careful not to declare himself on the subject of Communism. As an example, ████████████████████ Mr. PHINNEY ████████ Idaho, where he, PHINNEY, made a short talk before a Service club. PHINNEY asked afterward of ████████ if anything in his talk would be interpreted by those who heard it as reflecting Communism. ████████ said he had heard the talk and had not interpreted any part of it as containing anything of Communist character or "line". ████████ states that this one mention of Communism is the only time he can recall that PHINNEY has even mentioned the subject to him.

In ████████ opinion, PHINNEY does not belong to the Communist Party nor has he any desire to install such a system on the reservation or to influence the Indians in that direction. ████████ has never seen any periodicals or books of a questionable nature that might indicate Mr. PHINNEY's interest in Communism.

Mr. PHINNEY does not discuss politics and has merely acknowledged living in Russia. He has spoken to ████████ very briefly about hardships he found in Russia, in connection with housing, while he was there. He also has indicated that the so-called "iron curtain" was noticeable during the time he was in Russia, indicating that he was not allowed to see everything that was going on. He has never heard PHINNEY praise the system of government in Russia.

PHINNEY'S policies have been aimed at the best interests of the Indians. One of his policies has been to get the Indians back on their land and working it instead of leasing it. ████████ said he believes this is an over-all policy of the Department of

Interior as well. PHINNEY has had great influence, and has been able to carry through almost all of his plans and [policies] without opposition from the Indians. The one exception has been when the Indians of the Nez Perce tribe at Lapwai voted against adopting a constitution. PHINNEY was disheartened by this vote and released a newspaper article, published at Lewiston, Idaho, in which he criticized the Indians for not being progressive enough to vote in favor of the proposed constitution. PHINNEY asked ▆▆▆▆▆▆ if he had read this article and PHINNEY said something to ▆▆▆▆ to the effect that he surely "told them off" in the article. ▆▆▆▆▆▆ said PHINNEY was much upset by this turn of events and seldom expresses himself as loudly as he did on that occasion. Ordinarily Mr. PHINNEY is very quiet, conservative and "tight mouthed."[25]

Later in this same report, another informant at the North Idaho Indian Agency in Lapwai, Idaho, told the FBI that

he could not recall of any acts or statements by ARCHIE PHINNEY that would indicate Communistic tendencies. He also stated that there is no more dissension among the Indians of the area now than there has been under past Superintendents. He said there are always some few who have differences with the agency. He said the proposed constitution that was voted on by the Indians contained nothing of a Communistic nature whatsoever. He said that perhaps some of the Indians were suspicious of the constitution and voted against it more from a lack of understanding than for any sound reason. He said PHINNEY has made talks at various civic organizations, some of which he has heard, and that on none of these occasions has PHINNEY stated anything that would indicate a learning toward Communism or a Pro-Russian attitude.

He related that a number of fine buildings on the agency grounds at Lapwai have been ordered to be disposed of by the agency by either tearing them down or by having them removed. He recalled that PHINNEY thought it would be a good idea if these buildings were made into homes or apartments and the Nez Perce Indians live in them in a sort of community on the grounds. He was unable to sell this idea to the members of the tribe, who seem to prefer a more independent way of living in scattered shacks and homes throughout the large reservation. █████ thought that possibly someone might have interpreted this idea as being Communistic, but said he doubted that PHINNEY had any such intent. ████████ interpretation of the idea was that PHINNEY thought the building could be put to a good use in the manner and that the buildings would furnish better housing conditions than many of the Indians now enjoy.[26]

The suggestion that Phinney's attempt to gain maximum use of these available resources cast a shadow of communist suspicion on him indicates the extent to which knowledge of his years spent in the Soviet Union later colored interpretations of even the most mundane decisions.

A Portland Bureau FBI report (23 March, 1948) contained the results of an interview with an acquaintance of Phinney who reported Phinney stated that the "U.S. is obsolete and unfair to laboring classes and favors the capitalists; is all wrong; is run by the capitalists; government should be changed and will be changes; there will be an upset in this country some day; the government should own everything and operate everything."[27] This same individual reported that Phinney held an "utter disregard for laws" and was known to violate traffic and liquor control laws frequently.

Regardless of how many statements and testimonies that Phinney's "greatest interest appeared to be making the Indians more self-reliant, and having the White people receive the Indians without a feeling that the Indians were an inferior race, and also wanting the Indians to live in a manner that would make them acceptable to the White people," the FBI insisted on focusing their attention on claims that he had "allegedly made pro-Russian statements and attempted to antagonize Indians on his [Idaho] Reservation against the U.S. Govt."[28] It did not matter how many individuals reported that they had never heard Phinney say anything indicating that he was either pro-Russian or pro-communist; the FBI kept searching until they could find a few individuals who would report him as such.

The FBI's interest in Phinney ended with his sudden death in 1949. Had Phinney lived longer, as a federal employee he likely would have been called before Congressional loyalty and security hearings. His years spent in the Soviet Union, as well as his efforts to try and bring a more communal structure to various Indian reservations would have provided McCarthy and others with excellent opportunities for anti-communist diatribes.

EVERYTHING'S ARCHIE

The FBI's investigations of Archie Phinney were not routine employee background investigations; these were "Domestic Security" investigations. This is indicated by the FBI's record system classification code of "100" indicating a Domestic Security investigation, the FBI code most commonly used in FBI investigations of suspected communists. The nature of the FBI's investigation and ongoing surveillance of him and his activities—particularly their persistent attempts to link his tribal managerial reform efforts to communism—indicates a high level of Bureau concern with monitoring Phinney, but their efforts to investigate him also spread currents of fear and suspicion which appear designed to help undermine his credibility in ways similar to later COINTELPRO efforts to marginalize other progressive leaders.

Several factors converged with the FBI's investigation of Archie Phinney. First, simply working as a federal employee opened the door for the FBI's investigations of him—though few records in his file indicate that the FBI devoted much effort to this type of routine background investigation. Second, the FBI was intensely anti-communist, and the mere fact that Phinney had lived for several years in the Soviet Union raised suspicions that he was either a communist or was pro-communist. Third, Phinney's vision for the possibilities of tribal economics went beyond normative notions of what could be done with collective property and profits. That Phinney advocated for tribal pooling and community reorganization of tribal funds suggested to the FBI that these actions were part of a larger communist plot. The FBI lacked any historical or anthropological perspective concerning traditional native political-economic redistributional systems among American Indian peoples, so these actions were only seen as the importation of foreign ideologies, rather than the playing out of alternative native redistributional systems. But even off the reservation, the FBI was suspicious of almost any citizen working to provide alternatives to capitalism's rules of ownership and profit, undertaking investigations of citizens organizing Public Utilities Districts (community-owned non-profit energy cooperatives) and buying cooperatives in the 1950s.[29] Finally, the mere fact that Phinney was an activist, dedicated to improving the lives of minority populations was enough for the FBI to consider him worthy of an investigation. The FBI has a long history of investigating and marginalizing activists working to improve the plight of minority peoples.

The FBI's inquiries concerning Phinney on the Lapiway, Fond du lac, and Nez Percé Reservations should be interpreted not simply as acts of investigations, but also as acts of FBI harassment and intimidation. The visible and skulking presence of the FBI sent clear messages throughout these reservation communities that Phinney was a controversial person who was likely involved in wrongdoing of some sort, and others should steer clear of him and his proposals. As such, these inquiries were part of an FBI campaign to intimidate native peoples and to discredit individuals who had the skills and potential to organize other Indians in opposition to the policies of the dominant white culture. The FBI's efforts to discredit Phinney were in part linked to his advocacy for such progressive programs as "enterprise leasing," or more localized community-based forms of resource management.

Archie Phinney's FBI file raises a number of questions to which we do not have answers. I do not know if he was ever a member of the Communist Party, though it seems likely that he was a Party member at least during the 1930s. As a highly educated member of a persecuted minority group in his own society, the promises of communism in the 1930s may have seemed to offer a badly needed hope. In the end, the truth of Phinney's past Party membership mattered not at all, what mattered was Phinney's activism. Like Phinney, other activists affiliated with organizations tied to communist and socialist political organizations came under FBI scrutiny in the postwar period, and the boogieman of Party membership became a useful excuse to root through the private lives of any individuals dedicated to fighting for racial and economic equality. If communists were uncovered during this rooting, so much the better, but accusations and the resultant fear were the currency of these witch-hunts. During the McCarthy period, it mattered little whether Party membership was uncovered when these public humiliation rituals served to purge labor organizations and frighten concerned citizens from becoming active in the fight against Jim Crow racism.

Phinney's efforts on the Nez Percé Reservation to ratify a constitution increasing the collective power of the tribe while weakening individual property rights can be seen as not only existing along a continuum of Marxian approaches, but as also containing core elements of more traditional Indian political economic systems stressing group rather than individual processes.[30] And from an extended political perspective, the FBI's monitoring and harassment of native anthropologist Archie Phinney must also be seen as part of an extended FBI campaign to monitor, weaken, and discredit Indian political activists fighting for the rights of their people.

It should not be surprising that the FBI would view a Native American using his education and governmental position to try and empower other Indians and trying to help them regain control over their land as un-American. If we understand U.S. government policies against Indians and the history of treaty violations and theft of native lands as fundamentally *American activities*, we can clearly see how Phinney's legal efforts to empower Indian communities were in a very real sense *Un-American activities*. As a protector of these policies, the FBI's efforts to monitor and undermine Phinney were all part of a long history of government suppression of native autonomy and native rights.

6

The FBI's History of Undermining Legal Defenses: From Jury Panel Investigations to Defense Lawyer Surveillance Programs

A foundational premise of the American judicial system is the claim that all are equal under the law. As part of this claim of equality, when charged by the state, all people have access to lawyers who can develop the best possible defense for them without governmental interference. As part of the United States Department of Justice, the FBI claims to uphold these principles of fair play. Yet there are many ways that the FBI historically undermined the work of defense attorneys, while assisting prosecutors. Sometimes this has been simply withholding evidence from prosecuting attorneys, but there are other ways that the Bureau has used its investigatory files and surveillance abilities to aid prosecutors, hamper the defense, or even to conduct surveillance operations on defense attorneys.

Local police forces and prosecutors routinely cooperate in criminal trials. Under these arrangements, police collect statements and evidence that support the charging of individuals with crimes, and once charged, prosecuting attorneys take over the case and move towards a trial—or most frequently, towards a plea bargain. While police and prosecutors both represent the interests of the state, basic rules of evidence sharing and other procedural practices require that the police share evidence with the prosecution and defense in some neutral ways.

As a federal law enforcement agency investigating criminal activities, the FBI interacts with federal prosecutors in somewhat similar relationships as local police engage with prosecutors. Yet, the FBI's federal domain and extensive powers, as well as the Bureau's ability to operate under conditions of unusual secrecy, have repeatedly led the FBI to use its unique surveillance capacities to influence or interfere with judicial proceedings beyond what might be thought of as the normal scope of Bureau procedures.

This chapter draws on FBI files released under FOIA to examine two ways that the FBI has historically used its surveillance capabilities to impact or interfere with judicial processes. The first of these involves a poorly understood program under which FBI agents provide federal prosecutors with confidential records—from the Bureau's massive inventory of FBI files—on prospective jurors for federal trials. The second instance involves the FBI conducting surveillance operations on attorneys representing clients who have been the subject of extensive FBI investigations.

FBI Director Hoover studied criminal law in law school, but his general disdain for criminal defense attorneys became institutionalized within the FBI. One record of the FBI's institutional contempt for criminal defense attorneys is seen in a 1936 four-page FBI memo from FBI Agent R.E. Joseph to Clyde Tolson summarizing an *Esquire* article on F. Lee Bailey's approach to criminal defense, where Special Agent Joseph wrote that "portions of this article might be helpful to the Director in making future addresses, at which time he might desire to point out how unscrupulous criminal defense lawyers stimulate disrespect for law and influence crime conditions."[1] Historically, the Bureau's disdain for defense attorneys meant that the FBI did not consider its surveillance of lawyers conferring with their clients as unscrupulous behavior. Agents rationalized these acts as necessary to protect the American judicial system, even while engaging in acts that undermined its claims of legitimacy.

A 1977 lawsuit by the National Lawyers Guild (NLG) against the DoD, CIA, FBI, and NSA led to the release of over 300,000 pages of documents. These documents revealed various government agencies had monitored and harassed the Guild for decades. The Guild found that the FBI's harassment campaign resulted in "the Guild's membership decreas[ing] substantially and the organization lost public support and financial contributions."[2] Released records documented numerous NLG lawyers had been placed on the FBI's Security Index.[3] These FBI files detailed the Bureau engaging in "2,573 separate acts of trespass, burglary conversion, entry upon premises by false premise, obtaining documents by false premise, surreptitious copying of documents, and acts designed to cause of loss of membership and contributions."[4] This surveillance and attacks on the Guild succeeded in spreading distrust and suspicion of the organization, which led to loss of clients and declining public support.

The FBI targeted the NLG for surveillance because of the Guild's long history of representing members of the radical left, from anti-government subversives to victims of McCarthyism, Black Panthers, groups challenging the actions of the CIA or FBI, and various activist groups accused of terrorism. The FBI targeted numerous progressive groups and individuals simply because the Guild served as legal counsel, and this surveillance interfered with the rights for accused individuals and groups to privately consult with legal counsel. As Traci Yoder argued in her 2014 NLG report, *Breach of Privilege: Spying on Lawyers in the United States*, "Surveillance of the legal profession compromises the once sacrosanct attorney-client privilege—the ability to speak with a lawyer. The constitutional right to privileged attorney-client interactions is often ignored when a client's actions challenge the status quo of government and corporate power."[5]

Yoder found that the U.S. government conducted surveillance operations targeting lawyers representing detainees at Guantanamo Bay Detention Center, monitoring conversations between lawyers and their clients. The U.S. government used "microphones and cameras … disguised as ordinary objects like smoke detectors in meeting rooms" which they placed in rooms where attorneys met with clients. The Guild established that similar surveillance of lawyers representing clients accused of terrorism occurred at New York's Metropolitan Detention Center, and that the NSA spied on lawyers representing Sulaiman abu-Ghaith, Osama bin Laden's son-in-law.[6] During the trial of attorney Lynne Stewart, evidence obtained under a FISA warrant included recordings of what she had believed to be private attorney-client privileged conversations, in this instance a FISA warrant was used to listen to conversations between an attorney and her client.

One of WikiLeaks founder Julian Assange's legal advisors, Michael Ratner, reported the U.S. government allowed "the mass surveillance of my conversations overseas with all my clients who I assume are all under surveillance by the government, whether it is Julian Assange or Guantanamo families or others." Ratner complained that his ability to defend Assange was compromised because "all of our legal advice to clients is taken in by the NSA."[7] Ratner was also under FBI surveillance during his many trips to Cuba, including his legal work for Haitian refugees at Guantanamo Bay.[8] Documents leaked by Edward Snowden confirm that the NSA uses its surveillance capacity to listen in on attorney-client communications on a global scale.[9]

Yoder's report concluded that "government surveillance of legal professionals creates a chilling effect on lawyering, dissuades attorneys from taking on political clients, compromises their ability to represent people, erodes public confidence in the privacy of communications with attorneys, and requires precautions to ensure that communications between attorney and clients are secure."[10]

FBI JURY PANEL INVESTIGATIONS

One institutional legacy J. Edgar Hoover left the FBI grew from his insistence that agents collect and compile detailed information on all those who crossed the FBI's path. Hoover required that all such information collected by FBI agents be filed and cross-indexed in ways that could be retrieved and used at some future unknown point in time, for reasons unknown to those collecting this information. This feature of omnivorous collection of information linked to names is one of the obsessive features of the FBI as the Bureau extends its reach into imagined futures where, as an act of faith, it believes these collected scraps of knowledge might have some value. This meant that as the FBI collected and compiled information on persons of interest in an investigation, these agents also compiled information on the secondary and tertiary people who crossed their path along the way. Neighbors, coworkers, customers, job references, relatives of suspects, landlords, friends, distant acquaintances, and random associates of individuals subject to FBI investigations had their names, along with certain details, indexed and entered into the FBI's file system, under the assumption that this information might be of use at some later date.

The FBI's reasons for opening files on individuals have historically been far broader than might be assumed. For example, a wide range of government employment requires background checks undertaken by FBI agents—during wartime, these investigations have been widespread and ongoing. I have read hundreds of FBI files detailing FBI agents showing up unannounced (the FBI's favorite approach) at someone's home and informing the resident that they would like to conduct a background check interview on an acquaintance. In most instances the FBI agent is invited into the home and seated in the living room or at a dining room table and the agent interviews the references. The FBI tells them their responses will be confidential, then they are asked basic questions about how they know the job applicant, how long they have known them, whether they know anything suspicious about the individual or have any reason to suspect their loyalty.

Many of the FBI summaries of these background check interviews are brief, consisting of a short paragraph noting how long the informant knew the subject, stating they have no derogatory information, perhaps including a sentence characterizing some aspect of their personality demonstrating loyalty. But in some FBI reports, the agents record suspicions about the interviewee, noting information the agent gained during this background interview process; this being a free-ranging intelligence gathering feature of FBI culture. Sometimes these can be notes about reading material the agent observes in a living room, or during the 1940s, 1950s, and 1960s, concerns about interracial friendships maintained by the interviewee. At times, these concerns or questions could cause an ambitious FBI agent to open an investigation on these secondary subjects. Usually this just meant creating a short file noting whatever details caught the FBI agent's attention and placed this individual on their radar, which then brought checks of the FBI's indexes and cross lists of things like memberships in groups or subscriptions to publications viewed by the FBI with suspicion. During the 1940s, 1950s, and 1960s it did not take much to draw the FBI's attention.

FBI dossiers, files, and lists have a way of taking on a life of their own. During the McCarthy period if a large list of names included a known or suspected communist or two, everyone appearing on the whole list became suspect by the FBI. Because Hoover's FBI maintained its collected information in cross-indexed retrievable files, this large body of data was sometimes selectively provided by the FBI to federal prosecutors (without sharing with or alerting the defense team) when selecting jurors for upcoming trials. This occurred under an FBI program known as the Jury Panel Investigations Program.

SECTION 51: JURY PANEL INVESTIGATIONS

The FBI's Jury Panel Investigation program was established in 1924. Jury Panel Investigations are sanctioned Bureau operations that use FBI agents to compile information from the Bureau's private files to produce dossiers on prospective jurors who may be seated for an upcoming federal trial. To compile this list, the FBI cross-checks a list of potential jurors provided by a federal prosecutor with their FBI file indexes. When the FBI identifies files pertaining to perspective jurors, it makes these files available to federal prosecutors preparing for upcoming jury selection.[11]

Jury Panel Investigations have historically been relatively rare undertakings. Haines and Langber report only 520 cases at Headquarters (555 field cases, which likely mirror these same HQ cases), with 42 field offices reportedly opening cases between the years of 1924 and 1980. They also report that our ability to document the impacts of this program are reduced because "there has been substantial destruction" of FBI records from this program even though the National Archives' disposition recommendation is that records from FBI Headquarters (including these) should be microfilmed and retained, while all field records should be "destroyed."[12]

The FBI's Manual of Investigative Operations and Guidelines (Section 51) states that under the Bureau's policy and procedures these FBI Jury Panel field operations should only be undertaken after a U.S. attorney has requested the investigation to the Attorney General. Authorization from FBI headquarters is also required, and there must be a "specific written request from appropriate

Assistant Attorney General."[13] Once a Jury Panel Investigation is authorized, according to Bureau guidelines the FBI's investigations are "ordinarily ... restricted to ascertaining arrest records of the individuals and checking their names through the field office indices." But because the FBI has historically kept and indexed so much secondary information on individuals encountered during investigations, the FBI's files contain a broad range of information far beyond that collected on individuals under criminal investigations.

The use of credit reports in these investigations was prohibited in 1970, following the establishment of the Fair Credit Reporting Act. The FBI's procedures specify that "no inquiries should be made concerning a person's religious or political beliefs, or his membership in, or affiliation with labor unions or other organizations. No neighborhood inquiries should be made and no surveillance of any type should be conducted."[14] While these procedures prohibit making inquiries about a prospective juror's religious or political affiliations, should existing files contain such information this already collected information could be added to the Jury Panel Investigation report supplied to the U.S. attorney. Historically, the FBI has not always followed such recommended protocols when it thought it had a suspicious person of interest.

FBI RECORDS FOR PROSECUTORS, NOTHING FOR THE DEFENSE

Among the famous trials where the FBI pulled investigatory records on prospective trial jurors was the 1951 trial of Julius and Ethel Rosenberg, when the FBI supplied the prosecuting attorney, Irving Saypol, with dossiers of prospective jurors.[15] These FBI Jury Panel Investigations have occurred in various organized crime trials. The FBI's 1955 Jury Panel Investigation into the backgrounds of potential jurors for the upcoming trial of *United States v. Herman M. Greenspun*[16] dug unusually deep into the lives of prospective jurors. The FBI's report included statements on reports of jurors' reputations, associations with other individuals of interest to law enforcement, racial profiles, and other personal information.[17] In a 1963 organized crime case, the FBI provided prosecutors with records on prospective jurors for the upcoming trial of Anthony Provenzano, an associate of the Genovese crime family. These FBI records included information on the prospective jurors' occupations and private affiliations.[18]

The most extensive documentation of these practices I found occurred during an FBI Jury Panel Investigation documented in the 5,000-page FBI file of NKVD spy and anthropologist, Mark Zborowski. For years, Zborowski successfully infiltrated Leon Trotsky's inner circle and betrayed his movement to the Soviets as an NKVD agent, operating first in France, then continuing as a Soviet agent after he fled the Nazis, finding refuge in the United States in the 1940s.[19]

Once in the United States, Zborowski's anthropology training helped him find work on projects overseen by Ruth Benedict and Margaret Mead as part of Columbia University's Research in Contemporary Culture Project. He later worked at Cornell Medical School, all the while continuing to report to a Soviet NKVD officer on the activities of Trotskyites in America. His identity was eventually betrayed, and during a series of long FBI interviews and interrogations he admitted to some past NKVD spying but insisted, both to the FBI and then later to the U.S. Senate Internal Security Committee, that he had never been an NKVD spy while living in the United States. But unbeknownst to him, a Soviet double agent had already confirmed Zborowski had continued spying while living in the United States. Having caught Zborowski lying under oath, but not wanting to expose the CIA and FBI's methods and sources in an espionage trial, the U.S. government only tried Zborowski for perjury.

As the date of the trial approached, the FBI secretly provided federal prosecutors with dossiers summarizing material previously collected in the FBI files on prospective jurors. The defense and jurors were unaware that this collection of unverified FBI materials was being used by the prosecutors in the jury selection process.

Serious legal and procedural issues are raised by a prosecutor's exclusive access to secret FBI dossiers, and the breadth of the FBI's files on these random Americans' private lives is a chilling measure of the mid-century FBI's surveillance reach in the lives of Americans. These dossiers also illustrate that despite years of

McCarthyism's efforts to homogenize American political dissent there remained an impressive record of progressive political action and social nonconformity. Out of the 600 prospective jurors the FBI investigated in their files, they found FBI files on over one hundred of these individuals.[20]

Think of these FBI file summaries as a sort of non-scientific political sample of New York City's population from a lost age of surveillance. The FBI compiled subversive files on about 18 percent of this sample—and while a few of these entries were for reactionary right-wing subversive activities, such as records on individuals remaining fascistic public admirers of Hitler or Mussolini a bit longer than Charles Lindberg or *New York Times* foreign correspondent Anne O'Hare McCormick, the vast majority of these files chronicled leftist political activities.

Though the FBI admitted it was uncertain in some instances that the individuals identified in their files were those of the same name being summoned to jury duty, it still passed along these file summaries, with the obvious desired outcome being to reduce these individuals' chances of being seated on Zborowski's jury.

Ever focused on the prurient and personal, the FBI collected information on anything relating to extra-marital sexual activities or non-heterosexuality, compiling files identifying individuals as "homo-sexual" or involved with pornography. The FBI reported that one "professor G," a physicist associated with Yale University and the Atomic Energy Commission, had seen a psychiatrist over "sexual difficulties," and had scheduled appointments at Yale's Mental Hygiene Clinic two or three times a week "because he felt that he was not fully realizing his potential in physics and because he had a mental block which was keeping him from concentrating."[21] The FBI warned prosecutors that the parents of this physicist admitted to the Atomic Energy Commission belonged to the International Workers Organization.

The FBI identified individuals they believed were members of the Communist Party, former members of Communist Party youth groups, socialists, or members of what were believed to be communist front groups like the Institute of Pacific Relations. Any involvement in organized labor brought the FBI's suspicion, whether it was once working as a foreign correspondent for the

Allied Labor News or working in a teachers union.[22] The FBI warned federal prosecutors of such threatening minutiae as potential juror and Teachers Union member Ruth Adler's authorship of "a feature article regarding sweater designs for October 1955 *Woman's Day* magazine."[23] The FBI claimed that prospective juror Kirschner "conducted a 'sabotage school' during a strike in 1938 along with four other members of the Local 150, United Machinist of the Needle Industries, CIO."[24] Dozens of prospective jurors were blacklisted for signing petitions: petitions opposing military actions, petitions to place progressive or radical candidates on local or national ballots, petitions for peace, petitions supporting a fair trial for the Rosenbergs. Dossiers reported memberships in peace groups, the American Committee for the Protection of the Foreign Born, or the National Committee for the Defense of Political Prisoners. The use of these FBI surveillance dossiers to remove free-thinking individuals from a jury in a perjury trial is a sobering measure of the power of the FBI's surveillance complex. While the FBI was supposedly prohibited from using collected information about the political activities of potential jurors, collecting information on a juror's involvement in these political groups is a clear example of how the FBI used this sort of political information to help the prosecution politically screen juries.

The FBI compiled records on several men who had avoided the Selective Service Board during the Second World War and Korean War, moving without notifying the Board, and skipping out on the draft.[25] Some of the FBI reports warned of one individual's unusual interest in international affairs, and there were cautions that another individual had lived abroad while not stationed in the military.

The traits categorized as "deviant" by Hoover's G-Men almost reads like a deleted draft stanza of Ginsberg's *Howl*, with deviants hosting a Soviet embassy employee at a social event, a communist traveling salesman, pornographers, a man illegally wearing an Army uniform, art dealers hosting progressive political benefits, race track employee characterized by business associates as "immoral and unethical in his business dealings," a man whose name appeared in the address book of a suspected Hollywood communist, someone whose name appeared in the address book of a Nazi general, someone caught by U.S. Custom agents in 1957 with "an arms cache" believed destined for Cuban rebels, a National Lawyers Guild member, an FBI impersonator, someone whose father had been falsely accused of being a Japanese spy during the Second World War, the sponsor of an advertisement advocating for the defeat of the Mundt Bill, opponents of the Smith Act, Alcoholic Anonymous members, and a paranoid who had contacted the FBI numerous times reporting his belief that he was being followed by Russian spies. None of the consulted records indicate whether the federal attorney tried to use this last piece of information to seat this anti-Russian paranoiac on the jury.[26]

Using governmental records to selectively assist the prosecution raises significant questions of government misconduct in Zborowski's trial, and other cases that relied on these FBI methods. Such practices seem to violate the spirit, if not the letter, of the Attorney General's Guidelines for Domestic FBI Operations—but this was Hoover's America, where such concerns did not matter. The FBI routinely stalked citizens engaging in legal political dissent, collecting gossip and innuendoes that were often nothing more than artifacts of the FBI's institutional paranoia. Excluding the defense from access to these FBI summaries denied them the opportunity to object to the selection of jurors whose FBI files indicated political views aligned with the prosecution. Such secretive state action raises questions of violations of basic rights, as potential jurors' expectations of privacy and the state's use of select FBI monitoring of citizens engaging in lawful political activities were exclusively used by the state.

Zborowski's trial was a straightforward affair. The government produced transcripts from Congressional hearings documenting Zborowski's ever-shifting version of events and showed him lying about his contacts with his NKVD handler (and FBI informer) Jack Soble. The defense team tried to discredit Soble as a witness, and even while Soble's then-unstable mental health raised some doubts of his reliability, the jury soon found Zborowski guilty of perjury.

After Zborowski was found guilty, his lawyers moved that he remain free on bail while appealing the verdict, and the five-year prison sentence. Anthropologist Ruth Bunzel came forward and posted Zborowski's $10,000 bail while his appeal was under consideration.[27] Bunzel had attended each day of Zborowski's trial.[28] This caused the FBI to investigate Bunzel, and they determined that the

> current NYC Telephone Directory listed the same telephone number to Rosalind Zoglin, Ruth Bunzel and Andree Emery. Emery was the wife of Roy Hudson and both Hudson and Emery were Communist Party functionaries. NY files show that Zoglin's name appeared on a membership list of the Greenwich Village Club of the CP as of August, 1944.[29]

Zborowski's appeal argued that prosecutors had illegally withheld records from Soble's testimony at Grand Jury proceedings—records that they argued would have allowed a defense attacking Soble's mental stability and reliability as a witness. This appeal succeeded, but federal prosecutors were committed to retrying him, and did so over three years after his first trial.

In November 1962, Assistant Attorney General J. Walter Yeagley asked Hoover for FBI records on prospective jurors, and FBI dossiers were again made available to Richard Casey, the assistant U.S. attorney prosecuting the case.[30] The FBI again produced dossiers on prospective jurors that identified political activities, or elements of their lifestyle that had come to the FBI's attention, and this information was secretly used by federal attorneys to select the jury. The second trial went much like the first, and Zborowski was again found guilty of perjury.

FBI SURVEILLANCE OF DEFENSE ATTORNEYS

There are other ways that the FBI historically used its surveillance power to assist prosecutors and undermine the power of defense attorneys. The FBI had no qualms about spying on other lawyers defending the rights of those hounded by the FBI. Some FBI files record the FBI conducting surveillance operations monitoring defense lawyers representing individuals belonging to groups targeted by the FBI. For example, the FBI file on radical attorney William Kunstler documents the Bureau spying on and trying to undermine Kunstler's work.

The FBI targeted William Kunstler with surveillance for decades. The Bureau used wiretaps, physical surveillance, mail monitoring and monitored his public appearances for many years and placed him on the Security Index and the FBI's Agitator Index.[31] Notes in Kunstler's FBI file document the Bureau doggedly monitoring him and aggressively tracking him in his public and private life.

One 1970 FBI entry in his file shows the Bureau recording Kunstler's distaste for the American justice system, which these watchers were so deeply a part of. The FBI wrote that:

> Kunstler was critical of the judicial system in this country. He stated that he had no faith in the higher courts of the land and in their decisions.
>
> Subject claimed that the Federal Government is using the so-called crime of conspiracy to punish people for their fantasies rather than for what they have actually done. He said the purpose of conspiracy trials is to scare people into conformity.[32]

For years, the FBI monitored Kunstler under their "Key Activist Program." This program was secretly established by the FBI in 1968 to focus investigation on individuals in various leftist political movements "who engage in extensive travel and are most vocal in statements denouncing the United States and calling for civil disobedience and other forms of unlawful and disruptive acts."[33] Because so much of Kunstler's lifework was devoted to fighting the legal system's structural racism, the FBI's campaign targeting him was one more dimension of the Bureau's racism.

Kunstler's early civil rights work for racial equality established his career trajectory of fiercely fighting for those the legal system most often targets, ignores, or routinely convicts without due process. He first gained national fame as the lawyer for the Chicago Seven, which earned him a 40-month contempt of court sentence for his behavior during the trial. After this he soon became a legal presence in some of the most significant legal fights by underserved groups. He represented prisoners staging the Attica Prison riots, defended the radical anti-war Catholics known as the Catonsville Nine, and members of the American Indian Movement occupying Wounded Knee. He later took on highly public cases with less obvious appeal to American liberals and conservatives alike—successfully defending accused cop killer Larry Davis, and El Sayyid Nosair, the accused assassin of Rabbi Meir Kahane; clients who earned Kunstler the dubious distinction of being known as "the most hated lawyer in America."[34]

Later reflecting on this high level of FBI surveillance during the 1970s, his wife Margaret Ratner Kunstler recalled that "we knew [the FBI] was around us, because we'd walk around the corner and they'd confront us, but we didn't know they'd taken an apartment across the street. That was something we found out many years later."[35] But, they weren't just spying on Kunstler in his private life; the FBI pried into his legal work. FBI agents conducted surveillance operations on Kunstler while he was discussing legal strategy with the defendants in the Wounded Knee case, and at the end of the trial the trial judge sanctioned the FBI for withholding evidence from the defense, conducting illegal surveillance, and witness tampering. Zia Akhtar's study of the FBI's misconduct in the Pine Ridge trials found that

> During the Peltier trial, the FBI produced approximately 3,500 documents and claimed that these were all the files that were in existence. Through a FOIA request, Peltier's defense team discovered that some 12,000 documents had been withheld. Six thousand of these papers were then released. More recently, information has come to light that the FBI's claim that only 6,000 full documents related to this case remain undisclosed which the Bureau claim are merely "administrative" documents, and are of no use to the defense team.[36]

Attorney William Schaap's FBI file documents he was under FBI surveillance while acting as defense attorney for members of the Students for a Democratic Society, Yippies, Black Panthers, and the Weather Underground. Schaap would later be the cofounder of the anti-CIA magazine *Covert Action Information Bulletin*, and director of the Institute of Media Analysis. His FBI file documents very little about this part of his career,[37] though the FBI focused surveillance operations on him while he was legal council for members of the Black Panthers.

The FBI secretly tracked Schaap's movements, associations, and political activities for years. In 1970, the FBI designated Schaap "as a potential Weatherman legal support individual, New York [FBI agents were] instructed to conduct investigation and consider him for inclusion in ADEX."[38] The FBI noted Schaap's affiliation with the National Lawyers Guild, his contacts with Jerry Rubin, Stewart Albert, and various Communist Party members. The FBI's interest intensified when he became the lawyer for five members of the Weather Underground, known as the Electric Ever-Expanding Number, arrested for a plot to firebomb a First National City Bank in New York City on December 4, 1970.[39] On May 15, 1972, the FBI placed Schaap on the ADEX, the FBI's "Administrative Index" listing individuals to be detained in a national emergency. He was listed as a Category III risk, and the FBI described him as "a revolutionary attorney and sympathizer who, during a time of national emergency, would be likely to seize the opportunity to commit acts inimical to the national defense."[40]

The FBI's surveillance of lawyers undermines FBI claims to uphold due process and law and order. These ongoing efforts to interfere with accused individuals' rights to legal counsel and trials before juries of their peers demonstrates the Bureau's fundamental loyalty has historically been to maintain the *order* of the status quo. The Bureau's history of undermining the accused's right to a fair defense before the law clarifies the shallowness of the Bureau's devotion to due process under the law.

ALL'S FAIR IN LOVE AND *VOIR DIRE* WAR

While federal prosecutors appear to have launched a limited number of Jury Panel Investigations, the FOIA document releases from some of these investigations show this mechanism to be one more way that the FBI has historically used its free-ranging collection of information about Americans in very selective ways. The FBI's role in these Jury Panel Investigations is explicitly designed to selectively benefit the prosecution, and by withholding this information the FBI sought to harm the accused's defense. In practical terms, such a secretive use of FBI files by prosecutors rewarded the FBI for collecting broad information on U.S. citizens that would not have been collected had the Bureau greater concerns about civil liberties or rights to privacy.

Exclusively providing these FBI documents to the prosecution appears to be legal, but it hardly seems fair or ethical to have these documents—which were not produced by the prosecution but were given to them by a branch of law enforcement—withheld from the defense team. The prurient nature of the FBI's previous inquiries, completely unrelated to these individuals serving on a jury, leading the Bureau to compile these records was all part of the FBI's culture of unreflexive collecting and monitoring. If portions of these FBI dossiers were collected through illegal FBI activities, their use in these trials is improper.

Because FBI files used to inform jury selections have historically included heavily biased content—such as identifying individuals appearing on the Attorney General's list of subversive groups, or subscribing to publications deemed by the Attorney General as being subversive—the FBI's cataloguing of this information could in these instances lead to the removal of jurors-sympathetic-to-the-defense, who would not otherwise have been removed. This was a goal of this program: to give the prosecutors an edge in ferreting out information that would be useful to their position. Yet when this is *political* information of the sort that they would not have been allowed to openly inquire about during *voir dire*, this takes on new meaning, and shows one more example of how the FBI's collection of disjointed information could later be repurposed in ways not conceived of as it was being collected.

FBI operations monitoring defense lawyers clarify that during a national emergency the very lawyers most needed to defend detainees whose constitutional and human rights would be threatened would themselves be detained under these emergency programs and would thus be unavailable to defend detainees. The danger this potentially presents in the United States can be seen clearly when we consider how easily such a national emergency could be engineered. Simply consider how easily the attacks of September 11, 2001, or even January 6, 2021, were engineered by a relatively small group of people drawing on small enough amounts of financial support that personal credit cards could cover expenses and consider how easily a president or Congress could have used such crises to declare a national emergency. That the FBI for decades planned to lock up the very lawyers who would be most likely to provide robust legal defenses for those arrested *without specific charges leveled against them* is a significant measure of the disdain with which the FBI holds the American legal system's commitment to the right to a free trial. Placing lawyers on these security indexes, because they competently defended clients whose politics the FBI despised, shows that the Bureau literally believes that lawyers providing aggressive defenses for accused criminals are threats to national security.

These instances of prosecutors relaying on the FBI's Jury Panel Investigation Program and of the FBI spying on criminal defense attorneys provide an important view of the FBI. This view reveals the Bureau acting as an arm of the U.S. government as it collected, stored, then later used a broad range of what would otherwise have been private political data about individuals. This private data includes such things as involvement in union activities or free associations of group memberships. When this data was ultimately later used by the state to judge individuals' fitness to serve on a trial jury we find the FBI secretly trying to determine if these individuals were aligned or opposed to the Bureau's peculiar interpretations of American justice.

7

Agents of Apartheid: Ruth First and the FBI's Historical Role of Enforcing Inequality

I became interested in Ruth First after reading about her anti-apartheid writings which drew heavily on anthropological forms of participant observations and analysis. She researched her books and articles by living amongst the people she wrote about, and her analysis brought the sort of bottom-up perspectives gifted ethnographers strive to produce. Some of her approach appears to have come from her personality, but some elements derived from her academic training at the University of the Witwatersrand in the 1940s, which included anthropology courses. This time living with those she wrote about had a profound impact on her work, and in later life she wrote about the formative impacts on her life of doing field research for her books and articles documenting the brutalities of apartheid.

In response to FOIA requests for records on Ruth First, the Department of State claimed it had no records, the CIA used exemption claims to avoid meaningfully responding, and the FBI reported that its relevant records originated at an "other governmental agency," which, while unidentified, appears likely to have been the CIA. The FBI eventually released these records to me. The released FBI documents were a mix of FBI reports and memos originating in other unidentified governmental agencies—most likely the State Department and CIA.

Ruth First was born in Johannesburg in 1925, to immigrants Tilly and Julius First, whose socialist political orientation shaped her early critique of apartheid. As a university student, her early exposure to sociological critiques of power relations and anthropological methods of bottom-up inquiry shaped elements of her later work. As a student, she joined the Communist Party and helped form an activist group known as the Federation of Progressive Students, which challenged the basic assumptions of apartheid. She worked as a social worker, labor union organizer, taught in Black schools, and honed her writing skills while reporting for various newspapers including the Communist Party's Johannesburg paper *The Guardian*. When *The Guardian* was banned in 1951, she created new journalistic outlets to publish important series of articles showing South Africans and the world the realities of apartheid. Her investigative journalism often involved dangerous stints of first-hand fieldwork observation, during which she spent significant periods of time in rural settings, documenting the daily degradations of life, and problems facing the African National Congress (ANC) in South Africa.

As the leadership of the ANC came under increasing attack by the South African government, her husband, Joe Slovo, was imprisoned and in 1952 he was charged with treason. Despite such risks, Ruth First continued to publish important investigative pieces, and during 1961 she conducted extensive fieldwork for her book, *South West Africa*, work that combined journalistic, ethnographic, and historical research to document the harsh impacts of settler colonialism. She was arrested in August 1963, two months after the arrest of Nelson Mandela and other ANC leadership. She was held in solitary confinement for 117 days under South Africa's 90-day detention Act. After her release she lived abroad, in England and elsewhere, fighting apartheid in exile for the rest of her life. In 1977 she became the Director of Research at the Center for African Studies in Mozambique, where she continued to write and she became a focal point for international critiques of apartheid, until she was assassinated by a mail bomb sent to her by South African government operatives on August 17, 1982.

In 2007, former Special Branch and South African Bureau for State Security (BOSS) agent, Petrus Swanepoel, self-published a remarkable memoire, *Really Inside BOSS*, detailing South Africa's extensive surveillance and harassment protocols and shedding important new light on how the state security apparatus focused on activist writers like First.[1] Swanepoel also detailed some of the ways that the CIA and other security agencies interfaced with apartheid. One section in Swanepoel's book described his security force's clumsy efforts to follow Ruth First while she conducted interviews for her 1963 book *South West Africa*.

Swanepoel recounted how one morning in Windhoek he became aware of Ruth First, who he described as "a strange woman in town, or rather a woman who was acting strangely"—asking locals political questions. He followed her as she visited

> newspapers, the archives, the Administration Buildings and the very liberal American, Robert Mize, who was bishop of the Anglican Church in Windhoek [South West Africa; which became Namibia in 1990]. In fact, Robert Mize's house was her office. She lived in the Stadrt Windhoek Hotel, but when she was not out visiting, asking questions and giving us the jitters, she was at the bishop's house, doing God knows what.[2]

BOSS assigned three local detectives to follow First, but she quickly spotted and ditched them. Later, with help from some local residents, BOSS operatives followed her. At one point Swanepoel himself followed First to her hotel, where he pretended to nonchalantly read a newspaper in the lobby until she confronted him, and asked him what "do you think you're doing?" He sheepishly replied, "I suppose you might say I'm trying to follow you." When she asked him why he was following her, Swanepoel told her it was because she was a well-known communist working on a book. She admitted she was working on a book, but she assured him her work had nothing to do with the Communist Party. She then bluntly asked him to stop following and embarrassing her.

Swanepoel replied that he "could not promise anything," but if she would promise that she was not doing "communist work," his men would "try to be more discreet." By Swanepoel's account, First chided him, saying that she had already told him that her work "has nothing to do with communism, with communists or with the Soviet Union," which he later determined was in fact the case.[3]

Years later on reading First's account of his bungled surveillance in her book, *South West Africa*, Swanepoel was relieved that she had not identified him by name as she mocked his efforts, as she wrote that

> The detectives on duty that first week-end wore shorts and rugby socks, and childish smiles on their faces as, in the prowling police car, they outdistanced me, the footslogger, on the way to an appointment. In the beginning there were two, later four, and even five and six on duty, working in pairs, padding along the pavement six paces behind me, or on the opposite side of the road, sitting at the next table of the open-air coffee house. There was, this time, no midnight thump on the door. On the contrary, there was even an uncomfortable air worn by the more intelligent of the detectives, as it became obvious that talks to White town councilors and Herero Chiefs, businessmen and administration servants, with walks down main streets and to historical monuments, constituted a normal enough programme for a visiting journalist.
>
> But the scrutiny never faltered: the trail to the dry-cleaner and the shoemaker, the skulking next to the telephone booth, both ends of the road and every exit of the hotel patrolled, detectives following me to the airport, to the post office to buy stamps, watching me at breakfast, interviewing people I had seen— "What does she want from you?"
>
> Most Whites were too polite to comment on the chase. They remained accessible, but were guarded and reticent.
>
> Africans were bursting to talk. Bystanders in the street showed by smiles and winks that, if the Special Branch was on my heels, they were on my side.[4]

Rather than frightening away prospective local interviewees, the Special Branch's obvious surveillance of First had the opposite impact. She observed that while some whites became reticent to talk to her because of the surveillance, the "Africans were bursting to talk" showing solidarity with her and willingness to share their story with one taking such risks; that her work garnered the concern of the state's surveillance apparatus increased the promise of its value.[5]

Swanepoel noted that unbeknownst to First, the publication of her book, *South West Africa*, was indirectly subsidized with CIA funds.[6] This was because the Penguin African Libraries series publishing her book received funds from the Congress for Cultural Freedom; which was exposed as a CIA front in 1966, three years after *South West Africa* was published.[7] If true, this reflects the 1960s CIA's desire to use funding to establish links (even ironic links) to a broad range of individuals and groups, not on the work First produced. Agent Swanepoel also described discovering that another CIA front, the Farfield Foundation, financed the *Cultural Events in Africa* newsletter, an African news transcription service, and travel in Africa for anthropologists and other academics.[8] Given the extent of the CIA's covert funding of foundations and publishing projects, the funding of work countering regimes backed by the CIA was not unusual in this period and stands as a marker of the breadth of CIA infiltration rather than detracting from the significance of First's work.

Swanepoel also described reading an advertisement appearing in *New Africa* magazine (which would later be disclosed to have received CIA funds) for a London-based organization known as Transcription Feature Service Limited, which sponsored the publication of a newsletter known as *Cultural Events in Africa*, which also received funds from the Farfield Foundation, later confirmed to be a CIA front foundation, which provided cultural programming for African radio stations, funded the travel of African artists, and financed reading rooms in strategic locations in Africa, where Westerners made friendly contact with local artists and intellectuals. The Farfield Foundation spread around a lot of money; in 1965 alone it financed over $1.2 million in grants to various programs. Among the Western intellectuals, unwitting of CIA funding, participating in the discussions hosted by the Transcription Center was anthropologist Godfrey Lienhardt, speaking on African oral traditions.[9] As with many of the CIA-linked funding programs of this era, it is difficult to untangle the range of information directly useful to the CIA that was produced by Farfield Foundation grants, or whether the most significant CIA outcomes were of a secondary nature derived from hidden contacts the CIA may or may not have established with awardees. Many of the specifics of these relationships remain unknown: but new bodies of useful general knowledge were produced—knowledge which at times included analysis that was independent of the state systems it informed; in many ways, much more critical than that produced today by funding systems more openly linked to state military and intelligence apparatus.

Swanepoel's account of intelligence agencies monitoring an activist researcher, and of CIA funds being used to finance the work of an unwitting critical scholar are not unique to this instance. The South African intelligence services' monitoring of critical scholarship was not a unique occurrence: not unique in South Africa, nor among state intelligence apparatus around the world. For example, in 1959 the FBI was so concerned with the political implications of anthropologist Oscar Lewis' fieldwork in Mexico that they used a secret FBI informer in this community to spy on Lewis and to report on what questions Lewis was asking in the community.[10] In *Threatening Anthropology* I described FBI files reporting on the FBI spying on Lewis as he conducted fieldwork in Mexico and Cuba—including FBI efforts to monitor the information Lewis collected in his Mexican fieldwork on rural poverty. Other FBI files documented the FBI obsessively monitoring American anthropologists speaking out against American foreign or domestic policies. These files document the FBI monitoring anthropologists' remarks at rallies, recording phone logs, classroom comments, and private correspondence.

Released FBI documents indicate the U.S. government monitored Ruth First's political work, and expressed concerns, and increased surveillance as her activism and writings became increasingly well known and her work brought her into contact with Americans. Backchannel intelligence sharing between the CIA and South African intelligence services is well documented. The CIA provided intelligence to the South African government for decades, including intelligence directly used to capture Nelson Mandela; and this relationship between the CIA and South Africa continued even after U.S. sanctions against Pretoria were adopted as U.S. federal law in 1986.[11]

The first series of partially redacted FBI documents on First originated from March and April 1955. These included a redacted "registered airmail" letter from J. Edgar Hoover to an individual, only identified in un-redacted portions of the file as "My dear Commissioner." The first seven lines of the letter are completely redacted, but portions of Hoover's letter show the FBI was responding to a request for information from Bureau files on Ruth First. An internal FBI note typed at the bottom of this document reads: "NOTE: Classified Secret to conform with incoming. [FBI files] reflect First is an active Communist in South Africa but no indication she has ever been in U.S., or in contact with anyone in U.S. Internal Security Section unable to identify P.T.I. on basis info furnished."[12]

The FBI's interest in Ruth First from half a world away is one measure of just how much activism matters. Hoover's concerns about First were multiple. The Bureau's history of racism and discrimination is well documented; Hoover's agents routinely investigated and harassed activists for racial equality as communists, regardless of whether they had any ties to the Party; that Ruth First *was* a communist and that her writings and activism impacted American activists struggling for racial equality increased Hoover's concerns. While her communist affiliation was enough to garner the FBI's attentions, the FBI's dossier shows the Bureau was more concerned with the possibility that she would raise American awareness of apartheid's brutalities than she might recruit communists while visiting the United States or corresponding with Americans.

During the early to mid-twentieth century, the FBI played a significant role limiting what foreign ideas the American public should be exposed to by international visitors. For decades the FBI worked in tandem with the anti-communist head of the State Department's Passport Division, Ruth Shipley, who played a crucial role in deciding which Americans could travel abroad. Through such means, the FBI regulated American travel, and at times controlled who could travel to or live in the United States.

As we will see in the chapters discussing the FBI files of Alexander Cockburn, André Gunder Frank, and others, the FBI routinely provided the Immigration and Naturalization Service (INS) with information that was at times used to keep foreign writers and activists out of the United States, effectively black-

listing leftist activists entry into the United States.[13] The maintenance of these secret blacklists was one of the reasons why the FBI
monitored the work of international activists like Ruth First. These
monitoring campaigns of leftist public intellectuals show how the
FBI worked with the INS to try and secretly keep radical writers
out of the country. Hoover's correspondence about First was part
of this larger ongoing campaign to limit Americans' contact with
radical voices.

Four months after J. Edgar Hoover's initial memo concerning
Ruth First, he again wrote this "Dear Commissioner," this time
passing along information on First gathered from the FBI's New
York Office. This partially redacted document included references
to an FBI file on the "Infiltration of United Nations by Subversive
American Citizens, Internal Security, Racial"—reflecting the FBI
long-standing unofficial position that American employees within
the UN adopting anti-colonialist or anti-racist positions were likely
part of an international communist movement.[14] New York City
FBI agents sent Hoover a September 25, 1949 article written by
First on the "African Slave Market" that had been published in the
Communist Party's newspaper, The Worker.[15] Hoover forwarded
this and a report with additional (redacted) information expressing his "desire to cooperate in all matters of mutual interest."[16]
Hoover was not concerned about the revelations in First's article
that South African labor markets were effectively a form of modern
slavery, he was concerned that this was published in a communist
newspaper, and that her anti-racist views could agitate against the
American status quo. Another "Secret" FBI memo from this period
had the subject headings: "RUTH FIRST, aka: Mrs. RUTH SLOVO,
POLICE COOPERATION, FOREIGN MISCELLANEOUS" and
included inquiries pertaining to someone [redacted] linked to the
Press Trust of India, apparently living in New York City, and an
American economist known to her who had taught in Russia; both
of these individuals had links to Ruth First.[17]

Ruth First's FBI file indicates the Bureau received several
telegrams pertaining to her in mid-December 1970 relating to
concerns within the FBI and other agencies that First would soon
travel to the United States. One National Security Council staff
member from this period described her "as a communist and

the wife of a member of the Communist Party of South Africa," living in London in exile from South Africa. The FBI believed that she planned on visiting the United States to appear on a National Education Television (NET) "discussion-type program" as part of a television series on South Africa. The FBI expressed concerns that American audiences would be exposed to her critique of South African apartheid. The FBI learned that First had applied for a U.S. visa in order to appear on the Boston-based program, *The Advocates*, produced by Millie Teichols.[18] Her FBI file relating to this scheduled visit is incomplete and notes in her file indicate the FBI destroyed further Bureau records from this period.

First does not appear to have appeared on *The Advocates*, though she did come to the United States in 1971 to speak at the National Youth Conference in St. Louis, Missouri, in 1971.[19] The FBI approached the Public Relations Office of WGBH-TV, seeking information on their program, *The Advocates*, and on First. The FBI learned that *The Advocates* received grants from the Ford Foundation and the Corporation for Public Broadcasting; the program's format was described as

a pair of skilled spokesmen present strong cases for each side under the guidance of a well-informed moderator. Each advocate uses a full range of media to make the most powerful persuasive, and dramatic case. He may incorporate actual evidence, expert witnesses, documentary films, and even live dramatization of it makes a point most effectively.[20]

The FBI was concerned about a format allowing unfiltered radical views. The FBI reported that Ruth First had not participated in the two previous 1970 programs on South Africa.

The FBI recorded Ruth First's presence at the Second World Black Power Conference (aka International Conference on Racism and War).[21] The FBI collected several reports generated by other U.S. governmental agencies, during the early 1970s, including a series of FBI memos from the American embassy, London, pertaining to First's application for a U.S. visa. One memo reports FBI interviews with unidentified individuals about her "membership in the Young Communist League in South Africa from 1943 to 1946 and the Communist Party of South Africa from 1946 to 1950."[22] Once in the United States, the FBI monitored some of her activities, and filed a report on a talk she presented at the University of Denver on May Day 1974.[23]

On August 18, 1982, Ruth First was killed by a mail bomb in Maputo, Mozambique. The bomb arrived as she was organizing an international UNESCO-sponsored academic conference in Maputo bringing Western academics to discuss the problems of apartheid and neo-colonial Africa. Her FBI file contains an August 20, 1982 teletype report titled "Allegations of U.S. Link in First Killing" (the headline of a *Rand Daily Mail* wire news story) which largely consists of wire service accounts detailing published news stories on her assassination, including news speculations that the mail bomb had been delivered to her inside a package sent from the USAID-funded South Africa Development Information/Documentation Exchange (SADEX). News clippings in her FBI file quoted the Portuguese News Agency as reporting "that despite the alleged SADEX address, Mozambican authorities were 'not reduced in the conviction that South Africa's Secret Service was entirely responsible for the killing.' It quoted an unidentified source saying that the possibility could not be excluded that South African agents used SADEX mailing service to embarrass the U.S. government."[24]

A decade and a half later, in testimony given to South Africa's Truth and Reconciliation Commission South African agent provocateur, Craig Williamson, admitted to ordering the assassination of Ruth First because her activism threatened the security of the South African state.[25] Williamson, a one-time Major in the South African police force, in 1970 infiltrated the ANC by using contacts at the International University Exchange Fund (IUEF) of Geneva, connections which he used to fund South African students—who he would "befriend" and use as unwitting intelligence sources for the South African war on the ANC. He used the IUEF to fund the establishment of the South African News Agency, which spied on the ANC while spreading anti-ANC propaganda. In 2000, the Amnesty Committee of the South African Truth and Reconciliation Commission granted amnesty to Craig Williamson and Roger Raven for their roles in the murder of Ruth First. The Commission found that they had received sanctions from the minister of police for the murder as part of a campaign to destabilize the ANC, and therefore, qualified for amnesty.

In South Africa and internationally, there remains some ambivalence surrounding the outcomes of the Truth and Reconciliation hearings. There's ample research showing that the process helped the country move forward in ways that avoided a tide of what seemed to be an otherwise inevitable bloodbath of retribution. Yet, the substitution of the drama of admission and contrition without punishment, and the formal granting of broad immunity for the confessed murders and lesser crimes committed over decades of white rule leaves open questions of justice. Still, in principle, the truth and reconciliation process was a positive development needed for South Africa to move forward. I know this on a gut level, and have read enough academic analysis of the difficult but positive outcomes of this process to understand this is a viable route for post-revolutionary justice. While I intellectually understand this, something hit me hard when I was researching online, looking up news reports of the Truth and Reconciliation Commission hearing that granted amnesty to Ruth First's confessed killers. I found a report in the South African press detailing the amnesty for her killers, but it was a small addition to the end of the account that I found myself returning to in my thoughts.

After describing the Commission's decision to grant amnesty to Williamson and Raven, Ruth First's assassins, the story described the outcome of another individual coming before the Commission. The Commission decided to not grant immunity to another security police operative, Michael Bellingan, for the theft of checks in the mail of a union group he monitored, and for the murder of his wife—who he claimed was going to leak information of his intelligence operations to the ANC, and that "he decided to kill her because she was a security risk."[26]

I understand the logic of the Commission's decision to not grant immunity to this other killer, having concluded this murder was likely not carried out as an act of political violence of the sort protected by the Commission. Yet, this contrast in a single, simple, news story bares open the contradictions of a system setting free admitted state agents of oppression, whose acts prolonged the living hell of a national majority, while simple murderers and check-thieves were tried as criminals.

The forms of tracking and surveillance of Ruth First fit the general patterns of surveillance documented in other chapters here as these different individuals separated by continents are connected by commitments of activism and critique. There are recurrent patterns within the records of surveillance campaigns and shared tactical efforts to stifle various democratic movements for social change. While different regimes develop different tactics or surveillance practices, with some agencies very openly monitoring and attempting to frighten activists in ways that marginalize them as dissidents and mark them as so socially contaminated that they are removed from the normal boundaries of societies, other surveillance strategies are less obvious and remain unknown at the time.

The released portions of Ruth First's FBI file show American governmental agencies maintaining records on her political activities, and upon receiving word that she might be coming to the United States to be interviewed by public media, or to participate in academic conferences, the FBI passed along their information to other unidentified governmental agencies—who appear most likely to include the CIA and Department of State.

Historian Alan Wieder argues that the South African government chose to murder Ruth First during a conference gathering activist scholars focusing on the crimes of the South African government, "because they knew that ideas are important" and because she had organized this conference as a way of challenging the legitimacy of the South African state.[27] Journalist Joseph Hanlon argued that her murder was meant to scare off academics and activists, telling them "they should not attend conferences like the one Ruth organized, and they should not support or practice research or teaching that calls for socialist transformations."[28] These FBI records affirm that activism matters, and the FBI's concerns over Ruth First's contact with academics and the general public is one measure of the power and significance of her work.

PART III

Monitoring Pioneers and Public Intellectuals

Manufactured stupidity does more than depoliticize the public. To paraphrase Hannah Arendt, it represents an assault on the very possibility of thinking itself. Not surprisingly, intellectuals who engage in dissent and "keep the idea and hope of a public culture alive," are often dismissed as irrelevant, extremist, elitist or un-American. As a result, we now live in a world in which the politics of disimagination dominates; public discourses that bears witness to a critical and alternative sense of the world are often dismissed because they do not advance economic interests.

—Henry Giroux, "Public Intellectuals Against the Neoliberal University," 43–4

8

How the FBI Spied on Edward Said

After Edward Said died in 2003, I filed FOIA requests to access his FBI file because I assumed that his effectiveness in speaking out for Palestinian rights and critiquing colonialism could be at least in part measured by the FBI's surveillance of him. Had his work on Orientalism ended with discussions in literary circles, then his file would either be nonexistent or his surveillance trivial. Most of Said's file documents FBI surveillance campaigns of his legal, public work with American-based Palestinian political or pro-Arab organizations, while other portions of the file document the FBI's ongoing investigations of Said as it monitored his contacts with other Palestinian-Americans. The FBI's monitoring of his legal political activities and intellectual forays clarifies not only the FBI's role in suppressing democratic solutions to the Israeli and Palestinian problems, it also demonstrates a continuity with the FBI's historical efforts to monitor and harass American peace activists.

In Edward Said's 238-page FBI file, there were some unusual gaps in the released records, and it is possible that the FBI still holds far more files on Professor Said than they acknowledge. Some of these gaps may exist because PATRIOT Act and National Security exemptions allow the FBI to deny the existence of records; however, the released file provides enough information to examine the FBI's interest in Edward Said, who mixed artistic appreciations, social theory, and political activism in powerful and unique ways.

When I approached Edward Said's wife, Mariam, and told her about the basics of the file, she wrote me that she was not surprised to learn of the FBI's surveillance of her husband, adding, "we always knew that any political activity concerning the Palestinian issue is monitored and when talking on the phone we would say 'let the tappers hear this'. We believed that our phones were tapped for a long time, but it never bothered us because we knew we were hiding nothing."[1]

After I published an initial analysis of Said's FBI file, Said's longtime friend, Alexander Cockburn wrote in his *Beat the Devil* column in *The Nation* that he assumed that the FBI

> was probably tapping Edward Said's phone right up to the day he died in September 2003. A year earlier, when he was already a very sick man, Said was scheduled to speak at an event at the Kopkind Colony's summer session near Guilford, Vermont. The morning of Friday, August 2, the day Said was due to arrive, the colony's John Scagliotti picked up the phone at the colony's old farmhouse and found it was dead. He went to a neighbor to report the fault.
>
> "Within half an hour," Scagliotti remembers, "there was a knock at the front door, and there was a man who said, 'I hear you have phone problems.' Now, I am a gay man. I know what a phone service repairman is meant to look like. The phone man is a gay icon. Tool belt, jeans, work shirt, work boots. This man has a madras shirt, Dockers, brown loafers. He goes to an outside junction box, and a few minutes later the phone is working. Off he goes."
>
> A month later, in the course of a complaint to the phone company about an unusually high bill, Scagliotti suggests that the trouble may have stemmed from something the repairman did. After further checking, the phone company tells him they never sent a repairman that day. As it happened, shortly there-after Said's assistant called in to say he was too sick to make the five-hour drive from New York. But had he done so, we can opine with near certainty that the FBI would have been ready to monitor whatever calls he may have placed from rural Vermont.[2]

While the FBI has yet to release files establishing any involvement in this particular episode, the files they have released under FOIA show decades of surveillance of Dr. Said as he rose to prominence as a respected voice of Palestinian justice.

The FBI's first record of Edward Said appears in a February 1971 domestic security investigation of another unidentified individual.

The FBI collected photographs of Said from the State Department's passport division and various news agencies. Said's "International Security" FBI file was first opened when an informant gave the FBI a program from the October 1971 Boston Convention of the Arab-American University Graduates, where Said chaired a panel on "Culture and the Critical Spirit." Most of Said's FBI records were classified under the administrative heading of "Foreign Counterintelligence," category 105, and most records are designated as relating to Middle East International Security.[3]

Large sections of Said's file remain redacted, with stamps indicating they remain Classified Secret until 2030, 25 years after their initial FOIA processing. One 1973 "Secret" report is now "exempt from General Declassification Schedule of Executive Order 11652, Exemption Category 2," and is "automatically declassified on indefinite." Such administrative stonewalling diminishes our ability to understand the past and further complicates our ability to document the FBI's role in undermining domestic democratic movements.

In February 1972, New York FBI agents produced a report listing Said's employment at Columbia University, his home address and phone number, including a notation that his home telephone service was provided by New York Telephone Company; information that was later used to request listings of all toll calls associated with Said's home phone number.[4] A July 1972 FBI report indicates Said received a phone call from someone who was the subject of intensive FBI surveillance. The NYC agent wrote that "reasons for phone call, activities of the professor, and his sympathies in relation to ████████████ matters have not been ascertained."[5]

In the months after the attacks at the 1972 Munich Olympics there was a flurry of FBI interest in Said and other Palestinian-Americans. In early October 1972, the NYC FBI field office investigated Said's background and citizenship information as well as voting, banking, and credit records. Employees at Princeton and Columbia Universities gave FBI agents biographical and educational information on Said, and the Harvard University Alumni Office provided the FBI with records on him. As Middle East scholar Steve Niva observes, "looking back, this post-Munich period may have marked an historic turning point when statements in support of the Palestinian cause became routinely equated with sympathies for terrorism."[6]

The FBI spoke with their "Middle East informants" in Boston, Newark, and New York to gather information on Said. One report indicated that "several confidential sources who are familiar with Middle East ███████████ in the United States were contacted during 1972 and 1973, but were unable to furnish any information pertaining to Edward William Said." During this investigation, FBI agents located and read a 1970 *Boston Globe* article headlined "Columbia Professor Blames Racist Attitude for Arab-Israeli Conflict."[7]

One FBI report detailed events at the fifth annual convention of the Association of Arab-American University Graduates (AAAUG) held in November 1972 in Berkeley. Said was living in Lebanon at the time and did not attend the conference, but because he was a member of the AAAUG Board of Directors, the FBI included their convention report in his FBI file. There was a significant FBI presence at the conference, and the FBI's released records include the conference program indicating presentations from a selection of Arab-American scholars such as anthropologists Laura Nader and Barbara Aswad.[8]

The extent of the FBI's surveillance of the conference is seen in the FBI's list (provided by a "reliable" FBI informer) of all AAAUG convention's attendees staying at the Claremont Hotel. Why the FBI collected information on conference attendees' accommodations is not clear. Was it to break into participants' rooms to plant listening devices, search for documents, or to monitor attendees? The redacted report does not say, but the FBI's well-documented reliance on such "black-bag jobs" during this period raises this as a likely possibility. The Bureau's policy for these illegal operations was to maintain separate filing systems for them. The FBI's report contains summaries of several talks, including a detailed account of Andreas Papandreou's keynote address, writing,

> The main theme of Professor Papandreou's lecture was the impe-rialistic forces of the United States against the peoples of the Middle East, Greek and Arab peoples alike. According to source, Papandreou expressed an intense hatred for the United States

Government and its policies and claimed that the Nixon foreign policy of blood and bloodshed in Vietnam is very much like his policy to Greece. Furthermore, the United States, in its support of Israel, is undermining the oppressed peoples of the Middle East, and Western tiers of the Mediterranean. Papandreou of the United States, concluding that the United States should be removed from the Middle East with violence, if necessary.[9]

The FBI's report recorded that in January 1973, the FBI undertook further criminal and biographical background checks on Said, and the New York Special Agent in Charge recommended in February that the case be closed. But an FBI investigation the next month of a "subject [who had] traveled in the United States in 1971" began a new investigation of Said as one of several individuals whose phone numbers had come to the attention of the FBI and were believed to have possible "connections with Arab terrorist activities." Such alleged connections remain unspecified as do Said's connections to such activities, but such vague associations are frequently used by the FBI to keep investigations active.[10]

FBI memos from this period discuss the creation of a LHM (Letterhead Memorandum, meaning a memo identified as coming from the FBI) that "should be suitable for dissemination to foreign intelligence agencies." The agency or country to receive this LHM report is not identified, but Israel's Mossad was a likely candidate.

A Classified Secret NYC report on Said and a second unidentified individual, from September 13, 1973 is partially redacted and designated as "exempt from General Declassification Schedule of Executive Order 11652, Exemption Category 2," and is "automatically declassified on indefinite," reports that in "February, 1972, a representative of the Illinois Bell Telephone Company furnished a list of toll calls charged to Chicago, Illinois, telephone number ███████████ listed to ████████████ It is believed that most of the calls charged to this number were made by ████████████. Among the toll calls was one made on December 29, 1971 to [Edward Said's NYC phone number]."[11] The report indicated that the New York Phone Company confirmed that this was Edward Said's home number.

During the aftermath of the Yom Kippur War the FBI collected several of Said's newspaper columns and interviews, and his file includes a *New York Times* column arguing that Arabs and Jews in the Middle East had historically been pitted against each other rather than against "imperialist powers." In 1974, the FBI learned that Said would speak at the Canadian Arab Federation Conference in Windsor, Ontario, and the Bureau again tracked Said's movements even though an FBI informer indicated that "he did not consider Said to be the type of individual who would be involved in any terrorist activity."[12]

The FBI made no entry in Edward Said's file in 1978, the year of the publication of his groundbreaking book, *Orientalism*. The meaning of this omission remains unclear. Given the FBI's historic practice of reading and interpreting the academic work of those they monitor, it is possible that such omissions are a sort of negative record of the FBI's non-release of all of Said's file, and somewhere in their records sits an analysis of Said's work.

A July 1979 FBI report summarized information on 36 individuals (names redacted in the released documents) preparing to attend the August 1979 Palestine American Congress (PAC) at the Shoreham-Americana Hotel in Washington, DC. The FBI noted that Said was an ex-officio member of the council. Snippets of paragraphs on other unidentified attendees mention past academic and political conferences attended, and one FBI informant is identified as being linked to the "pro-Iraqi Ba'ath Party." FBI offices receiving this report were advised to check their files for pertinent information on any of the mentioned individuals.[13]

The extent of the FBI's conference surveillance is shown in a partially declassified Secret Report Index indicating that attendee records had been consulted from FBI field offices in 25 cities listed alphabetically from Albany to Washington. This report contains sentence summaries on participants. Said's summary, for example, says, "EDWARD SAID Previously identified as being from Columbia University, New York City, New York, and as being deeply affiliated with the Popular Front for the Liberation of Palestine." Other released passages find the FBI preoccupied with tracing various attendees' PFLP sympathies.

The PAC was perhaps the most open and democratic deliberative effort by displaced American-Palestinians to address the goals of the Palestinian struggle. With great concern the FBI documented how the PAC "created a Preparatory Committee that empowered it to prepare a working paper on a proposed constitution for some mechanism for collaborative action."[14] In reading the FBI's report of this conference it is painful to see how the FBI's endemic paranoia conflated democracy with revolutionary action, actions that show the FBI's misunderstanding that decreased access to democratic solutions would lead others to more violent means.

The FBI noted some internal arguments about the legitimacy of some delegates coming from Arab communities with low Palestinian populations. The FBI reported that one delegate at the Congress "reminded all in attendance that the FBI has no legitimate interest in the activities taking place during the three-day convention. There was no reason to be afraid of one's presence at all functions of the PAC."[15] Without irony the FBI then noted with concern that some of the individuals they were spying on used false names to register their hotel rooms.[16]

Following opening remarks by Jawad George, another speaker described in the FBI report as a revolutionary Black male named Smith was reported to have

delivered a strong speech concerning Young's dismissal/resignation. Complained about the FBI, Israeli Intelligence Service, and other U.S. Government agencies for what had taken place surrounding the Young dismissal ... [Smith] expressed gratitude for Palestinian efforts on the West Bank and all over the world for their struggle against U.S. imperialism. "Ensured the PAC that the black Americans would render assistance to Arab revolution." No further comment on what exactly this assistance would be, probably moral support. This individual gave a brief history of black people in the United States and requested additional activities [on] behalf of the Palestinian cause since we (black/Arab) are working together for a revolutionary situation.[17]

Other speakers discussed in the FBI report included a member of the Organization of Arab Students and Ramallah Mayor Krim

Khlif speaking on efforts to establish a Palestinian State on the West Bank.[18]

The FBI report discussed problems arising at the conference's conclusion when there was "much discussion on just the preamble to the constitution. Strong disagreement on the wording of a sentence concerning return to its national homeland, to national self-determination, and to its national independence and sovereignty in all of Palestine, by the Arab peoples." Fights over the wording of the constitution's preamble continued, and several disputes "almost broke out into fist fights" between rival factions.[19] Said's FBI file contains a copy of the "Proposed Constitution of the Palestine American Congress" that had been distributed to PAC attendees, which the FBI marked as classified "Secret." This information provided by an FBI informant from this period has now been reclassified under the PATRIOT Act measures making the document classified "Secret" until the year 2029. In 2006 I launched a series of FBI in-house appeals to get these withheld records released, but these efforts met with failure.[20]

In May 1982, the New York FBI Special Agent in Charge sent a Secret report to FBI Director William Webster saying that Said's name had "come to the attention of the N.Y. [FBI Office] in the context of a terrorist matter." FBI headquarters was then requested "to contact liaison with State Department's Middle East section with regard to their knowledge of Said."[21] A week later, the FBI added a photo to Said's file showing him addressing the December 1980 Palestine Human Rights Campaign National Conference.[22] One 1982 newspaper clipping added to the file attempted to connect his wife Mariam Said and the PLO to the funding of a full-page anti-Israel advertisement in the New York Times.[23]

The FBI recorded that during the summer of 1982 an unidentified individual was arrested and deported from the United States, and the "INS obtained photocopies of all documents in his possession." Among these papers was a document with Edward Said's name and home phone number. Documents relating to Said and this deportation are still being withheld and are being vetted under National Security Classification review processes.[24]

On September 3, 1982, FBI Director Webster instructed FBI librarians at Quantico to use their computerized New York Times index to locate all past references to Said. This generated a 13-page report containing abstracts of 49 articles. These articles range from political columns by Said, features about him, to literary book reviews by Said. The *New York Times* Information Service was routinely used by the Bureau during this pre-Google age to compile dossiers on persons or organizations of interest. Using these simple means, the FBI produced a filtered analysis of Said's writings and public statements formed by the reports and prejudices of *Times* reporters and editors.

Said's released FBI file concludes with a few redacted reports (now reclassified until the year 2030) from 1983 and a highly censored Classified Secret memo from August 1991 that ends with the suggestions that the FBI "may desire to contact your Middle East Section for additional information concerning Said."[25] Curiously, Said's released file contains no information on the remaining dozen years of his life. Either the FBI stopped monitoring him, or they couldn't locate these files, or they won't release this information or even the fact that the information exists in the files. The latter two possibilities seem far more likely than the first.

It did not matter how frequently or clearly Edward Said declared that he "totally repudiated terrorism in all its forms," the FBI continued to focus its national security surveillance campaign on him. Had the FBI read the PAC's proposed constitution placed in Said's file in 1979, they would have seen the group's commitment to upholding the "basic fundamental human and national rights of all people and affirms its opposition to racism in all of its manifestations including Zionism and anti-Semitism." Instead, they kept searching for connections to terrorism.

The FBI's surveillance of Edward Said had similarities with their surveillance of other Palestinian-American intellectuals. For example, Ibrahim Abu Lughod's FBI file records similar monitoring though Abu Lughod's file finds the FBI attempting to capitalize on JDL death threats as a means of interviewing Lughod to collect information for his file.

Having read hundreds of FBI reports summarizing "subversive" threads in the work of other academics, I am surprised to find that Said's FBI file contains no FBI analysis not just of his book *Orientalism*, but of *any* of his academic work. This is especially surprising given the claims by scholars, like anthropologist Stanley Kurtz in his 2003 absurd testimony before the House Subcommittee on Select Education, claiming that Said's post-colonial critique left American Middle East Studies scholars impotent to contribute to Bush's terror war.[26] Kurtz even claimed that at Middle East Studies Centers on American campuses "the American government has been pouring millions of dollars into the pockets of the most anti-American scholars in the academy, vast chunks of which end up force-feeding America's children a steady diet of Arundhati Roy and Edward Said. Worse, since Sept. 11."[27] Given what is known of the FBI's monitoring of radical academic developments it seems unlikely that such a work escaped their scrutiny, and it is reasonable to speculate that an FBI analysis of *Orientalism* remains in unreleased FBI documents. I had originally requested Said's file because I assumed that his effectiveness could at least in part be measured by the FBI's surveillance of him. Had his work on Orientalism ended only with discussions in literary circles, then his file would either be nonexistent or his surveillance trivial.

Some known things are obviously missing from the released file. Chief among these are records of death threats against Said and records of the undercover police protection he received at some public events. But there are no good reasons for the FBI to withhold such records, and their absence gives further cause to not believe the FBI's claim this is his entire releasable file. The reasons for the temporal and thematic gaps in Said's file remain unknown. One explanation for such gaps is suggested in Kafka's *The Trial*, where reference is made to cases of suspects never cleared of vague accusations but who are instead given an "ostensible acquittal" under which the accused's dossier circulates for years, "backwards and forwards with greater or smaller oscillations" on "peregrinations that are incalculable."[28] Perhaps such Kafkaesque forces move within the FBI, empowered by post-9/11 legislation and desires to shield the public's eye from acknowledgments of past persecutions of Edward Said.

9

Seymour Melman and the FBI's Persecution of the Demilitarization Movement

Throughout the second half of the twentieth century, Seymour Melman was a visible critic of the military-industrial complex's takeover of the American economy. Studying industrial engineering and economics, in the postwar years Melman took seriously President Eisenhower's warning of dangers the world faced by the unbridled growth of the American military-industrial complex. Writing books like *Inspection for Disarmament* (1958), *Our Depleted Society* (1965), and *The Permanent War Economy* (1974) Melman presented publicly accessible critiques during the 1950s, 1960s, and 1970s of how Pentagon-capitalism robbed America of opportunities to confront basic issues such as poverty, lack of universal health care, and comprehensive mass transit. Melman's command of financial data and his approach to complex systems produced rich critiques filled with data and arguments questioning the logic of American militarization. He was fond of pointing out not only the sheer waste, but the illogic of a military economic system devoted to producing so many nuclear weapons when "not even the largest military budget allows you to kill a person more than once."[1]

Melman was Professor of Industrial Engineering and Operations Research at Columbia University from 1949 to 2003; he died in 2004 at the age of 87. Melman's training, experience, and lifelong critical political engagements broke outside the mold and expectations of his engineering training, and his life as a public intellectual showed the promise of the roles to be played by thinkers in a free society; just as the FBI's monitoring of him, his private life and public advocacy shows the role the FBI has long fulfilled as enforcer of the American corporate status quo. In response to my Freedom of Information Act request the FBI released 219 pages of Melman's FBI file, which records how the mid-twentieth century FBI conceived of those challenging the economic sustainability of military-industrial capitalism as possible enemies of state.

The FBI first investigated Melman in 1955–56 as part of a standard background check for his work as a consultant for Senator Harley Kilgore's Senate Subcommittee on Copyrights, Patents, and Trademarks. The FBI learned that during 1939–40 Melman traveled in Europe and Palestine. The Bureau showed concern over his past membership in the American Student Zionist Federation but did not discover that Melman had been involved in Avukah, the socialist-Zionist student movements that put him in contact with linguist Zellig Harris, who later supervised his Second World War work for an Army Specialized Training Program (ASTP) language project. When the FBI interviewed Zellig Harris, in January 1956 as part of this employee background check, he did not mention any political connections with Melman, instead only reporting that

> Melman was introduced to him by an undergraduate student at [University of Pennsylvania] in 1941. Melman later wrote [Harris] asking if he had some work he could do. Melman knew the Arabic Language and in that the university was handling ASTP, he hired Melman to give lectures ... and he considered him to be of good character, a loyal American and would recommend him for a position of trust.[2]

When I asked Noam Chomsky if he knew anything about these Avukah links, he wrote me that

> Melman and Harris certainly had Avukah connections. I'd have expected that Harris would have kept to the minimum cooperation with the FBI, and that much probably only not to prejudice Seymour's future. Can't imagine that he would have raised these contacts, or mentioned anything, if not explicitly asked. And I rather doubt that he used the phrase "loyal American."[3]

The FBI expressed concerns that Melman had been hired by Columbia University "at the request of Professor Walter Rautenstrauch, who was described as having been in several [Communist Party] Front Groups, and who was one of the principals involved in the Communist conspiracy to subvert the Methodist Church for Communist purposes." Despite these concerns Melman was cleared to work for Senator Kilgore's committee, but possible "loyalty" concerns raised during this investigation were added to his file where they echoed for decades.[4]

In 1959 the FBI learned that Melman planned to meet with Nikolai Smelyakov, Soviet president of the Amtorg Trading Company, during Smelyakov's U.S. visit.[5] During this 1959 investigation of Melman, the FBI's suspicions multiplied upon learning that the previous year he had published a book entitled *Inspection For Disarmament*, which advocated for nuclear disarmament. Melman's research and writing on nuclear disarmament kept the FBI's attention for decades.[6]

In 1958, one FBI informer (a former Communist Party member) reported that an unidentified Columbia professor had said that the Committee for the Study of Peace and War, a committee led by Melman at Columbia, "had discussed a plan to smuggle 'fake hydrogen bombs' into the U.S. and Russia in order to demonstrate how insecure the world is today." When the FBI then learned that Melman had been scouting industrial machine shops, they assumed that this activity could be part of these rumored efforts to build a fake hydrogen bomb—as if this might be the only reason that an industrial engineer might seek out an industrial machine shop.[7]

In 1960 an employee of the Library of Congress wrote to FBI Director, J. Edgar Hoover to report some private correspondence he had with Melman regarding a manuscript on automation in the USSR. This library employee told Hoover that in a recent article Melman advocated what he considered to be pro-Soviet views on industrialization. This informer added that an unnamed Colonel, working at the Pentagon was so addled by Melman's article that the Colonel considered writing a rebuttal to Melman's arguments for publication in the *New York Times*. But with the able assistance of this librarian-informer, the Colonel found a far more satisfying means of attacking Melman: raising suspicions of Melman's loyalties with the FBI. This Colonel worried that "in view of Melman's position as a Professor at Columbia University … [Melman's] views might have a dangerous influence on the students there." In the coming years, the FBI would repeatedly recycle this disgruntled Colonel's complaint that Melman's article was "an espousal of the Communist Party line."[8] The long life of this critic's conjectural attack illustrates a fundamental danger of these FBI files, where a single biting comment, or a baseless speculation takes on an eternal life of its own; often re-spun in files until baseless speculations become presented as facts.

As Melman began publishing popular books written for the American public on the negative effects of Cold War military spending, the FBI assigned employees in its Central Research Section to read and analyze his work. In reviewing his 1962 book, *The Peace Race*, the FBI concluded that

> Melman believes that under-developed nations consider the Soviet economy to be more realistic although they desire freedom. He asks the question "can we offer to underdeveloped nations a plan which combines (Soviet) economic planning with Western personal freedom?" His answer is: Yes, by industrializing these countries and encouraging the workers to form autonomous, independent organizations which will have a voice in economic decisions.

The FBI summarized Melman's argument that the United States could win the international battle for hearts and minds if it would engage in unilateral nuclear disarmament. The FBI wrote:

> Realizing that the U.S. must have a plan to take care of its industrial capacity after disarmament, Professor Melman suggests that the capacity can be used to raise living standards in under-developed areas of the U.S., for production for "public sectors" of the economy, and to industrialize the 'rest of the earth.' The areas of the economy which would be expanded through central government planning would include health functions, transportation, water supply, electricity and natural resources, scientific research and housing.

This FBI book critic concluded: "It is quite evident that Professor Melman would side-step Patrick Henry's cry 'Give me liberty, or give me death' with the statement: In order to have liberty, there must first be life."[9]

The FBI monitored Melman's interactions with various political groups throughout the 1960s, including Students for a Democratic Society (SDS), the Committee for the Sane Nuclear Policy (SANE), Columbia University teach-ins, and his work with Noam Chomsky and Benjamin Spock in opposing the draft for the Vietnam War. As the FBI increasingly monitored Melman's public criticism of the Pentagon, one 1964 near-Dadaist file entry simply reads: "The Defense Department recently denied Melman's charges that the United States had stockpiled more than enough nuclear weapons needed for a full scale war."[10] The absurdity of this Pentagon denial can be seen by considering that the National Resources Defense Council's Archive of Nuclear Data now estimates that 1964 was one of four record high-water-mark years with an estimated record 30,751 stockpiled U.S. nuclear warheads.[11]

A 1967 FBI "Russian Espionage" report claimed a

KGB officer, had regular contact with a very well-known professor in the United States. This professor wrote a book about the economic consequences of disarmament. Source believes his name begins with 'S'; however, the source cannot recall the complete name. This professor's KGB code name is [Mansha]. Source stated that he is not an agent of the KGB, but an individual with whom the KGB has established a trusted relationship.

The next month an FBI informer claimed that "Melman is one of the most dangerous Communists in the U.S. She felt that Melman was an extremely important key in the Communist conspiracy to weaken the U.S. government by fostering unilateral disarmament. According to [this FBI informer] Melman heads a conspiracy to weaken the industrial might of the U.S."[12]

A few months later another FBI report, admitted that "as is evident, Melman has espoused some views which have long been popular with the Communist Party and related groups, however, Melman has never been identified as a CP member or actively associated with any front groups"; thereby offering the FBI's classic rationalization for investigating any American whose free opinions were counter to narrow views of FBI agents.[13]

On January 19, 1968 the New York City FBI Office issued a "classified secret" comprehensive review of the information the FBI had collected on Melman. This report included extensive reviews of newspaper and magazine articles chronicling his work with SANE, Benjamin Spock, Noam Chomsky, Columbia University's Teach-in movement, and an advertisement in the Communist Party's *Daily Worker* listing Melman as a sponsor of the 1965 March on Washington, DC.[14]

Once the FBI collected the sniping comments of FBI informers and disgruntled colleagues, these reports were rehashed and repeated within FBI reports for decades repeating rumors until what appeared as speculations in initial reports were reified as facts. The way that these rumors were transformed and took on lives of their own is shown in what happened during the decade and half between the FBI file repeating the initial 1958 report that Melman was part of an activist group considering smuggling *fake* hydrogen bombs into the United States and USSR to demonstrate the insecurity of nuclear states had been transformed into a plot to smuggle *real* hydrogen bombs, and the transformation of this into a 1972 FBI report claiming: "A group at Columbia University discussed plans to smuggle a few hydrogen bombs into the United States and Russia in order to show the potential insecurity of the world. The group was believed to be called the 'Group for the Study of Peace and War' and to be headed by [Melman]."[15]

This FBI report refers to an undated (but likely January 1968) FBI interview with Melman that took place in his office at Columbia. The agent conducting the interview seems to have been assisting Attorney General Ramsey Clark's efforts to build federal cases against Melman's colleagues Benjamin Spock and the Rev. William Sloane Coffin for conspiring to destroy selective service documents. The FBI reported that they told Melman

that the specific purpose of this interview concerned possible violations of Section 462 of Title 50 of the United States Code relating to counseling, aiding or abetting another to refuse or evade registration or service in the Armed Forces.

Professor Melman claimed that he had "never directly given counsel to any individual" to violate Selective Service laws and that no one has ever come to him for advice relating to his draft status.

He claimed that his appearance as a peace delegate at the Department of Justice in Washington D.C. on October 20, 1967, was as an individual and not as a representative of any specific group. He referred to this appearance as "a moral act" on his part to protest the illegality of the Vietnam War and to request the Department of Justice to investigate war crimes which have been committed by the Armed Forces in Vietnam and even by the "Commander-in-Chief."

He produced a research paper which he stated consisted of six hundred pages of documentation of the United States behavior in Vietnam in relation to the laws of war. He referred to United States Army Field Manual Number 27-10 page 178 which states that every violation of the laws of war is a war crime. He claimed that the constitutionality of Selective Service itself has never been tested in court. It was his opinion that because of the illegality of the Vietnam War certain actions taken by Selective Service could be considered violations of the laws of war.

Professor Melman stated that he did not "approve or condemn" the act of destroying or handing in draft cards to the Department of Justice. In this regard he stated only that on October 20, 1967, he was aware of "pieces of paper" which could have been draft cards being collected on the steps of the Department of Justice building prior to their meeting with an Assistant Attorney General. He declined to discuss participants in this act and claimed that he was unaware of the actual contents of a briefcase offered to the Assistant Attorney General in his presence.

Investigation conducted by the FBI regarding possible Selective Service Act violations on the part of Seymour Melman and others reflected that Melman was one of an eleven man delegation who appeared at the United States Department of Justice, Washington, D.C., on October 20, 1967, and met with Deputy Attorney General John Van De Kamp. During this meeting

Melman observed that the war in Vietnam is illegal and that people are justified in attempting to stop this war and in refusing to comply with the Selective Service Act. Melman stated that he supported the student newspaper at Columbia University when it called upon all students to resist the draft. Melman stated that the young men of this country are refusing to be drafted on the grounds that the draft is invalid because the war in Vietnam is illegal and immoral. Melman stated that it is incumbent upon members of the older generation to support this position.[16]

The report concluded with a (redacted) summary of the January 5, 1968 indictment of Benjamin Spock and Rev. William Sloane Coffin Jr. by a Federal Grand Jury in Boston for "conspiring to counsel young men to violate the draft laws."[17]

In 1971 the FBI intercepted, copied, and analyzed Melman's correspondence relating to the Pugwash Symposium held in Leipzig—including his visa application and personal correspondence to his wife, Ruth Sager, mailed from Berlin; filing these intercepts under "International Security." The FBI's last entries in Melman's file discuss information on a Russian exchange student who was Melman's advisee at Columbia. The FBI planned to interview Russian-American contacts in the student's residence, and upon learning of Melman's contacts with the Soviet student, the FBI fantasized about ways to limit the academic freedom of Melman and others writing that: "the Bureau may wish to discuss with State Department officials at the appropriate time and place the folly of having academic advisors with the reputation of Melman participating in an official East-West Exchange program."[18]

An undated airtel from NY Special Agent in Charge (SAC), John Malone to Hoover with the subject heading: "Balnchain, ESP-R" is in Melman's file, but released information reveals little beyond that this concerns KGB information and an individual from the People's Republic of China. The next report in the file states that: "While there are no known connections between Seymour Melman and the PRC, it is believed that he should be considered a logical suspect in the ███████ case"—and the report then goes on to summarize Melman's known connections with the American anti-nuclear weapons movement.[19]

In 1974 an FBI memo from NY SAC to Hoover, under the heading "IS-R [International Security] (Student)" describes the FBI's interest in one of Melman's student advisees at Columbia. This student may have been a Soviet exchange student. The FBI wrote that the New York Office

> will attempt to develop sources close to the subject in spite of the obvious obstacles ... It should be noted that this endeavor will be somewhat restrictive as subject resides at a hotel housing Soviet families almost exclusively and he attends a university [e.g. Columbia] which can be described as somewhat less than sympathetic to the Bureau.[20]

The record of the FBI's monitoring of Melman suddenly ends in November 1974, a cut-off consistent with the sudden drop in FBI records of other American dissidents during this period. The paper trail's sudden end is likely related to investigation limits enacted during the post-Watergate moment when the Church Committee and other Congressional actions installed safeguards limiting the FBI's monitoring of Americans' political activities. While it is unknown what sort of off-the-books domestic FBI investigations continued after the establishment of these mid-1970s safeguards, we do know these safeguards were swiftly obliterated with bipartisan adaption of the PATRIOT Act in October 2001.

FBI files generate and sustain an internal logic that amplifies suspicion into fictive-substance by fetishizing the fragmentary information in the files; creating faux-gestalts of guilt wherein the repeated shards of rumors are reconstituted in ways that cast shadows of guilt greater than the whole of facts sustain. FBI files during this period frequently sustained a logic justifying monitoring progressives working on issues ranging from racial equality, disarmament, economic justice as having (as it appears in Melman's file) "espoused some views which have long been popular with the Communist Party and related groups" even while the FBI repeatedly acknowledged that these individuals had not violated any laws, or in Melman's case, had "never been identified as a CP member or actively associated with any front groups." But these free-ranging FBI investigations were not about investigations of law breaking, they were about monitoring dissent; as such they mark not only the borders of orthodoxy, they mark effectiveness or the perceived threat of a critique. By this measure, Melman's critique of the economic damage of the American military economy was effective.

Decades ago, sociologist Steven Spitzer argued that the determinant of what would be considered deviant in a given society would be that which threatens the society's dominant economic forces; and Melman's critiques of the damage wrought by the excesses of military spending and his opposition to the nuclear arms race cut to the core of the military-industrial complex's interests that the FBI so loyally protected.[21] Melman's file demonstrates the FBI's functional role as an arm of a state secret police apparatus designed to sniff out and mark deviants threatening to undermine the political and economic interests of what used to be called the Power Elite. That such a critic of the American nuclear state would be tainted with baseless accusations of being a spy should be expected in such contexts.

10

Traces of FBI Efforts to Deport a Radical Voice: On Alexander Cockburn's FBI File

During the dozen years before his death in 2012, while writing pieces for *CounterPunch* documenting FBI monitoring of American activist intellectuals, I had several conversations with Alexander Cockburn about FBI surveillance of political radicals. He took it as a matter of course that a nation's secret police would keep tabs on critics, visionaries, and troublemakers. Yet, ever the undeterred optimist, when considering the possibility of such surveillance directed at himself, Alex maintained a nonchalant buoyancy, insisting he did not give this possibility much thought because his continued ability to freely write remained unfettered. If the FBI was monitoring him, it had not limited the freedoms of expression he claimed for himself, so he wasn't going to waste time worrying about such matters. While acknowledging the FBI and others routinely monitored radical political writers such as himself, he was not going to restrain or mute his critiques over such eventualities, acknowledging their likelihood while also noting his continued freedom to engage in these critiques.

It's not that Alexander Cockburn underestimated the power of the FBI to disrupt political movements. Over the years he wrote critically of the FBI's infiltration of environmental activists, the Black Panthers, his friend Edward Said, COINTELPRO, and topics such as the dangers of post-9/11 data mining. He just didn't let such possibilities alter the course or force of his critical work.[1]

In July 2012, a few days after Alexander's death, I filed Freedom of Information Act requests for records pertaining to him with the FBI and CIA. The FBI eventually notified me that their record search revealed one set of documents that had previously been moved to the National Archives for storage. I refiled my FOIA request with the National Archives and in November 2012 I received a small collection of FBI documents, only 17 pages, spanning the years 1973–75. The FBI claimed these documents comprise Alexander Cockburn's complete FBI file.

It is surprising to find as outspoken a critic of American capital and corruptions of empire as Cockburn to have such a paltry record of FBI attentions. There are good reasons to wonder if this release truly represents all FBI records pertaining to him. The FBI is notoriously sloppy and inefficient, and its responses to FOIA requests show recurrent patterns of inconsistently searching for records. Given the outdated state of the FBI's older record system, it is likely they hold yet to be identified records on Cockburn. Unfortunately, during the first Bush and Clinton administrations, a broad range of historic FBI records was destroyed rather than moved to safe storage at the National Archives. The extent of this damage to the historical record is not well understood by FOIA scholars. Over the past decade I have received several notifications of destroyed records in response to FOIA requests, and there are routine reports of the FBI acknowledging the destruction of FBI files on prominent writers like Hunter S. Thompson.[2]

But even with unresolved questions about the completeness of Cockburn's FBI record, these released 17 pages combined with what is known of FBI efforts to limit political discourse during this period provide a disturbing view of how the FBI and Immigration and Naturalization Service (INS) used McCarthy era legislation to try and limit political discourse in America.

1973 COCKBURN IN NEW YORK

Cockburn's released FBI file (FBI 100-HQ-478026) was catalogued under the FBI's Central Records Classification System number "100," indicating he was the subject of an FBI Domestic Security investigation. This is the same FBI designation used for its numerous investigations of suspected communists, anarchists, socialists, and other national security subversives since the Bureau's creation. The cumulative total of FBI "Domestic Security" investigations is unknown, but in the early 1990s the FBI disclosed it had to date undertaken over 1,300,000 "Domestic Security" investigations, producing files occupying over 22,000 cubic feet of space.[3] We can only guess at the growth in size of these files in the post-9/11 era.

The FBI opened its initial record of Alexander Cockburn on August 15, 1973, with a brief report describing him and his work carrying a disclaimer that it was to be

made available to the Immigration and Naturalization Service only on the understanding that under no circumstances will it, or the identity of the originating agency, be disclosed to the public, to the subject of the report or to his representatives or employer, in any administrative or judicial proceedings without the written prior consent of the originating agency.[4]

Cockburn moved to the United States in 1972 to work as a freelance journalist. The FBI described him as a

leading figure of the "New Left," a group of revolutionary Marxist academics centered round the "New Left Review," since 1966. Although closely associated with members of Trotskyist and Communist groups, he is not known to have been either a Trotskyist or a Communist himself, and is probably best described as a Revolutionary Marxist.[5]

The FBI's report included a copy of Cockburn's INS application requesting Permanent Resident Status in the United States.

The following week, the FBI's New York Special Agent in Charge (SAC) submitted a report to FBI Director Clarence M. Kelly summarizing the Bureau's knowledge of Cockburn. This investigation occurred during the midst of significant administrative upheaval within the FBI, coming just 15 months after J. Edgar Hoover's death, with Kelly now the FBI's third post-Hoover director. The memo header listed Cockburn's name along with the FBI subject heading "SM—SWP," FBI shorthand meaning: Subversive Matter—Socialist Workers Party, a designation likely revealing more about

FBI predilections for inventing political affiliations than Cockburn's actual party ties at that time.

The FBI reported Cockburn had submitted a request for an "adjustment in immigrant status" and referenced information coming from a "confidential source abroad," writing that "a review of files at [FBI] Headquarters indicates that Cockburn edited 'Student Power,' a British publication relating to student protests. No other pertinent information is available in Bufiles [Bureau Files] in addition to that furnished by confidential source abroad and enclosed herewith."[6] The report conceded that Cockburn "has never been known to have been a member of a Trotskyist or Communist Organization as such."[7]

The New York SAC wrote FBI Director Kelly that his office would review its files, incorporate any relevant details along with information from their confidential sources and submit this on a Letterhead Memo (LHM) to FBI Headquarters and the INS, stressing that the restrictions protecting the identity of MI5's informer be maintained with the INS. This reference to a LHM indicated FBI plans to release a memo designed to be distributed with attribution outside the Bureau, in this case, the outside agency receiving this LHM was the INS.

An October 3, 1973 FBI memo referenced eight copies of a LHM, including one copy sent to the INS.[8] This LHM described Cockburn as a "revolutionary Marxist," and included biographical information on him and his father, Claud Cockburn, and his mother, Patricia Arbuthnot (née), while stressing his links to the *New Left Review* and Marxist academics. The FBI included the summary of a 1954 interview with Claud Cockburn's former wife, identified by the FBI as Mrs. Robert Gorham Davis, who described Claud's journalism career. This FBI investigation occurred during the heyday of the FBI's McCarthyism anti-communist crusades. Davis had told the FBI of Claud's work for *The Week* and writing for "the London counterpart of the 'Daily Worker,'" and she told the FBI that while she herself was a former communist, she believed that "Claud Cockburn was not a CP member during the period of their marriage and while she feels he embraced the philosophy of Communism because it reflected his own social thinking, he would not have become a CP member."[9] FBI reports attempting to chronicle familial ties to radicalism have long been a routine Bureau practice.

While the FBI LHM portrayed Alexander Cockburn as a subversive involved in radical socialist movements, no released records indicate further FBI action or interest in him in 1973. The reasons for the FBI or INS's lack of further activity immediately after this initial 1973 series of memos is unclear, but given the rise of Watergate investigations, with the impeachment resolution introduced in Congress months earlier, and the beginning of scrutiny into a broad range of FBI activities, rapid shifts in FBI leadership, and accounts in memoirs of a range of FBI insiders, we know that the FBI was adopting a new posture of historically relative caution and was not perusing radical political activities as aggressively as it had just a few years earlier.

The next entries in Cockburn's FBI file would come in 1975, but before discussing these records, some historical information contextualizing the FBI and INS's roles in monitoring, deporting, and denying entry visas to suspect writers is in order.

FBI HOUNDING AUTHORS

The legal foundation of the INS and FBI's mid-1970s investigation of Alexander Cockburn was the 1952 Immigration and Naturalization Act, more commonly known as the McCarran-Walter Act. This McCarthyism era law includes provisions for barring entry to the United States to subversives and allowing the deportation of those involved in subversive activities. Though the Act was vetoed by President Truman, his veto was overridden by both House and Senate votes. The Act has been revised several times; 1990 revisions removed some political exclusionary restrictions, but the McCarran-Walter Act remains in place, now with post-9/11 political manifestations.

There is a long history of the FBI monitoring authors the Bureau believes are subversive. Hundreds of American authors including John Steinbeck, William Carlos Williams, Langston Hughes and Alan Ginsberg were tracked by Hoover's FBI, and the Bureau at times worked with the INS to revoke visas of foreign authors residing in or visiting the United States. When Michel Foucault applied for a visa to come to the United States in 1972 to present a series of lectures at Cornell University, the Paris LEGAT notified the FBI's acting director and the INS of the visit, noting Foucault's "former membership in the French Communist Party".[10]

The breadth of this surveillance remains unknown, but back in 1991 Tim Weiner documented in a *Philadelphia Inquirer* investigative series that U.S. immigration authorities then maintained a "blacklist" identifying over 367,000 individuals not to be allowed into the United States. Weiner determined that "ninety-six percent of those names were tacked onto the list for ideological reasons." Among those writers denied entry to the Unites States identified by Weiner were Carlos Fuentes, Farley Mowat, and Doris Lessing. McCarran-Walter has been used to deport Graham Greene from Puerto Rico, and to deny Marxist sociologist Thomas Bottomore an entry visa to the Unites States.[11] The FBI undertook a "cryptographic examination" of Aldous Huxley's *Brave New World*, looking for hidden subversive materials,[12] and Gabriel García Márquez' writings led to his being listed as a subversive writer, and being blacklisted from U.S. entry until explicitly removed during the Clinton presidency. In 1991 Weiner discovered that "the law still allows the Secretary of State to exclude foreigners on the basis of their words and ideas if he thinks it is in the national interest. Immigrants from socialist countries can be barred if they were members of the Communist Party within the last five years."[13]

Such uses of McCarran-Walter powers to limit intellectual and political discourse are not an archaic practice from a past age. In 2007 Dr. Riyadh Lafta, the Iraqi scientist who coauthored the 2006 *Lancet* study estimating the number of Iraqi deaths resulting from the American invasion exceeded over 600,000 people was denied entry to the United States when he was invited to present an academic talk at the University of Washington. In 2011, the U.S. State Department denied a visa to German journalist Gabriele Weber (well known for her anti-Nazi research, having thousands of records on Adolf Eichmann released), seeking to conduct research at the U.S. National Archives.[14] During this same period covered in Cockburn's FBI file, John Lennon waged a protracted legal battle with the INS, who sought to deny him a permanent visa in the United States for political reasons.[15]

It is this historical pattern of the INS and FBI working in tandem to monitor progressives or radicals, and at times denying entry or even deporting non-American writers or others that the context of these FBI records takes on significance. The FBI and INS interest in Cockburn was part of an ongoing application of the McCarran-Walter Act to limit American political discourse.

1975 FBI AND INS DEPORTATION PROSPECTS

Alexander Cockburn came to the FBI and INS's attention during a period that his writings were making a significant splash in American journalism. His "Press Clips" column in the *Village Voice*, co-written with James Ridgeway, was pioneering a new form of media criticism, and his regular contributions to *The New York Review of Books*, *Harper's*, *Esquire*, and other publication were expanding American political discourse.

After 14 months of inaction, in January 1975 the FBI began administrative proceedings to release information detailing Cockburn's involvement in subversive activities that could lead to his expulsion from the United States by the INS. A January 20, 1975 memo from Henry E. Wagner, Assistant Director of Investigations, to the New York FBI Assistant Director in Charge, requested the disclosure of the identity of the individual who had made accusations to MI5 against Cockburn in an FBI LHM dated October 3, 1973.[16] Wagner wrote that this information could be used for "deportation proceedings" against Cockburn.

Five months later (June 18, 1975), the INS's Assistant District Director for Investigations wrote to the FBI's Assistant Director in Charge reminding him that in January, the INS had requested the release of the identity of Cockburn's 1973 informer. This request was to have been sent to the FBI's Liaison Division.[17]

Released internal FBI Records Branch slips document FBI Headquarters' personnel searching central records for information on Cockburn, locating apparent references in at least five other FBI files. These files were indexed relating to: domestic security, foreign counterintelligence, "miscellaneous-nonsubversive," research matters, and income taxes.

A declassified July 1975 FBI memo that referenced a 1973 MI5 report of a confidential informer provided unspecified damaging information on Cockburn. This memo stated that the INS wanted to interview "the original source of information for possible use in deportation proceedings."[18] The memo requested permission to identify the source of the information on Cockburn for use by the INS in possible deportation proceedings. Among the recipients of the memo was "Legat, London," the American embassy in London's Legal Attaché, a member of the embassy personnel staff who is an FBI agent and would certainly have had contacts with the CIA officer stationed at the embassy.

The released summary of the MI5 report states:

NOTE: MI-5, in 1973, provided information on Alexander Claud Cockburn and we, in turn, provided that information to INS, INS now wishes to interview the original source of information for possible use in deportation proceedings. This communication is being directed ▮▮▮▮▮▮▮ to determine if they interpose any objection to our release of their identity as the original source of information … Delivered to Washington Representative of ▮▮▮▮▮▮▮ by pld.[19]

A July 29, 1975 memo declared that it was impossible to disclose the identity of the individual providing deleterious information on Cockburn.[20] The FBI redacted information on the individuals and agencies cited in this document under FOIA exemption (b)7-D, an exemption allowing the withholding of information that could identify informers, or intelligence agencies conducting national security investigations.

The next month (August 14, 1975), FBI Director Kelly informed the INS that the FBI was "unable to obtain authorization to reveal the identity of the source in this matter and, therefore, the source will not be available for interview."[21] This ended FBI and INS interest in Cockburn in files so far released under FOIA. Whatever the nature of the information collected by MI5, it did not interfere with Alexander Cockburn becoming a U.S. citizen, while retaining his Irish passport, in June 2009.

Alexander's brother Andrew Cockburn confirmed Alexander had protracted legal difficulties with the INS during this period, adding that "Alexander believed that at least one of the deportation efforts was sparked by a request from Rep. Peter Rodino, then chair of the Judiciary Committee, which controlled the INS budget." He recalled Alexander hired a top immigration lawyer, Stanley Mailman, "who drove them off."[22] While the specifics of the referenced MI5 information remain unknown, Andrew Cockburn speculated to me that

> MI5's interest in Alexander might have come from his work with Ralph Schoenman, former secretary to Bertrand Russell, who controlled a lot of money donated by Russell and put it to use in the antiwar movement in the late 60s. At one point Schoenman, banned from Britain, smuggled himself in and was looked after by Alexander who among other things took Ralph, who was being actively hunted by the authorities, to Number 10 Downing Street and photographed him standing between two smiling coppers at the front door, said picture appearing in *The Times* the next day.[23]

Andrew Cockburn mentioned other possibilities, writing to me that

> in 1969 Alexander met and talked to many in the IRA (this was before the official/provisional split) in connection with an article for the Sunday Times magazine. Shortly afterwards Official Sinn Fein occupied Lismore Castle in County Waterford, Irish seat of the Dukes of Devonshire and a suitable emblem of residual colonial occupation. Once they had secured the premises (politely ejecting the housekeeper) they called Alexander in London for advice on further action.
>
> "Put out a press release" he told them, which they did, and left.
>
> I can just see how in the palsied imaginations of the secret police this could be translated into a terrorist mastermind issuing instructions to his minions.
>
> I bet you're right about there being further files. MI5 claim that our father's file was closed in 1953, clearly a lie.[24]

But in the end, speculation about absent files can only be speculation.

SECRET EVIDENCE

These FBI documents suggest that the reason why deportation proceedings against Cockburn were not undertaken was the FBI's refusal to disclose the identity of the MI5 informer. During the mid-1970s, constitutional safeguards, such as that most basic of Sixth Amendment protections allowing those accused of wrongdoing to face accusers, prevented the INS from using secret evidence to deport individuals from the United States. Today, post-9/11 policies now routinely allow the use of secret testimony in INS deportation proceedings.

Jaya Ramji-Nogales writes in a 2008 *Columbia Human Rights Law Review* article that while conditions of secrecy make it impossible to know how widespread governmental use of secret evidence is, the use of secrecy in immigration cases has increased since 2001. Ramji-Nogales observes that

> the government has not presented statistics on the use of secret evidence in immigration court since 2000, and because records of immigration proceedings are not publicly accessible, it is practically impossible to obtain this information independently. We do know of consistent efforts in Congress to expand the use of secret evidence in immigration proceedings as part of immigration reform legislation.[25]

The timing of Alexander Cockburn's move to America likely played a role in limiting the FBI and INS's action against him. These records of the FBI and INS weighing deportation options coincided with a period of administrative upheaval within the FBI following J. Edgar Hoover's death, the rise of Congressional investigations of FBI abuses of power, and during an era when basic civil liberties mandating the right to face accusers still prevailed. The FBI's 1975 renewed interest in exploring the possibility of deporting Cockburn coincided with the rise of the U.S. Senate Church Committee and the House's Pike Committee's hearing investigating FBI and CIA's illegal interference in domestic and international political activities, and it is possible that these larger historical processes limited the FBI's ability to strike in ways that it had routinely done just a few years earlier.

Given the pleasure that Alexander Cockburn found arguing that Gerald Ford was America's greatest President (largely because Ford's short term of office transferred "the Hippocratic injunction from the medical to the political realm, he did the least possible harm") I imagine he would have savored the historical point that it was the Ford administration's adherence to standards of fair play and the rule of law that prevented his deportation from the United States.[26]

It is difficult to assess the impact on American letters and political life had the INS undertaken deportation proceedings and expelled Alexander from the United States. Certainly his critique would have flourished elsewhere, though without the American flavor he developed and the unique independence he found living for years in Petrolia along the California Lost Coast; but certainly American political and intellectual life would been much the poorer had the decidedly un-American activities of the FBI and INS prevailed.

ON THE QUESTIONS OF A BRIEF FILE

The brevity of Alexander Cockburn's main FBI file raises more questions than it answers. Either the FBI has more files which they have either not located or have and intentionally won't release, or it is possible that no further FBI files on Alexander exist. It is tempting to speculate whether either outcome is a measure of FBI incompetence: either a recent incompetence in the Bureau's ability to search, identify, and release existing files, or a more ancient incompetence in evaluating the threat that was Alexander Cockburn. Having studied the extent of FBI surveillance during this period, I am betting on the former, though both remain possibilities. While FBI noncompliance with FOIA requests is a measure of the Agency's contempt of the law and a lack of Bureau professionalism, the federal courts do not look at such incompetence lightly. On October 17, 2012, U.S. Federal Judge Edward Chen awarded FOIA researcher Seth Rosenfeld $470,459 in legal fees accrued in decades of Rosenfeld's legal efforts to access documents (from an uncooperative FBI) relating to FBI political oppression at UC Berkeley during the 1950s and 1960s.[27]

One of the problems that FOIA researchers face when arguing administrative appeals for unreleased files is that because it is impossible to know whether further records actually exist, or in some cases, what the nature of withheld records is, we must construct the best arguments we can arguing with unseen but presumed records. In filing my administrative appeal with the Department of Justice's Office of Information Policy I made a multi-pronged appeal, arguing that:

> First, my reading of the released Cockburn files indicate there are other FBI entries relating to Cockburn that were not adequately searched for by Justice Department staff; I am requesting that your staff look more carefully for files not previously located or disclosed. Second, I am specifically requesting that you search in the FBI NY LHM-100-178981 (10/3/73 and other dates), for information relating to Alexander Cockburn (referenced in the 6/18/75 FBI materials released to me by the NAA). Third, search for information pertaining to Alexander Cockburn in files 100-478026 and 1-100-789 (as indicated in 100-478026-3 7/11/75). Finally, I am requesting that personnel specifically search for materials pertaining to Cockburn in the following files, referenced in the July 25, 1975 memo released to me: 100-478026, 105-169446, 94-64180, 62-112228-265.[28]

During the last two decades I have filed several hundred FOIA requests, and recurrently received initial responses claiming there were few or no files, only later to have several thousands of pages released upon appeal. This appeal led to the identification of 15 more pages of FBI records relating to Cockburn, eleven of which were released to me. These consisted of items the FBI collected, including a reproduction of a handbill announcing a book talk for *Corruptions of Empire* on April 3, 1989 at New York City's Martin Luther King Jr. Auditorium—and a clipping from a 1989 Queens Peace and Solidarity Council's *Action Bulletin* newsletter announcing the talk. A highly redacted 1982 Secret FBI cable appears to list

Cockburn being in contact with an unknown individual of interest to the FBI. Another listed Alexander Cockburn in a paragraph with several other well-known journalists (Mike O'Neill, Editor, *New York Daily News*; Harrison Salisbury, Editor, *New York Times*; James Fallows, Editor, *The Atlantic Monthly*; A.M. Rosenthal, Executive Editor, *New York Times*; Mila Andre, Assistant Editor, *New York Daily News*; Victor Navasky, Editor, *The Nation*; Allen Wolper, Editor, *The Soho News*; Alex Cockburn, Editor, *The Village Voice*) and included the following passage:

[New York FBI Offices] DO NOT REFLECT ANY DERROGA-TORY INFORMATION CONCERNING THE MEDIA PEOPLE OR THE TWO STUDENTS, WITH THE EXECPTION FOR ALEX COCKBURN, WHO WAS ONCE THE LEADER OF THE NEW LEFT MOVEMENT AND WAS UNDER INVESTI-GATION BY THE NYO.

FBIHQ IS REQUESTED TO CHECK INDICES ON THE ABOVE MENTIONED PERSONS. IN THE ABSENCE OF ANY DERROGATORY REFERENCES, APPROVE INVERVIEWS WITH ALL OF THE ABOVE, WITH THE EXCEPTION OF ALEX COCKBURN.[29]

Recognizing that Cockburn was the only name among this list of journalists that they dare not approach for an interview was one instance of the FBI showing good judgment—lest their inquiries lead to a public raking over the coals in true Cockburn style.

A 1989 Secret memo from the Boston Special Agent in Charge summarized some of the papers and discussions at a recent Cambridge conference on "Anti-Communism and the U.S.: History and Consequences." This was a large conference, with over a thousand in attendance, and speakers included Carl Bernstein, Abby Rockefeller, Philip Agee, John Stockwell, Gus Hall, William Styron, and other members of the intelligentsia. The New York FBI office had requested the Boston FBI office investigate the confer-ence, and they later mailed six tapes of recordings from the con-ference to the New York office.[30] The FBI collected newspaper reports on the conference from *The Washington Post*, *The Harvard*

Crimson, The Union Leader, The Boston Herald, and *The Soviet Observer,* and the report stated that:

> As the clippings will attest the conference was a rather one sided affair attended by and large by those of the same opinion on the government's roll [sic] in representing the Soviet Union and communism to the body politic. While ███████████████ ██████████ etc. may have participated they can hardly be said to have had a major influence on the Conference, its participants or whatever conclusions were arrived at.[31]

The FBI discussed presentations and comments by Jagan, Howard Zinn, Gianfanco Corsini, and others whose identities are redacted. The FBI reported that:

> Alexander Cockburn noted that years ago Averell Harriman suppressed favorable reporting on the USSR by strong arm tactics at "Newsweek" magazine. He characterized anti-Communism as a deliberate class policy which tries to obscure the universal reality of taking money away from rich people ... Alexander Cockburn commented that Jesse Jackson was the victim of tremendous racism in the press and cited examples. He went on to cite other world leaders who were regularly made victims of anti-Communism by the American press.[32]

The FBI reproduced *The Soviet Observer*'s article on "Conference on Anti-Communism Draws Big Crowd in Cambridge" (November 15, 1988).

The final document is a highly redacted page of an unidentified file with all lines withheld except for a sentence reading "In 1990, Alexander Cockburn, a columnist for the Nation, summarized his perspective of Mr. Emerson in the Wall street Journal: 'Mr. Emerson's prime role is to whitewash Israeli governments and revile their critics,'" a quote taken from Cockburn's (June 14, 1990) *Wall Street Journal* column on journalist Steve Emerson.

Though these additional documents were released, several other pages were withheld under claims that almost 40 years later these materials still must be protected under National Security Exemptions: Title 5, United States Code, Section 552 (b)(1), wherein three pages are "specifically authorized under criteria established by an Executive order to be kept secret in the interest of national defense or foreign policy." These documents originated with another federal agency, and given the contents of the released files, it is likely that this agency might be the CIA or INS. When researchers file FOIA appeals we are often required to advance a coherent argument about the contexts of a black box which may or may not exist. Facing the doublebind of appealing for the release of unknown records that are being withheld under unknown conditions, I filed the following in-house appeal with the FBI. My appeal argued that

> Because the FBI has released no information about these three pages, I logically remain limited in what arguments I can make when appealing for their release. I do not know if these documents (about which the FBI "consulted with another Governmental agency") relate to the INS, CIA, or another agency (though these agencies are suggested in the other, released, sections of Mr. Cockburn's FBI file), nor do I even know the topic covered in these withheld pages. These designed Kafkaesque conditions limit the arguments I can make in my appeal, and if my administrative appeal is denied by your office, I intend on filing a legal appeal in Federal Court arguing that this withholding is an improper use of 552 (b)(1), and will ask the courts to determine for itself whether the government is now abusing this exemption to improperly shield the government from public disclosure of past surveillance activities, or other abuses of governmental power.
>
> My appeal argues that these three pages of old records are not properly being withheld to protect the interests of national defense or current foreign policy as claimed, but are instead improperly withheld because their release could embarrass governmental agencies today. Obviously without reading these documents, this is conjecture, but after two decades of FOIA research, and reading tens of thousands of FBI files released under FOIA, such an abuse of 552 (b)(1) would fit an ongoing pattern for the Bureau's (ab)use of FOIA exemptions.[33]

This appeal had little impact, leading to the release of a trickle of more FBI documents. But there is little surprise in this outcome and as with the cumulative knowledge that comes from most FOIA requests, we know enough about how the surveillance of Cockburn worked to understand the government's monitoring of this critical voice. All this brings to mind Alexander Cockburn's essay about American journalists' "hunt for the smoking gun" as "a process by which our official press tries to inculcate itself and its readers against political and economic realities" that have long been made clear, yet claims of a lack of a "smoking gun" are used to perpetuate assertions that we don't know what happened.[34] Even without whatever materials the FBI, CIA, and others are withholding, Cockburn's writings and these released scraps of FBI surveillance provide all the smoking gun we need to understand how and why the FBI monitored him and his work.

11

Medium Cool: Decades of the FBI's Surveillance of Haskell Wexler

American cinematographer Haskell Wexler (1922–2015) transformed Hollywood and independent filmmaking. His use of natural light and sound and innovations mixing scripted action with the unscripted world, and pioneering use of handheld cameras raised the bar decades before the coming of the *Dogma 95 Manifesto* or Soderbergh's films. Wexler won academy awards for his camerawork on *Who's Afraid of Virginia Woolf*, and *Bound for Glory's* groundbreaking use of the Steadicam, while his unprecedented mixing of documentary and fictional modes and his choice of the political subjects in *Medium Cool* broke artistic and political boundaries. With the FBI's release of Wexler's 175-page FBI file, we can see how his politics and art brought him decades of FBI surveillance.

He was born in 1922, into a wealthy Chicago family. His father, Simon Wexler, owned Allied Radio Corporation of America, a large company manufacturing radios and selling electronic components. Haskell's FBI file documents FBI concerns over Simon Wexler's donations to Chicago's Abraham Lincoln School, sponsorship of events at the Chicago Council for American Soviet Friendship, and funding local events backed by Harry Bridges.[1] While raised with the luxuries of privilege, Haskell came of age in Depression era Chicago surrounded by progressives. He attended the elite, progressive Francis Parker School where he befriended classmate Barney Rosset, who founded the *Evergreen Review* and became publisher/owner of the Grove Press, where he waged important anti-censorship publishing battles that brought D.H. Lawrence's *Lady Chatterley's Lover* and Henry Miller's *Tropic of*

Cancer into print. Young Wexler befriended Studs Terkel, who he considered one of his greatest teachers.[2]

While still a student Haskell helped organize a labor strike at his father's radio manufacturing plant,[3] and worked for photographer Mickey Pallas, photographing striking workers in Chicago.[4] He briefly attended college at Berkeley, dropping out to join the Merchant Marine, and during the Second World War was aboard a ship sunk in the Indian Ocean by German torpedoes leaving him afloat in a lifeboat with other survivors for two weeks before being rescued.[5]

One FBI report includes notes from a 1943 selective service registration, with a note explaining:

apparently the [draft board] questionnaire was filled out with the aid of the subject's father as at the end of it there was a statement as follows: "I have assisted the above named registrant in preparing this questionnaire because I am his father and he is too jittery to write." Signed Simon Wexler. It is noted that there was no social security number listed in the file and the explanation given in the file was that it was lost at sea when his ship was torpedoed.[6]

Throughout the 1940s, the FBI tracked Wexler's radical politics. They recorded his membership in the Convoy Club of the Young Communist League and his wartime membership of the Seamen's Branch of Communist Party, New York City.[7] In 1948, the Bureau considered placing him on the FBI's Security Index; the FBI catalogued various political activities and otherwise mundane activities ("he operates a photographic laboratory in the apartment") with suspicion, and filed reports on Wexler for decades.[8]

Reports of communist involvement led to ongoing FBI investigations. The FBI recorded that "a relative by marriage described Wexler in 1954 as a communist sympathizer."[9] One inquiry to previous landlords produced assurances that Wexler and his wife Nancy were "communists because they had a large picture of Stalin in their room and talked along Communist lines." The FBI tracked him and his wife Nancy as they attended meetings of various communist front organizations, like the American Youth for Democracy, and his subscription to *The Daily Worker, New Masses*, and other Communist Party linked publications.[10]

After the war, his father provided substantial funds to equip his own film studio in Illinois, and he began making films in earnest.[11] His early works included commercial projects as well as some with leftist political messages—working on union documentaries and a film supporting Henry Wallace's presidential bid.[12] During this period, the FBI tracked Wexler's car being parked at various leftist political events in Chicago including Communist Party meetings (1948, 1950), Progressive Party meetings (1949–50), the 1951 World Peace Congress, and the 1952 meeting of the Veterans of the Abraham Lincoln Brigade.[13]

When Wexler applied for a passport in 1954 to travel to England and France for work on a documentary film on Shakespeare, the State Department denied his request because of allegations that he had been a communist—advising him that he had 30 days to respond to these charges. He did not challenge this finding, then four years later he reapplied for a passport for a leisure trip to Europe, and was issued a passport.[14]

A January 1961 State Department Passport Division report notified the FBI of Wexler's plans to travel to Brazil to work on a film.[15] An FBI agent telephoned Wexler Brothers Productions, Inc. in Hollywood and used a fake name and pretext to gather information on his planned trip to Brazil to work on the (1961) film *The Fisherman and His Soul*. The FBI compiled a brief dossier on Wexler Brothers Productions, Inc., detailing its 1958 incorporation, stock value, capitalization and assets, office locations, and the corporate accounts held at the Chicago National Bank.[16] The FBI reported:

> Haskell "Pete" Wexler is a motion picture cameraman who belongs to Local 666, Chicago, Illinois. He comes from a very wealthy Chicago family, and is rumored to be a millionaire in his own right. However, he has a burning desire to be a first cameraman and has threated to sue Local 659 for a million dollars since the Local has denied him first cameraman status. He does, however, work out of the Chicago Local as a first

cameraman on motion picture productions which are made in areas not under the jurisdiction of Local 659, Los Angeles.

He is allowed to work out of Local 659, Los Angeles, as an assistant cameraman or operator. His most recent motion picture assignments as a cameraman were "Studs Lonigan," a motion picture which was photographed in the Midwest and completed at Hal Roach Studios, Culver City, California, and one other picture the name of which was unrecalled by ██████████, Wexler has not as yet, produced a motion picture, but has no hesitancy in investing money in motion pictures on which he can serve as a cameraman.[17]

One FBI informer claimed "Wexler's father left his sons a large number of shares of Superior Oil Company valued at $30.00 per share, which they later sold for $1800.00 per share." The FBI learned the Wexler brothers inherited ownership of the family business, describing it as "one of the largest electronic firms in the United States." Another FBI informer reported the Wexler brothers had "'terrific' financial connections throughout the United States and have no difficulty in obtaining funds for investment in motion pictures." FBI memos noting Wexler's financial independence highlight this freedom removed the normal constraints facing others in the film industry.[18] The FBI's interest in Wexler's wealth exemplifies the FBI's long history of investigating left-leaning elites in ways that right-leaning, even openly fascist, elites were seldom monitored. Such investigations highlight the FBI's institutional role as American Class Police. This shows a similar pattern of FBI alarm that appears in the FBI files of other wealthy progressives; such as appears in the FBI file of candy magnate Fred Haley (see Chapter 13), whose support of unionization at his Almond Rocca factory, or his support for racial equality and academic freedom in the public schools in the 1950s garnered intense FBI investigations that showed the FBI's interest intensified by his status as a financial leader of the community.

After FBI informers in Hollywood's Professional Cultural Section of the Southern California District of the Communist Party reported they didn't know Wexler,[19] the FBI called Wexler's mother, pretending to be a former Merchant Marine shipmate passing through town, to gather information about his activities.[20] After this flurry of investigative activity, in February 1961, the Bureau decided to not place Wexler on the Security Index or Reserve Index at that time—the Bureau's secret list identifying radicals for ongoing monitoring, and prioritizing them as subject for detention during times of national emergency.[21]

Still, the FBI continued to collect information on Wexler and his associates. The FBI reported that Haskell's first wife Nancy Ashenhurst had attended meetings of the American Youth for Democracy, and his second wife, Marian Wexler was "a free-lance artist, also of a wealthy family is reported to be in sympathy with the communist movement" who subscribed to the *Daily Worker* and had contributed to the Chicago Committee to Secure Justice in the Rosenberg Case.[22]

In July 1961, the FBI contacted Wexler and requested an interview "to determine his nationalistic sympathies, and if he merits consideration for placement on one of the Bureau indexes."[23] Wexler told the FBI that he was upset by this contact, and that he wanted to speak with his attorney. Days later Wexler contacted Special Agent Parker, saying his attorney advised him not to speak with the FBI without his attorney present. Parker reported that despite the attorney's advice, he kept Wexler on the phone chatting, telling Wexler about

> the confidential nature of much of the Bureau's work and the matter to be discussed with him did involve internal security, and for this reason it was felt it would be best that he and the Agent talk privately. Eventually as a result of discussion, Wexler agreed to discuss the matter with [the] Agent with the provision that it would be kept confidential and that his attorney ███████ would never be told that he had talked with the FBI against his wishes and without his being present. Wexler was assured that the entire contact was confidential insofar as the FBI was concerned, and he stated he knew this was true, and he likewise would keep it confidential.[24]

Wexler told the FBI he joined the Communist Party in 1943 or 1944, and resigned near the end of the war "because he could not withstand the regimentation." The FBI reported that "Wexler stated that he is opposed to Communism, is a loyal American, and would fight for this country against the Soviet Union or any other country. He stated that if information came to his attention regarding the CP or CP members, he would voluntarily furnish this information to the FBI."[25]

Some of what Wexler told the FBI was demonstrably false and appears as an effort to reduce the FBI's perception of him as dangerous. Wexler told the FBI that

> when he was a young boy his father was an ultra-conservative and this caused him to rebel and assume the position of a radical. He stated probably this had something to do with his joining the Communist Party. He stated that while he realizes Communism is wrong and it stands for everything he abhors, he still considers himself a person wanting other[s] to have a better life too. He stated that he was appalled at some of the poverty which exists in Latin-American countries, and pointed out that while he was in Brazil he let his beard grow and some of the peasants when they saw him would cheer him and call him "Fidel." Wexler stated that it is things like this which make him concerned because our country is not doing enough to assist the Latin-American people and he is afraid unless something is done, they will go Communist.[26]

Wexler told the FBI that "he would like to maintain contact with them" in case he came across information the FBI should know about, stating that he "considered espionage a very serious crime"—and admitted he knew Martha Dodd and Alfred Stern (convicted Soviet spies who in 1957 had fled the United States), and that he had been in their home and even introduced their son to the woman he would eventually marry.[27] These admissions suggest Wexler feared the FBI falsely suspected him of having connections to espionage.

If Wexler's admissions of past communist connections and limited contacts with known radicals like Dodd and Stern were efforts to reduce FBI suspicions, this approach worked. The FBI report concluded that "no recommendation is being made that

Wexler be placed on any of the Bureau's indexes" and his case was closed in the LA office; the FBI made no further inquiries about Wexler for three years.[28]

In April 1964, the FBI noticed a story in the UCLA *Daily Bruin* about Wexler's work on the film *The Bus* (1965), documenting civil rights activists' bus trip from San Francisco to Washington, DC for the 1963 March on Washington. The FBI later learned Marlon Brando and Harry Belafonte were "promoting the group from Hollywood."[29] One FBI informer reported Wexler had "so much film that he did not know what to do with it" and that he was considering making three films from the trip. The FBI's opposition to the Civil Rights movement spawned more surveillance of Wexler, and the Bureau's usual decision to file these reports under the heading "SECURITY—C" (C for "Communist") demonstrates the FBI's belief that the Civil Rights movement was a communist threat to American security. A year later, the FBI reported that Wexler hired a German translator in San Francisco to translate a letter from East Germany relating to Wexler's failed effort to retrieve a copy of his film *The Bus* that he had shipped to East Germany a few months earlier.[30]

Internal FBI reports described Wexler's 1968 masterpiece *Medium Cool* as "anti-establishment and anti-law enforcement in nature,"[31] and the Bureau filed reports on news stories appearing in *Daily Variety* about the film. The Bureau monitored Wexler's involvement and financial support for a Hollywood organization known as, Entertainment Industry for Peace and Justice (EIPJ), which the FBI described as dominated by Jane Fonda and Donald Sutherland.[32]

In 1969 Wexler first collaborated with Saul Landau (see Chapter 19) on a documentary, filming *Fidel*—a collaborative relationship that would span decades, with overlapping political critiques and interests in documenting global injustices, they collaborated on films *Brazil: A Report on Torture* (1971), *Land of My Birth* (1976), *Target Nicaragua* (1983), *The Sixth Sun: Mayan Uprising in Chiapas* (1995), and *Paul Jacobs and the Nuclear Gang* (1979).[33]

In 1972, the FBI finally placed Wexler on the ADEX Security Index, under the subversive designation "Category IV," identifying him as "potentially dangerous because of background, emotional instability or activity in groups engaged in activities inimical to U.S."[34] Wexler's placement on ADEX followed a visible shift in the political orientation of his films, moving away from edgy but mainstream works like *The Loved One* (1965), *Who's Afraid of Virginia Woolf* (1966), *In the Heat of the Night* (1967), to more radical works as he took on the role of director—the three films he completed before being placed on ADEX were *Medium Cool* (1969), *Interviews with My Lai Veterans* (1971), and *The Trial of the Catonsville Nine* (1972). Edward Albee's critique of twentieth century marriage was one thing but presenting the Barrigan brothers' radical anti-war views in a sympathetic light was another thing altogether. The FBI collected and filed clippings on Wexler from sources ranging from *Daily Variety* (1968, 1972) and *People's World* (1972).

One apparent acquaintance of Wexler wrote to U.S. Secretary of State William P. Rogers, after Wexler had mailed this person a copy of a Chilean leftist pamphlet entitled "frente brasileño de informaciones," telling Rogers he had received this and other pamphlets from Wexler, noting that the Secretary of State might want a copy of this or to pass it along to the CIA. Secretary Rogers sent these materials to the FBI which added them to Wexler's file.[35]

In 1974 the FBI collected reports of Jane Fonda, Thomas Hayden, and Wexler's plan to travel to North Vietnam to film a documentary that would eventually be released in November 1974 as *An Introduction to the Enemy*. FBI agents stationed in Paris and LA tracked Wexler as the cameraman traveling with Fonda and Hayden to film in North Vietnam.[36] After Hayden, Fonda, their infant son, and Wexler returned from North Vietnam, the FBI pieced together the steps of their trip; learning they first claimed they were traveling "to Thailand and Japan for purpose of filming for three weeks," but instead traveled from Bangkok to North Vietnam.

The FBI routinely develops short biographical summaries of individuals that are recycled repeatedly in future reports; these often contain sensationalist accusations or quotes. Hayden's recycled summary listed SDS activities, status as one of the Chicago Eight, and re-repeated an interview quote in which Hayden said, "when the time comes for bombings, when people can understand bombings, I will be the first one to load a truck full with explosives and drive it into a building ... I am not kidding and you can quote me so that you can remember this day."[37]

A May 1974 memo to FBI Director Kelly justified ongoing investigations into Wexler, Fonda, and Hayden traveling to North Vietnam, arguing this constituted advocating the overthrow of the government, insurrection, seditious conspiracy, or violations of the Internal Security Act of 1950 and the Communist Control Act of 1954. Prior to the release of *Introduction to the Enemy*, FBI Headquarters advised the New York Bureau that they "should be alert to any press reviews concerning this production, reporting same in form suitable for dissemination, if such press reviews indicate the nature of this production is contrary to the best interests of this nation."[38] The film received mixed reviews and political attacks in the mainstream media. The FBI took no further action in this matter, and Wexler continued working on both independent and mainstream Hollywood projects.

In 1975 Wexler began work as cinematographer on *One Flew Over the Cuckoo's Nest*, and he later claimed he was fired after the FBI made inquiries on the set about him and his politics. But there are no indications in Wexler's released FBI file that the Bureau made inquiries with anyone associated with *Cuckoo's Nest*.

This absence raises two possible, conflicting, interpretations. The first explanation is that the FBI did not release all files pertaining to investigations of Wexler. The second is that no FBI intrusion on the set occurred, and that Wexler was fired for his well-documented, strongly expressed artistic differences and clashes with the director. If so, this would not be the first time he'd have been fired for such clashes. He was fired two years earlier as cinematographer on one of the greatest surveillance films of all time: Francis Ford Coppola's *The Conversation*—with all of Wexler's footage reshot except for the amazing multi-camera complicated central surveillance shot in San Francisco's Union Square. In Pamela Yates' documentary *Rebel Citizen*, Wexler admitted having provided acting directions, and rewriting dialogue for Jack Nicholson and others off set on *Cuckoo's Nest*, because of what he saw as the failures of director Milos Foreman—acts undermining the director and supporting the likelihood that he was fired for these intrusions, as producer Michael Douglas claimed.[39] Perhaps the best evidence supporting the FBI story as a face-saving explanation comes from director Irving Kershner, who said he never heard the FBI story at the time of Wexler's firing—despite his own political alignment and friendship with Wexler.[40]

Whatever the cause of this firing, the FBI certainly investigated Wexler's work filming fugitive members of the Weathermen for the then forthcoming documentary, *Underground*. Filming with director Emile de Antonio, Wexler shot *Underground*, interviewing five Weather Underground fugitives hiding at a safe house at an undisclosed location, filming in ways obscuring their faces. Wexler's released FBI file includes few references to this, and given Wexler's later lawsuit against the FBI alleging illegal surveillance and theft, the FBI likely withheld these files when they originally processed files to release to Wexler. These reports have yet to be released under FOIA.

In 1981, former FBI agent Wesley Swearingen disclosed that an employee of the sound studio editing the film *Underground* had surreptitiously copied the film's audio track and provided a copy to the FBI, who tried to use it to locate the filmed fugitives. Wexler had worked with the sound studio owner, Terry Walker, when producing TV commercials, and he introduced de Antonio to him with a cover story that de Antonio was a psychiatrist working on a new form of "existential transaction analysis." He claimed that the sound tape being processed was thus very confidential and because no one else should hear the content of the tapes, special arrangements were made for de Antonio (the presumed psychiatrist) to do the studio audio editing and transfer of soundtrack himself—while paying Walker the full studio rate that would normally include the fees for a sound technician. But Walker became curious and after listening in to the content of the soundtrack, he became worried. Walker secretly duplicated about three hours of portions of the soundtrack—which the lawsuit argued was a breach of contract—and Walker then called the FBI and gave them his tape. Swearingen reported that the FBI copied and transcribed the tapes provided by Walker, which de Antonio and Wexler's suit argued was copyright violation.[41]

In the early 1980s Wexler and de Antonio brought suit against the FBI, though they failed to get the courts to make the FBI release these allegedly stolen materials; and no record of these tapes appeared in Wexler's released FBI files.[42]

While de Antonio's FBI file, released under FOIA, revealed orders for a "discreet FISURE" operation (FBI speak for a covert physical surveillance operation), no reports from this operation appear in Wexler's FBI file, further evidence that the FBI has not released his complete file.[43] De Antonio's FBI file includes a report from May 13, 1975 detailing the FBI's mail watch program intercepting de Antonio mailing a copy of Paul Schrader's script for the film *Rolling Thunder*, which was examined by FBI cryptanalysis experts. U.S. Assistant Attorney Robert Bonner told the FBI he would authorize the arrest of de Antonio on felony charges of harboring fugitives and concealment of a felony, and considered filing charges of rebellion, insurrection, seditious conspiracy, and unlawful possession of firearms, explosives and incendiary devices—presumably simply for speaking with fugitives accused of these activities.[44]

According to Emile de Antonio's biographer Randolph Lewis, de Antonio was aware of ongoing FBI surveillance after filming *Underground*, and he later recounted that in May 1975, after being followed by FBI agents, he called the FBI office and asked, "Would you get your fucking gumshoes off my back please[?]" As if in reply to his comment, two FBI agents appeared several days after at his Manhattan offices. The agents asked him where they could serve a subpoena on his wife, Terry—'A graveyard on Long Island,' he told them."[45] The following month de Antonio was subpoenaed, and told to surrender all shot footage, sound recordings, and rushes that Wexler and he had shot on the Weathermen.[46] Fortunately, they had already preemptively burnt all the footage and sound recordings that had not been used in the final cut.

President of the Screen Directors Guild Robert Wise, and the ACLU, opposed the subpoena as a violation of First Amendment freedoms. Hollywood stars, including Mel Brooks, Sally Field, Rip Torn, Shirley MacLaine, Jack Nicholson, William Friedkin, Terrence Malick, Arthur Penn, Peter Bogdanovich, and Elia Kazan issued statements of support.[47] The confluence of shady legal ground, a strong team of defense lawyers, and high-profile supporters led the government to withdraw its subpoena, and de

Antonio was not required to testify.[48] De Antonio later learned that Terry Walker's

> sound-editing company, Sound Services, Inc had provided the FBI with a copy of the soundtrack, Evidently, the owner of the lab had not believed de Antonio's story about "transactional analysis" and had reported his suspicions to the FBI. In a letter of March 7, 1976, to the U.S. attorney general, Edward H. Levi, FBI director Clarence Kelley noted that "a cooperative individual in Los Angeles was willing to make a copy of the voice tapes available to us." The ACLU of Southern California filed suit on de Antonio's behalf against the firm on September 16, 1980, claiming violation of federal copyright law as well as its contract with the filmmaker.[49]

When *Underground* was finally released, it received mixed reviews, many reviewers stressed the undeniable plodding unchallenged narrative, though most lauded the daring will of the filmmakers. Yet, it mostly remained an unseen film, having great difficulty getting distribution, with film festivals fearing getting involved in the controversies surrounding it. A 1981 *LA Times* article covering Wexler and de Antonio's suit against the FBI for theft and copyright infringement is the final entry in Wexler's released FBI file, yet Wexler continued to make provocative political films until his death in 2015.[50]

Even without a lifelong involvement in radical political causes, the FBI might have monitored such a genius of *cinéma vérité*. Wexler's films often feel ethnographically raw, missing an artificial luster that dominated American film, his audiences see more of the poverty, inequality, and injustices of our world. I don't know which is more remarkable, that he shot such gorgeous scenes while color-blind, or that he was able to portray his radical vision and remain working with mainstream studios. Such unvarnished creations seem bound to attract the attentions of a Bureau maintaining American power relations of injustice. Yet with Wexler it was his activist insistence of this unglossed vision of an unjust world that so anchored him in his cinematic approach, the stories he chose to tell, and decades of FBI surveillance.

12

Blind Whistling Phreaks and the FBI's Historical Reliance on Phone Company Criminality

In 1971, Ron Rosenbaum's *Esquire* article, "Secrets of the Little Blue Box," introduced the world to phone phreaks, a subterranean network of geek explorers who probed the global phone system as the world's largest pre-internet interconnected machine. The star of Rosenbaum's piece was Joe Engressia, a blind telephonic hacking pioneer with perfect pitch, an unusually inquisitive mind, and the ability to seize control of phone systems by whistling pitches into telephone receivers.[1]

Before the introduction of modern phone-switching technology, audible tones were used to connect phones with distant destinations. As a young child, Engressia was obsessed with the telephone, finding comfort within the steady blare of the dial tone. At the age of five, he discovered he could dial the phone by clicking the receiver's hang-up switch, and at seven, he accidentally discovered that whistling specific frequencies could activate phone switches. From there, experimentation, brilliance, networking, and perseverance led Engressia to probe weaknesses in the network that allowed him to make free phone calls. His mastery over this global machine was liberating, if not obsessive.

As Rosenbaum was completing his 1971 article, Engressia was arrested for theft of telephone services. At the time it appeared that the phone company had only recently become aware of his activities—though a few years earlier he had been expelled from the University of South Florida for selling fellow students long-distance calls for a dollar each.

Rosenbaum's 1971 piece put the spotlight on Engressia, and soon a variety of newspapers, magazines, and television programs ran features on him and his activities. Engressia became a cultural icon, or proto-hacker stereotype, as characters with his abilities were written into cyberpunk novels and Hollywood screenplays with characters like *Sneakers'* Erwin 'Whistler' Emory.

Engressia had a high IQ, but as an adult he wished to live as a five-year-old, founding his own church, the Church of Eternal Childhood. His wish to remain an eternal child appears to be linked to the repeated sexual abuse he received from a nun at the school for the blind that he attended as a child, as well as the academic pressures that led him to miss out on childhood playtime. In 1991, Engressia legally changed his name to Joybubbles. Until his death in 2007, Joybubbles ran a phone "story line" in Minneapolis, where callers would call and hear him tell a different children's story each week—adopting a cadence and personal style reminiscent of his hero, Mister Rogers.[2]

When Joybubbles died in 2007, I filed a FOIA request for his FBI file, mostly just to see what the FBI had made of this explorer who had loved and wandered through the telephone's pre-internet global network. I figured there might be something in his file relating to his 1971 arrest, but I hadn't expected to find an FBI and phone company investigation of him from two years before this arrest.

An August 28, 1969 FBI General Investigative Division report describes an investigation by Kansas City telephone company of three subjects in Kansas City, Miami, and Chicago who had "discovered a means to intercept and monitor WRS and Autovon" phone lines. Autovon (Automatic Voice Network) was a Defense Communication Agency telephone network used for non-secure military phone communication. The FBI's report mistakenly claimed that Autovon was a "top secret telephone system utilized only by the White House," when in fact Autovon was really a non-classified military telephone system, designed to link military installations even under the unpleasant conditions of nuclear annihilation.[3]

The FBI believed that Engressia was "the 'brains' in this matter and was an electronics genius with an I.Q. of one hundred ninety." Even though the FBI's investigation had "not revealed any national security aspect to their activities" and phone company officials stated that this group's use of free phone calls had been "strictly for their own amusement and [the] harassment of [the] phone company," the FBI's investigation reports were filed under the heading: "Security matter—Espionage: interception of communications."[4]

The FBI thought a blue box may have been used to avoid tolls, though they realized that Engressia "was capable of orally emitting a perfect twenty six hundred cycle tone, which could be used to direct distance dial any phone number in the country."[5] The FBI reported that without any authorization from law enforcement personnel, an employee of Southern Bell Telephone & Telegraph had contacted Engressia, interviewed him, and later gave information from this interview to the FBI. This employee told the FBI that

Joseph Engressia, age twenty and blind, [was] interviewed and he admitted intense interest in telephone company systems and equipment. He is familiar with the practices as to test numbers, circuits, and operations of telephone companies. Engressia exhibited ability to whistle twenty six hundred cycle notes which is utilized by telephone company in toll network. He claimed he learned majority of information by trial and error using his touch-tone instrument. He claimed he did not wish to violate any law and that his activities with the telephone were for amusement and education.[6]

The FBI viewed Engressia as a significant threat. On August 29, 1969, J. Edgar Hoover sent a summary memo regarding Engressia's activities to John Ehrlichman, counselor to President Nixon, to Melvin Laird, Secretary of Defense, and to James J. Rowley, the Director of the U.S. Secret Service. While Hoover apprised these governmental bodies of his investigation and expressed concerns that Engressia had the power to undertake undetectable wiretaps, the FBI had no actual evidence that Engressia intercepted any phone calls, they only had concerns he might have such powers.[7]

Fortunately, the FBI employees processing my FOIA request accidentally revealed parts of the identities of the two phone phreaks mentioned in Engressia's file. An individual referred to as "also known as 'Tandy Way'" is identified as another blind radio and telephone enthusiast living in Miami, and a "Mr. Jacobs" is revealed as the Kansas City resident accessing free phone calls to talk with Engressia. Jacobs had first met Engressia after seeing him on the *Huntley-Brinkley* TV show, and contacted him first by letter, then by phone.

The FBI report indicates that the phone company had known about Engressia's abilities for about a year:

> Joseph Engressia Jr. first came to the attention of the SBT&T Company in the summer of 1968. At about the same time there was a routine trouble report in the middle of August 1968, that was received by ████ showing a "blue box" in use on the telephone number ████ Miami subscribed to by ████ Miami. ████ explained that a "blue box" is a device that can be used to defraud the telephone company of the revenue from long-distance toll calls. This device produces multi-frequency tones which enable the user to make long-distance telephone calls and circumvent the billing equipment in the long-distance network.[8]

It is not clear if Engressia was using an actual blue box (an electronic device designed to make free calls by generating 2600 Hz through a speaker) or if he simply whistled into his phone to produce the same results. This September 1, 1969 report includes an account of a Canadian operator reporting Engressia for selling long-distance phone calls for $1.00 each at the University of Southern Florida. Engressia was suspended and fined $25.00, "however, he was reinstated with full honors shortly thereafter."[9]

An August 29, 1969 FBI memo states that an employee "of the Florida Bell Telephone Company in Miami, Florida, illegally monitored conversations on Joe Engressia's telephone # 274-0760. It is further alleged that these monitored conversations were divulged by ████ [presumably the Florida Bell employee] to an unnamed FBI Agent in Miami, Florida."[10] Later interviews confirmed that "the results of the monitoring [were] furnished to a Miami FBI Agent." Another FBI memo reports that an FBI source, employed at Southwestern Bell Telephone Company, learned undisclosed information "by monitoring telephone conversation between [Jacobs] and Engressia."[11]

On September 3, 1969, Jacobs wrote the FBI a detailed two-page letter extensively citing chapter and verse of the Communications Act and accusing the phone company and the FBI of violating wiretapping sections of the statute. He wrote that:

> I believe there has been a serious violation of the Communications Act of 1934, Section #605. Several days ago, FBI Kansas City agents ██████ and ██████ visited my home and repeated back to me excerpts from a private conversation I had with a Mr. Joe Engressia (Tel: 274-0760) of Miami, Florida. Mr. Engressia for some time believed his phone was being monitored and in order to get the tapper to tip his hand, mentioned many words that might be of interest to the supposed tapper such as Autovon, etc. It is my information that a ██████ of the Florida Bell Telephone Company has illegally monitored, recorded, and transcribed telephone conversations without the permission of the receiver and/or the sender and without a court order. ██████ then divulged this conversation in the form of a written transcript to a Miami gent ██████ who passed it on. Mssrs. ██████ and ██████ were good enough to confirm, in their visit to my home, that there had in fact been monitoring of a telephone line contrary to 47 USC 605.[12]

Jacobs then threatened to expose the FBI's complicity in this illegal wiretap. He asked the FBI if they would fulfill their legal obligations to investigate his "allegations even though an FBI agent may indeed have been a part to the violation of 47 U605." The letter closed with a request that the FBI advise him what a U.S. attorney will do with this information.

The FBI released no memos or files from the following few days and then, five days later, there was an odd series of unconvincing memos that appear designed to establish a paper trail of plausible deniability, claiming (in contradiction to FBI report from August 29, 1969) that the FBI had been given records illegally obtained by the phone company. A September 8, 1969 memo from the Kansas City Special Agent in Charge to Hoover shows the agent then claiming he doubted that the information the Bureau received from the phone company employee was reliable.

The next day the FBI produced a memo designed to formalize its "story," changing some key details establishing a paper trail obscuring illegal acts. A Miami FBI agent wrote to Hoover claiming, "when interviewed Aug. 28 last by Bureau agents Miami, Re: Activities of Joseph Carl Engressia Jr. and [Jacobs] ██████ did not reveal telephone company had monitored telephone conversations between [Jacobs] and Engressia." Given that previous FBI reports stated that their conversations had been illegally monitored by the phone company and illegally shared with the FBI, this report appears to be a ham-handed effort to manufacture records later to be used if Jacobs pushed for an investigation of illegal wiretapping.[13]

In 1967, the Supreme Court ruled in *Katz v. United States* that Fourth Amendment protections against unreasonable searches extended to telephone conversations, but the following year Congress added provisions to the 1968 Omnibus Crime Bill seeking to undermine the court's decision by identifying a list of specific crimes (kidnapping, organized crime, marijuana distribution, etc.) meriting wiretaps. But the phone company's spying on Engressia was clearly illegal under existing 1969 laws.

For a few days, the FBI recirculated several versions of this same report; the FBI was obviously feathering its nest in case of further legal inquiries at some point. The projected faux sotto voce tone of the FBI memos attempts to "establish" the absence of records of illegally intercepted calls is comically damning. These track-covering memos are the last records appearing in Engressia's file.

It seems curious that an incident, which a matter of days earlier had been of such urgency that the counselor to the President, the Secretary of Defense, and the Director of the Secret Service had been alerted, was so suddenly dropped so quickly and quietly, never to be mentioned again. That such a formerly urgent matter would be so quickly scuttled, set aside and forgotten is a strong measure of the threat Jacobs' accusations represented to the FBI and their special relationship with the phone company.

In those years, before Judge Harold Green broke up the phone monopoly and birthed the baby bells, it was easy for Hoover's FBI to maintain a special arrangement with the phone company—an arrangement under which the FBI ran warrantless wiretaps and pen registers largely as Hoover saw fit and with the phone company's compliance. No questions were asked. The public inspection of such matters would have threatened Hoover's special relationship with the phone company.

Fearing public disclosure of its illegal eavesdropping on Engressia, the phone company waited until 1971 to drop the bag on him, once some time had passed and Jacobs' threats were no longer in play.

But this tale, even five decades later, has relevance beyond the particulars of an ingenious blind renegade phone whistler. It is but one artifact of the largely unexplored history of the FBI's symbiotic enabling of the phone company's illegal wiretapping—a history with increasing relevance in the present, as Congress continues to provide immunity to a historically abusive industry, long protected by the sort of formal arrangements with law enforcement documented in these files.

13

The FBI and Candy Man: Monitoring Fred Haley, a Voice of Reason during Times of Madness

The Brown and Haley Candy Company was founded in 1914 by Harry L. Brown and Jonathan Cliff Haley in Tacoma, Washington. When the Great War brought large numbers of soldiers to train at nearby Ft. Lewis, demand for candy increased and the company had strong sales to soldiers until the war's end. In 1923, sales rose again with the introduction of Almond Roca, which would become the company's signature candy. A few years later Jonathan Haley bought out his partner Harry Brown, deciding to keep Brown's name on the business for reasons of continuity.

Cliff Haley's children grew up working at the candy factory, and his son Fred worked in the family business after returning from serving in the U.S. Navy during the Second World War, taking over the running of the business in the 1950s. Fred soon became a visible civic leader, associated with progressive political causes and speaking out on issues of civil liberties even as McCarthyism and Red Baiting frightened many Americans into remaining silent instead of speaking in favor of political positions, like racial equality, labor rights, or supporting inter-racial marriage; issues that right-wing political figures and the FBI routinely characterized as communist positions. Fred Haley's 188-page FBI file's reports show that he did not succumb to fear and silence, while the FBI monitored him for decades, and as a form of political intimidation the FBI at times let those around him in powerful political positions or in the business community know Haley was being watched.

Fred Haley first came to the FBI's attention in 1947, when he spoke out against Washington State Senator Albert Canwell's Washington State Interim Committee on Un-American Activities hearings.[1] Haley and a group of other Tacoma progressives wrote public letters complaining about Canwell's grandstanding tactics—tactics that would be a blueprint for the anti-communist show trials of Senator Joseph McCarthy in the coming years. Haley issued public statements condemning Canwell, and he helped organized a group of Canwell critics. Haley's FBI file includes copies of a news account from *The People's World* (the Communist Party's west coast newspaper) dated April 7, 1948, reporting on "a meeting of forty Tacomans who disapproved of the attack by the Canwell Committee on University of Washington professors. It was reported that the group approved a resolution condemning the Canwell 'method of investigation.'" The FBI noted Fred Haley's criticism of Canwell, and Haley's election as Chair of this group.[2]

The next entry in Fred Haley's FBI file occurred in 1950 as part a U.S. Navy Intelligence "Espionage and Subversive Activities" report which grew out of the FBI investigating reports that Fred's brother, Jonathan Clifton "Cliff" Haley, had illegally traveled to Spain to fight the fascists during the Spanish Civil War as a member of the Lincoln Brigade. Cliff Haley's time in Spain did not work out well for him; he went AWOL after a short time after disobeying orders to join an infantry unit facing certain death and casualties. A 1938 *New York Times* story told of U.S. State Department inquiries into Cliff Haley's welfare after he was arrested by Spanish Loyalists while attempting to leave Spain.[3] *The New York Times* described Cliff Haley as a "volunteer machine gunner in the Spanish Loyalists forces" who had abandoned the fight and "tried to get on a tanker at Barcelona in hopes of getting to Port Arthur, Texas," but had instead been arrested by Spanish Loyalists. The article reported that the U.S. State Department sought assurances from Spanish Loyalists that Cliff Haley (the son of "a candy manufacturer in Tacoma") would not be harmed, while his "father feared the boy might be shot."[4] He was eventually allowed to leave. While the FBI's investigations collected rumors that he had been allowed to leave due to arrangements made by his father, the FBI found no proof of this. Having deserted the fighting, Cliff Haley's name does not appear among any of the records or memorials of the Abraham Lincoln Battalion.

During the Second World War, Fred Haley was investigated by Military Intelligence after mistakenly believing he, instead of his brother Cliff, had fought with the Abraham Lincoln Brigade, and later determined he had not.[5]

The FBI reported Fred Haley had taken over the management of the family candy business after his father had suffered a stroke. Two years later, in November 1952, Naval Intelligence again sought FBI information on Cliff's involvement with the Lincoln Brigade and his claims that he had "lost" his passport, a common ploy used by Lincoln vets to avoid problems when returning home; the FBI believed that some of those claiming to have lost passports were part of a larger plot in which Soviet spies "used the identities of Abraham Lincoln Brigade members and their lost passports in establishing illegal agents in foreign countries."[6] The FBI assisted the Navy's investigation; one agent examined the *Tacoma News Tribune*'s "morgue files," searching for any stories relating to any members of the Haley family. The FBI reported that the newspaper's files

> reflect extensive articles concerning the activities of Jonathan Clifford Haley, Jr. while a member of Loyalist forces during the Spanish Civil War. Files on Fred T. Haley reveal that Haley is generally active in numerous civic organizations in Tacoma, including Community Chest, Red Cross, and the Tacoma Symphony Guild. Included in the file of Fred T. Haley is an item dated 6/1/52, reflecting that Haley was a candidate for Representative in the 26th District, Washington State Legislature on the Democratic ticket. (Later files reveal he was defeated in the Primary election.)[7]

The FBI reproduced letters to the editor written by, or responding to, Fred Haley on a variety of political topics.[8] One of these letters is reproduced in full to provide a sample of the style and arguments Haley used as he advocated for the maintenance of due process under the law and fair play, the sort of arguments supporting due process that caused the FBI to investigate him for years:

To the Editor: In his letter of April 11, an able and respected citizen, Mr. A. B. Comfort, complains of the tendency for a group of "honest, earnest and loyal Americans … found almost exclusively in our most highly educated classes—the college trained," to be critical of un-American activity probes.

Mr. Comfort's dilemma, it seems to me, lies in the facile and unfair assumption that a group defends un-Americanism, or Communism, by its conviction that civil liberties must be defended, and orderly processes of law upheld. It would be quite as sensible to argue that the current rash of McCarthy and Canwells are agents of the Kremlin in the provocation of fear, suspicion and uncertainty in the minds of Americans, which all too evidently plays into the hands of Russia.

Would Mr. Comfort argue that those lone champions of law and order in our lawless west a few years ago were defending cattle-rustling, when they insisted, often at great personal peril, that the suspected cattle rustler be found legally guilty and punished, rather than strung peremptorily by the neck from the nearest tree?

Does he think that Wendell Willkie was defending communism when he argued the defense of Schneiderman before the Supreme Court in Schneiderman vs. U.S.?

There are, indeed, Americans who believe that the Anglo-Saxon concepts of equal justice under the law, slowly and painfully evolved through the centuries and forged into the American Bill of Rights are too precious a heritage to be thrown carelessly aside in an hour of panic.

In truth, many honest and loyal Americans, observing the mischievous spread of legalized thought control from points of infection in the Congress to state legislature after state legislature, fear for the realization of historical American purposes, for the articles of our faith, which are beliefs in the dignity of the individual, freedom of mind and thought, freedom of the press and assembly, and in the inherent American principle of fair play.

There are those loyal American who think that the techniques of smear by association, slander under the cloak of Congressional immunity, and the steady erosion of civil liberties under the guise of their preservation are wicked and fraught with danger to all Americans. The roads suggested by such tactics, I submit, are those which in the past have led to the persecution of scientists, of scholars, of religious minorities, and indeed, all groups who may have, at a particular time or place, been unpopular with the majority.

For my part, Mr. Comfort, I hope I may always have the capacity of indignation and the courage to defend a fellow citizen's own efforts and those of the Dem-(Type error) [sic] whatever his station and however unpopular his views, when that defense is the defense of his civil rights and thus your rights and mine.

Fred T. Haley[9]

Haley's arguments were polite, reasonable, and logical; unfortunately during this time of fear, these sorts of arguments were rarely seen in such public arenas. For Haley, patriotism involved supporting the Bill of Rights, not spouting slogans and accusations. His suggestion that McCarthy and Canwell (and perhaps by extension, A.B. Comfort) were doing the Kremlin's work, that those calling for due process and rule of law were the loyal Americans, did not appear to make the FBI aware that the Bureau had strayed from their legal duty to not interfere with legal political discourse, and to uphold the law. Instead, Haley's commitment to due process assured his status as a target of FBI investigations; and his letter spawned another episode of FBI inquiries. Internal FBI file checks found that Fred Haley was chairman of the Tacoma Chapter for Academic Freedom, when it passed "a resolution condemning the Canwell 'method of investigation.'"[10]

The FBI's investigation led Naval Intelligence to again review Fred Haley's Naval Reserve records. Naval Intelligence noted that three of Haley's listed references (Eugene Linden, Chauncey L. Griggs, and Allen R. Benham) had links to subversive organizations.[11] Naval Intelligence expanded its investigation of Fred and Cliff Haley, and their investigator interviewed Alvin H. Brown, President of the Rogers Candy Company, Seattle—Brown was the son of Harry Brown, the former partner with Jonathan C. Haley, Sr. of Brown and Haley Candy Company. Brown said that "he is well acquainted with all members of the Haley family and described the Haley family as being very eccentric and a family of definite convictions; that each of the family are so definite in these convictions that they stand up and fight for them regardless of public opinion."[12] Brown told the investigators that "once in Spain, Cliff Haley had become discouraged and disillusioned" and when his father learned of this change of perspective, he "spent thousands of dollars to have him returned to the U.S ... [and] used considerable influence and untold amounts of money in order to suppress any publicity on his son's service with the Communist armies in Spain." Brown claimed that the senior Haley's health problems stemmed from the shame and heartbreak of the eventual publicity coming from the news of his son's time in Spain.[13]

Brown described Fred Haley's reputation in the local business community, reporting that many "businessmen viewed Fred with considerable bewilderment due to his political beliefs which Brown described as being 'definitely liberal.'" Brown characterized Haley as a "Roosevelt New Dealer" and a Truman "Fair Dealer," noting that Haley remained pro-Union even while assuming a leadership position at his family's factory.[14]

In August 1953, Naval Intelligence conducted a "thirty day mail cover" investigation, monitoring the mail Fred Haley received at his Tacoma home which "failed to develop receipt of any correspondence from this brother, Jonathan Clifford Haley, Jr."[15] When Naval Intelligence learned that Fred Haley worked to support progressive Democratic issues, FBI suspicions intensified as agents tried to gather names of Democratic Party organizations he associated with.

SCHOOL DAYS: HALEY ON THE TACOMA SCHOOL BOARD

Fred Haley was elected to the Tacoma School Board in 1954, and he used this position to defend the civil rights of one of the district's primary school social workers, Margaret Jean Schuddakopf's (known as Jean). After Schuddakopf was accused of being a member of the Communist Party, she used her Fifth Amendment protections to avoid testifying before a traveling version of the

House Committee on Un-American Activities (HUAC) convened in Seattle. Haley and fellow Tacoma School Board members James Boze and Ray Kelly voted against firing Schuddakopf, arguing that all Americans have the right to take the Fifth Amendment, and in doing so she had broken no laws. Conservative groups organized significant public pressure to fire Schuddakopf, at one point "more than 20,000 residents had called for her firing."[16]

As an employee of the Tacoma School District, a few years earlier Schuddakopf had signed a loyalty oath declaring she was not (then) a member of Communist Party, which she declared was still a true statement. Schuddakopf (née Wheeler) came from a radical northwest family, her parents had been socialist activists and organizers in eastern Washington and her brother Donald Niven Wheeler was an active member of the Communist Party.[17] Jean had a history of activism stretching from her childhood, through her years as an undergraduate at Reed College, and included anti-racist and anti-nuclear weapons protests. Her non-compliance with the militaristic and racist norms of the Cold War period, and her family's radical leftist politics made her an obvious and easy target for the reactionary forces of the 1950s. The only thing that was unusual about this episode was that Fred Haley appeared so comfortable taking on the wrath of a fearful community being whipped up into an anti-communist frenzy. Haley later reflected that while these were frightening times, even at the time he understood that "far from being anti-American, I was being *American* by defending her rights."[18]

After a reactionary conservative group took out advertisements in the *Tacoma News Tribune* attacking board members Boze, Haley, and Kelly, Haley purchased his own counter-advertisements in the paper explaining his position. In these ads Haley advanced civil libertarian arguments supporting Bill of Rights protections and challenged anyone to provide proof that Schuddakopf had committed perjury or broken any laws. Haley argued that baring any evidence of illegal activity she must retain her position. The controversy spawned a call to boycott Brown and Haley Candy, and there were economic repercussions at the Candy company.[19] Haley later said that this reactionary stance caused him to never join other local business leaders in becoming a Rotarian or Kiwanian.[20]

As a result of growing political pressure, eventually School Board member Ray Kelly gave into the mob's pressure, reversed his vote, and Jean Schuddakopf was fired. Despite political pressure from local conservative political groups, the State Superintendent of Education, Pearl Wanamaker, eventually ruled that Jean Schuddakopf could not be fired for refusing to testify before HUAC under Fifth Amendment protections. By the time Schuddakopf's position was upheld she had taken another job elsewhere, though she was provided with backpay following Wanamaker's ruling.[21]

The FBI also collected 1954 news accounts of Haley denouncing a book burning incident, in which copies of Frank A. Magruder's *American Government* textbook were burned in a rally at Tacoma's Stadium High School. Right-wing groups attacked this book for its progressive views on race, and these Tacomans were part of a larger homegrown American fascistic political movement burning Magruder's textbook in other communities. One news story from Idaho's *Lewiston Morning Tribune* reported a small rally burning 20 books.[22] Haley's FBI file included a story published in the Communist Party's west coast newspaper, *The People's World*, titled "Bonfire in Tacoma: School Board President Raps Book Burning."[23] *The People's World* quoted Haley saying:

"We know that two years ago, this community was whipped into a frenzy over an issue of civil liberties," Haley said. Haley was referring to the American Legion inspired controversy around Mrs. Jean Schuddakopf, school counselor, who refused to cooperate with the House Un-American Activities Committee. The school board refused to fire Mrs. Schuddakopf who was later ousted by the county superintendent. The case is still in the courts.

Haley added that "we know that sometimes men do sad sad things in times of stress and tension. I don't think we're looking for scalps, I suggest instead, we save our energies for the job at hand our indignation for the next time that academic freedoms are under attack in this city, as they most surely will be."[24]

But such calm philosophical approaches were out of step with the times, as Cold War developments helped nurture public fear, and sensationalist media reports and political campaigns fed reactionary responses from the public.

THE FBI, FRED HALEY, AND THE TACOMA
BUSINESS COMMUNITY

As the CEO of a large local business, Fred Haley occupied an important position in the Tacoma business community, and while some of his progressive views were at odds with many of his fellow capitalist business owners, he belonged to the usual sort of social networks befitting a civic business leader. One 1957 entry in his FBI file reported:

On 6/20/57, [a Tacoma businessman who was an FBI Informer] advised that he is a member of a Masonic luncheon club which meets once a month in a downtown restaurant. He stated that some of the leading citizens of Tacoma including Judge Burtil Johnson and [others] ... are among the members. [The Informer] states that the club discusses current issues during the luncheon meetings and he was of the opinion that the stand taken by [a local insurance man], and member of the Tacoma School Board, Fred Haley ... seems to him at times to practice the [Communist Party] line. [He] stated that on one occasion [this person] volunteered to bring a recording which he described as being an authentic recording of procedures taken during the Congressional hearings inquiring into Red activities during the time that Senator McCarthy headed the committee. However, when [he] began to play the recording it was clearly and obviously a recording manufactured to discredit McCarthy and was definitely not a recording made during the actual hearings. The recording was a planned and rehearsed thing which had the form of that type of hearing but which ridiculed and discredited Senator McCarthy and this type of hearing. [The Informer] stated that the members did not even let it play through to its conclusion and most of the membership was outraged because [the joking member] had misrepresented the recording and brought it into such a club. He added that [the member ridiculing Senator McCarthy] went to a great deal of trouble to bring a machine into the Model Restaurant, where the luncheons are held.

[The Informer] went on to say that both [███████████] and Haley were extremely outspoken during the Korea Conflict, stating that the United States had no business in Korea and they appeared to be in favor of our withdrawal no matter what the cause. He added that he noted that both ███████ and Haley were noticeably silent during the Hungarian uprising and the events which transpired wherein the Russians were involved in suppressing the revolution.[25]

Haley's openness to working with unions, his progressive political views and support for freedom of speech and other civil rights raised the suspicions and concerns of some of his peer local business leaders; and the fears propagated by the Red Scare helped Haley's cohort see him as a potential danger.

On June 27, 1960 J. Edgar Hoover alerted Seattle's Special Agent in Charge of a transfer of funds from an account at the Bank for Foreign Trade of the Union of Soviet Socialist Republics in Washington, DC apparently (given the context of the memo, which remains partially redacted) to Fred Haley, or perhaps to Brown and Haley.[26] This transfer of funds again intensified FBI interest in Haley's activities. Another redacted memo sent later that day records FBI speculations that the Soviets might be "establishing an illegal agent in this country" in some way connected to Haley.[27]

But two months later the FBI determined these Soviet funds were likely "a routine refund of funds in connection with [Fred Haley's recent, April 1960] trip to Russia."[28] The FBI launched a thorough investigation of all countries visited by Haley since he was first issued a passport in 1936, listing each of the 23 countries he had visited while traveling in 1936, 1952–53, 1957, and 1960. A September 1960 FBI report noted with concern that Haley had traveled to Russia and other European countries "for the purpose of examining the educational systems of these countries with the view of applying good features observed to Tacoma schools where possible."[29] Haley's FBI file contains a copy of an October 1, 1960 article "Candy Capitalist Sees Soviet Schools," in the Communist Party's newspaper *Peoples' World* describing Haley's recent trip to the USSR to visit Soviet schools. Haley described the Soviet educational system as based on egalitarian principles, stressing that he was able to visit the schools he chose and was not shepherded about only seeing the schools his hosts wished him to see.[30]

While Fred's brother Cliff had a youthful dalliance with radical politics, his other two brothers and his sister were political conservatives. A 1960 *Tacoma News Tribune* feature headlined, "Five Haleys Take Pride in Rival Political Views," detailed how Fred was the only sibling to be supporting Albert Rosellini's campaign as a progressive Democrat for Washington Governor; with other siblings taking out an opposing ad in the newspaper.[31]

When Fred Haley gave the keynote address to the 1961 Washington State School Directors Association, the FBI analyzed the *Tacoma News Tribune* coverage of his talk describing his recent trip to the USSR. Haley reported seeing that "like our own, their society is modeled to the 'pursuit of excellence' and … in this fact lies the hope and the threat alike of the Russians in the world today."[32] His file contained an article Haley published in the WEA's *Washington Education* (April 1961), in which he explained that what he feared most about the Russians was that

> their educational system will continue its rapid improvement while ours stands still, and that as a result the ideas which characterized the high-water marks of our western civilization—of the Age of Pericles, the Renaissance, and the 18th century of Voltaire—will be lost to the world. The baton has come down to us through the British, the French, the Italians and the Greeks, and I don't want to hand it to the Russians and let the heritage of Byzantium, of the Tartars and the East, fix the values for the 21st Century. If there is a threat in the Russian system as I see it, this is it, and not the economic system they call communism, which we regard with such rigid and unyielding ferocity.[33]

His WEA article showed Haley's interest in the Soviet system was motivated by a desire to understand what strategic edge the Soviet's pedagogy might present, not as a call to adopt their economic model; but his attacks on the conservative political posturing of Washington school administrators was confrontational, attacking individuals and the anti-intellectual nature of the second Red Scare sweeping Tacoma area schools. The FBI collected and filed a *Tacoma News Tribune* news article (September 17, 1961) headlined, "Haley Takes Jab at State School Policy on Reds" which reported Haley's attack on the neighboring Clover Park School Board, ridiculing them for adopting a district policy limiting what students could be taught about communism. Haley criticized the neighboring district board for uncritically adopting a policy compiled by the state Office of Public Instruction, arguing that

> there are plenty of things wrong with the statement, though most of it could be ignored as when a rude person belches in company. This I think is a public belch, betraying the social indigestion which brought it up. Isn't it the gaseous result of the forced ingestion of the same warmed-over mess we've been choking down since the end of World War II? Its cooks call it Americanism, but it's the 200 per cent variety known at various times as Canwellism, McCarranism, McCarthyism, and now John Birchism, is it not? Vile stuff. Terrible.[34]

Fred Haley lampooned the Clover Park School Board, and other Washington boards as mindlessly operating in lockstep with a totalitarian state superintendent of public instruction who argued that freedom of speech and thought must be limited to protect freedom of speech and thought. He absurdly argued that "it should be unmistakably understood that this freedom of inquiry in our classrooms remains intact as long as it is not too freely exercised."[35]

One indicator of how McCarthyism's paranoia became normalized is found in records of the invisible army of citizen-informers it created who felt it was their duty to report thought crimes to the FBI. One early 1960s letter to FBI Director Hoover, written by a member of the Bremerton Education Association, reported on a recent address by Haley to the Association, noting rumors that Haley had been investigated by the FBI several times. This host turned informer expressed concerns about Haley's loyalty and asked whether or not Haley had ever been investigated.[36]

The Seattle FBI office monitored the Brown and Haley Candy Company's 1962 charitable contributions to a student "peace group" building a float for Tacoma's Daffodil Parade. When the student group first asked the carpenters union to donate labor to construct the float, the union's Executive Board initially agreed, but when they learned that someone involved in the float was from a family "connected with some sort of subversive group" that union withdrew their support and voluntarily provided the FBI with an account of these events.[37]

In September 1962 a Pierce County School Board member attacked Haley for his critique of the board adopting state policies limiting class discussions of the Soviet Union; the *Tacoma News Tribune* printed exchanges between Haley and members of the Pierce Board. In a rebuttal, Haley argued that students needed free thought, not state-directed indoctrination, writing:

> Students must be encouraged and aided in free inquiry, in arriving at conclusions only after an examination of all available evidence, in detecting propaganda and in respect for facts. Conclusions resulting from this type of study will be much more meaningful to students than any which may be imposed upon them. Conclusions thus reached bring about strong and abiding convictions which will enable students to act loyally, discriminatingly and calmly in resolving great problems.[38]

The FBI collected news clippings reporting Haley joining the 1963 civil rights march on Washington, DC (August 29, 1963), and an FBI informer reported on him speaking at a September 1964 NAACP regional conference.[39] The FBI monitored Haley's frequent funding and endorsements of progressive causes; such monitoring of domestic political activities was exactly the type of oppressive FBI surveillance that was curtailed by legislation following revelations of the Church Committee in the early 1970s; limitations that were again removed under the USA PATRIOT Act. Haley's name appeared on the letterhead of groups like "Free Prisoners Bail Fund of Seattle" in 1967, a group which provided "bail to those indigent persons who are held in detention by virtue of punitive or discriminatory attitudes on the part of administrators of justice or by unconstitutional laws."[40]

SWEETNESS AND POWER

I got to know Fred Haley during the early 2000s after he came to my aid following an incident where I had been asked to present a position paper for a prominent Washington State politician considering a run for the U.S. Senate, and my views ran afoul of those of the wealthy individual hosting this event in his Seattle mansion. Fred Haley (and Seattle journalist, Mike Layton) came to my aid and stopped our host from ejecting me from his home, and forced an apology from our host in what must have been a humiliating moment for him. Immediately after this incident, Fred Haley took me to lunch, and we were soon friends; later meeting at several political meetings (meetings from which I returned home with large bags of delicious misshapen candy for my kids); from others I learned of some of his political activities, but I hadn't known what I'd find in his FBI files. When I first read his FBI file, I was struck by how much time, energy, and money the Bureau devoted investigating an outstanding citizen who was doing nothing illegal, and who had largely come under investigation for fighting for the constitutional rights of individuals being harassed by individuals in the FBI and supported by the FBI.

When Fred Haley was asked in 1986 how he came to develop such progressive pro-union views as the owner of a large industrial operation, he said it was a combination of forces that included experiences he gained "working in the woods, probably listening to the kinds of arguments that I did during the Depression, among loggers who had cause to hate their bosses."[41] He also credited his Tacoma Stadium High, and Dartmouth University education, where he was exposed to the civil libertarian writers of the Enlightenment, singling out Locke, Rousseau, Voltaire, John Stewart Mill. He directly credited his activism as rooted in his education reading these thinkers, observing that "it would be much more extraordinary if having the educational background, and whatever thoughtfulness I had, if I hadn't felt the way I did and been willing to put my head on the [chopping] block if I had to."[42] Yet there had to be something more than his education at work, as most of his agemates who received this same education remained silent as the Red Baiting and the silence before its bullies flourished in the postwar period.

These FBI records of Fred Haley's ongoing governmental surveillance document the shallow limits of freedom afforded Americans in the mid-twentieth century; those individuals recognizing and resisting the oppressive forces of their age and who were not afraid to speak out in opposition to these limits were regularly placed under surveillance and monitored. Because these governmental surveillance campaigns frequently used the FBI to interview individuals known to the subjects of these campaigns, the awareness of this surveillance naturally stigmatized these individuals. As Fred Haley's FBI records show, the knowledge or even suspicion that activists, or individuals asserting their basic constitutional rights to free speech and association, were being monitored by the FBI was all that was needed for third parties to disengage from working with these stigmatized individuals. In Haley's file we find a labor union withdrawing its offer of free labor for building a student peace group's parade float, and numerous instances where the FBI contacted Haley's peers of local businessmen, asking probing questions about Haley's private comments—questions which would obviously raise suspicions and help ostracize him among his peers. Likewise, the FBI's use of morgue files at the *Tacoma News Tribune* to gather information on Haley planted seeds of sensationalist suspicion among reporters, who naturally carried these suspicions in their future reporting.

Even with these governmental efforts to lant Fred Haley and to stigmatize his efforts to speak out about un-American efforts to limit the free speech of American teachers and students, he continued to advocate unimpeded, speaking out publicly for these and other causes. Fred Haley was later recognized for his strong positions on these and other progressive social issues, being awarded the William O. Douglas Award by Washington Chapter ACLU (1985), and being appointed by Democratic and Republican governors Albert Rosellini and Daniel Evans to Washington State Board Against Discrimination (1964, 1967), and he remained a popular member of Tacoma School Board, serving eleven years on the board, from 1954 through 1965.

Haley's position as an elite obviously offered him several protections not afforded to other Americans during the Cold War in the 1950s and 1960s—but it is important to recognize that he did not squander the privilege he was afforded like so many of his contemporaries did. The FBI's probing questions to other business leaders must have led to fewer invitations to dinner or parties, but such inquiries could not lead to him getting fired, as was often the case among wage laborers subjected to such damaging FBI inquiries. The FBI implicitly understood that as a privileged elite, Haley had easy access to lawyers and public officials, and such knowledge had to impact their treatment of him and the nature of their public inquiries. This recognition of Fred Haley's position of privilege does not diminish his accomplishments, but this context helps us understand how such FBI campaigns of open surveillance and soft harassment, using investigations of legal activities to silence dissent and mark those using their basic civil rights, were effective tools for managing citizens whose livelihood could more easily be threatened. Haley could have comfortably remained silent, as most Americans did during these oppressive times, but he was not easily intimidated and retained his critique despite the obvious risks of governmental surveillance and harassment.

14

David W. Conde, Lost CIA Critic
and Cold War Seer

In 2018 I stumbled across references to an obscure twentieth century journalist, author, and CIA critic named David W. Conde and began tracking down some of his published work. The more of Conde's work I read, and the more I learned of his backstory, the more I kept thinking about Kilgore Trout, the underappreciated science fiction writer in Kurt Vonnegut's fictional universe. Trout spent his life publishing stories in obscure outlets, most frequently crude pornographic magazines uninterested in his prose, printed by publishers seeking verbiage to fill magazine pages simply to reduce production costs. Because Kilgore Trout only published in the most out of the way places, except for rare obsessive fans often at the core of Vonnegut's novels, his work was destined to be ignored—regardless of the profundity of his observations. Trout was a prophet without honor in his time, publishing pearls of wisdom in places where few could be influenced, making him an absurd hero in a world that cared little for him regardless of the truths he uncovered. And while there are limits to the similarities between Kilgore Trout and David Conde, their shared marginal status, lack of concern with mainstream conventions, ability to make startling observations out of step with their time and place, and comfort publishing in the most obscure outlets link them in very concrete ways.

I first learned of David Conde while researching a book examining 1950s and 1960s links between The Asia Foundation and the CIA. While working through a massive archival collection of Asia Foundation papers at Stanford University's Hoover Institution, I found a memo mentioning Conde's previous directorship of the U.S. Motion Picture and Theatrical Branch (MPTB) in occupied postwar Japan. This 1953 internal Asia Foundation staff memo summarized the MPTB's postwar work censoring and promoting movies in occupied Japan, producing focused propaganda messages, and then described someone—I later determined to be Conde—while being unable to recall his name, declaring him a communist, writing:

> ... as is to be expected the Japanese communists early recognized the value of the movies as a means of mass-communication and moved into the field immediately after the cessation of hostilities and the beginning of film production. The communists were aided in early occupation days by several Americans who were either card carrying commies themselves, or fellow travelers of heavy red tinge. Two of these individuals (Roberts, and a man with an Italian name I have forgotten [this being David Conde]) were directly assigned to the motion picture unit in the [Civil Information and Education Section] organization. These lads spread the commie line with sufficient diligence to be given credit by many for really establishing the strong leftist foundation upon which the new industry grew.[1]

The possibility of radical Americans greenlighting left-leaning Japanese films under MacArthur sparked my interest, and after a bit of triangulating I determined Conde was the referenced "man with an Italian name." I tracked down a rare copy of one of the dozen books he authored, and eventually visited the University of British Columbia archives which housed the remains of his collected papers. The paper scraps remaining of the man I found were intriguing, and like Vonnegut wrote of Trout, he comes off a bit like "a cracked messiah," though many of his observations about CIA surveillance and international activities would find support in governmental hearings of the post-Watergate 1970s.[2]

CONDE'S BACKSTORY

David W. Conde was born in 1906 in Ontario, Canada, where he spent his early childhood. In the early 1930s, he moved with his family to California, becoming a U.S. citizen in the early 1930s.

During the Second World War, he worked on Allied propaganda operations within the U.S. Office of War Information's Psychological Warfare Branch, specializing in writing and producing anti-Japanese propaganda radio broadcasts. He was recruited by OWI after they became aware of a series of radio plays he had written, produced, and broadcast by shortwave radio for Japanese audiences during the early 1940s. He later wrote that at the OWI he was

> asked to work on "surrender" and demoralization leaflets to be dropped on Japanese troops in New Guinea. I was also assigned to work on Rakkasan (Parachute News), printed also in Japanese and for similar purpose. I had been in the Brisbane office for about two months (in Spring 1944) when I was asked to move from the civilian OWI part of the office to the PWB-military section.[3]

Conde later described himself as "one of that small group of men who had served with General MacArthur all the way from Brisbane to Japan. The only difference perhaps was that I was not a soldier. I was a civilian 'Japan Specialist' picked and hired by the State Department."[4] Conde wrote that his propaganda broadcasts stressed "the errors, cruelties, and crimes being committed by the Japanese militarists, paying particular attention to the role of the *Tokko Keisatsu* [elite Japanese police unit monitoring political groups] within Japan." Conde insisted that it was this war propaganda work that prepared him to analyze postwar CIA propaganda targeting Japan. He wrote that because of his war work "against the thought control police of Japan, it was natural that I should be aware of and know the dangerous-to-liberty role of the CIA when it was born just after World War II."[5]

After the armistice, Conde applied his propaganda skills at the occupation's Film, Theatrical and Music Section, where he oversaw the production of Japanese films, assuring these films fit the guidelines established by General MacArthur. Conde was married and his wife and two daughters lived in Oakland, California, while he remained in Japan at the war's end. In the book *Allied Occupation of Japan*, Eiji Takemae observed that "Conde was known for his radical ideas, a zealous determination to reform Japanese cinema and a short temper. Under his leadership, the Motion Picture and Drama Branch revitalized Japanese film-making and theatre by encouraging anti-militaristic and democratic themes."[6]

One of the many film productions Conde supported was *Those Who Make Tomorrow*, a 1946 feature film co-directed by Akira Kurosawa (along with Hideo Sekigawa and Kajiro Yamamoto), a pro-union story portraying the heroic labor struggle of members of a Japanese film studio. Rumors of a surviving print of the film persist, though known copies have not been found. Details of the plot are known, and Conde's radical sympathies are clearly represented in this story of a labor union struggle. Film writer Patrick Galvan observed that during "the early years of the occupation, labor unions were viewed as a metaphorical spit in the face to the allegiance-demanded beliefs prevalent in the war … In other words, labor unions represented individual rights: something the occupation forces very much wanted to push." Conde supported the film for its pro-union message, while the Film Section's policies endorsed the union's threat to the pre-war social order. However, the rushed production, and reportedly crude message and delivery resulted in an awkward film that Kurosawa later omitted from his own credits and failed to even mention in his memoir.[7]

Conde also backed one of the occupation period's most popular pro-democracy films, Akira Kurosawa's 1946 Film *No Regrets For Our Youth*, inspired by the true life story of Hotsumi Ozaki, the only Japanese citizen executed during the war. He was executed for aiding a Soviet spy ring and for trying to undermine Japanese imperialism. Conde shepherded *No Regrets* through the censorship process, helping bring to life the most mature of Kurosawa's early films.

In July 1946, Conde left his position as Chief of the Films Section over disagreements about the political messages of some of the Section's films, and because of growing rumors that he was a communist sympathizer. Conde's "resignation" appears to have been un-voluntary. He was likely fired for backing Fumio Kamei's eventually banned film, *The Japanese Tragedy*, a work described by film historian Kyoko Hirano as a "Japanese documentary critical of capitalism and of the imperial system, which the American military censors found objectionable." Conde later wrote of his firing that "in spite of this blackmark I feel that the history of Japanese humanist 'great' films made in the period 1946 to 1950, were in part the result of my friendly intervention."[8]

After his firing, Conde was soon hired by Reuters as a news reporter covering the International Military Tribunal for the Far East. While reporting on the Tribunal, Conde collected a significant body of trial transcripts, prosecution documents, POW documents, wire stories, and notes. Without these war crime tribunal documents to anchor his collection of papers, it seems likely that his many typed published and unpublished book manuscripts, hundreds of articles and correspondence would have been discarded after his death instead of being deposited at the University of British Columbia archival collection.

Conde's war crime tribunal reports for Reuters were often as focused on those who escaped justice as they were on those sentenced. He wrote about Prince Fuminaro Konoye who committed suicide before he could be tried, and about how Japanese crime boss Yoshio Kodama was initially "arrested as a war criminal for his great crimes in China but strangely—mysteriously—Kodama escaped all ordinary punishment heaped on those guilty of crimes against some part of humanity." News reports speculated that Kodama later used the *yakuza* to smuggle for the CIA in Asia. For Conde, the selective prosecutions of the tribunal revealed a U.S. deal helping establish American regional dominance in the postwar world. Conde later reflected that

> it is at this point that my interest in the CIA story begins, with *Tokko Keisatsu* [political police], plus my knowledge of Yoshio Kodama as a war criminal. And it was at this time, before the War Crimes Trials were completed that I was given ten days to leave Japan, in the name of General MacArthur, and under the instructions of his semi-Nazi G2 head General Charles A. Willoughby.[9]

After publishing a story in the *St. Louis Post-Dispatch* criticizing the strict limitations General MacArthur imposed on reporters covering the tribunals, MacArthur and Willoughby quickly expelled Conde from Japan. Conde resented his deportation, and members of the international press covering the tribunal protested his expulsion. After MacArthur ordered Conde expelled from Japan, Conde wrote that

> Reuters stated flatly that they wanted me to continue to be their correspondent in Japan. The Press Club went unanimously on record as opposing MacArthur's action and demanded normal human rights for the press. It was voted to send a three-man delegation to the General to ask for a reversal of the expulsion and to attempt to find out the truth for this highhanded arbitrariness.[10]

Conde's fellow reporters wrote to Congressional representatives back home complaining about Conde's treatment, and Conde later claimed that MacArthur had interfered with an inquiry by Senator Tom Connally.[11] Conde complained that MacArthur's General Headquarters' "secret police" assumed that once he was expelled from Japan, he would return to the United States. He instead moved to China, spending time in Shanghai and Taiwan, where he became friends with Anna Louise Strong, and other progressive Western writers in exile.

Conde returned to the United States the following year, where he became convinced that he was "watched every day by the secret police as though I was truly dangerous"—and FBI records at the National Archives indicate the Bureau began investigating Conde as a suspected communist in 1947, with investigations continuing until 1980.

Conde returned to California to his wife and daughters in 1947, after his time in Shanghai. He joined the local branch of the World Affairs Council and began delivering public talks about Asia. Soon after his return, his wife of 15 years filed for divorce. He later learned that during this period, "the FBI had been pressuring my wife to get her to accuse me of being a red."[12] He did not want a divorce and resisted finalizing the divorce for some time, eventually taking his daughters with him to Canada to stay with his sister in Ontario.

Conde then moved to Minneapolis and began working for Sears. He rapidly advanced up through the ranks at Sears, eventually rising to a position in the main office as a chief buyer. In 1952 he remarried and moved back to California. In California he interviewed for a position at the Montgomery Ward West Coast office, and on his second visit to the office he was told that "they had been advised reasons why Ward's should not employ me," and he later learned this was due to the FBI's efforts.[13] Soon after his second wife was visited by the FBI and CIA, she filed for divorce saying she wanted nothing to do with Conde. In San Francisco, Conde became a successful salesman at a scaffold manufacturing company, where he remained under FBI surveillance.[14] He worked on a variety of jobs until returning to Japan in 1964, where he worked as a journalist, writing for several news outlets including the *Far Eastern Economic Review* and several Japanese publications.

CRITICISM OF U.S. HEGEMONY IN JAPAN

Back in Japan, Conde's years writing and analyzing propaganda for the OWI continued to inform his analysis, and he wrote a series of articles for Japanese publications examining how the United States was reshaping Japanese news media in ways aligned with American interests. His articles examined how the Asia Foundation, USAID, and Rockefeller and Ford Foundations funded programs chose specific types of journalists and scholars over others for funding or seminars. Those chosen learned to produce works aligned with American narratives of power. Conde argued that these forms of U.S.-aligned support selectively stifled critiques of Western intervention in Japan during the 1950s and 1960s. Conde described himself as "a CIA watcher," and he wrote numerous articles trying to identify CIA assets in Japan, one article even claiming to have identified the CIA's Japan headquarters to be located "in the Mantetsu Building across the street from the U.S. Embassy," estimating that they employed about 50 workers.[15]

Conde's archived papers include thick files of political news clippings from the mid-1960s to mid-1970s on political topics including Nixon, Kissinger, CIA revelations and governmental hearings into CIA activities, and a Japanese-CIA bribery scandal. Many of these clippings have detailed hand-scrawled notes and highlighted passages preserving Conde's methods of working directly from these newspapers, Reuters and TASS press wire teletype printouts, and wire service transcripts of political speeches. Conde used these sources and published reports to write investigative articles tracking funding of U.S. Army programs at Japanese universities and institutes, and to analyze how U.S. aid shaped the production of knowledge at these universities and Japanese news outlets.

Conde wrote hundreds of articles for Japanese magazines and newspapers, frequently writing political analysis, originally in English then having it translated into Japanese. He published articles in Japanese magazines, frequently Japanese men's magazines, on topics like: "The Revenge Motive in Post-War Japanese Films," "How Nixon Sold Pepsi to Moscow," "Will Nixon use the A-Bomb in Vietnam?" Many were prescient, unreserved critical analysis of American hegemony in Asia, though some betray an overzealous CIA obsession steering him into untethered territory where paranoia sometimes overtook his interpretation of the shards of what he believed to be larger stories revealing covert CIA connections. An example of this is seen in his 1972 *Pynchonesque* piece, "Was Mao Tse-tung a CIA Agent, Opening China for Nixon?" attacking Mao for *détente* with the West—entertaining the unlikely possibility that Mao had been duped by a CIA plot. Yet even with such occasionally wild analyses, the larger body of Conde's prose and analysis remained engaging and many of his claims about CIA connections to foundations would later turn out to be not as farfetched as they might have seemed.

The UBC archival materials include complete and partial Conde manuscripts, and references to a dozen books (eight surviving book manuscripts, five missing) that were self-published overseas at low-budget presses. He published *CIA—Core of the Cancer* at a small New Delhi press.[16] *Core of the Cancer* was the only Conde book that I was able to locate in libraries or online booksellers, while the UBC archives contain partial and complete manuscripts, and references to another seven Conde books. Conde's dozen books include the titles: *American Dream Is Ended, The American Nightmare Begins, America in Despair, The Atomic Samurai, How America Ate Japan, CIA: Core of the Cancer, Indonesian Invisible Coup d'état,* and *Mud on the Kimono.* Most of his book manuscripts were reworked versions of articles he had published in Japanese newspapers and magazines, though some were new works. I read his long unpublished manuscript, *A Structured History of the United States*, an unpublished textbook, apparently written in the 1960s, highlighting class conflict and struggles in U.S. history. Like Conde's other writings, it showed a radical critique of power relations, and argued for liberation, and followed themes similar to those later explored by Howard Zinn in *A People's History of the United States*.

CONDE'S VISION

Conde's most significant critique came from his clear vision that after the press exposed various programs in the late 1960s receiving CIA funding, these programs were not necessarily suddenly transformed by receiving new non-CIA funding sources. What Conde did, and so many others at the time failed to do, was to focus on the desired outcomes of these programs from a perspective assuming there were continuities of neo-colonial desires that were independent of funding sources. He did not care that many of these programs were simply scholarships, research fellowships, academic exchanges, or library programs, he remained focused on the larger issues of political control he saw at work. Conde had no way of knowing that behind the scenes, following the rapid exposure of various academic CIA fronts in the late 1960s, there were panicked discussions within the Executive Branch, and within the Rockefeller and Ford Foundations, seeking to deal with the crisis of what were internally referred to as "CIA widow and orphan foundations" created by these exposures. Yet Conde's analysis did an exceptional job of independently intuiting empire's desire for continuity, regardless of the end of CIA funds.

After investigative journalists exposed dozens of CIA funding fronts during the late 1960s, Conde predicted these revelations would cause the U.S. government to increasingly use other "safe sounding" governmental and private agencies to fund similar projects to those the CIA had covertly funded. For example, in *CIA—Core of the Cancer*, Conde wrote, now, as the CIA is preparing to change its name—to shed its skin—to confine itself to actual spying and transfer its "educational" tasks to other private business' organizations, it becomes obvious that such activities of the Rockefeller, Ford, the Asian and other U.S. Foundations are intertwined with the CIA, and that it is this "American way of life" that is the "enemy."[17]

As USAID and other State Department agencies became new sponsors of projects following CIA funding revelations, many programs designed by the CIA were now funded by these "clean" funding sources, as if the source of funds were the only problem, not their links to political intervention abroad.

After a March 1967 *New York Times* article revealed the Asia Foundation had been receiving CIA funds, the Foundation responded quickly, admitting it had received some funds, and stated it would no longer do so. The Foundation made misleading statements minimizing how much CIA funding it had received, though it did stop receiving CIA funding as a result of this exposure. Most journalists covering the story acknowledged this change in funding and moved on, but Conde's analysis of the Foundation during its pre- and post-CIA-linked years focused on both the leadership and activities of the Foundation, as well as the continuity of programs after these revelations. He analyzed the significances of a CIA-linked foundation stacking its board of directors with capitalism's captains as a way of representing the economic interests the CIA sought to preserve. Corporations placing their CEOs on the Foundation's board highlighted symbiotic relationships between capital and "security" such involvements nurtured. When discussing other symbiotic relationships allowing the CIA access to Asian students, Conde observed that

> The Asia Foundation took particular interest in Asian students, seeking to influence the younger generation and make friends of the U.S. Scholarships were offered for American universities and carefully screened students were brought to America to study approved subjects. A most careful system was set up to guide these students from the time they left their homes in Asia until they reached their selected school in the U.S. Counselors

accompanied them on shipboard to prepare them until they left the shores of the United States bound back to their homeland. Forever after they were in the "files" as a future contact.[18]

Conde argued that before 1968 the CIA had used the Asia Foundation to finance the Japanese Federation of Bar Associations and other international judicial organizations (such as the International Commission on Jurists) because "most law is concerned with property and the purpose of this organization to inculcate respect for law, is in a sense, seeking to retain the sanctity of existing contracts. As half the world is deeply in debt to the United States, and facing both the repudiation of contracts, bonds and currency, the mobilization of world opinion to support some possible U.S. forceful action, appears most desirable from the U.S. view."[19]

In *CIA—Core of the Cancer*, Conde critiqued CIA efforts to covertly influence foreign governments and cultural movements. He analyzed how the CIA-funded Congress of Cultural Freedom (CCF) sponsored the Japanese magazine *Jiyu* ("Freedom"), which presented Japanese views aligned with American political messages. Conde observed that after the CIA links to CCF were exposed, the Ford Foundation made up for the lost CIA funding and the program continued as before. Conde argued that because of the continuity of desired outcomes, the entire project must be rejected. Conde pointed out that one measure of this continuity was seen in the fact that McGeorge Bundy, who was "formerly top CIA man in the White House, [was] now head of the Ford Foundation" overseeing the continuity of these arrangements.[20] Conde also argued that the Japanese readers of *Jiyu* magazine were not the CIA's only target audience, instead,

A most interesting part played by such a magazine is their role in deceiving the American public. Articles published in *Jiyu* are most frequently translated by the American Embassy service and supplied to Japanese English-Language newspapers, particularly Yomiuri, Mainichi and the Japan Times, and thus serve to give the English-reading public in Japan the belief that such material is typical—which it is not—of the views of Japanese magazines. Additionally, copies of these translation are sent to Washington and they serve to give the impression there that the Japanese press supports the U.S. position—a far cry from the truth. The Embassy's use of *Jiyu's* "viewpoint" is most deceptive and in a sense is but reflecting the Washington line back to Washington as in a distorted mirror.[21]

Conde viewed American academics as largely complicit with CIA efforts to steer academic inquiry. He pointed out that when the CIA began using funding fronts to shape and limit discourse, and

thousands of U.S. professors and scientists, imbued with the "free idea of success" and a "high standard of living" accepted CIA and Pentagon "subsidies" and "research grants," bettering their family income but thus contributing to the corruption of educational ethics. Rather than being seekers after objective truth with a concern for mankind, a larger percentage of "scholars" became employees of the CIA-Pentagon, committed to the anti-Communist cold war.[22]

After Praeger Press was exposed for having secretly published CIA-sponsored books for years, Conde observed that

the books of Praeger have served to "educate" a whole generation of all those who sought to learn the truth of what the world of liberation meant. Many U.S. professors have been guided in their writing and publications of books on foreign affairs, totally unaware that the CIA stood behind their publisher, assuring that the end product would meet cold-war standards.[23]

Because of these critical views of the CIA and American activities in Asia, the FBI investigated Conde for decades claiming to suspect he was a communist, though producing no evidence backing these claims. His writing frequently moved far beyond the usual progressive critiques of American hegemony that were usually enough during this period to garner FBI suspicions, to occasional praise of Joseph Stalin for his refusal "to bow to the dictates of U.S. monopoly" after the atomic bombing of Japan.

He described McCarthyism's Red Scare as simply recycling Hitler's anti-communist hysteria. One of the rumors collected by the FBI of his supposed communist links stretched back to the postwar occupation of Japan; this was a story claiming that Conde had been visibly upset that newsreel footage he reviewed as a film censor did not more prominently feature Japanese Communist Party leaders that General MacArthur released from prison.

Conde corresponded with other radicals around the globe. His archived correspondence includes exchanges with Julius Mader, the East Berlin writer who in 1968 authored the book *Who's Who in the CIA*—a scattershot effort to publish names of CIA employees, which was filled with inaccuracies but pioneering many of the techniques later used in the 1970s at *CounterSpy* or *Covert Action Information Bulletin* to identify CIA agents.[24] His correspondence with Mader shows Conde's general paranoia not inhibiting his critique or engagement with others struggling against the CIA.[25]

What remains so unique about Conde was not that his analysis of the reach, methods, and goals of the CIA was flawless or heavily documented (it wasn't either of these)—there are clear instances where he was wrong, or his paranoia led him astray; it is instead how he drew on his Second World War OWI intelligence experience, studying American and Japanese intelligence practices, to interpret postwar developments and extrapolate what the CIA was likely covertly doing. In some sense, his wartime experience studying cultural manipulation by an empire struggling to expand its reach across Asia shaped his analysis of the next global power who tried to expand across the region. His war years committed to fighting fascism left him politically prepared to challenge the forms of corporate fascism the CIA soon aligned to protect as it opposed anti-colonialist liberation movements all over Asia.

With the hindsight offered by a half century of historical research and FOIA revelations we can see that at times his analysis went too far or wandered off in strange directions, but all told, even with his errors and occasional paranoid miscalculations he did a better job of interpreting CIA motivations and activities in Japan than did most of the mainstream press or academics, whose work generally downplayed these persistent CIA interventions. That he was a marginal figure tells us as much about the inevitable status of those rare lone voices unconcerned with making their analysis fit with commonly accepted views than it does about the truth of what he found.

PART IV

Policing Global Inequality

The Difference between the CIA and the "good" agencies such as the Peace Corps, [United States Agency for International Development] and [the National Endowment for Democracy] are like those between Coke and Pepsi—one has a little more sugar, each has different packaging, but neither has nutritional value worth a damn.

—Covert Action Information Bulletin Winter 1991–92,
back cover

15

E.A. Hooton and the Biosocial
Facts of American Capitalism

During the early and mid-twentieth century, physical anthropologist E.A. Hooton found a comfortable, nurturing academic home at Harvard University. He helped keep forms of racialized "science" alive by writing for academic publications, popular magazines, and making public appearances in which he championed forms of eugenics or produced studies that helped justify America's racialized and ethnically marked inequities. Hooton's writings supported beliefs that race was an inherent biological state, and that intelligence and social worth were tied to genetic ancestry. Hooton's significance in twentieth century anthropology in part derived from the number of physical anthropologists he trained at Harvard, though few of his students championed his eugenic-ish and racialized theories. While Hooton's notions were challenged by other contemporary anthropologists like Franz Boas at Columbia University, Hooton's work articulated racist folk models about human variation and notions that stratified social phenomena could be linked to biological differences.

In 1998, after I read Hooton's 1943 proposal for the Allied forces treatment of postwar Japan ("exile, imprison and sterilize all members of the Royal family," while letting China oversee a postwar occupation, "forbid purely Japanese marriages," etc.), I filed FOIA requests seeking a copy of Hooton's FBI file. The FBI eventually sent me the few pages of records they had on Hooton. His file consisted of only two pages: a crude photo-static reproduction of a 1943 newspaper article summarizing an article by Professor Hooton written for a general audience, and a short memo by an FBI agent accompanying the article's internal FBI circulation.

On July 27, 1943 FBI Special Agent L.B. Nichols sent Clyde Tolson an internal memo drawing Mr. Tolson's attention to a United Press wire newspaper story appearing earlier that week in the *Washington Daily News* under the headline "Supervised Child Breeding Urged by Harvard Expert." This article drew on quotes from a recent article in the popular *Woman's Home Companion* magazine by Professor Hooton.

Nichols sent Tolson and others within the FBI a copy of the *Washington Daily News* article along with an internal memo that was marked (and ignored, given that I was sent a copy from Hooton's file), "INFORMATIVE MEMORANDUM—NOT TO BE SENT TO FILES," which read:

> You will recall Dr. Hooton has always been a first-rate fool. His latest, on scientific child breeding as set forth in the attached clipping is one for the books. It is too bad that some epidemic cannot strike a lot of our college professors.
>
> Respectfully, L.B. Nichols[1]

The *Washington Daily News* story (included in Hooton's FBI file) reads as follows:

> Supervised Child Breeding Urged by Harvard Expert
>   By United Press
>   Dr. Ernest Hooton, a noted Harvard University anthropologist today proposed that the Government undertake the improvement of its citizens by a program of supervised breeding, sterilization of the unfit, and increased control over the development and education of its future parents.
>   "If the Government has to take care of all the infirmed, aged, unemployable, and chronically antisocial, why should it not be allowed to take measures to prevent the multiplication of undesirables and to produce better human quality?" he wrote in the current issue of the *Woman's Home Companion*.
>   Stating that only medical men were qualified to undertake the job, but that only Government had enough authority and resources, Hooton proposed the setting up of a Department of

Population headed by a Cabinet officer who was a doctor with four bureaus.

MARRIAGE BUREAU

The first would be the Bureau of Adult Rehabilitation. This would remake adults below the age of 50 years insofar as they need rehabilitation. "The young and the middle-aged men and women are our breeding stock."

The second would be a Bureau of Marriage and Genetics. This would fill our "supreme social need ... The scientific improvement of marriage, reproduction and the home." It would function in four ways, 1. Medical and genetic supervision of marriage to prevent matings "bound to produce inferior offspring thru heredity or environment." 2. Subsidization of parents proved capable of breeding superior children to remove the economic pressure on them to practice birth control. 3. Sterilization of the feeble minded, the insane, and the habitually anti-social. 4. "Intensive and extensive studies of human heredity to learn exactly what produces bad and good human individuals."

The third bureau would be known as Growth and Nutrition. "Its task would be to supervise the medical, physiological, psychological and nutritional care of the population from birth to maturity. A larger order." Hooten said, "but we cannot leave the development of children wholly to the efforts of parents of variable things man does, but rearing them properly is the hardest."

The fourth bureau would deal with educational and vocational guidance and would be charged with "fitting the individual with a curriculum based upon his ability, personality, and social adaptability."

Hooton said that those who opposed his program with cries of fascism and communism are those who are "determined to retain power over the masses ... these are the real opponents of individual betterment. These are the veritable fascists."[2]

If the governmental human breeding bureau proposal itself did not suggest Professor Hooton might be off his rocker, his preemptive declaration that anyone who considered his proposed final solution to be fascistic or communist were the true fascists, broadcast a tone of righteous instability. Yet his position at Harvard made this not just the smug declaration of a garden variety street corner kook shouting to the rooftops, but an authoritative declaration affirming a certain sort of mid-century American elite power, with ideas that themselves aligned well with the injustices of America's economic order.

There's also something in Hooton's proactive defensive proclamation that connects with more contemporary crackpot defenders of racialist science. It has similarities to popularized forms of racist pseudoscience that more recurrently have been foisted off on the American public by a range of writers coming from fields such as general science, genetics, or evolutionary psychology. In many ways, the writings of J. Philippe Rushton, Steven Pinker, Charles Murray, and Richard Hernstein are more contemporary versions of this sort of racialized pseudoscience.[3] One of the best examples of this sort of popularized racially biased work appeared in Nicholas Wade's dismissive attack on the over 100 professors from population genetics, evolutionary biology, and other fields who denounced Wade's book, *A Troublesome Inheritance: Genes, Race and Human History* in which Wade adopted a Hooton-like tone,[4] accusing the scientists who denounce his misuse of their work and the work of colleagues of ignoring science, which apparently only he, a journalist, could seem to see.[5]

Professor Hooton's final defensive claim that he was neither communist or fascist is worth considering. It would of course be wrong to call Professor Hooton a communist; his views do not align with communist philosophy. Professor Hooton was a capitalist, and his proposed solutions on how to deal with surplus laborers demonstrates his alignment with the spirit of American capitalism. On this count he was correct: he was no communist.

But Professor Hooton also raised (if only to dismiss) whether his proposed establishment of government run breeding boards overseeing the forced sterilization of the "feeble minded" was fascistic. In the original August 1943 *Woman's Companion* article, Hooton cavalierly stated that "only an extreme optimist could estimate more than one half of our population to be physically and mentally fit." Because fascism links governmental functions primarily with supporting the needs of corporate owners over the needs of workers, there are elements of Hooton's dystopian vision that align well with fascist philosophy insofar as Hooton's views of surplus humanity aligned with capital's formations of surplus labor. Whatever philosophical links to fascism Hooton's vision may have held, it was certainly totalitarian to the core.

The problem with Hooton's modest proposal wasn't that he contemplated governmental programs concerned with reproductive issues, the problem was his complete anthropological failure to understand how a society's demographic dynamics are linked to its economic formations. Hooton's fallacy was that he understood "feeble-mindedness" to be a simple independent variable that caused low economic productivity and other "drains" to the efficient society he aspired to create. He failed to understand how culture helped shape the conditions under which (he imagined) only half of the American population met his criteria for being allowed to reproduce. It is difficult to imagine a less anthropological perspective, but Hooton's anthropology had thematic links to a deep history of Harvard racist scientistic studies stretching back through Theodore Stoddard's 1920 *The Rising Tide of Color Against White World-Supremacy*, which fostered notions of biological racial categories, and argued for Nordic Aryan superiority using flawed data and bigoted arguments conveniently portraying Northern Europeans as those worthy of drinking dry martinis on the veranda at the top of the evolutionary ladder, while darker imagined less-evolved races cluttered the vast landscape below. And while the rhetoric of these arguments has shifted, Professor Hooton's inability to consider the social causes of differing participation in intellectual activities connects his project, Stoddard's project, and Nicholas Wade's more contemporary work. Each of these works justifies social inequalities with misguided claims about biological natures not in evidence.

Given the FBI's propensity to open files on virtually anyone who came to their attention for beliefs they found deviant, I was initially surprised that the FBI did not open an investigation on Hooton or his research. Perhaps the decision to not investigate Hooton was related to the other activities the FBI was engaged in during the war, but given some similarities between Hooton's vision of responsible breeding with those of the Nazi administration, it is surprising that FBI records do not include standard records checks to see if Hooton held ties to Nazi organizations—which I don't imagine he did, but the FBI routinely made these checks under such circumstances. I suppose the jocular suggestion that an epidemic wipe out a swath of college professors simply shows the FBI's interest in this news story as being on par with absurd news stories many of us share with coworkers today by email. Even the FBI, with its own institutional racism and class-based enforcement practices, could recognize the absurdity of Hooton's proposal.

In the end, Hooton, Wade, and others who view human intelligence or social worth as an immutable biological property are inevitably finding answers ready-made for a technologically sophisticated outsourced capitalist society that decreasingly has uses for human beings. If unemployment can be blamed on biological inferiority—not outsourcing jobs to robots; imprisonment on genetics—not surplus labor or racism; academic failures on racial differences—not differences in opportunities and a collapse of public education; then the wisdom of the market remains unquestioned, and market forces can be left to take care of human needs.

At the end of *God Bless You, Mr Rosewater*, Kurt Vonnegut has Kilgore Trout speechify on just this topic, as Trout ponders a world where capitalism and technological sophistication produces a social system despising the underemployed whose jobs have been taken by the machines they were promised would liberate them. Trout identifies this as

... a problem whose queasy horrors will eventually be made world-wide by this sophistication of machines. The problem is this: How to love people who have no use?

In time, almost all men and women will become worthless as producers of goods, food, services, and more machines, as sources of practical ideas in the areas of economics, engineering, and probably medicine, too. So—if we can't find reasons and methods for treasuring human beings because they are *human beings,* then we might as well, as has so often been suggested, rub them out.

Americans have long been taught to hate all people who will not or cannot work, to hate even themselves for that. We can thank the vanished frontier for that piece of common-sense cruelty. The time is coming, if it isn't here now, when it will no longer be common sense. It will simply be cruel.[6]

Vonnegut understood how the social facts of American capitalism blame those who are surplus labor for their plight.

This old article mentioning Hooton's crackpot breeding ideas, and the more recent forms of popular racialized "science" efforts show the strains on a broken economic system that no longer needs the meaningful labor of so many of its people even as it exploits and criminalizes the poverty of would-be workers. In a world where cellphones broadcast the brutal consequences of policing the dispossessed, these brutalities need justifications of the sort supplied by the Hootons and Wades of the world to maintain the imbalances of a system that champions market forces over human needs.

16

Walt Whitman Rostow and FBI Attacks on Liberal Anti-Communism

During the Cold War, economic historian Walt Rostow's Modernization Theory became a powerful ideological tool used by academics and policy makers to rationalize economic interventions in the underdeveloped world. Rostow is today remembered as an architect of the Vietnam War, and his modernization work is frequently critiqued for its links to ineffective international aid projects during the Cold War. Despite Rostow's multiple policy failures, core elements of Modernization Theory remain attractive to liberal and conservative U.S. policy makers.[1]

Rostow's FBI file documents inform us how during the Cold War it was not enough that prominent Americans be anti-communists. In order to remove the paranoid suspicions and ongoing monitoring by the FBI, one needed to be a *conservative* anti-communist. Rostow's FBI file reveals that while there was a long clear record of his academic and political anti-communism, because his approach to undermining communism was through liberal foreign aid programs designed to weaken foreign support for communism, the FBI suspected him of secretly being a communist.

To cure global poverty, Rostow's Modernization Theory prescribed technology infusions to underdeveloped nations with promises of transforming them into prosperous market-based economies. His 1950s work at the CIA-financed MIT Center for International Studies provided an intellectual foundation for the coming establishment of Cold War soft power international economic aid programs at the United States Agency for International Development.[2] Rostow had a missionary's zeal and clear vision of evolutionary progress for underdeveloped nations to achieve the pinnacle of modernization: a lifestyle of high mass consumption. Modernization Theory prophesized the coming gospel of Zippy the Pinhead and the Coneheads' dogma of mindless shopping and consuming mass quantities.[3] As Marshall Sahlins observed, Rostow was "among the first to perceive that the culmination of human social evolution was shopping."[4] Modernization's insistence that postwar America was the apex of cultural evolution that must be emulated by other, less evolved nations, proclaimed an American narcissistic view of historical destiny.

Modernization Theory provided an important faux intellectual veneer for policy makers to rationalize neo-colonial ventures in the post-colonial world. Rostow's advocacy for increased international economic aid became a key component of U.S. Cold War counterinsurgency strategy. He advocated large-scale U.S. economic assistance for modernization programs, most often in the form of technological infusion loans claiming to improve agricultural or industrial processes or bringing improved roads or sanitization facilities; programs which usually delivered minimal goods or services but established crippling debts that could be used by the United States to manipulate domestic policies in these debtor nations.[5] During the Cold War, American social scientists routinely worked as Modernization Theory's foot soldiers, interacting with local populations and working out logistical problems or trying to engineer local support for development projects.

Rostow's *Stages of Economic Growth* claimed that if the world's underdeveloped countries would only follow the same historical stages of economic development that were taken in the West— with foreign aid birthing their technological development—they too would prosper. Rostow's Modernization Theory was a key rationalization for USAID's early programs and supported the false consciousness needed for many participating in the sort of Third World rip-offs described by John Perkins in *Confessions of an Economic Hitman*.[6]

When I filed a FOIA request for Rostow's FBI file, I expected to find the usual background investigation for high-level federal employment relating to his service in the Kennedy and Johnson administrations. I did not expect to find records of Hoover and the FBI's deep institutional paranoia so completely misunderstanding Rostow as advocating projects that would be used to enslave the underdeveloped world through massive debt generating "development" programs. Rostow's almost thousand-page FBI file is a monument to the paranoid irrationality of FBI Director J. Edgar Hoover. It documents the FBI's inability to understand that Rostow's programs functioned not to bring a socialist revolution, or even to actually enrich underdeveloped nations. They instead maintained an imbalance of power and debt that would create neo-colonial relationships between patron and client nations, all while trying to make the rest of the world a little bit more like Texas.

Rostow's FBI file begins with early 1950s FBI employment background investigations related to his work as a governmental economic consultant. The FBI was concerned over Rostow's father and his aunt's involvement in radical politics long before he was born. The FBI described his aunt, Sarah Rostow Rosenbaum, as "a very active member of the Communist Party in New Haven" and FBI records indicated that his cousin Ruth Roemer had joined the Party in the early 1940s.[7] As the FBI conducted background investigations on Rostow for various sensitive positions in 1942, 1951, 1952, 1953, and 1960, the Bureau repeatedly focused on his father and aunt's radical politics.[8] FBI records show no indication that they ever understood that his father's family's Marxist leanings apparently dialectically predisposed him to espouse forms of anti-communist beliefs with the sort of vehemence one sometimes encounters with the anti-alcohol fanaticism of the children of alcoholics. The FBI instead viewed familial contact with Marxism as a contagion to be identified and isolated.

FBI interviews with prominent economists traced Rostow's academic career. These scholars noted his early studies under economists Gunnar Myrdal and John Maynard Keynes. Aaron Victor Abramson told the FBI in 1952 that the agency where he worked (identified only as "an unidentified government agency," often an FBI euphemism for the CIA) was concerned that Rostow shared "pro-Russian views" with Myrdal and others. Another employee of this unidentified agency stressed they found nothing suggesting Rostow was pro-Russian or a communist. In 1953, another unidentified employee of "another governmental agency" recited a long list of political positions held by Rostow which he believed indicated an unnatural alliance with Russian positions and indicated Rostow was unfit to hold a governmental position of responsibility, calling Rostow a "poor security risk."[9]

In 1955 the FBI added a copy of Rostow's *Harpers* article, "Marx Was a City Boy: Or Why Communism May Fail" to his file.[10] No FBI analysis of the article survives in his file, but given Rostow's rabid anti-communist arguments in this article, it is difficult to understand why the Bureau continued to suspect Rostow of being a communist after reading this article, which argued that Marx's greatest failure was his inability to understand the world of peasants. Rostow argued that peasant farmers would be unlikely communists in the long run, writing that "perhaps the most dangerous enemy of communism is the stoic, passive peasant in Eastern Germany, Poland, the Soviet Union itself, China, and Northern Vietnam. He will certainly not revolt on his own under present circumstances; but even a police state cannot make him increase his output on the scale communist plans require."[11]

Rostow's claim that peasant farmers in Northern Vietnam and China were natural enemies of communism highlights how his political commitments shaped much of his analysis. Rostow rejected Marx's prediction that, as he put it, "history would make of the farmer simply an industrial worker of one sort or another" (a prediction later fulfilled by the spread of corporate agri-biz), and he instead predicted these farmers would inevitably become discontent with communism as they worked under the demands of state managed communism. Rostow predicted that the brutalities of forced rapid collectivization would necessarily create tensions, and that centralized demands for increased agricultural productivity to meet Five Year Plans would lead to farmer revolts against centralized communist governments. Rostow argued that the superiority of free market capitalism over the shackles of communism was apparent if one contrasted the economic advances coming to China and India, writing:

These two great nations are simultaneously attempting a radical transformation. Over the next decade they plan to put themselves in a position where economic growth will be relatively automatic. Throughout Asia, and throughout the vast under-developed portions of the world, the relative performance of Communism and Democracy at this monumental task will be closely watched and weighed.

Even Communist totalitarianism cannot afford enough policemen to follow the peasant about in his daily rounds and make him produce what economic growth requires. The devices of a police state, which work with tragic efficiency in urban areas, adapt with difficulty to the countryside.[12]

Despite the FBI's awareness of Rostow's publications on the failures of communism, the Bureau remained obsessed with finding communist tinctures within Rostow's pro-capitalist philosophy. When Alice Widener attacked Rostow in her neo-fascist newsletter, *USA, an American Bulletin of Fact and Opinion*, her attacks fed FBI paranoia about Rostow's politics. One 1956 FBI report somehow characterized Rostow as a "Marxist economist who, although he may not be a communist and may be at variance with the Kremlin, does foster economic goals which, in her opinion, follow the Communist Party line." Misunderstanding how aid fed American hegemony, Widener criticized Rostow and Millikan's proposals to use international aid to further U.S. international interests, interpreting aid projects as part of a Marxist plot. Widener did not understand that Rostow's development programs were designed to undermine the economic assistance programs of the Soviet Union and China. In ignorance, Widener's paleoconservatism called for scrutiny of Millikan and Rostow "in relation to Lenin's and Stalin's pronouncements on the need for equalizing the economies of the backward and advanced countries."[13]

A 1957 internal FBI memo detailed the bizarre allegations of General Arthur S. Trudeau on the "Infiltration of Fabian Socialists into High Policy Making Areas of the United States Government." General Trudeau alleged that thousands of crypto socialists had silently taken over the government taking jobs as governmental workers where they were launching a socialist takeover of the country. Trudeau sent the FBI documents containing "over 5,500 references" and a listing of 122 suspected Fabianists, with

Walt Rostow prominently included in this paranoid list. Trudeau's understanding of social scientific analysis was so crude that he was unable to understand obvious differences between Marxian critiques of capital and Rostow's efforts to spread American style capitalism abroad, and the FBI did not appear to have a much better understanding of the anti-communist nature of Rostow's work.

General Trudeau was not alone in suspecting something was dangerously wrong with liberal anti-communists. William F. Buckley wrote an impassioned 1957 column in *National Review* attacking Rostow and others at MIT's Center for International Studies (CENIS) for distributing CIA propaganda. Buckley wrote that MIT's "Center for International Studies, according to persistent rumor, was set up and financed for the most part by the Central Intelligence Agency."[14] Buckley of course was himself a former CIA agent, having worked for E. Howard Hunt in Mexico just a few years earlier, but as a *conservative* anti-communist, he distrusted liberal CIA anti-communists. Buckley argued that CIA liberals at MIT were breaking the law, established in the CIA's charter, by conducting domestic CIA operations and producing propaganda for domestic consumption.[15] Buckley's critique marked not only a shift in American conservatives' stance towards the CIA, but it also shows how comfortable Americans have today become with what even Buckley correctly understood as the inevitable polluting effects of secrecy and intelligence work on the production of academic knowledge in American institutions of higher learning.

In 1959, an unidentified individual who had been corresponding with Cambridge University professor, and rival development economist, Péter Tamás Bauer, provided the FBI with a copy of a long letter in which Bauer described his dislikes and suspicions of Walt Rostow. Bauer and Rostow had fundamental academic differences. Bauer believed that centralized economic planning undermined economic development, which no doubt contributed to Bauer's nasty assessment of Rostow's intellectual capacities. Bauer's four-page letter[16] described his recent exchanges with Rostow who was then spending a sabbatical in Cambridge writing *Stages of Economic Growth*.[17] The letter opened with a description of Bauer's recent lunch with Rostow and his efforts to learn more about Rostow's work and politics.[18] Bauer noted Rostow's contacts with

American Democrats such as the Kennedys and Adlai Stevenson, adding that Rostow "clearly implied that Kennedy's advocacy of massive aid to India was based largely on his (Rostow's) own ideas." Bauer wrote that Rostow

claims to be a staunch anti-Marxist and says that ever since his undergraduate days it has been his prime intellectual ambition to show up the weakness of the Marxist system and replace it by another system. It is perfectly true that he does criticize aspects of Marxism, but he is nothing like fundamental enough in his criticism. Of course, although he is a critic of Marxism, the policies he espouses are designed to create societies which are largely or completely dirigiste and very vulnerable to the communist appeal.

Although his phenomenal success and contacts owe a great deal to the teamwork of the leftists and to their control of the intellectual transmission lines, I am sure that there are other factors behind it. The man is very largely a faker. He is essentially on the surface, but he has certain perceptions and insights and an excellent gift of expressing them. He is, in fact, a good journalist. When I analyzed his and Millikan's book for you I said that I thought he correctly assessed what kind of programme, what sort of mixed appeal to idealism and self-interest was most likely to influence American opinion. I think I was right. Again, the phrase "the national style" (which he coined) is I think a very apposite one to describe a certain way of setting about things in the U.S.A. and elsewhere. I asked him what struck him most in England on his return after eight years' absence. He said promptly: "the middle class has re-asserted itself," which is a plausible and in some ways perceptive judgment, pithy and vividly express, though it does not go deep. He perpetrates the most elementary economic errors and his knowledge of history is superficial, but he has a remarkable feel of what sort of ideas, and manners of expressing, them are likely to sell currently, or in the near future. He also has the gift of putting a half a quarter truth pithily in a sentence which it takes two pages to demolish completely.[19]

With this individual's sharing of Bauer's correspondence, this dislike of Rostow moved from idle personal gossip to a political attack. Another FBI report quoted Bauer as describing Rostow as "an indoctrinated Marxist."[20] The FBI collected these reports and reexamined and recirculated them in future reports when Rostow became an advisor to Presidents Kennedy and Johnson.

In the weeks after the 1960 presidential election, the FBI consulted Bureau files for information on Rostow as they vetted files of potential White House appointees for the incoming Kennedy administration. One internal FBI memo discussed concerns raised by Kennedy's press secretary Pierre Salinger, Special Counsel to the President Ted Sorensen, and Presidential advisor Lawrence O'Brien concerning the FBI's intrusive background investigations; stating concerns that the FBI would be collecting, compiling, and keeping all information and gossip they gather for future uses, which is exactly what the FBI did.[21]

On December 5, 1960 General Robert Cutler, Rostow's OSS supervisor during the Second World War, provided the FBI a strong recommendation for Rostow but he also told of how in 1953 or 1954 Rostow had been asked to serve in an advisory role related to Cutler's then service on the National Security Council. Rostow had agreed to serve, but when an FBI investigation discovered Rostow had communist family members, Rostow was asked to excuse himself from service on the NSC.[22]

The FBI received a letter from an unidentified concerned citizen reporting that while a houseguest in one of the Rostow family members' homes they found a Communist Party membership card while snooping around, supposedly looking for a comb. The redactions on the released document shield which family member's home this was (possibly his aunt, cousin or father), or when these events reportedly occurred. The informer "advised that he had not considered this matter again until he learned of Rostow's present position and he felt that because of this position, his knowledge should be made available."[23]

A December 1960 memo by Kenneth O'Donnell, Special Assistant to the President-elect, expressed concerns over possible difficulties associated with Rostow's pending appointment, but O'Donnell told the FBI that

Allen Dulles of the CIA has been pushing vigorously for this appointment. Prior to submitting this matter to the President-elect for a decision, O'Donnell said it would be most helpful if there could be made available additional details with regard to any loyalty hearings afforded Rostow, which matters were referred to in the summary for the new administration which was submitted on 12/8/60.[24]

There are no records in Rostow's FBI file indicating the Bureau had any awareness that Rostow had just published his most significant book, *Stages of Economic Growth: A Non-Communist Manifesto*, and this lack of awareness of the fundamentally anti-communist elements of his writings helped the FBI continue believing Rostow might somehow be linked to some international communist conspiracy. The FBI's institutional privileging of secretive back-channel intelligence gathering over open source intelligence available to any literate person who knew how to use a public library has repeatedly led the Bureau to misunderstand the individuals and groups it investigates.

USAID was created in March 1961 as an agency representing the Kennedy administration's liberal anti-communist strategy of trying to win the hearts, minds, and loyalties of the underdeveloped world by essentially implementing core features of Rostow's Modernization Theory. But Rostow was not brought into Kennedy's Camelot to oversee or advise international development programs. He was instead appointed Deputy Special Assistant for National Security Affairs under National Security Advisor, McGeorge Bundy.

While not directly involved in the planning or implementation of Roger Hilsman and Sir Robert Thompson's Strategic Hamlet Program, Rostow's Modernization Theory influenced this early counterinsurgency project of the Vietnam War. As James Tyner and Chris Philo observed, "in principle, from the perspective of McNamara and Rostow, the Strategic Hamlet Program would deny the NLF its ability to socially reproduce itself ... Apart from the perceived military gains, the Strategic Hamlet Program also conformed to Rostow's promotion of democracy and development in Vietnam."[25]

Rostow's move to the inner circles of Washington placed him within high-level closed-door policy discussions, and it thrust him into discussions and debates about the application of armed and unarmed counterinsurgency operations in Southeast Asia and elsewhere. After Rostow advocated massive bombing of North Vietnam in 1961, President Kennedy removed him from his White House staff and placed him on his Policy Planning Council, a move that brought new FBI investigations when he needed a "Cosmic" security clearance to represent the United States at a 1962 conference in France.[26]

After a 1963 news story mentioned Rostow's work for the Kennedy administration, the FBI received a letter from someone claiming that he was a New Haven neighbor of the Rostow family back in 1937 who "recalled that common gossip in the neighborhood indicated that the mother of Mr. Rostow was a secretary of either the Communist Party or Socialist Party."[27]

In 1965, D.J. Brennan, Jr., senior official in the FBI's Domestic Intelligence Division, wrote a secret memo to W.C. Sullivan raising concerns about Rostow's soft stance on communism. Brennan analyzed sentiments in Rostow's State Department whitepaper on "Communist Parties in Western Europe Today."[28] Brennan claimed Rostow's State Department Planning group "allegedly plays a key role in forming U.S. foreign policy, we may find the enclosure not only interesting but decidedly alarming, bearing in mind that if the views of Rostow are followed, developments could have a bearing on Bureau interest."[29]

Brennan outlined seven points in Rostow's paper, detailing changes in Western European political developments and shifts in the acceptance of the Communist Party in European elections. In his summary of point 4, Brennan wrote:

With regard to the goals of European communists, Rostow recognizes that the communists have not renounced their belief in the "ultimate triumph of socialism" but he takes the position that they are increasingly disposed to see this end as attainable only by gradualist and revisionist tactics as against militant, revolutionary methods. He raises this question: "Are European communists becoming respectable" and comments that of the fifteen noncommunist governments in Western Europe, only three imposed a ban on their Communist Parties, which attests to a certain degree of official acceptance. He states that European Communist Parties will henceforth give greater heed to national objectives and he gives several instances as evidence that communists are being increasingly accepted into political life of various countries.[30]

But point five pushed Hoover to consider Rostow as something more than a liberal policy advocate, raising the absurd possibility that he was taking orders from the Soviets. Brennan summarized point five, writing that

> Rostow feels that it is now appropriate to examine our postwar attitudes and policies respecting communism in Western Europe. He refers to our past policy where we have sought to isolate the communists and reduce their influence. He now thinks that we should take into account the realities of "the developing situation." Referring to the increasing role of communists in Western Europe, he does not think that we should seek to ostracize or exclude them from political life. He states, "whatever its utility in the past, such a policy is no longer likely to serve any useful purpose."[31]

J. Edgar Hoover added a handwritten note at the end of the file stating: "Sounds as if it came directly out of Moscow. Let me have summary on Rostow." The resulting re-re-investigation rehashed the same old files, once again unearthing the old claims that Rostow's 1952 position when working with the UN's Economic Commission had been shown to be "Pro-Russian," while the CIA's 1953 Loyalty Review Board found no reason to doubt his loyalty. But the FBI's review of these records noted that Director Hoover had jotted the notation "Certainly a dubious conclusion" on this report.[32]

After President Kennedy's assassination, Rostow hoped the new administration might listen to plans for a massive bombing campaign targeting communists. As Hoover fantasized about Rostow holding crypto-Soviet links, Rostow worked with General Maxwell Taylor to convince the Johnson administration to launch

Operation Rolling Thunder's ferocious bombing campaign on North Vietnam. Along with Rolling Thunder's hard power, Rostow advocated capturing the hearts and minds of the South Vietnamese by funding development schemes for the lower Mekong Delta that would "provide food and water and power on a scale to dwarf even our own TVA."[33]

When Rostow joined Johnson's National Security Council in 1966, the FBI conducted another security screening,[34] and during this process State Department undersecretary for Economic Affairs, Thomas C. Mann, told the FBI that Rostow was "an idealist" and an "'irrepressible optimist' who does not take a 'soft line toward Communism.' Mann heard the appointee discuss the Viet-Nam situation about one year ago. At that time, the appointee advocated a 'tough line' against North Viet-Nam including bombing of North Vietnam."[35] Robert and Teddy Kennedy praised Rostow to the FBI,[36] and Archibald Cox reported Rostow had "always impressed him as a person of high intellectual ability who has a large capacity for work." In 1966 Rostow was given a "Q" clearance with the Atomic Energy Commission.

In the *Washington Post*, Drew Pearson[37] and Jack Anderson attacked Rostow for advising President Johnson to not honor his previous offer to meet and talk peace with the North Vietnamese anywhere, anytime; as the North Vietnamese offered to meet with the United States in Warsaw. Pearson and Anderson wrote that

around the State Department it's said that Walt Rostow suffers from two things: First, he has been trying to live down the fact that his father was a Socialist; second, Walt Rostow was the man who originally recommended to President Kennedy that he send large scale troops into Vietnam. Ever since, Rostow has been trying to prove this policy was no mistake.[38]

As Johnson left the White House, Rostow retreated to a life of academia where he continued to advocate liberal anti-communist policies linked to Modernization Theory. While little in Rostow's approach to communism changed, with his exit from governmental service, the FBI's interest in Rostow ended.

THE FBI'S PARANOIA OF LIBERAL ANTI-COMMUNISTS

It is important to recognize that American Cold War anti-communism was not limited to the sort of right-wing attacks undertaken by Republican Senator Joseph McCarthy. Many of McCarthy's basic guilt by association and list building anti-communist techniques had already been developed by Democratic President Harry Truman in his shameful red hunting federal loyalty oath program.[39] And because liberal anti-communist programs had little chance of being supported by conservative Republicans in Congress, the CIA ran wild with a broad variety of liberal covert anti-communist programs. Many of these CIA anti-communist programs used covert funding fronts, and funded liberal organizations like the National Student Association, American Friends of the Middle East, the Asia Foundation, or the Congress for Cultural Freedom, which funded various groups abroad using soft power to try and win friends and influence people in ways that undermined communism.[40] But as Rostow's FBI file shows, the anti-communist nature of projects was of less interest to the FBI than were concerns about his involvement in non-confrontational international activities.

There was nothing hidden about the Cold War role which Rostow believed Modernization Theory would play in fighting communism. He literally proclaimed this view when titling his magnum opus a *Non-Communist Manifesto*; yet it is striking how governmental agencies, such as USAID, implementing the programs based on Modernization Theory's propositions are not uniformly viewed as implementing *counterinsurgency* programs. Many individuals working on global development projects have been uncomfortable acknowledging Rostow's own ideological end-goal for world development—they have instead preferred visions of Third World self-sufficiency which ignore the hard reality of development's serial disasters and legacy of debt.

Rostow's FBI file instructs us about the sprawling nature of the Cold War's National Security State. The state's inability to recognize Rostow as a helpful anti-communist servant provide us with views of the Cold War FBI evolving into an appendage so large, awkward, and inefficient that it could not tell the difference between friend or foe, devouring and damaging both without distinction as its paranoiac fuel and simplistic thinking drove it to distrust and destroy those who haphazardly crossed its path.

It wasn't enough that Rostow supported indiscriminate killing of the North Vietnamese through war crime levels of carpet bombing of Rolling Thunder, his support for liberal soft power aid programs in South Vietnam kept the FBI digging for clues that this might mean he was somehow secretly a communist. No amount of surveillance would persuade the FBI to reevaluate their suspicions, and the Bureau's inability to understand something as obvious as the fact that liberal anti-communists were not communists underlines the simple fact that broad FBI's investigations have a long history of being designed to ignore information that contradicts Bureau prejudices.

The FBI's institutional paranoia created distortion fields that warped its institutional understanding of fellow anti-communists like Rostow. But even more significantly, the FBI did not understand that Rostow's larger project provided the base of America's most significant counterinsurgency strategy for the latter half of the twentieth century. The FBI saw things so simply that they could not see past Rostow's father's old time socialist politics—that led him to name his sons Eugene V. Debs Rostow, Ralph Waldo Emerson Rostow, and Walt Whitman Rostow. In the end, the national debts created by Modernization Theory's development projects had a considerably greater societal impact than the demographic, social, health, or agricultural benefits they claimed to produce. Development strategies built on debt's dependency damaged the autonomy of underdeveloped nations as the creditors set and manipulated national policies ranging from food prices to determining the debtor nation's participation in unpopular wars.

17

André Gunder Frank, the FBI, and the Bureaucratic Exile of a Critical Mind

The FBI's surveillance of the economist André Gunder Frank demonstrates how the Bureau's investigative powers historically were used to try and limit the influence and impact of intellectuals critical of American foreign policies. The FBI's intrusions into intellectual matters have not been limited to McCarthy or Cold War era grandstanding, but have occurred in ways large and small, before, during, and after the Cold War, domestically and abroad. One of the many ways the CIA and FBI seek to shape academic discourse is by helping limit which foreign voices are allowed an audience in American halls of higher learning. The FOIA release of 190 (of an acknowledged 298) pages of André Gunder Frank's FBI file illuminates not only the extent of his FBI surveillance, but how the U.S. government's active interest in a scholar's political critique can spawn efforts to limit the domestic impact of their scholarship.

Throughout his career Frank was a peripatetic scholar traveling under a German passport. His itinerant status was the result of many factors: his love of travel, a deep distrust of authority, a reluctance to compromise, and a concerted effort by the INS, FBI, and other U.S. agencies to not allow him to renew his Resident Alien status for purely political reasons. During the 1960s and 1970s Frank's writings transformed academic understandings of global inequality. Frank's Dependency Theory explained how the poverty of underdeveloped nations was the inevitable outcome of global capitalism's "development of underdevelopment," not the product of haphazard misfortune. Frank's work chronicled how centuries of empire and colonialism extracted wealth from afar for uses in the core.[1]

The threats Frank's work presented to the American interests the FBI protected can be seen by contrasting Frank's Dependency Theory with Walt Rostow's Modernization Theory. As discussed in Chapter 16, Walt Rostow's Modernization Theory pitched debt generating development programs for poor nations with claims that all societies could become wealthy by aping the stages of historic development undertaken by the United States.[2] The catch was that the United States managed these projects like a huckster right out of the musical *The Music Man*, offering aid in the form of loans to assist nations as they leapfrogged up an imagined evolutionary ladder to a top rung where every nation could engage in mass consumption.

Frank attacked Rostow for ignoring the roles of debt and patron-client relations that derived from modernization's aid programs. Frank instead argued that these were not "accidental" outcomes. A declassified 1954 CIA memo on "Notes on Foreign Economic Policy" demonstrates that even as Rostow was initially developing the public altruistic arguments for modernization, he was privately confiding to the CIA more mercenary motivations for these programs. In 1954, Rostow knew it was "extremely doubtful that we can maintain in the United States a free and growing economy unless the free world economy of which we are a part is also growing," and that modernization's programs would lead to "lower prices for American consumers."[3] With these divergent public and private goals for programs supported by Modernization Theory, it became a vital ideological component of postwar international relations; with time André Gunder Frank's work developed a prominent critique of Walt Rostow's Cold War work.

Frank's FBI file contains records from a 1962 U.S. Army investigation of his father, the famous German novelist Leonhard Frank. His father's file detailed his involvement in the failed 1919 Berlin communist revolt, noting his political affiliations, writings, and how he and his family fled Berlin for the United States in 1933. The FBI recorded that at the age of four André (born in Berlin in 1929 as Andreas, Gunder was a high school nickname) came to the United States with his parents, received his schooling in California and Michigan, eventually writing his doctoral dissertation on Soviet Ukrainian agricultural production at the University of Chicago under the tutelage of Milton Friedman in 1957.[4]

The FBI's first file entry on André Gunder Frank records a 1957 memo by an Omaha FBI agent requesting permission from J. Edgar Hoover to open an investigation on Frank's activities at Iowa State University. This request was spawned by Professor Frank's analysis at a campus Social Science Seminar of the "Soviet governmental process" where he "rudely" remarked

> that the Politburo is no different than the Security Council we have as an adviser to the President … [Frank] advised that the general tenor of democratic action in Russia [was as] in the United States. [Frank] argued that the Russians have a legislative branch in the Presideium which fulfills the same place as our legislative assemblies.

The agent's report did not include a comparison of KGB and FBI methods of monitoring dissident scholars. The FBI informer appears to have been one of Gunder Frank's ISU colleagues. The FBI made further inquiries among ISU faculty concerning Frank's loyalties, and the FBI assembled a dossier on Frank—noting with concern his writing for the *American Socialist*.[5] One Iowa State FBI informer reported that Gunder

> appears to be retiring by nature and he tries to make up for this by being belligerent and rude. He stated subject is brilliant in his field … He advised that none of the persons contacted felt that [Gunder] was favorable toward Communism or that he tried to influence the students to lean toward Communism.[6]

The FBI's interest in Frank's politics was satiated by this brief campus investigation. That spring, Frank resigned from Iowa State and took a position at Michigan State University, where he taught for five years before resigning to travel for several years in Europe and South America. During the 1960s he held university positions in Brazil, Canada, Chile, and Mexico.[7]

The FBI next investigated Frank in 1961 when his and his mother's names appeared in FBI and CIA investigations related to the arrest of Soviet UN delegate, Igor Melekh, on charges of espionage. Frank's mother, Elena Frank, had known Melekh in her capacity as a translator at the UN; she had introduced André to Melekh, and the FBI believed that Melekh and Frank had corresponded. Hoover sent CIA Director Allen Dulles summaries of FBI intelligence on André Gunder Frank's contacts with Melekh.[8]

In 1961 an FBI agent interviewed Frank at his home, and concluded that "apart from Frank's comment that Melekh's character did not lend itself to espionage, he made no statements which would give any insight into his sympathies. He was noticeably cautious in his selection of words and volunteered no information on which his sympathies might be evaluated." Frank told the FBI that Melekh had been generous to his mother and had made kind inquiries after her health during a period of illness, "a gesture for which Dr. Frank was very grateful." Frank had asked Melekh for introductions to Soviet scholars who might help him during a research visit to the Soviet Union in July 1960, but Melekh had not provided any contacts. Charges against Melekh were later dropped and he returned to the USSR with his family.[9]

In March 1962, the FBI's Bern Legal Attaché sent FBI Director Hoover (and CIA and FBI liaisons in Bonn, Paris, and Rio de Janeiro) a heavily redacted memo reporting that "the American Consulate General, Geneva Switzerland, is being contacted for any information it might have with respect to the allegation that Frank was responsible for the poisoning of ███████████." The following half-page is redacted and the meaning of this reference is unclear, but if there was any evidence supporting a poisoning claim the FBI would have pursued this, and this is the only reference in his released file.[10]

In August 1962, the FBI intercepted a letter Frank wrote from Guatemala to his mother. He wrote of his unsuccessful efforts to move to Cuba, his disinterest in teaching at U.S. universities, and efforts to teach in Europe. He ended the letter writing, "I am getting ready to retire also—from the world. I don't think I like it. I don't know why my father put up with it so long." FBI reactions are partially redacted, but one later FBI commentary noted "that the subject's father was a suicide."[11]

In 1962 Frank married Chilean Marta Fuentes, whose radical political views helped Frank further develop his critique.[12] After his marriage, Frank increasingly focused on how American and European policies extracted wealth from South American nations. In 1963 a Rio de Janeiro FBI agent reported to Hoover that Frank had written a letter to the embassy criticizing American policy in Brazil. Frank wrote the ambassador that "Americans in Brazil are engaging in 'spoilage.' He has further made the remarks, according to the Political Section, that he does not feel that the help that has been given to Brazil has done any good." The FBI then launched a more extensive FBI investigation, which mostly rehashed old information and brought new efforts to trace his movements, but this time the FBI noted his developing academic critique of how the United States manipulated South American political and economic developments.[13]

In 1996 Gunder told me he believed that a letter he had written, mimeographed, and sent to about a dozen U.S. friends in 1964 had been turned over to U.S. authorities, possibly by one of the recipients. He wrote me that "the INS people cited that letter as 'grounds' for my exclusion from the U.S. because of what I said in that private letter, and in an article published in the *Monthly Review* about my 'ideology.'"[14] Frank noted the possibility (suggested by a third party) that one of the letter's recipients who had been critically mentioned in this letter had been a "conduit of the letter to the U.S. government." However, nothing in Frank's released FBI file referenced this letter—though other intercepted letters are reproduced or summarized.

This July 1, 1964 letter was a typed, ten-page single-spaced impassioned dispatch combining detailed explanations of Frank's ideological transformations with a notice of his desire to return to the United States to rejoin an academic world he had abandoned. This letter shows Gunder Frank's fierce independence, his commitment to pursuing truth, and his unwillingness to compromise. In some 2007 correspondence with anthropologist Sidney Mintz discussing Gunder Frank's contributions and life, Mintz wrote me that he thought that

Gunder deserves thoughtful and serious treatment for several reasons. For one (and like Chomsky, I believe), he distrusts all authority. He was not afraid to take any position he believed in. But he was equally prepared to abandon any he distrusted. He didn't have a party or a party line. For another, as far as I can tell, he was absolutely above pandering for *anything*. Neither poverty nor hardship nor gumshoes frightened him. To the best of my knowledge, the one thing he did need was love. Finally, I think he deserves such treatment because he is one of a disappearing species.[15]

These core traits of distrusting authority, not being "afraid to take any position he believed in," no compromising, and willingness to endure hardships for a position he believed in shine through in this July 1, 1964 letter to his American friends and colleagues. Gunder wrote that:

It has been four years since I left the United States, except for three couple-month visits in 1961 and 1962. In June 1960 I went to the Soviet Union on a one month American research grant. 1960–1961 I was on research of absence from Michigan State University and spent it in Cuba, West Africa, and Eastern Europe looking into political determinants of economic Development. More generally, I was trying to get a better perspective on development problems than I had been able to acquire at home. I then resigned from Michigan State University because I felt that the political basis of the professional climate there and in the U.S. generally oriented me—and others—to pursue directions in my teaching and research on problems of economic development and social change which could never bear fruit in speeding up development in underdeveloped countries and serves, on the contrary, only to retard it. I decided, therefore, to remain for further study in the under-developed countries or the socialist ones and to look for a political-intellectual climate which could influence me to at least ask more nearly the right questions of my chosen problem of development.

In the spring of 1962[,] I went to Latin America to pursue my search and research. I intended to go to Cuba to work. While waiting to arrange something in Cuba, and in case I could not as indeed I have not been able to so far, I wanted to do three things in Latin America: To come to know it in a general way as a preliminary to future research on this area; secondly, to learn how one might go about doing research on the political determinants of development and underdevelopment (as an erstwhile economist I had long since shifted my attention from "economic" to "social" factors in development and thought that it was high time to get to the evidently immediately more important political ones, but I lacked any theoretical guide for doing so though I did know, as I am sure you will agree, that asking the American political scientists is a sure way never to find any); and thirdly, should Cuba prove to be unavailable to me, I wanted to find an alternative institutional working environment whose political orientation would steer me in the right and not drag me in the wrong direction. Thus, I spent upwards of a month each visiting, doing informal interviews in, reading about, and beginning to write about Mexico, Guatemala, Venezuela, Peru, and Chile. In the latter country, I did not learn much because I spent three months getting married instead—to Marta Fuentes, on December 21, 1962.[16]

Gunder described how from Chile, he and Marta traveled to East Germany and Brazil, where in 1963 and 1964 he began to develop foundational elements of his Dependency Theory as his "focus changed from 'development' to 'underdevelopment' and it was changing from studying the determinants of one or the other of these to examining how historically each of these determined and still continues to produce the other."[17] He became friends with members of the Brazilian left, who would soon be jailed or exiled in the spring 1964 coup.

Gunder wrote that all of this travel hindered his ability to write detailed academic articles, but what it did provide him was a powerful comparative perspective on the forces of the underdevelopment. Instead of peer reviewed articles, he wrote journalistic pieces for outlets that included *The Nation*, *Revolution*, and *Monthly Review*. His break from the Chicago school was complete and final, writing that:

I recently read Milton Friedman's *Capitalism and Freedom*; and its disingenuous mixture of fallaciously muddled logic with unscientific selection of some and crass disregard for other facts makes me marvel at how I could ever have been led, as other still are, to think that the guiding spirit of the economics department in which I revied my PhD deserves his reputation of exceptionally able theoretician and empiricist.[18]

His work now focused on "the development of underdevelopment no less than that of development itself is a necessary consequence of capitalism and that under capitalism this process continues today essentially as it did in the past." His non-partisan independence led him to

criticize the very similar policies of the Alliance for Progress and the Communist Parties in Latin America, both of which are associated with very similar but quite erroneous analysis of Latin American reality in terms of dualism and feudalism and both of which demonstrably have, for Latin America, disastrous results of retarding over-all development and increasing underdevelopment still further.[19]

After describing some of the reactions to his research thus far—including reports that Chinese newspapers had reprinted some of his work criticizing the self-serving uses of U.S. aid programs—Gunder addressed his own transformation, writing that:

I can no longer distinguish political from professional aspects and maybe also from personal relations in my life and work. I have long thought that the liberal positivist creed or ideology of trying to separate one's politics from one's social science is not only politically and morally but also scientifically objectionable in that the supposed political and moral dispassion, far from permitting objectivity, condemns to scientific failure. But for a long time also I did not know how to avoid it and led a schizoid existence like many of us in which political and moral ideas and feelings were effectively compartmentalized and separated from work as a social scientist. A major purpose of my work abroad, of course, has been to overcome this weakness; and I think I am now well along the way to a cure. My "unliberal" identification of science with politics, let alone with my politics, would not be very well received in the United States of course. Furthermore, though I would not and do not do so, better Marxists both south and north of the equator now call me one of them. I have not devoted myself to studying the great books—though I am belatedly getting around to reading some of them—but according to these Marxists I think like a Marxist dialectician and perceive and study the world around me so differently from my liberal friends and erstwhile colleagues that we hardly seem to be living in the same world. As a person I must support the present Chinese position on major world problems and that of the most militant black nationalists such as Malcolm X and Robert Williams on American domestic ones because as a social scientist I see that it is their positions which most nearly reflect the world's realities and necessities.[20]

Gunder Frank outlined writing projects he hoped to soon complete which examined fallacies of Friedman's work, Keynesian economic models of international inequality, and a reexamination of Lenin's theory of imperialism. He wrote that this work "implies the rejection on empirical and theoretical grounds of the entire basis, conception, exposition, and application of the Rostonian stages of growth approach to the problems of development."[21]

He wrote that his transformation in his understanding of underdevelopment "inevitably affects my teaching profoundly" to a point where he could not continue to teach as he had before. He now understood this would make it very difficult for him to again teach in a U.S. university, where Modernization Theory was on the rise. He wrote that

if I teach courses on development—that is on underdevelopment—or on sociology or economics—that is on the nature of the society and economy which produces among other things development, underdevelopment, race problems, and the threat of nuclear destruction—I have to pose the questions, to say nothing of any possible answers, quite differently than do colleagues and books at home and to a large extent abroad.[22]

Because of this "difference in political-intellectual framework" it would be impossible to teach students in a U.S. university, and he asked his friends to let him know if they believed this was true. He also wrote that he believed it was more important that he direct his teaching to those in "capitalisms underdeveloped periphery," who might use his critiques to improve their plight, and clarified that his position "may involve, of course, fighting with more than a pen as weapon."[23]

After discussing what he saw as the inevitable difficulties he would face with colleagues and students in an American university economics department, he wrote there were also "difficulties with the [U.S.] government." He worried that the U.S. government

might try to interfere with or to prevent my work along the aforementioned lines, particularly inasmuch as I am a foreigner. In fact, my relations with the government already render difficult and maybe even impossible my reentry into the United States. For various technical reasons and my refusal to be drafted, I already had serious difficulties in traveling and returning from abroad while I was permanent resident of the U.S. without citizenship.[24]

At this point, Gunder Frank had given up his U.S. resident status, having stayed abroad too long, and he was in limbo waiting for five months to hear back on his application for a new resident visa, and suspected (correctly) that the reasons his visa was not forthcoming were political. Two years later he authored a *Monthly Review* article on "The Development of Underdevelopment," which he believed created new even more serious problems with the INS, because of his argument that underdevelopment "was and is generated by the very same historical process which also generated economic development: the development of capitalism itself."[25] After Frank's death in 2005 *Monthly Review*'s editors wrote that this essay "was seen by the U.S. government as constituting a threat to its empire in the Americas and he was sent a letter from the U.S. attorney general telling him that he would not be allowed reentry into the United States."[26] Though his FBI file does not reference Frank's July 1, 1964 letter, it does describe what appears to be another 1964 letter discussing his political orientation.

In November 1964, an unidentified woman, who had met Frank's mother the previous summer on a flight returning to NYC from a visit to Chile, reported to the FBI that she had translated a letter written in Spanish, "which Mrs. Frank had received from ███████ in Chile. According to Mrs. Frank ██████ is ██████ of Andreas Frank, who is the son of Mrs. Elena Frank."[27] While the identity of the letter's author is redacted, the context possibly suggests André's wife Marta Fuentes—though Fuentes' own radical politics conflict with the summarized contents of the letter. The FBI's summary of the letter states that the writer

> was very much opposed to communism and the pro-Castro type of Government in Cuba and strongly disapproved of … communist sympathies and ideologies. [The letter's author] indicated in the letter that she wrote to Mrs. Frank, in order to determine whether anything could be done to change the political feelings of Andreas Frank.

The FBI's summary reported that she

> indicated in the letter that she wrote to Mrs. Frank, in order to determine whether anything could be done to change the political feelings of [Andreas] Frank. ███████ Said Mrs. Frank also very strongly disapproved of her son's political activities, but she indicated there was no way for her to change him. Mrs. Frank said her son had commented that social and political changes needed to be made in the western world in order to incorporate socialist and communist type Governments, and he was willing to live in squalor and sub-standard conditions in order to accomplish this end. When he visited Mrs. Frank about two years ago in New York City, he criticized his mother for having nice furnishings in her apartment. He felt she should give up such luxuries in order to further the cause of socialism and communism.[28]

Without access to the original letter or the letter author's identity it is difficult to interpret this letter's meaning, which may have been nothing more than a daughter-in-law's efforts to maintain cordial relations with her relatively conservative mother-in-law. Whatever the contextual meaning of the letter, to the FBI it corroborated their belief that Frank's loyalties were opposed to dominant U.S. interests.

One 1965 FBI report concluded,

> There is no doubt that FRANK is thoroughly anti-American and pro-Communist and would represent a danger to this country were he present. His activities should be investigated if he were to return to this country. Accordingly, Detroit will contact INS, Detroit to determine final action taken on the hearing afforded the subject on his admissibility to the U.S. in 1962. There is some indication he was again furnished permanent residence status in the U.S. which he subsequently lost by remaining out of the country more than one year. His mother, however, has stated he was "blacklisted" from returning to the U.S. Detroit also furnish subject's INS alien registration number and photograph, if available, from his INS file.[29]

The FBI was incapable of understanding the independence of his critique. As the FBI monitored Frank's correspondence with his mother, they learned that he had asked her for some publicly available UN documents from the 1964 "Trade and Development Conference in Geneva."[30] Another 1965 memo records a Detroit agent telling Hoover that "every effort will be made to prevent [Frank] from returning to the United States," but that there was "a problem concerning the matter of the wording of the denial of [his] application for re-entry."[31] "INS Lookout Notices" were generated.[32] A Bonn FBI agent alerted Hoover to an article by Frank in *The Nation* criticizing U.S. policies in Brazil.[33]

An unidentified FBI informer from Brooklyn wrote to the American embassy in Bonn, claiming that Elena Frank had recently returned from Germany after receiving $10,000 in "illegal money" from the German government. The informer claimed that both mother and son Frank were communists, and that Edena was leaking secrets from the UN. The handwritten letter to the American embassy read as follows:

> Brooklyn, N.Y. 5/14/65
> American Embassy:
> For your information and I think it is my duty as an American citizen to tell you about Mrs. Elena Frank who returned to Germany March 29th just to get illegal money, $10,000 from the German government. Mrs. Frank was born in 1899 in Kiev, Russia naturalized American citizen worked about 15 years for the United Nations as a Russian translator. Mrs. Frank and her son Andreas Gunder Frank are both 100 proof communists and all the time Mrs. Frank was working for the United Nations gave her son always Information about all military secret. Her son is at present in Mexico, this letter was found in her apartment to give you proof she is now in Germany pretends to be a very sick person but will try to get her son to Germany to start trouble there ... All people here are disgusted that the American government has to pay this woman all kinds of benefits who should not really receive a penny from the United States and we have to pay the taxes for draft dodger Andrew Frank.
> Sincerely,
> ████████ [34]

As Frank intensified his work on *Capitalism and Underdevelopment in Latin America*, the FBI's commitment to keeping him out of the United States increased. In the summer and fall of 1965 the FBI received reports that Frank was in Mexico City and it used local informers working in communist circles and FBI agents to try and find him.[35] The FBI appeared convinced that Frank's critique was part of a foreign Communist Party's efforts; several FBI memos record efforts to tie his critique to Socialist Workers Party doctrine; in a memo on a "Chinese Communist Intelligence Biographical Data Album" a New York agent conceded there was not enough data to connect Frank with Chinese communism.[36]

After the American embassy in Lima issued Frank a three-month U.S. visa in 1966, the INS issued a "lookout notice," but by August the FBI concluded that he had not returned to the United

States and the FBI monitored his bank account in Mexico City in an attempt to track his movements.[37] After the publication of *Capitalism and Underdevelopment* (1967) the FBI renewed their past investigations of Frank. An unidentified 1968 newspaper clipping in his file reported Frank was not rehired at Montreal's Sir George Williams University "because of his Marxist political ideology" and for supporting a student strike.[38]

In 1968 Frank joined the University of Chile's Centre for Socio-Economic Studies where some of Latin America's most influential Marxists, dependency theorists, and liberation theologians worked until the 1973 coup overthrew Allende's socialist government and pushed Frank and his colleagues into exile. Curiously, Frank's released FBI file contained little information from this period, though such international monitoring was increasingly becoming the task of the CIA—which did not release files on Frank in response to my FOIA request.

The CIA's monitoring of Frank is suggested by a 1970 memo from J. Edgar Hoover to DCI Richard Helms passing on a copy of the underground newspaper (*News from Nowhere*) containing information on Frank.[39] The FBI's released files on Frank are blank for most of the rest of the 1970s and 1980s when he taught in Belgium, Chile, China, England, Germany, Holland, and the United States. The INS and State Department did not allow Frank back into the United States until 1979 when Senator Edward Kennedy intervened on his behalf so that Frank could teach a seminar at Boston University.

Frank's file ends with a summary of the legal findings from the 1990 case of *National Lawyer's Guild v. U.S. Attorney General*. The case was settled with the U.S. admitting that prior to 1977, the FBI engaged in COINTELPRO type operations against National Lawyer's Guild (NLG) members—activities that included wiretaps and other surveillance. Because the NLG assisted Frank in his efforts to reenter the United States, his communications with Guild lawyers may have been subjected to surveillance. While the record of U.S. government surveillance of Frank is still incomplete, released documents establish the FBI monitoring Frank after his ideas were identified as opposing U.S. policies, and they show the FBI assisting INS efforts to prevent his return to American campuses.[40]

But Frank's file is more than a dusty footprint of past FBI efforts to monitor and keep threatening scholarship distant; it also warns of the likelihood of similar FBI actions today. Post-9/11 visa restrictions for critical foreign scholars wishing to visit American universities and conferences allow the functional quarantine of critical foreign voices who might otherwise inform us. As the FBI, during the last two decades, has taken on increasing "security" roles on campuses, their institutional past should make us question exactly what they are protecting—in the 1960s they "protected" American universities from Frank's Dependency Theory; today, the FBI's "Counterintelligence Domain Program" tries to get American universities to restrict unspecified public research that may be of use to unknown enemies. Just what this unspecified research is remains intentionally unclear, but if the past is any guide these "dangers" might include critical writings that question the foundations of American empire.

18

Angel Palerm and the FBI: Monitoring a Voice of Independence at the Organization of American States

At the time of his death in 1980, Angel Palerm Vich was Professor of Anthropology at the Universidada Iberoamericana of Mexico. He lived a rich and varied life, born a Catalan native, he fought the fascists in the Spanish Civil War, eventually acquiring Mexican citizenship and establishing his career as a Mesoamerican anthropologist. He published significant research on New World prehistoric irrigation complexes, and anthropological analysis of the impacts of contemporary land reform. Eulogizing Palerm, anthropologist Eric Wolf wrote that he had viewed "anthropology at once as a critical model of inquiry and as a means for realizing the aspirations of the Mexican Revolution."[1] While widely viewed as a significant figure in Mexican anthropological research and as a scholar whose Marxist analytical roots informed his anthropological analysis, his FBI file shows the U.S. Department of State and the FBI viewed Palerm's years working within the Organization of American States as presenting a communist threat to American interests.

Angel Palerm Vich was born in Ibiza, Spain in 1917. He earned his bachelor's degree in History at the University of Barcelona before the outbreak of the Spanish Civil War. He joined the Republican Army as a Catalan nationalist and fought the fascists as a committed socialist, holding the position of Commissar, becoming a division commander, and was eventually seriously wounded in battle.[2] After the war, he fled Spain first to France, then immigrated to Mexico in 1939, becoming a Mexican citizen in 1941. One FBI report claimed that in Mexico

> he was active in Mexican Communist Party youth groups in 1940 and attacked a splinter group of Catalan Communist Party as being against Third International and against the Catalan Communist Party and Communist Party of Spain, [organizations in which] he was active for about 2 ½ years. He broke with Communist Parties because he could not accept Spanish dictatorship over Catalans.[3]

Even with this knowledge that Palerm had split from the communists, the FBI concluded that "if he could achieve an important position in the communist movement, he would collaborate with communism."[4] Palerm enrolled at the Universidad Nacional Autónoma de Mexico, while simultaneously studying anthropology at the Escuela Nacional de Anthropología e Historia, where he worked with Dr. Isabel Kelly, and began fieldwork studying the Totonac of Tijin. He later undertook archaeological excavations and working on the importance of irrigation in Mesoamerica, often with ethnohistorical sources and engaging with the work of Karl Wittfogel on the rise of hydraulic societies and claims of an Asiatic Mode of Production.[5]

While the FBI's interest in Palerm first grew from his employment with the Organization of American States, the FBI's awareness of his Marxist political orientation kept the Bureau monitoring him for decades.[6] The first 150 pages of Angel Palerm's released FBI file show a repetitive rehashing of reports about him fighting fascists in the Spanish Civil War, then being exiled to Mexico, followed by speculations that he may have been a communist during the war or in the present. The FBI interviewed dozens of Palerm's acquaintances about his politics, and the reports from these interviews show the Bureau's general distrust of anti-fascists.

PALERM MOVES TO WASHINGTON, DC

In 1951 Angel Palerm and his wife Carmen moved to Washington, DC where he took a position as a social science specialist at the

Pan American Union (PAU) within the Organization of American States (OAS). Palerm worked in PAU's Social Science Office and took on editorial responsibilities of its journal, *Ciencias Sociales*. Under Palerm's leadership, *Ciencias Sociales* became a significant bilingual anthropological journal and later, as the founder of the OAS's Department of Social Affairs, he coordinated social science research within the OAS. The FBI opened their investigation of Palerm in August 1952, with a report from the U.S. Immigration and Naturalization Service notifying the FBI that Palerm was preparing to move to the United States to work for the OAS in Washington, DC. During Palerm's first year in the United States, the FBI wrote several memos reporting basic biographical information and highlighting his history of anti-fascism.

In February 1954 the FBI contacted several U.S. anthropologist colleagues of Palerm for background interviews. Though the identities are redacted, details in files indicate two of those contacted were Oscar Lewis and George Foster; neither Foster nor Lewis reported any derogatory information.[7] A later FBI document reported that Oscar Lewis told the Bureau that

Palerm's main interest, to his knowledge, has always been Anthropological. [Lewis] stated that what discussion he has had with Palerm concerning politics leave him with the impression that Palerm is extremely anti-Communist ... [he] advised that Palerm once made the remark that Spaniards who had gone to the Soviet Union had been badly mistreated by the Communists there. In addition [Lewis] advised that Palerm once commented that if it hadn't been for the Communists the Spanish Republic would not have lost the Spanish Civil War.[8]

But because the FBI had absurdly been investigating Oscar Lewis as a suspected communist since 1949, these assurances were likely met with FBI skepticism.[9] Unidentified anthropologists in Mexico were also interviewed concerning Palerm's politics and background[10] and FBI informants in Mexico with knowledge of Mexican Communist Party activity reported never having heard of Palerm.[11] While his identity is redacted, the context and released information show the FBI interviewed anthropologist John Murra in May 1954. While the FBI concluded Murra knew Palerm, they thought it inadvisable to ask Murra about Palerm, fearing "that he may possibly reveal to Palerm the fact that Palerm is being investigated by this Bureau."[12]

The FBI also opened a file on Angel Palerm's wife, Carmen Viqueira Landa Palerm. For years the FBI monitored her support for progressive causes, noting her protesting the execution of Julius and Ethel Rosenberg and her involvement in other leftist causes. Such FBI file entries became standard file fodder, and the FBI's observations of her political activities were repeated and amplified during the next several years in Angel Palerm's FBI file.

In 1958 Palerm became executive assistant to the Secretary General of the Organization of American States and he left this position in 1961 to direct the newly created Department of Social Affairs of the OAS, where he remained until 1965. The FBI reported that in May 1961, someone posted anti-Castro, anti-communist signs at several OAS buildings in DC, buildings of the Pan American Health Association, and on the lawn of Palerm's home in Falls Church, Virginia.[13]

A June 1961 FBI memo summarized a report from an unidentified anti-Castro Cuban emigre mentioning Palerm. The report explained communist techniques for bureaucratically seizing control of existing organizations in ways that allowed communists to remotely run the organization. This Cuban exile believed Angel Palerm had used classic techniques of communist subterfuge to seize control of the OAS Council. He told the FBI that "what has been at stake is a complete change of ideology. The first stage was to prevent the development of programs through 'red tape' and thus paralyze all activities."[14] The second stage of Palerm's operations was supposedly then underway, with a coming large-scale reorganization with the assistance of consultants, who would instruct the OAS to create an independent Social Science Department that could carry out communist activities. The third stage involved hiring strategic personnel, bypassing normal procedures of receiving the council's approval and canceling programs at odds with private agendas, establishing programs for international exchange of university professors in the name of improving scholarship. All this supposedly would help achieve the communists' clandestine goal of establishing links between labor unions and farmers. This Cuban exile presented the FBI with a picture of Palerm as a gifted silent operator remotely guiding developments at OAS for the Communist Party.[15]

After describing several incidents where Palerm convened special meetings, used handpicked consultants to advise changes within the OAS, and helped develop new broad powers for the OAS executive, this FBI informer added that

> A part of the communist plan is to discredit OAS. To this end, Palerm did not allow any of the technicians of his department to present any project of activities to be fulfilled during the fiscal year 1961–1962, which did not have a direct bearing on the Bogota Act. He thus rejected with that excuse a project on "A Social Security Program and its implications on the Latin-American common market."[16]

These efforts to support anthropological research made this informer suspicious that Palerm was trying to simply waste OAS funds to discredit the organization. This contradictory claim that communists wanted to both discredit the OAS and use it to achieve their goals was not critically questioned in the FBI's report. Instead, the FBI appeared receptive to these claims. Some FBI reports recorded ridiculous arguments claiming that Palerm's work was a form of sabotage designed to undermine OAS credibility. This FBI informer complained that Palerm was wasting resources conducting anthropological research establishing chronologies for pre-Columbian cultures. The informer claimed this archaeological research was part of a conspiracy to undermine the credibility of the OAS. The informer claimed that Palerm understood that "when it is known that OAS is studying 'pre-Columbian cultures,' and later publishes its report, Latin-American people will lose faith in an organization that does not concern itself with more urgent and pressing problems."[17] Among the claimed programs Palerm failed to support was a Brazilian rural electrification program that was not funded in favor of a librarian training program in Puerto Rico. Critiques that funding social science research was necessarily part of left-leaning political programs were common features in the United States during the early Cold War period; elements of this critique prevailed during failed early efforts to fund social science through the National Science Foundation, and show the general skeptical view of applied social science programs during the 1950s and early 1960s.[18]

Under an FBI mail monitoring operation, the U.S. Post Office provided records of return addresses on all mail Palerm received.[19] The FBI used a trash cover operation to read and inventory Palerm's trash, but these plans were abandoned once the FBI "determined that the methods employed by Fairfax County [trash collectors] make such coverage extremely difficult."[20] The FBI also monitored Palerm's banking records and tracked his whereabouts in the United States and abroad.[21]

The FBI believed Palerm's position at the OAS allowed him to control agendas favoring communists. FBI efforts to monitor Palerm and to intervene in OAS political matters underscore the Bureau's role not as a law enforcement body but as a political arm of American capitalism, enforcing what the Bureau saw as a particular type of justice favoring U.S. capital's interests over the interests of neighboring countries. The FBI's focus on individuals they identified as opponents' lawful use of existing rules and power structures as somehow being an unfair weapon of the global communist conspiracy finds the U.S. top law enforcement agency contriving to interpret those using existing rules to assert their will as somehow cheating. In a report from October 1961, an FBI informer (who told the FBI that Palerm was not a communist) examined the sort of power Palerm held within the OAS, claiming that

> In the field of labor, Palerm intends to pay attention to the problems of the urban labor force in Latin America under the pretense that this is where the communists are gaining power and where social programs ought to be emphasized.
>
> Controlling the budget of the economic and social department of the Department of Technical Cooperation, and of part of the Department of Cultural Affairs, Palerm has enough money to send agents of his own ideology as experts in any of the departments' fields. He can, on the one hand, discredit the OAS and on the other, through his experts promote unrest. Controlling

the social programs of the Director of Social Affairs and the economic programs by default, since no head of the Economic Department has been appointed, controlling the granting of fellowships and professorships as well as other technical cooperation programs, Palerm practically has in his hand half of the PAU's budget. Controlling the Bureau of Personnel and the Fiscal Office, he can hire personnel of his choice.[22]

While the FBI insinuated something sinister in Palerm's power within the PAU, his control over budgets and agendas was no more than any other administrator of his stature. Still, the FBI made inquiries in Madrid and began searching for any records the fascist government in Spain had on Angel and Carmen Palerm.[23]

In January 1962 Palerm visited the Dominican Republic on an OAS mission establishing scholarships for students at the University of Santo Domingo. During the delegation's visit to the University, the FBI reported that

violent political disorders were in progress in Santo Domingo ... requiring the intervention of the Dominican armed forces. While this was going on ▮▮▮▮ received a telephone call from a group of Dominican University students who brusquely announced that they were en route to the university with guns to kill Palerm, ▮▮▮▮▮▮▮▮▮ because they were communists from the OAS. ▮▮▮▮▮▮▮▮ hurriedly telephoned for aid from the Dominican armed forces but was told that the troops were in use and could not be sent immediately. ▮▮▮▮▮▮▮▮ thereupon left his office and soon personally confronted a group of angry Dominican students armed with submachine guns in an outer courtyard of the University. During the ensuing parley, ▮▮▮▮▮ dissuaded the students from pursing their announced purpose by pointing out that such an act would bring great disgrace not only to the University of Santo Domingo but to the struggling new Dominican Republic.[24]

In June 1962, the FBI interviewed an individual working at the Library of Congress' Hispanic Foundation who had known Palerm since the early 1940s when they met while he was conducting research in Mexico. After Palerm moved to Washington in 1952, they had renewed their friendship. This source told the FBI that

> PALERM has on several occasions told him that in his youth in Spain, he fought in the ranks of the Spanish Republican forces in the Monserrat area near Barcelona during the Spanish Civil War. ███████ recalled that PALERM had told him of blowing up a bridge in the Monserrat area ... ███████ said that he had gathered from Palerm's comments that Palerm was then and probably still is a Catalan Nationalist and an agnostic as far as religion is concerned. ███████ advised that he has the impression from his talks with Palerm that Palerm may have been permanently declared persona non grata by the Franco Government for having been guilty of a so called "crimes of blood" during the Spanish Civil War. ███████ indicated that he assumed that this designation had resulted from Palerm's military activities in Spain on behalf of the defeated Spanish Republican forces. ███████ went on to indicate that he does not know whether or not Palerm was a communist in Spain commenting that even if Palerm had been a communist in Spain this would not prove much as regards Palerm's current political views.[25]

The informer told the FBI he was sure Palerm would now be a U.S. citizen if this would not mean he would lose his current job at the OAS. He said the claims that Palerm was a communist were just false rumors. Other informers told the FBI that they were convinced that Palerm had been a communist in Spain and that he remained a communist while in Mexico and while working for the OAS in the United States.[26]

In July 1962, a woman affiliated with the OAS's Inter-American Commission of Women in Washington, D.C. told the FBI that earlier that year the Colombian government had objected to Palerm visiting Colombia as an OAS representative because they considered him to be a communist. She told the FBI that "she had been in Spain and had personally viewed official Spanish records there which proved that subject was a militant communist when he lived in Spain, his native country. The informant promised that she would arrange a confidential, personal interview of SA

█████████ with █████████" But when the FBI later tried to interview her, she would not cooperate because a new government had come to power in Colombia and this "made such an interview perilous for her."[27]

Another individual told the FBI he was considering using this Colombian incident to remove Palerm from the OAS. In August 1962, the FBI reported that following this incident this individual had "recommend to PAU Secretary General Jose A. Mora that Palerm be made the Director of the PAU Centro Interamericana de Vivienda y Planeamiento in Bogota," as a means of moving Palerm out of his position of power at OAS headquarters.[28] Here, the FBI stepped beyond simply monitoring OAS activities, and towards passively acquiescing in the assistance of a coup within the PAU.

The FBI learned in late August 1962 that

the panel of nine international experts, the so-called "Nine Wise Men" who were appointed in December 1961 as economic advisors to the Alliance for Progress Program, had been engaging in secret meetings under the █████████ one of the nine) for the purpose of preparing measures and arguments for effecting the transfer of their operations from Washington, D.C. to Mexico, D.F. The Source said that the panel hopes to effect the action during the meeting in Mexico of the Inter-American Economic and Social Council of the Organization of American States (OAS). This meeting is presently scheduled to take place in October, 1962.

The informant said that inquiry into this proposed move has indicated that Angel Palerm Vich ... probably is behind this proposed action by the panel. The informant explained that such a move, if successful, would go a long way toward disrupting the overall activities of the PAU, sharply reducing United States influence over the organization and, at the same time, enhancing the influence of Mexican leftist and pro-communist elements in its affairs. The informant said that if the panel of experts were successful in accomplishing the move, it would be only logical for the PAU Department of Economic Affairs, Social Affairs, Cultural Affairs, and of Technical Cooperation to follow, since these are the principal departments used by the panel of experts in their work.[29]

The informer admitted to having no direct information that Palerm was the instigator of this plan, though Palerm supported such actions and reportedly favored moves leading to "the evisceration of the PAU and the OAS, or their capture by leftist and pro-communist elements." It was reported that "Secretary General Jose A. Mora of the PAU is inclined to believe that Palerm has had far more to do with this proposed action by the panel than is apparent."[30] This informer claimed that "Palerm is reputed to be expert in bringing about a broad action without his ever appearing clearly as its instigator or even as its supporter."[31] Palerm's denials of supporting these developments were viewed by the FBI as in character with such maneuvering.

Another FBI informer claimed "Palerm is now dedicated to thwarting the success of the Alliance for Progress," and he reported that

recent maneuvers on the part of Palerm appear to have increased suspicion of OAS Secretary General Jose A. Mora that Palerm is a cunning and dangerous bureaucrat who is aiming for either the destruction of the Organization of American States (OAS) and its permanent Secretariat, the OAS, as an effective instrument for Inter-American cooperation, or the subordination of these organizations to anti-United States, if not communist influence in Latin America.[32]

There were further claims that Palerm was behind efforts to move the OAS out of the United States to "Mexico or other Latin American countries" and there were speculations that once the possibility of such actions became known, Palerm cynically renounced such plans and used this as an opportunity to try and sidle up to OAS's powerbase. This unidentified informant told the FBI that:

Secretary General Jose A. Mora has recently indicated that in view of Palerm's alleged past communist connections in Spain, and in view of the widespread feeling among Latin Americans that

Palerm may still be pursuing disruptive, if not pro-communist tactics in his current work in the PAU in Washington, consideration will be given to transferring Palerm from his present PAU post in Washington, to some other OAS post, preferably outside the United States. The informant explained that such a transfer might minimize Palerm's influence of PAU structure and activities, and possibly bring out into the open his alleged pro-communist tendencies.[33]

The FBI continued to monitor Palerm's mail and his banking activities.

Another FBI informer claimed Palerm was a progressive liberal, not a communist. Palerm told this informant that he thought Castro was an "egomaniac" and that he despised dictators of the left and right. In discussing the execution of Spanish communist Julian Grimau (the previous month) he reportedly said that "the only real error committed by the Franco Government was in failing to afford Grimau a public trial. Palerm did not question the justice of the execution indicating that he was convinced that Grimau amounted to a bandit disguised as a politician."[34] But no matter how many reports the FBI collected of Palerm criticizing communists, the FBI continued to investigate him as a suspected communist.

Finally, after a decade of investigations, in June 1963 an FBI Special Agent proposed that the Bureau close its investigation of Palerm, acknowledging that "searching inquiries conducted over a span of some ten years have failed to show that Palerm has been a communist or a secret agent for communism during this investigative period."[35] After recounting various suspicious reports about Palerm that the FBI had collected over the years, the report concluded:

The fact that Palerm is a controversial figure is evidently the reason why the USDS has repeatedly requested investigation of him. These requests seem to originate in a hope that investigative results might resolve the political problem posed by Palerm's continued tenure as an important OAS official.

Since careful and extensive investigation has failed to accomplish this, it seems valid to conclude that continued investigation cannot be expected to delineate Palerm as something other than what he evidently is in his present position.

It would further appear that the results already accomplished by investigation should be sufficient to form the basis of a political decision by the USDS as to whether Palerm should be allowed to continue in his present post.[36]

Even with this conclusion, the FBI continued to collect material for his file, compiling another 100 pages of reports. Instead of dropping its investigation, the FBI dug deeper into its old files where it found and rehashed an old October 14, 1953 report alleging that Palerm "had been an officer assigned to the General Staff in the 'Red Army' during the Spanish Civil War and his duties had been such as to make it evident he was Secretary General of the Communist Party in Ibiza, Spain."[37] The resulting report recycled a decade's worth of rumors about Palerm using his position in the OAS to advance radical policies. It mattered not that these were old unsubstantiated rumors: the FBI used these to continue to monitor Palerm.

During this period Palerm increasingly used his position at OAS "to promote the use of the social sciences to help solve some of the major problems of the day," as he funded international programs designed to improve agriculture, urban planning, social programs, and land reform.[38]

In early 1964, the FBI learned that an employee of the U.S. Department of Labor had filed a complaint against Palerm concerning an incident at a Latin American development conference. An FBI informer reported s/he had heard directly from Secretary General Jose Mora "that there has been a complaint made against [Palerm] by an unidentified official of the U.S. Department of Labor. [The FBI informer] was not aware of the nature of the complaint except it came as a result of Palerm's association in an official capacity with officials of the Department of Labor."[39] A later FBI report noted

that in light of Palerm's conduct which stimulated the complaint and also in view of the fact that ████████████████████████████

it is the informant's opinion that the Secretary General of the OAS, Jose A. Mora, would probably give favorable consideration to any overture by the United States Department of State seeking the dismissal of Palerm from his job at the OAS.[40]

A later FBI memo indicated that the complaint against Palerm stemmed from his failure to provide the U.S. delegation with English translations of labor policy documents that had been under consideration at the meeting of the Committee on Labor Matters of the Inter-American Economic Social Council meeting as required by meeting agreements.[41] The United States complained that this made it impossible for U.S. delegates to consider policy items on the meeting's agenda. One FBI informer interpreted this incident as revealing that "Palerm's desire is to eliminate all United States interest and influence in Latin American labor matters."[42]

In May 1964 an FBI informant reported Palerm's transfer to Lima, Peru, where he was Special Representative for Field Operations for the Assistant Secretary for Economic and Social Affairs of the PAU.[43] A June 1964 FBI memo summarized a meeting between J. Edgar Hoover and Ambassador Thomas C. Mann, a prominent anti-communist U.S. statesman with a long history of attacking South American leftists. Mann complained to Hoover that the OAS was "loaded with pro-Castro people" and he insisted that the FBI should investigate the OAS. FBI memos indicate they shared this information with the "CIA and other interested intelligence agencies."[44] Another FBI report accused Palerm of using the OAS to provide scholarships for pro-Castro students from Peru. Increasing hostilities between Secretary General Jose Mora and Palerm, and Mora's communications with the FBI clarify Mora disliked Palerm.

"COMMUNIST INFILTRATION AT THE OAS"

On April 9, 1965, an FBI informer gave the FBI a five-page report titled "Communist Infiltration at the OAS." The document's author was unknown to the FBI, and it was believed to have been written around 1962.[45] Below are excerpts from this document—which appears to be a multi-generation primitive photocopy of a copy, and is so washed-out that some passages are difficult to read.

Communist Infiltration at the OAS

Until recently the communists were not interested in the OAS which they considered a tool of the United States. Since the emergence of Castro, however, and the possibility of gaining a foothold in the Hemisphere the communists have been trying to infiltrate the Organization of American States (Secretariat of the OAS) in order to influence the programs, the policies and even the delegates to the Organization.

The Communist Cell

The likely head of this cell is Angel Palerm, Spanish refugee, Mexican citizen, who has risen very rapidly in the Secretariat in the last two years, from an intermediate-level post in the Department of Cultural Affairs—he is an anthropologist-to Executive Officer of the Secretary General, with the rank of Department Director. In this post he has been in effect the Secretary General, and Dr. William Sanders, the Assistant Secretary General. With strong hand Palerm has even overruled decisions of the Secretary General. He has been hiding from him certain facts. Palerm operates through a faithful clique of staff members of communist tendencies, left-wingers, fellow travelers and others who are merely opportunists.

On 18 January 1961 Palerm was appointed Director of Social Affairs. In order to accommodate him, the Secretary General has split the Department of Economic and Social Affairs into two parts: one social and one economic, with the aim of creating two separate Departments when the OAS Council approves his proposal. In this new post Palerm is to administer all the Social programs of the OAS which have been given priority as a result of the provisions of the Act of Bogota.

Palerm's group control the most sensitive programs of the OAS. The main [personalities] of the group as ███████ (an American), ████████████ (Spanish refugee), ██████████████ (Spanish refugee) ██████ the OAS; ████████ (an American) in the Department of Technical Cooperation; ████████(an American)

████████ (an American) ████████ (an American) ████████ they use some Latin Americans of low intellectual caliber when they have given responsible positions and utilize [them] as puppets, such as ████████.[46]

The report listed reasons why the United States had remained ignorant of the communist infiltration of the OAS. These reasons included general lack of awareness of communist tactics, key individuals' fondness of Palerm, the State Department's lack of attention to non-economic programs of OAS, and a general lack of concern because of the OAS's relatively small budget. It then speculated on the communists' master strategy for the OAS:

The communist plan

On January 20 Palerm took over the effective head of the Department of Social Affairs which will comprise work in the following roles: community development, agrarian reform, education, labor, social security, cooperatives, general social aspects of housing. His aim is not to be successful in any of these fields. In land reform, he has a program which will take a long time, merely collecting a bibliography, buying books on the subject, and collecting statistics. He is well aware that this type of program ... will be blamed for sponsoring such inaction. In community development he intends to fail as other programs in this area have already failed ... because if the failure is well advertised the conclusion could be reached that institutions cannot be changed through persuasion and that the only system which is effective in improving levels of output and which means swift changes is the system of the Chinese communes. In the field of cooperatives he can advertise the so-called Cuban cooperatives which are in fact Government-controlled states.

In the field of labor he is going to pay attention to the problems of the urban labor force in Latin America under the pretense that there is where the communists are gaining power and where social program ought to be emphasized.

Controlling the budget of the Economic and Social Departments, of the Department of Technical Cooperation and of part of the Department of Cultural Affairs he has enough money to send agents of his own ideology disguised as experts in any of the Department's fields. He can, on the one hand, discredit the OAS and others, through his experts provoking unrest. Controlling the social programs or the Director of Social Affairs and the economic programs by default since no head of Economic Department has been appointed, controlling the granting of fellowships and professorships as well as other technical cooperation programs Palerm practically has in his hands half of the Organization of American State's budget. Controlling the Bureau of Personnel and the Fiscal Office he can hire personnel of his choice. At present the appointment of several Chilean communists, who are in Cuba advising Che Guevara, to the sensitive position of experts in fiscal conferences sponsored by OAS, ECLA, Interamerican Bank and Harvard Group.

Suggestions for action

The OAS is promoting Castro's [agenda] in the Continent [and it will continue to] unless Palerm and his group is removed from office. While he was Executive Secretary to a Secretary General it was practically impossible to remove the man who has the greatest confidence of S.G. Now that he is head of an inexistent Department, the U.S. could disapprove of the measure of splitting the Economic and Social Affairs Department into 2 Departments under the excuse that it needs a revision of the Charter, which it is true. If at the time the position of Director of Economic Affairs is still open and Palerm wants to be appointed to it the U.S could interfere on the grounds that he is not an economist. A better solution however, would be to appoint a truly politically conservative anti-communist as Director of Economic Affairs and at the due time suppress the Director of Social Affairs.

At this time and place it is not advisable to let any communist have a word in the OAS. Otherwise the Organization which budget is 60 percent paid by the U.S. will be financing communist activities in the Continent.[47]

A May 1965 FBI memo included an informer's statement claiming to have seen a letter written by Palerm in which he admitted to having been a member of the Communist Party from before the

Spanish Civil war until 1956, and that while no longer a communist, he is a socialist.[48]

An FBI informer reported that on May 3, 1965 Palerm

had been appointed as a special representative of the Secretary General of the Organization of American States, Jose Mora. The informant noted that the above was a move to downgrade Palerm within the OAS and place him in an "exile" position. The informant said it was the consensus at the Organization of American States that within two years Palerm would be eased out of that Organization completely.[49]

From 1965 to 1966, Palerm was Special Representative of the Secretary General of the OAS, working in several Latin American countries. Eric Wolf wrote in Palerm's *American Anthropologist* obituary that during this period, Palerm "was becoming increasingly disillusioned with the role of the United States in Latin American affairs, especially after United States intervention in the Dominican Republic," so he returned to Mexico, where he took up a professorship in anthropology at the Escuela Nacional de Anthropología e Historia—where he taught until resigning in 1969 in an act of solidarity with faculty fired during student protests.[50]

The final entries in Palerm's FBI file are brief communiques recording information gleaned from contacts within the State Department relating to Palerm visiting the United States to attend anthropological conferences—and a 1974 invitation for a visiting professorship at the University of Texas, Austin.[51]

CONCLUSIONS

It is significant that the FBI's investigations of Angel Palerm were undertaken in coordination with the U.S. Department of State, whose relationships with the OAS drove these investigations. In response to my FOIA requests, the Department of State released a few dozen pages of documents on Palerm.[52] Most of these chronicled State and FBI efforts to determine the extent of Palerm's contacts with or sympathies towards communists. These State Department records included correspondence between the State

Department and FBI, summaries of FBI investigations in Mexico not included in the released FBI records,[53] and a July 1961 letter from Emery J. Adams, Department of State's Office of Security to FBI Director Hoover expressing concerns that Palerm and another individual at the OAS were communists. One confidential 1965 report claimed to substantiate Palerm's high-level status within the Communist Party, and included an account by an OAS employee claiming Palerm said that during the Spanish Civil War he had been personally responsible for protecting a Spanish castle owned by the employee's family. The confidential memo argued that the rank of Chief of Staff required for such commands would have necessarily been held by a communist during the Civil War, and that when responding to such questions,

> Palerm showed the jacket of his Spanish War uniform—it had the three bars of a Captain. ▮▮▮▮▮▮ asked how he could have been Chief of Staff with that rank, Palerm said [he] had another mark of rank. ▮▮▮▮▮ says that such mark was Commissar badge, and that then it was possible for mere Captain to be C. of S.[54]

In response to my FOIA requests the CIA refused to release any records on Palerm.

Angel Palerm's FBI file demonstrates some of the ways the U.S. government investigated, monitored, and sought to control mid-twentieth century intellectuals involved in political activities and documents how the FBI tried to limit the political independence of America's southern neighbors. This is part of the FBI's long history of viewing normal forms of political maneuvering as conspiratorial or even criminal when undertaken by members of the political left. The FBI claimed Palerm used his position of authority to do things like set agendas, to favor specific proposals over others, or to reorganize the sections of the bureaucracy he oversaw. Each of these were within his administrative power, yet, because his work was interpreted by the FBI as essentially countering the Monroe or Truman Doctrines, these actions were viewed as so conspiratorial that the FBI encouraged his removal from power.

Like other veterans of the Spanish Civil War, his early engagement fighting fascism raised suspicions among FBI and State Department personnel.[55] Palerm's ongoing involvement in progressive causes stoked the FBI's interest in monitoring him for years to come. The FBI obsessed about whether Palerm was, or had been, a member of the Communist Party which led the Bureau to unearth conflicting records about his past and present sympathies and disdain for communism. While the FBI obsessed about these matters, Palerm's status as a possible Communist Party member mattered less to the FBI than the work he produced. One measure of this work was the sort of anger the FBI reported coming from Ambassador Mann who was outraged that Palerm's work reduced U.S. hemispheric hegemony.

The proper roles of the FBI in investigating the OAS or its staff members should have been very limited—as the host nation housing the OAS, the U.S. government took on specific responsibilities involving protecting OAS employees and of conducting some security-related activities pertaining to OAS properties and the organization itself. The Bureau was not officially authorized by OAS to undertake the political policing we find in Palerm's FBI files. But during the Cold War, the FBI understood its charge to include aggressively pursuing anyone thought to be influenced by communist or Marxist thought—and Palerm's efforts to limit U.S. control over the OAS intensified FBI concerns.

Like many other mid-twentieth century leftist intellectuals investigated by the FBI, the Bureau's interest in Angel Palerm was raised to the level of the sort of monitoring they undertook only because he was actively engaged in moving beyond theoretical Marxist critiques and attempting to try to change the world. That Angel Palerm merited this decade of extensive monitoring is a testament to his commitment to working for a better world which limited the role of U.S. intervention south of its borders.

19

The FBI's Pursuit of Saul Landau: Portrait of the Radical as a Young Man

Saul Landau was a prolific author, documentary filmmaker, and public intellectual—publishing 14 books, making 40 films, and serving as a fellow at the Institute for Policy Studies since 1972. He was a close friend of sociologist Cecil Wright Mills, helping Mills with his post-Cuban revolutionary experimental novel *Listen Yankee*, and traveling in Europe and the Soviet Union with Mills during the last year of Mills' life. He worked quickly, rapidly producing films on topics like Castro in Cuba, the Zapatistas in Mexico, the Cuban Five, or Brazilian torture, working at an accelerated pace, reaching audiences with timely critical information in a pre-internet age, where things like secret wars or bombing campaigns could still happen, and when Americans could still be shocked by such atrocities. He worked with Haskell Wexler (see Chapter 11) on several films, like *Paul Jacobs and the Nuclear Gang*, *The Sixth Sun: Mayan Uprising in Chiapas*, or *Brazil: A Report on Torture* under a symbiotic partnership that enhanced the work of both filmmakers.

When Saul Landau died in September 2013, America lost one of its brightest public intellectuals. After I filed a FOIA request with the FBI, the Bureau acknowledged significant file holdings on Landau totaling over 14,000 pages, but they have so far only released about 600 pages of his files. The CIA has not fully responded to my FOIA requests, and what few records they've made available are mostly copies of newspaper reports from their clipping files.[1]

These initial releases of his FBI files show the Bureau monitoring a young Saul Landau and present an intriguing portrait of a young radical coming of age as seen through the eyes of an oppressive governmental agency monitoring political analysis that challenged the narrow choices of mainstream American politics. The story arch within this FOIA release of Landau materials finds the FBI monitoring Landau as a student in the 1950s involved in what would become the roots of the New Left, with growing FBI concerns over his socialist critiques and support for the Cuban Revolution.

Landau emerged as an important critical public intellectual voice, a writer, investigative journalist, social critical, and filmmaker—changing public discourse on issues ranging from Cuba, the 1976 Washington DC assassination of former Chilean ambassador Orlando Letelier, and the CIA's covert war in Nicaragua. The earliest entries in his FBI file show him developing progressive political views as a student studying history and politics at the University of Wisconsin, Madison, earning his BA in 1957, and his MA in 1959.

THE YOUNG RADICAL

Landau's FBI file opened with a March 1956 report from Washington, DC FBI agents sent directly to FBI Director Hoover. These agents observed two men, one a "white male, 26–28 yrs., 5'8", 140 lbs., black hair" and "horn-rimmed glasses," the other a "negro male" entering the Soviet embassy, then emerging 16 minutes later, driving away in a 1954 Ford with Wisconsin plates registered to Saul Landau.[2] FBI investigations determined Landau was then enrolled at the University of Wisconsin. A campus FBI informer reported Landau had joined the Madison Chapter of the Labor Youth League (LYL).[3] Landau later recounted how he had been recruited for the LYL by Henry Wortis, a housemate in Madison who had left copies of the *Daily Worker*, *Masses and Mainstream*, *Political Affairs*, and the *Guardian* in the bathroom, and engaged Landau in political discussions.[4] Landau's time in the LYL was a formative period for him; he later reflected that

Once in the LYL, which was divided into cells so that an individual would know only the names of those few students in his own unit, I began to learn not only the ABCs of Marxism and Leninism but the basics of organizing in the political and cultural arenas. Secrecy was maintained because the party leadership believed at the time that McCarthyism was just a short step away from full-blown fascism and that therefore members of even the unofficial party youth organization had to be protected.[5]

A Milwaukee FBI agent reported on a 1955 letter to the editor of the *Daily Cardinal* written by Landau defending the LYL, in which he wrote that "the Attorney General and the Subversive Activities Control Board have proved nothing against the LYL except that the group does not go along with U.S. Government Policy." The FBI reported, "LANDAU further stated in references to the LYL, 'It is called subversive for what it says, for wanting to end segregation, establish arms control, live in peaceful co-existence, and study Marxism. These are not subversive acts. They are beliefs which don't conform to 'good American' views."[6]

FBI records listed Landau's name among Wisconsin citizens opposing a Subversion bill in the Senate Judiciary Committee, and the Bureau collected biographical information on Landau and his family; noting Landau's involvement in the National Student Association—a left-leaning national organization that would later be revealed as secretly coopted by the CIA at the national level; revelations of this would not be public until the publication of a 1967 *Ramparts* exposé.[7] Within a few months the FBI determined Landau and the unidentified Black male also observed entering the Soviet embassy had attended the Washington, DC NAACP convention, as representatives of their campus chapter. The FBI tried to determine which of the Black males traveling with Landau had entered the Soviet embassy.

For several months during 1956, a series of Kafkaesque FBI reports flowed between Washington and Madison trying to determine exactly how the Madison office knew Landau was affiliated with the LYL. Missing documents cast doubts on the sourcing of the agent's initial report, and the informer originally identified as saying Landau was a LYL member could not recall making this report; this led to an internal FBI investigation resulting in senior Special Agent Alexander D. Mason being disciplined for filing a mistaken report.[8] The FBI's report recommended censure and "administrative action be taken" for other identified failures. The FBI determined Landau was a member of the Wisconsin Student Peace Center.[9] The FBI's obsession with tracing the source of this information seems odd given the overall laxity of agents in such matters, including the common practice of inventing sources to support agent's hunches, even trolling names from cemeteries or phonebooks for names of fake informers—as described in former FBI agent Wesley Swearingen's memoir *FBI Secrets*.

While the FBI determined Landau was a member of the Wisconsin Student Peace Center, the Bureau's failure to confirm his LYL membership led to a rejection for a request to place Landau on the Security Index—the FBI's national list of subversives, who were to be monitored, and in the event of national emergencies, detained. At its height, the FBI's Security Index held the names of half a million Americans—including luminaries like Martin Luther King, Dorothy Day, Dalton Trumbo, Lillian Hellman, and James Baldwin. The Security Index became a register of visionary nonconformity, a monument to the FBI's foundational paranoia, and a muted proclamation of American un-Freedom.

The reliability of the FBI's initial report identifying him as a LYL member was not fundamentally different from other field reports from this period—perhaps more accurate than most, given that Landau *was* in fact an LYL member. Decades later, Landau described the high level of secrecy governing Madison LYL meetings, where members were organized in secretive cells because of Party concerns of government surveillance and fears of a coming crackdown. In an interview with Mathew Levin, Laudau later described elaborate ruses, where LYL campus leader Henry Wortis would "put on his trench coat, ask me to feed his dog if, for some reasons, he didn't get back in time, and then mysteriously leave the house often turning his head several times to check that no one was following him."[10]

Like many other U.S. university campus groups with ties to the Communist Party, the Madison campus branch of the LYL disbanded in 1956 following Khrushchev's revelations about Stalin. The campus Socialist Club soon rose in prominence for campus radicals, and sponsored campus talks and forums on political issues like U.S. interventions in Lebanon, Nixon's visit to Latin America, and the Cuban Revolution.

The Bureau's questions about Landau's LYL affiliation ended when Agent Mason filed a June 1959 report on Landau's activities in the Wisconsin Socialist Club; this report included details of Landau's attendance at the National Conference of American Socialists in Cleveland.[11] An FBI agent monitored Landau's campus talk at a forum sponsored by the Wisconsin Socialist Club, reporting that "a group of students gave extemporaneous speeches on the United States foreign policy with regard to the Lebanon situation. Several of the students were from Arab countries, and the Agents observed that some of the Arab students gathered together in a group around ███████████ another student who also spoke to the gathering." The FBI reported Landau discussing the "War Over China." In 1958, Landau was elected Chairman of the Wisconsin Socialist Club and he again attended the organization's National Conference.[12]

LANDAU AND CUBA

At a University of Wisconsin talk on October 30, 1960, the FBI learned Landau "had recently returned from a four month stay in Cuba, [and he] criticized the United States Department of State for such policies as a firm support of former dictator Batista and was markedly pro-Castro in his comments."[13] The FBI characterized Landau as a "prominent member" in the pro-Cuban advocacy group, Fair Play for Cuba, which was "beginning to create a stir across the nation."[14] Landau worked as an editor for the group's semi-monthly bulletin, and the FBI monitored his work organizing a trip taking groups of students to Cuba during the 1960 Christmas Break.

Because with hindsight we know that Fair Play for Cuba's most famous member would be Lee Harvey Oswald, reading these FBI files mentioning Fair Play for Cuba and Landau creates a growing tension, as dates of FBI reports count down towards the date of Kennedy's assassination, November 22, 1963.

In early 1961, the Bureau grew increasingly concerned that Landau may have moved to New York City and rented a room under the name of David Eakins.[15] After further investigation, the FBI determined Eakins was a student from Madison who worked with Landau in the Fair Play for Cuba group.

In his roles as editor of the Madison-based publication *Studies on the Left*, Landau was at the forefront of a wave of new political expression emerging to form what would become the New Left. Landau's involvement with *Studies on the Left* coincided with the rise in prominence of the publication and his interest in Cuba helped focus new attention on the revolutionary changes there. Mathew Levin later described the excitement of this moment:

> The excitement about Cuba in Madison and throughout the American left was reflected in *Studies'* decision to devote its entire third issue to the revolution and to print twelve thousand copies, more than three times the number for the first and second issues but still not enough to satisfy demand. Brushing aside concerns about the nationalization of American property and the threat of communism, concerns that had led American policymakers to quickly turn against Castro, the editors high-lighted their enthusiasm for the revolution, portraying it as a movement for freedom and an attempt to create a "humane society." "These revolutions," the editors wrote of the revolution-ary movements in the third world, including Cuba, "were not created by devils; they arose in fulfillment of the long-held aspi-rations of the hungry people of the world." In other words, the Cuban Revolution and other third world revolutions, despite official American opposition, were essentially just. Following Williams's lead again, the editors rejected a central foundation of American foreign policy, that American power was ultimately beneficial to the rest of the world. Their criticism of American power, or what Williams called "empire," meant an alternative perspective on revolution in Cuba and elsewhere in the world.[16]

Landau helped establish *Studies* as a leading outlet for campus free speech movements arising on American college campuses in the coming decade. Following Landau's vision, the third issue of *Studies on the Left* was an expanded issue devoted exclusively to the Cuban Revolution and Castro's efforts to address poverty.[17]

C. WRIGHT MILLS

Landau met American sociologist C. Wright Mills in Cuba in 1960. The two hit it off right away and Landau soon became the key interlocutor shaping Mills' understanding of Cuba. Mills' political critique had been building to a crescendo the previous few years, with his works on *The Sociological Imagination* and *The Power Elite* exposing how capitalism undercut American democracy. Working at a frenetic pace, Mills quickly cranked out a novel, *Listen Yankee*, describing positive changes in Cubans' lives following Castro's revolution.

Mills and Landau began working intensely together. In June 1961, the FBI learned of Mills and Landau's plans to travel together to England, Yugoslavia, Poland, and the Soviet Union, and "according to [an] informant, Landau was supposed to be helping Mills write a book" and the FBI learned Mills and Landau would "attend a Cuban Rally to be held in London."[18] In an effort to track Landau and Mills' travels, the FBI checked with New York American Express offices to see if travelers checks had been issued, but they failed to identify the purchase of any travelers checks. In July 1961, a postal carrier in Madison reported to the FBI that someone known to Landau [identity redacted] received a postcard mailed by Landau from Germany.[19]

Mills' years of hard living, manic writing binges, fast motorcycles, drinking, and smoking led to a serious heart attack at only age 44. This heart attack caused him to consider leaving his professorship at Columbia University for a position in England. Mills and Landau set out for Europe, stopping off in the USSR to see if Soviet doctors could offer Mills better medical options than he had received from American doctors. Landau accompanied Mills, traveling as his secretary.[20]

Landau later published an account in *Ramparts* of these travels, describing Mills' dissatisfaction with American liberalism and American universities, and writing that Mills had hoped the Soviet medical system could treat his heart condition—which would kill him, at age 45, half a year later. Landau captured Mills' critical approach to all social life, writing that while impressed with Soviet progress in some areas, on his last night in the USSR, Mills toasted a group of Party leaders, lifting his glass saying, "here is to the day when the complete works of Trotsky are published and widely distributed in the Soviet Union." His hosts were not amused.[21]

In the fall of 1961, the FBI learned Landau had written to the Passport Office requesting clearance to travel to Cuba on behalf of C. Wright Mills and Ballantine Books, "to gather facts and documents for defense of court actions" from Amadeo Barletta's lawsuit against Ballantine Books and C. Wright Mills.[22] Barletta's suit sought $50 million in libel damages, claiming that Mills' character in his novel *Listen Yankee* was clearly identifiable as him. Barletta had owned 42 radio and television stations in Cuba, and the suit claimed that Mills made false and damaging clams that Barletta was connected to the Dominican Republic's Generalissimo Rafael Trujillo and with organized crime before being ousted by the Castro regime.[23] The United States had no interest in helping Mills by allowing Landau to travel to Cuba to search for documents or testimony supporting Mills' depiction of Barletta as a crook, and his passport application was denied.

EARLY 1960S SAN FRANCISCO

The FBI tracked Landau's October 1961 move from Madison to San Francisco, noting Landau's work as a social worker.[24] The FBI's interest in Landau intensified, and a June 15, 1962 memo from SAC, San Francisco informed Hoover that Landau was being removed from the FBI's Reserve Index and was being placed on the FBI's Security Index.[25] Once placed on the Security Index, the FBI's monitoring increased, and his file shows the FBI monitoring his public talks. This monitoring included things like a Secret memo about a KPFA radio broadcast where the FBI reported Landau said that "U.S. congressmen foam at the mouth 'like rabid dogs' in their obsession to invade Cuba."[26]

A late 1962 document marks how quickly shifts in political consciousness can occur with social movements. With no inkling of the radical changes coming to American university campuses in just a few years, Landau's FBI file shows him, in 1962, worried about the conservative politics of American university students. The FBI reported that when speaking at an event sponsored by the

National Guardian, Landau said that he had spoken about developments in Cuba, and that "he said he found the hatred in the eyes of the students and felt that they wanted to lynch him. He stated many educators fear that the right wing is gaining control of the universities."[27]

A June 11, 1963 FBI memo listed Landau as a witness at upcoming proposed open hearings of the House Committee on Un-American Activities (HUAC), slated for a special Los Angeles hearing the following month.[28] Landau was to be subpoenaed by HUAC to testify about his contacts with Cuba in a proposed Open Hearing in Los Angeles or possibly San Francisco.[29]

The FBI appeared increasingly concerned that Landau planned to travel again to Cuba, even though such travel was now forbidden by the U.S. government. An update in his Security Index file shows the FBI monitoring his remarks at the July 16, 1963 public meeting of the Bay Area Opposition (BAO) group. The FBI reported that Landau

spoke concerning the Cuban situation with particular reference to the 59 students who had recently visited Cuba for the purpose of testing the law banning their travel. He described the ban as immoral and a restriction of the individual's freedom to travel. He suggested that the students be met at the airport and a reception be held in their honor. He further felt that a series of speeches throughout the country by these students would be enlightening. He further brought forth the idea that on the day of their return or shortly thereafter to have one of their number go to the passport office of the State Department and pay the $10.00 required for a visa to Cuba and at the same time have pickets posted outside the building with banners on the travel restrictions. Source advised that these ideas were presented to those present and voted on in the affirmative and that the Subject then picked several persons to head the committees charged with implementing his ideas.[30]

The FBI increasingly monitored Landau's movements. A September 1963 coded FBI Cablegram from the U.S. embassy in Mexico City to Director Hoover reported that Landau has been in Mexico City several months and plans to leave for Cuba in the near future to teach English literature and political science at University of Havana ... Source advised [in] September 24 [telegram] that subject has left Mexico to return to San Francisco briefly to wind up affairs, after which he will return to Mexico and proceed to Cuba.[31]

As the FBI intensified Landau's surveillance, J. Edgar Hoover wrote to the FBI's San Francisco Special Agent in Charge, expressing his desire that Landau be arrested on felony charges upon his next return from Cuba.[32] After establishing that Landau's passport had been stamped that it was invalid for travel to Cuba and other communist countries, one FBI report stated that:

Inasmuch as this subject reportedly intends to travel to Cuba in the near future, the San Francisco Office and Legal Attaché, Mexico City, should make every effort to develop all admissible evidence which would tend to prove the subject violated Section 1185 (b), Title I, United States Code, in the event he travels to Cuba. In this connection the Department has previously advised that in order to sustain a successful prosecution, the Government must prove the following:

1. Subject did not have a validated passport for travel to Cuba
2. The place of subject's departure and return to the United States
3. Evidence that he did, in fact, enter Cuba
4. Evidence of subject's intention to travel to Cuba at the time he departed from the United States
5. The subject had knowledge of passport restrictions for such travel at the time he departed

In this connection it is noted that records of the Passport Office, Department of State, reveal that Landau by letter dated 2-1-61 requested that his passport be validated for travel to Cuba and by letter dated 2-20-61 the Passport Office refused Landau's request.

The San Francisco Office should immediately ascertain the subject's current whereabouts in the San Francisco area and be sufficiently cognizant of his whereabouts in order that you may know when he departs for Mexico City. Your sources and informants should be alerted, particularly panel sources who could possibly testify concerning the possible travel of this subject, and every investigative technique of an admissible nature should be utilized to definitely develop a possible violation in the event this subject's travel is consummated. San Francisco Office should make every effort to provide the Bureau with advance information of the subject's travel to Mexico in order that the Legal Attaché, Mexico City, may be appropriately advised.[33]

The FBI arranged for one of Landau's neighbors to report his movements to the FBI. This neighbor reported Landau had not mentioned leaving San Francisco, and she assured the FBI she would promptly notify the Bureau if Landau left town.[34] The FBI monitored airline flights,[35] and in mid-October the Bureau monitored the mail at Laudau's home address.[36] Throughout the fall of 1963, the FBI was convinced Landau was about to travel to Cuba, but he remained in San Francisco and the FBI was not able to fulfill its plan of arresting and prosecuting him as he returned from Cuba. It is possible that news of Lee Harvey Oswald's connections to Fair Play for Cuba led Landau to suspect the likelihood that travel to Cuba was increasingly being monitored.

Two years later, on December 14, 1965, J. Edgar Hoover sent a confidential memo "concerning Presidential protection" to the Secret Service claiming that Saul Landau could present a danger to the safety of the President of the United States. Hoover filled out a form claiming that his concerns were raised, "because background is potentially dangerous; or has been identified as member or participant in communist movement; or has been under active investigation as member of other group organization inimical to U.S." and he designated Landau fell under the category of "Subversives, ultrarights, racist and fascists who met" the checked criteria of making "expressions of strong or violent anti-U.S. sentiment."[37]

It is difficult to interpret this as anything other than J. Edgar Hoover using another governmental agency to harass Landau. With this backhanded passive aggressive gesture, Hoover outsourced Landau's harassment to another governmental agency. Hoover wasn't stupid. He knew Landau posed no threat to the President's life, but with the assassination of Kennedy, Oswald's prominence in the Fair Play for Cuba group provided an easy form of remote harassment for Hoover to arrange. Hoover sent an identical Secret Service alert the following year, on November 15, 1966.

A March 1967 State Department report summarized Landau's past passport applications, including a 1965 attempt to travel to Cuba as one of three *Ramparts* reporters. These past passport application materials included his 1951 efforts to travel to Cuba to gather documents for C. Wright Mills' lawsuit, and this 1965 attempt as a *Ramparts* reporter. This report reproduced quotes from a letter from the Bureau of Security and Consular Affairs, U.S. Department of State from July 8, 1965 to (redacted) at *Ramparts* writing:

> in April you requested a passport endorsement for your ▮▮▮▮▮▮▮▮▮▮▮ to travel to Cuba on a similar news assignment which the Department subsequently authorized. In May, you requested that Saul Irwin Landau of your news staff be granted a validated passport for travel to Cuba on a like news assignment. Mr. Landau's application is presently pending. In your letter of June 21st, you say: "Rather than rely on others, I felt it incumbent upon myself as publisher and editor-in-chief, to take on the assignment." Does this mean that you will be replacing ▮▮▮▮▮▮ and Landau? Or is it your intention to travel to Cuba in addition to them, thereby assigning three Ramparts representatives to Cuba this summer for quite similar stories? The File bears the notation that Bureau of Security and Consular Affairs was advised on July 16, 1965, that Landau would not be going to Cuba and his application was withdrawn.[38]

In August 1967 Landau traveled with a KQED television documentary crew to Cuba, via Mexico City, to produce a film under a contract from National Educational Television on life in Cuba. The FBI consulted its records for background information on the documentary crew, noting that one of them had subscribed to the *National Guardian*. Someone at KQED, San Francisco's PBS station, told the FBI that Landau and others from the station left

San Francisco on July 14 on the way to Mexico City where they would then fly to Cuba, adding that "the occasion of the trip is KQED having received a contract from National Educational Television in New York to do a documentary on Cuban life."[39] The FBI searched its files for derogatory information on any of the crew on this trip, and listed gathered information on subversive publications to which some individuals subscribed. An FBI AIRTEL memo updated Hoover with a report based on a confidential informant providing information on Landau's travel to Cuba, and reported that "an F-1 stop has been placed with INS for [Landau's] return to the United States," and the FBI monitored flights between Mexico City and San Francisco, searching for Landau.[40] The FBI reported on Landau and the KQED crew's return to the United States from Cuba trip, via Mexico City on August 11, 1967. One KQED crew member told the FBI that

the filming done in Cuba was primarily concerned with the effects of the Cuban revolution on the peasant people of Cuba. He said that the filming crew was only denied the filming of military installations and were otherwise given a free hand as to what they wanted to photograph.

[The FBI informer] stated that the filming crew ran into no problems as far as getting to Cuba except some legal ramifications experienced in Mexico City. He said that the return trip earlier scheduled from Cuba to Spain and then to New York was only an alternate plan should entanglements be experienced as far as returning to the United States via Mexico City.[41]

On September 19, 1967, an INS inspector at LAX reported Saul Landau's arrival on a flight from Mexico City.[42]

The FBI monitored Landau's remarks at a UC Berkeley Stop the Draft Week rally, where he "urged the demonstrators to confront the Oakland Police Department" the following day, when demonstrators blocked the Oakland Induction Center.[43]

In December 1967, the FBI sent memos alerting agents of a Cultural Congress to be held the following month in Havana, featuring leftist artists, authors, and scientists from around the world. Among the listed Americans thought to be attending were

Paul Sweezy and Leo Huberman (both of the *Monthly Review*), and Saul Landau.[44] After Landau attended the Cultural Congress as a U.S. Delegate, one FBI agent argued that "Mr. Landau may have violated the affidavit he signed enabling him to go to Cuba as a 'professional reporter.'"[45] While Landau was kept on the Security Index, no move was made to prevent him from returning to Cuba that June to work on a KQED TV documentary.[46]

A series of September 1968 FBI Confidential memos reported that while Landau had traveled from Mexico to Havana on May 24, 1968, and had returned to the United States, one U.S. citizen, identity redacted, traveling with Landau had not returned to the United States.[47] The FBI tracked when Landau was scheduled to take his annual vacations, and during the summer of 1969 the FBI speculated he would likely try and enter Cuba with his month of accumulated summer leave from KQED; which he did, leaving the United States for Cuba on July 4, 1969.[48] The FBI noted that Landau's passport had only been endorsed in 1968, for a single round trip to Cuba, a trip which Landau had completed the previous year, but still the FBI took no action.[49]

In May 1970, a citizen-informer wrote J. Edgar Hoover a two-page letter, with a copy of a newspaper story appearing in *The Carletonian*, the student newspaper of Carleton College, to report that Landau and Professor Carl Weiner were spreading subversive ideas on American college campuses.[50] The letter's author, an employee of Caldwell Company of Sioux City, Iowa, nostalgically recalled having alerted Director Hoover, back in 1946, of campus activities on Carleton's campus organized by the American Youth for Democracy when they denounced the fascist dictator Francisco Franco.

In the spring of 1970, the FBI learned of the formation of the Center for Cuban Studies in New York City, and speculated that the Center might "be in violation of registration requirements if it is not registered with the Department of Justice," claiming that it was "a semi-official agency of [the] Cuban Government."[51] The FBI determined that eight out of eleven of the Center's Board of Trustees were subjects of FBI investigations. While this entry is partially redacted, these eight individuals under FBI investigation were described as:

- A (male) member of Stanford University's Department of Political Science.[52]
- (male) Playwright, Department of Drama, Columbia University.
- Saul Landau, filmmaker and author.
- A woman who was a member of the Polytechnic Institute of Brooklyn, Department of Social Science.[53]
- [Anthropologist Oscar Lewis, whose identity is redacted, but the FBI file number matches his file.] A male from the University of Illinois,[54] who was then "in Cuba working under a three-year Ford Foundation grant on follow up to study he made of Cuba families in 1946."
- [Lee Lockwood] Journalist and author from Boston. Wrote a 1967 book *Castro's Cuba, Cuba's Fidel: An American Journalist's Inside Look at Today's Cuba*. "The author's conclusions set forth at end of book pretend to be impartial and objective. Overall effect of the book is to picture Castro as benevolent savior whose ties with international communism are merely accidental." The book comprises interviews with Castro.
- Male, author, internationally famous author working on a book on Cuba. "Was removed from Security Index in 1956."[55]
- From University of Wisconsin.[56] Was secretary for Fair Play for Cuba Committee in 1961, 1965 advisor to University of Wisconsin Socialist Club.

Three other members of the Board were identified as not having FBI files; these individuals had affiliations with Random House, E.P. Dutton, and the *New York Review of Books*.

There are indirect artifacts in Landau's FBI file marking the end of Hoover's FBI reign. These records indicate shifts in emphasis such as the FBI's February 1972 monitoring of Landau boarding a February 18, 1972 flight from Mexico City to Havana, Cuba,[57] and a trail of memos a year and a half later, showing FBI policies shifting in the wake of Hoover's death, as criteria for placing U.S. citizens on the ADEX Index came under review. Landau was finally removed from the Index in August 1973.[58]

Without explanation, the FBI inserted a "deleted page information sheet" in these released records, reporting that 208 pages of

FBI documents were deleted at some undisclosed date. The next page of documents in this release is from January 22, 2009, 36 years later, and is a highly redacted "Secret" document indicating that "a separate investigation should be opened on each member of a Group under investigation, as well as on the Group itself," with no indication of what this group is.[59] Large sections of pages are redacted, but an identifying paragraph summarizing Landau reads:

(S) LANDAU works as an analyst for the Cuba-L Direct project. This project was started in 1986 by Nelson VALDES ████████████, and it is headquartered at the University of New Mexico. The objective of the Cuba-L Direct Project, aka Latin American Database (LADB) or the Electronic Information Collaboration Project, is to foster two-way information exchange between information providers in the United States and Cuba. LANDAU co-authored an article titled "Why the U.S. must help Cuba" with VALDES.[60]

These 2009 documents record the FBI increasingly relying on the open source intelligence offered by the internet for its surveillance. The collected records were on par with those that could be collected by the average 15-year-old Google-stalking hobbledehoy, with collected records of: Landau's California DMV records, photo and fingerprint (from California Department of Motor Vehicles website, January 28, 2009), car registrations, lists of Landau's writings, his website's address, email address, photocopies of book catalog copy of his books and films, Landau's Wikipedia entry (print out dated November 19, 2008), an AOL White Pages listing of his Alameda, California, home address and phone number, a web article by him on Venezuela and Cuba, and a 24-page detailed listing of Landau publications printed off the Transnational Institute's webpages.[61] The web simplified the collection of these materials documenting the public life of this public intellectual, but the FBI also increasingly used third party subscription resources, like Lexus/Nexus.

This period also records the FBI using less public means to monitor Landau. The San Francisco FBI office wrote to the Airlines Reporting Corporation (ARC) of Arlington, Virginia, requesting records of Landau's travel—referred to by the FBI as "requesting ARC Compass search for travel records."[62] ARC is a privately held business that provides escrow services for air travel ticket purchases, connecting travel agencies, airlines, and customers. ARC was founded in 1985, and is owned by nine airlines,[63] and four decades later it completed over $100 billion in transactions a year. The FBI's use of ARC to track the movements of American citizens shows one of the ways the FBI (and other intelligence agencies) increasingly piggybacks on the mechanisms of private industry's corporate data mining and surveillance for the FBI's governmental uses.

In 2009, FBI agents also undertook physical surveillance of Landau's Alameda apartment, noting that his building was surrounded by chain link fences with gated entrances, and that "within the parking area is a dumpster for the residents to dispose of their trash."[64] The FBI printed out 25 pages from the online edition of the *New Mexico Daily Lobo*, which included a listing on the site's calendar of the "Exhibit and Lectures Mark the 50th Anniversary of Cuban Revolution," which included the Saturday April 4th event, "Fidel and the Fiftieth: Film and Lecture on legacy of Cuban Revolution" featuring Landau's film, and talks by Nelson P. Valdes and Saul Landau.[65] A San Francisco FBI memo indicated that "FBI Albuquerque is planning on conducting surveillance of the event" on the University of New Mexico campus.[66] In June 2009, the FBI issued an order to place Landau on the Customs and Border Patrol's lookout list.[67] After this flurry of FBI monitoring activity in 2009, and a final, highly redacted FBI entry from July 30, 2009, the released FBI records on Saul Landau end.

In 2015, the FBI admitted identifying another 14,000 pages of files that they would process, but these records have yet to be released. Like many of the hundreds of FBI files I have read, these initial releases of FBI files document the narrowness of allowed political dissent in America, with narrative records depicting America's secret police's efforts to criminalize the human right of free movement, dissent from international policies, and advocacy for new approaches to democratic change.

But the knowledge that the state put such concentrated efforts into tracking his movements, work, and views could not have been surprising to Saul Landau. He understood the nature of struggle, and this knowledge did not slow him down or discourage his advancement; if anything, it was oxygen for the fire that burned within him and moved him to describe and confront the corruptions of power, and beacons of resistance that marked the times in which he lived.

Conclusion: Unbroken Chain— Connecting Seven Decades of American Surveillance and Harassment of Progressive Activists, Visionaries, and Intellectuals

The preceding surveillance vignettes document recurrent historical patterns in which federal agencies selectively monitored and harassed individuals believed to be threatening fundamental elements of the American way of life. It is vital that we consider what the threat was that these agencies believed these individuals presented. Most of these chapters document the FBI or others monitoring individuals challenging elements of America's system of stratification. In some instances, these forms of stratification involve: economic stratification, racial stratification, the differential power held by the military-industrial complex, union power, or American global hegemony. These surveillance campaigns inform us not only of the historical significance of political surveillance and harassment of American progressives, but they demonstrate a significant recurrent pattern in which the FBI historically protected America's dominant power formations from those who would organize to challenge the status quo. The individuals challenging the status quo came under surveillance because the FBI viewed this political surveillance as a routine feature of its institutional charge. These political surveillance operations became normal features of Bureau culture, and forms of political surveillance remain a constant element of FBI culture. They also inform us about the power and significance of activism.

Much of the information in these FBI files from past eras was collected without our internet age's capacity to constantly track and assess associations, readings, purchases, and desires. In today's new surveillance normal, the state's ability to monitor movements, reading habits, political expressions, and affiliations in real time or after the fact makes irrelevant many of the clumsy and labor-intensive methods described in these chapters on FBI history. And while some of these historical methods are now irrelevant, the uses to which such data collected by the surveillance state are put remain constant. The importance of the history recounted here has less to do with the ways and means of surveillance, than it does with the ongoing *desires* of the surveillance states and the atavistic trajectories the FBI and other agencies continue to follow as they monitor activists, public intellectuals, and others challenging the dominant political economic systems of the United States. These files show the roots of these intelligence desires; roots which continue to grow new surveillance operations that differ more in capacity and means than they do in fundamental desires to monitor and control.

Obviously, institutions can and sometimes do change. In some significant ways, the FBI of the 1950s is not the FBI in the 2020s; in other ways, little has changed. The Bureau is demonstrably more diverse, Bureau agents are no longer predominantly just the white men of the mid-twentieth century FBI, and some of the illegal practices of Hoover's FBI no longer routinely occur. The make-up of the FBI is certainly more inclusive than it was 70 years ago. Yet the fundamental alignment of the Bureau's investigatory priorities in some ways betrays a significant continuity with the past. While the FBI no longer focuses its attentions on suspected communists the same way as it did during the 1950s, many of these same attitudes and suspicions are now directed at environmentalist groups, animal rights groups, anti-war groups, and anti-corporate groups. While the personnel making up the FBI have become more inclusive and representative of America, but when the Bureau is viewed as a law enforcement agency devoted to protecting the reign of American corporate capitalism—which in the 1950s, communists and others hoped to disrupt, and in the twenty-first century the Occupy Movement and Land Protectors hoped to disrupt—significant streams of institutional continuity can be identified. Old agencies monitor new groups threatening power structures in new and old ways.

Historically, the FBI has interpreted its obligations to protect and serve as aligned with protecting some Americans and some American values over others. During the Jim Crow era, this meant protecting the color line, and those who challenged these racist conventions frequently found themselves under surveillance, either as accused communists or fellow travelers. This was an era when those working to dismantle racist institutions benefiting the few at the expense of the many came under surveillance. The FBI has historically protected American inequality; protecting the continued functioning of American capitalism over the rights of people striving to build a system that puts human needs over the needs of markets. This has long been an implicit feature of policing in America, but the FBI's ability to operate under a veil of secrecy across the country helped spread the sort of surveillance campaigns targeting activists recounted here.

The past documented and analyzed in this book is not *just* the past. In many ways this past sets the stage for the present and future political engagements and can instruct us on some of what we can expect in future American political struggles. Among the generalizations and themes that connect this past with present surveillance operations are: new surveillance technologies will be used to achieve similar ends; the political left is monitored significantly more than the political right; activism matters; once individuals becomes a surveillance target, data collection snowballs; it is often difficult to know what surveillance is happening at the time it occurs.

I briefly comment on these themes below and add some analysis connecting what we know about this past to what we can anticipate in present and future surveillance systems.

NEW SURVEILLANCE TECHNOLOGIES WILL BE USED IN SIMILAR WAYS

As the internet of things grows and becomes increasingly ubiquitous, new forms of surveillance we cannot now imagine will develop in tandem with these new technologies and media birthed by it. While trying to predict coming technological developments is always a dodgy business, the advent of new ways to fuse new technologies into our bodies seems as inevitable as it is invasive, and whatever the forms these new developments take, they will bring new invasions and means of monitoring and tracking those challenging the basic political economic order and power relations of society.

Speculating on unknowable technological features of future surveillance operations is less productive than commenting on how particulars of political economy determine which groups will be targeted by surveillance campaigns designed to monitor and limit their political actions. We know that states monitor their people in ways that make them visible and potentially malleable for the needs of state; and while socialist, communist, and capitalist cultures have historically developed surveillance apparatus to monitor deviant individuals or groups threatening to the social order, the particulars of deviant behavior in a given society can vary significantly. While the extent to which these activities threaten a given political economy vary, when these activities threaten the economic order of a given society they tend to be subject to surveillance and harassment. We can expect that whatever changes new technologies bring, this basic dynamic will remain.

The history of U.S. surveillance by the FBI and other agencies indicates that they conduct surveillance on groups trying to disrupt significant features of American political economy. Insofar as the basic tenets of fascism do not oppose principles of free market capitalism, it should not be surprising that fascist groups receive less surveillance and harassment than do socialist, communist, or even labor organizing groups. Similarly, as the U.S. economy is increasingly tied to industries linked to militarization and production of war goods, those who advocate anti-war or demilitarization positions, such as Seymour Melman, can be expected to come under surveillance. To the extent that groups or individuals protesting things like racism, gender discrimination, sexual orientation, and other forms of bias disrupt the flow of the U.S. economy, we can expect these people to be disproportionately subjected to surveillance and other forms of monitoring. These general patterns of the ways that past surveillance trends have been linked to political economy, targeting those who would disrupt a given stratified order, allow us to generally understand how coming surveillance campaigns will likely focus on those who challenge the dominant power systems, especially those favoring elites benefiting from these power relationships. While the forms of surveillance should be expected to change with developments of new technologies, these fundamental positions within the relations of production, and efforts to alter them, can be expected to remain similarly aligned, regardless of what technological developments are coming, so long as the basic formations of American capitalism remain in place.

THE POLITICAL LEFT IS MONITORED SIGNIFICANTLY MORE THAN THE POLITICAL RIGHT

The FBI has historically monitored and harassed individuals and groups from progressive and radical leftist political groups at levels significantly exceeding the Bureau's monitoring or harassment of right-wing domestic political groups. While the FBI has periodically investigated Nazis, neo-Nazis, the Klu Klux Klan, and other white supremacist and fascist groups and members of these groups, these investigations have been more usually tied to specific incidents under FBI investigation than they have been the sort of free-ranging ongoing campaigns documented in this book.

Put another way: given the FBI's institutional commitment to protecting capitalism as a way of life, it has historically not investigated pro-capitalist fascist organizations with the same ferocity it has investigated organizations with alleged or real ties to socialism or communism; or even more mainstream groups interested in reforming elements of American capitalism. White supremacists historically have had few fundamental complaints with capitalism itself (though adherents are prone to imagine Jewish capitalist conspiracies) and given law enforcement's racist practices, there have been ongoing alignments between white supremacists and law enforcement. While Hoover's FBI reluctantly investigated some atrocities such as the 1964 murder of James Chaney, Andrew Goodman, and Michael Schwerner, given COINTELPRO's widespread FBI surveillance and harassment of civil rights campaigners, such FBI investigations were by comparison rare and less significant than the Bureau's investigations of activists supporting racial equality.

As recently as 2019, FBI documents established that rather than primarily investigating the Klu Klux Klan, the Bureau was investigating U.S. civil rights groups protesting neo-Nazi groups.[1] These documents record the FBI investigating the California activist group, By Any Means Necessary (aka, Bamn), as a group possibly engaging in a "'conspiracy' against the 'rights' of the Ku Klux Klan and white supremacists."[2] Despite the KKK's long history as a terrorist organization, the FBI, as Levin observed, "considered the KKK as victims and the leftist protesters as potential terror threats and downplayed the threats of the Klan, writing: 'The KKK consisted of members that some perceived to be supportive of the white supremacist agenda.'"[3] Bamn's activism against police brutality was included as "evidence in the terrorism inquiry."[4] While disturbing, given the FBI's historical deep anti-leftist institutional practices, none of this should be surprising—and it of course raises serious questions about the Bureau's failures to investigate domestic fascistic hate groups.

Questions remain concerning whether the degree to which the political alignment with basic supporting tenants of American capitalism and new-right fascist groups like QAnon, the Proud Boys, Oath Keepers, or The Three Percenters will shield them from the same sorts of FBI surveillance and intimidation visited upon radical leftist individuals and groups whose views run so counter to capitalism. That some police officers privately belong to these fascistic groups further discounts the likelihood of disruptive monitoring.[5]

Still, the fact that historically U.S. surveillance campaigns have been launched or overseen by both Republican and Democratic presidents takes on increased significance following the January 2021 insurrection against the U.S. Congress, led by then President Donald Trump. Following this attack there were increased calls from the American left to use the FBI and other U.S. intelligence agencies to monitor and prosecute violent right wingers. Questions of whether the FBI and other branches of law enforcement should conduct surveillance on domestic fascist groups are answered differently by American civil libertarians, which champion civil rights over other concerns, and by those whose anti-fascism overrides these worries. Given the court's historical record in turning a blind eye to egregious violations of laws when the government spies on dissidents, we cannot necessarily expect the courts to sort this out, unless the American courts', after decades of Republican court stacking, alignment with fascist values brings sympathetic protections.

Recognizing this recurrent pattern of surveillance disproportionately targeting individuals on the left helps us consider how current and emerging forms of surveillance will likely be used by the FBI and other law enforcement agencies, who remain embedded within political economic formations and bureaucratic institutions tied to the surveillance episodes recounted here.

ACTIVISM MATTERS

One major lesson to be learned from these FBI files is simply that activism matters. As these records show, it matters so much that the U.S. government spent incredible energy and resources to monitor and try to confound those trying to change the world. This is a simple but important lesson.

While the causes that progressive activists pursue will change, as long as they continue to expose and challenge powerful forces aligned with dominant power structures, we can assume activists will be under surveillance in the sort of selective and harassing ways examined here. When researching the FBI's surveillance of American anthropologists during the 1950s McCarthy period, I found significant differences in the FBI's interest in various leftist anthropologists. Some of these anthropologists were far more interested in the epistemological dimensions of Karl Marx to *understand* the world, while those who were actively involved in trying to *change* the world came under much more intense surveillance and more frequently found themselves facing unemployment as their activism led to appearance before McCarthyistic headings.[6] Further, there were lots of anthropologists who really had no connections to Marx, communism, or socialism, who were accused of being communists simply for agitating for racial equality during the 1940s and 1950s. It was their efforts to change the world that brought them trouble, and no matter how much the technology and specific dynamics of American culture change, when these efforts to bring change threaten capitalism and the power elite, we can expect monitoring campaigns to be launched against those fighting the powers that be.

If these efforts to try and change the world, challenging the inequality of the day didn't matter, the FBI would never have devoted so much time and energy to monitoring, harassing, and trying to undermine these activists.

OCCUPY WALL STREET

From its earliest days in September 2011 in New York City, the Occupy Wall Street movement was monitored by police, and soon local police departments across the country and the FBI began monitoring Occupy encampments and meetings, and soon agent provocateurs appeared. In one incident in May 2012 in San Francisco, an Occupy march was hijacked by "clean cut, athletic, commanding" individuals wearing brand new outfits costuming them to look like members of the "black bloc" as they led the march while trying to incite violence.[7]

As the Occupy Wall Street movement developed, the FBI intensified surveillance of individuals and groups associated with these protests. Following established historical patterns, the FBI investigated individuals they believed to be leaders of this essentially leaderless movement, and the FBI used informers to compile files detailing activities, speeches, participants, and ideological developments and splits within the movement.[8] The FBI used this intelligence to coordinate crackdowns and arrests at Occupy encampments and private homes of activists across the country. Documents released by The Partnership for Civil Justice Fund demonstrate how police departments and the Department of Homeland Security worked cooperatively with banks as they targeted citizens peacefully protesting the damage being caused by these very financial institutions. Through such acts, the FBI fulfilled its traditional role as domestic intelligence collator; collecting, sifting, and organizing information on individuals and groups threatening the status quo economic order.

During the Occupy Movement's earliest months, the Department of Homeland Security asked local offices to gather information on "Peaceful Activist Demonstrations, in addition to reporting on domestic terrorist acts and 'significant criminal activity.'" Beginning in August 2011, FBI agents met with "the New York Stock Exchange to discuss the Occupy Wall Street protests that wouldn't start for another month. By September, prior to the start of the OWS, the FBI was notifying businesses that they might be the focus of an OWS protest."[9] Some of the surveillance of Occupy Movement protestors occurred at anti-terrorist "Fusions Centers" that were established with funds provided by the Department of Homeland Security across the United States to coordinate intelligence on developments that could possibly be linked to terrorist activities. Journalist Michael Isikoff determined that while Boston police's counterterror intelligence unit was devoting millions of dollars of surveillance resources monitoring the Boston Occupy Movement, they ignored two warnings concerning the likelihood of coming violence by Boston Marathon bomber Tamerlan Tsarnaev.[10] While spying on the legal protest activities of Occupy protesters, the police ignored tips about Tsarnaev.

A report issued by the group Rights and Dissent described a series of raids coordinated by the FBI and local police forces designed to intimidate and weaken protest organizers. The report found evidence that:

> The FBI and other law enforcement agencies conducted preventative actions in cities throughout the United States. Some were wholly unnecessary: "The FBI's Indianapolis division released a 'Potential Criminal Activity Alert' on September 15, 2011, even though they acknowledged that no specific protest date had been scheduled in Indiana," the PCJF report states. Other actions were entirely misplaced: the Richmond, Virginia FBI communicated information about the local OWS protest to the Joint Terrorism Task Force. The FBI obviously had not been there listening when New York City Mayor Michael Bloomberg, in a press conference held two days before the [Occupy Wall Street] demonstration began in Zuccotti Park, said, "People have a right to protest, and if they want to protest, we'll be happy to make sure they have

locations to do it." To their eyes, the protestors were potential, and likely, terrorists.[11]

While some politicians maintained that protestors had some rights to dissent, the FBI and police demonstrated the minimal limits of allowable dissent. Similar raids soon occurred at various Occupy protest locations across the United States. In the Pacific Northwest, raids in Olympia and Seattle, Washington, and Portland, Oregon, weakened organizing efforts, leaving activists facing Grand Jury investigations frightened and disrupting local protests.[12] In several of these raids, the FBI used intimidation tactics and tried to scare detainees with threats of vague guilt by association, accusations that were virtual replays of the sorts of tactics found in the files from the 1940s, 1950s, and 1960s discussed here.

GIBBONS' REPORT

In 2019 Chip Gibbons, the policy and legislative counsel for the group Defending Rights & Dissent, published a report on "The Enduring Problem of FBI First Amendment Abuse." This report critically evaluated FBI abuses of its surveillance and law enforcement powers as it monitored and harassed domestic political groups. Gibbons evaluated the previous decade's FBI abuses, and found that since 2010 the FBI had

repeatedly monitored civil society groups, including racial justice movements, Occupy Wall Street, environmentalists, Palestinian solidarity activists, Abolish ICE protesters, and Cuba and Iran normalization proponents. Additionally, FBI agents conducted interviews that critics have argued were designed to chill protests at the Republican National Convention or intimidate Muslim-American voters.[13]

Much of the information that the Bureau gathered on activists during this period came from FBI informants who had joined these groups that the FBI had under surveillance. The FBI routinely claimed concerns about terrorism to justify its surveillance of these legal political activities, repeatedly claiming the possibility that "lone wolf" members of political groups (most of the groups discussed in Gibbons report are progressive left-wing activist organizations) could commit acts of violence. While the FBI made claims of leftist potential violence, Gibbons noted that "no indication is given as to why these groups in particular warrant such concerns, however, the FBI continuously singles out peace, racial justice, environmental, and economic justice groups for scrutiny"—a pattern that finds continuity with the various surveillance vignettes collected in the previous chapters. Gibbons concluded that targeting these groups is part of a "decades-long pattern of FBI First Amendment abuses and suggests deeply seated political bias within the FBI."[14] This type of FBI domestic political surveillance operation had been prohibited in the mid-1970s after the Church and Pike Committee Congressional investigations, and COINTELPRO documents established that the FBI abused its power by monitoring and harassing domestic political organizations. These prohibitions on domestic political surveillance were rapidly lifted by the PATRIOT Act. Gibbons' report found that in the post PATRIOT Act landscape, the FBI was comfortable using its new "counterterrorism authorities to spy on a number of domestic advocacy groups, including Greenpeace, PETA, the Catholic Workers, and Thomas Merton Peace Center."[15]

Following the sort of recommendations established by the Church and Pike Congressional hearings of the mid-1970s, Gibbons recommended establishing mechanisms bolstering Congressional oversight of the FBI's investigations that risk violating American First Amendment rights. He also called for Congress to establish a statutory charter specifically limiting the FBI's ability to monitor domestic political activities of U.S. citizens.[16]

BLACK LIVES MATTER MOVEMENT

Activist leaders in the Black Lives Matter protest movement became targets of ongoing police and FBI surveillance operations. While this surveillance relies on internet-based forms of tracking, monitoring, and surveillance, it follows the basic principles of the old school surveillance campaigns targeting racial equity activists accused of being communists in the 1950s and 1960s.[17]

Law enforcement personnel portraying activists struggling for law and order and social justice as outlaws is an old routine, and while the basic motivations of law enforcement for monitoring contemporary activists connect with the history recounted here remain similar, the age of social media, email, texts, GPS signals, and apps with privacy settings that most users fail to comprehend creates hitherto unimaginable means of monitoring not only activist leaders, but all those who read their work online, follow them on social media, or attend talks or protest events. Police departments with technologies like Stingrays (cell tower simulators that allow police to monitor all cellphone transmissions in a given area) now capture all cellphone conversations, texts, emails, and social media posts in real time at protests or other political events. These technologies are also used by police to identify everyone who has their cellphones on at a protest event.[18]

The history of the FBI's surveillance of activists struggling for equal rights or opposing militarism teaches us that there is little hope that the collection of this data won't be abused. Today, cellphone surveillance data on anti-police violence activists and Black Lives Matter activists is being collected under the shadiest of legal circumstances in ways that almost guarantee it will be abused. These conditions connect present practices with mid-twentieth century American political police abuses, and this increasing political surveillance by law enforcement agencies leads to continued abuses of state power.

ONCE AN INDIVIDUAL BECOMES A SURVEILLANCE TARGET, DATA COLLECTION SNOWBALLS

Because of the premium that law enforcement agencies like the FBI place on personal and profiling data on individuals who become persons of interest to them, once data and metadata is collected, the simple existence of this data tends to facilitate the collection of more data for data's sake. As we see in many of the FBI files discussed in these chapters, there are patterns of recurrent reification, where the information initially appearing in individuals' files is repeated in various iterations of files, frequently amplifying vague observations or claims in ways increasing the interpreted significance of these reports, processes which often guarantee a magnification and growth of these reports.

Files, whether typed paper reports, physical newspaper clippings, audio recordings, or gigabytes of emails or other electronic documents, take on lives of their own. Once these files become classified, their believed institutional importance is rapidly inflated, further assuring the continued collection of information and circulation within the Bureau with little reconsideration of the accuracy of meaning of the collected material in absurd Kafkaesque iterations removed from the sort of corrective critique that occurs with public data. Secrecy protects inaccuracies that would easily be dismissed under public scrutiny. In these processes secrecy is the best infectant.

With the rapid growth of massive data server farms storing previously unimaginably large collections of metadata, current trends appear to be supporting systems of collection and analysis increasingly reliant on artificial intelligence. Much of the data collected by intelligence agencies *originated* as open sourced intelligence, and we know from the Snowden leaks that the NSA and CIA are also increasingly collecting more and more private corporate data and metadata.

Historically, once the FBI begins to focus attention on an individual and their political associations, the Bureau's focus and drive to continue to collect data takes on a life of its own. This has usually led to the collection of a wealth of surveillance information that is used to determine the movements, associations, loyalties, and possible threats presented by the individuals. In a very real sense, these investigations become a type of self-fulfilling prophecy, where those expressing deviant views come to be seen as threats, and the more data collected indicating an individual is challenging dominant political views, the more intelligence is collected, and the files grow. Both the collecting of information for files and what is done with this information are political matters, with decisions on who to monitor and what is done with what is collected usually having as much to do with who is monitored than with what was collected.

IT IS DIFFICULT TO KNOW WHAT SURVEILLANCE IS HAPPENING AT THE TIME

While far from a profound observation, it is important to acknowledge that the nature of surveillance is that we seldom know the presence or extent of governmental monitoring at the time it is occurring. While leaks and other revelations of the sort provided by Edward Snowden, or the Media, Pennsylvania FBI office break-in alerted the public to the existence of the FBI's COINTEL-PRO program, it is more generally true that we have little idea of what types of surveillance are occurring at a given moment.

But a combination of knowledge of how surveillance has occurred in the past, creative thinking about the technological possibilities for surveillance inherent in available technologies, and an understanding of how specific political economic formations target specific groups of people provides some basic guidelines for accurately theorizing what forms of surveillance are occurring, who are likely surveillance targets, and how this surveillance will be used— this last dimension is always a political feature of surveillance.

CORPORATE AND GOVERNMENT SURVEILLANCE CONVERGENCE

Beginning in the twentieth century there have been increased desires by governments and businesses to make populations legible and tractable. In the United States, electronic surveillance grew with the popularization of the telephone. This has been a long history of law enforcement and government officials trying to weaken public resistance to surveillance, even while corporations have avoided the limitations that at least theoretically limit the U.S. government's ability to monitor and track the populous.[19]

With the rise of corporate surveillance in many ways U.S. surveillance systems have become thought of as "voluntary" forms of surveillance, where people provide data willingly, while the "voluntary" nature of this system has increasingly shifted as it becomes a near necessity for anyone engaging with the technology of the twenty-first century economy. Notions of agency and voluntary consent in any cultural system are by nature problematic concepts, and when the dominant culture and economy increasingly revolves around online presence, purchases, and ponderings, choices to disengage from online systems monitoring and tracking our consumption, entertainment, and political preferences, and endless facets of our identity are limited.

The 9/11 terror attacks were a boon for U.S. government forces long seeking increased surveillance. The American government nurtured the public's fear even as global populations were being seduced by the convenience of commerce surveillance as the world's online lives were commodified, as the global village acclimated all to not fret about leaving digital footprints whenever they went online. But the U.S. post-2001 terror wars in Iraq and Afghanistan began incorporating surveillance and the sorts of big data profiling that were developing at home, in the battlefields where U.S. military and intelligence forces were operating. New efforts to amass data for culture hacking enemies developed, making bold promises that were never met in programs like the failed Human Terrain Systems that tried to amass data in centralized distant locations on individuals and cultures that U.S. forces were trying to manage and manipulate in battle settings.[20] None of it worked as promised, but these programs instruct us of military and intelligence agency desires, and we can expect the metadata generated by government and corporate surveillance to increasingly feed programs whose mission (of trying to sort out cooperative and hostile individuals and groups) involves similar forms of cooption and control.

CONNECTING PAST AND PRESENT

Our understanding of this past can help foretell and prevent future surveillance abuses. This knowledge needs to be part of our defense; and internalizing resistance and critique is one step in this process. But reckoning with this history requires us to perhaps skeptically assume that most Americans have not learned from past governmental abuses of surveillance powers. It also requires a healthy distrust of any promises that the supposed procedural safeguards of Western democracies offer meaningful protections from invasive surveillance operations.

There remains a common naive assumption that even while invasive surveillance technologies spread and become common-place, the established political mechanisms of Western democra-cies will somehow offer protections from government overreach. These views, while widespread, not only misrepresent the present surveillance situation, but they fail to come to grips with ongoing patterns of past invasive surveillance. Typical of these liberal and conservative claims is *London Review of Books* writer Neal Ascherson's conclusion to his review of anthropologist Katherine Verdery's excellent book on the Romanian secret police's massive surveillance file compiled on her during the 1970s and 1980s. After detailing the extensive record of this long-term invasive sur-veillance campaign, Ascherson falls back on the well-worn trope assuring his readers that it can't happen here, assuring us that "the big difference, plainly, is that in a liberal democracy we can launch investigative journalism against MI5 and stay free, whereas we might have perished in a labour camp for trying the same with the Securitatate."[21]

The comfortable blinders of ethnocentrism make it easy to not consider what happened to WikiLeaks cofounder Julian Assange for publishing leaked materials exposing U.S. military and intel-ligence agencies' overreach, or Edward Snowden having to flee the country after exposing massive presumably illegal surveil-lance operations capable of monitoring us all, or the persecution and prosecution of NSA whistleblower Thomas A. Drake, or John Kiriakou's prosecution for revealing CIA wrongdoing. True, none of these critics perished in labor camps (though Assange's legal team has produced documents showing concerns he could die in prison, the UK courts became so concerned over his health that they blocked extradition proceedings), but the address and precise severity of the life destroying state apparatus seems less significant than parallels in state abilities to limit press and whistleblower's disclosures about the severity, reach, and abuses of state security apparatus.

Our greatest hope of protections against state and corporate abuses of surveillance rests in strengthening public records access laws like FOIA, and strengthening protections for whistleblow-ers, leakers, and outlets publishing information about what those monitoring us are doing. We need to know what the FBI, CIA, and NSA are doing with all the surveillance data they collect. But with growing entrenched bureaucratic resistance to complying with FOIA requests and appeals, it would be difficult today to get the records released that I've compiled during the last quarter century some of which have been discussed here.

Our greatest hope for remaining free from oppressive political surveillance operations is for an informed public to demand greater transparency and accountability from government and corporate entities, even while knowing that such demands will themselves be collected in the very files we hope to eliminate. But in our sprawling computer age awash in metadata, something as basic as what is and isn't a "file" becomes increasingly amorphous, even as the need to gain control over the uses of this information increases.

Notes

PREFACE

1. Lanting was a medieval farming practice where farmers soaked seeds with stale urine (lant) to keep birds away from the seeds. See Addy, *A Glossary of Words Used in the Neighborhood of Sheffield*, 27; Price, *Threatening Anthropology*, 369, n3.

INTRODUCTION: CONTEXTUALIZING OLD PATTERNS AND NEW SHIFTS IN AMERICAN SURVEILLANCE

1. Price, *Threatening Anthropology*; Price, *Anthropological Intelligence*; Price, *Weaponizing Anthropology*; Price, *Cold War Anthropology*.
2. Scott, *Seeing Like a State*.
3. Weiner & Rahi-Tamm, "Getting to Know You."
4. Funder, *Stasiland*.
5. Schnell, "Snapshots at Random"; Price, *Cold War Anthropology*, 12–13.
6. Wright & Greengrass, *Spycatcher*, 51.
7. Haines & Langbart, *Unlocking the Files of the FBI*.
8. Mailer, *Harlot's Ghost*, 210.
9. DeLillo, *Underground*, 559.
10. For social scientists, the reason why adhering to ethical research practices is so important is that frequently the best way to find things out about research participants would be to use unethical methods; and this creates natural attractions for unethical methods. Rather than asking people questions in interviews or with questionnaires, if researchers instead bugged their phones, planted surreptitious cameras, lied to subjects to get close to them by pretending to be their friends, this could produce better data than using traditional methods and asking participants for their voluntary informed consent. In some very real sense, because the strictly methodologically "best" ways to gather data on people are often unethical, the importance of ethical research methodologies takes on a profound significance. Of course, law enforcement and intelligence agencies are not restricted by any such ethical concerns.
11. Michael, "Weaponizing Anthropology, the CIA and Publishing, with David Price."
12. Kirchheimer, *Political Justice*, 204.
13. D'Souza, "The Surveillance State."

14. Price, "Extra-Constitutional Proceedings."
15. White, *The Science of Culture*; Peace, *Leslie A. White*.
16. Agee, *Inside the Company*, 575.

1. J. EDGAR HOOVER AND THE FBI'S INSTITUTIONALIZATION OF SURVEILLANCE

1. An early draft of this chapter was initially written at the request of Alexander Cockburn for an edited book he planned but never finished that was to feature profiles of various monstrous public figures and was to be titled *The CounterPunch Book of Monsters*.
2. Powers, *Secrecy and Power*, 36–92.
3. Ibid., 39–40.
4. Theoharis, *From the Secret Files of J. Edgar Hoover*; Theoharis, "A Brief History of the FBI's Role and Powers."
5. Theoharis, "The FBI and the American Legion Contact Program, 1940–1966," 280.
6. Robins, *Alien Ink*, 293–4.
7. Powers, *Secrecy and Power*, 209.
8. Sullivan, *The Bureau*, 90.
9. Swearingen, *FBI Secrets*, 47.
10. Summers, *Official and Confidential*, 90.
11. Cf. ibid.; Theoharis, *J. Edgar Hoover, Sex and Crime*.
12. Summers, *Official and Confidential*, 94.
13. Theoharis, *From the Secret Files of J. Edgar Hoover*, 290–1.
14. Elias, "A Lavender Reading of J. Edgar Hoover"; Tucker, "Hist! Who's That?"
15. Summers, *Official and Confidential*, 84.
16. Sullivan, *The Bureau*, 172–3.
17. Theoharis, "A Brief History of the FBI's Role and Powers," 22.
18. Summers, *Official and Confidential*, 57.
19. Theoharis, *From the Secret Files of J. Edgar Hoover*, 102–3.
20. Kelley & Davis, *Kelley: The Story of an FBI Director*, 184, 276.
21. Gentry, *J. Edgar Hoover*, 28.
22. Powers, *Secrecy and Power*, 484.
23. Woodward, *The Secret Man*.
24. Churchill & Wall, *The COINTELPRO Papers*.
25. Theoharis, *From the Secret Files of J. Edgar Hoover*.
26. Journalist Drew Pearson; Summers, *Official and Confidential*, 100–1; Justice Felix Frankfurter; Summers, *Official and Confidential*, 38–9; poet William Carlos Williams; Robins, *Alien Ink*, 293–7, environmentalist Edward Abbey; FBI-121-40221; Groucho Marx; FBI 100-4665.
27. Theoharis, *From the Secret Files of J. Edgar Hoover*; Price, *Threatening Anthropology*.

28. Salisbury, "The Strange Correspondence of Morris Ernst and John Edgar Hoover, 1939–1964," 579.

29. Coulter, *Treason*.

2. MEMORY'S HALF-LIFE: NOTES ON A SOCIAL HISTORY OF WIRETAPPING IN AMERICA

1. Greenwald, "NSA Prism Program Taps in to User Data of Apple, Google and Others"; Greenwald, "Edward Snowden: The Whistleblower behind the NSA Surveillance Revelations."

2. Westin, "Our Double Standard of Privacy."

3. Tucker & Fingerhut, "American Warier of US Government Surveillance."

4. Willing, "Poll: 4 in 10 Americans Don't Trust FBI."

5. DoJ, *Sourcebook of Criminal Justice Statistics*.

6. Toner & Elder, "Public Is Wary But Supportive on Rights Curbs"; DoJ, *Sourcebook of Criminal Justice Statistics*.

7. Chomsky, "A Quick Reaction."

8. Cf. Barclay, *People Without Government*; Scott, *Seeing Like a State*.

9. Dissent, *Olmstead v. United States* 277 U.S. 438; Murphy, *Wiretapping on Trial*, 116.

10. Fischer, *America Calling*.

11. Murphy, *Wiretapping on Trial*, 13.

12. Berner, *Seattle in the Twentieth Century. Vol. 2: Seattle 1921–1940*, 84–8; *Seattle Times* February 20, 1926: 1; *Seattle Times* February 21, 1926: 1, 4.

13. Murphy, *Wiretapping on Trial*, 52.

14. *Olmstead v. United States* 277 U.S. 438.

15. Pacific Telephone and Telegraph Company brief, in Murphy, *Wiretapping on Trial*, 90.

16. Brandeis, in Murphy, *Wiretapping on Trial*, 120.

17. Murphy, *Wiretapping on Trial*, 125.

18. *New York Times* June 6, 1928: 24.

19. *Seattle Times* June 10, 1928: 6.

20. Arron Goings to David Price, June 15, 2013.

21. *Seattle Times* June 10, 1928: 6.

22. Murphy, *Wiretapping on Trial*, 126.

23. Summers, *Official and Confidential*, 112.

24. www.comicspage.com/dicktracy/history.html, accessed March 29, 2022.

25. Murphy, *Wiretapping on Trial*, 133.

26. Powers, *Secrecy and Power*, 466; Murphy, *Wiretapping on Trial*, 134–5.

27. Edwardson, "James Lawrence Fly, the FBI, and Wiretapping"; Summers, *Official and Confidential*, 112–13.

28. Sullivan, *The Bureau*, 218.

29. Schrecker, *Many Are the Crimes*, 223.

30. Murphy, *Wiretapping on Trial*, 150.

31. Dash, *The Eavesdroppers*.
32. Hochman, "Eavesdropping in the Age of *The Eavesdroppers*."
33. Rockefeller, *Commission on CIA Activities Within the United States*, 20.
34. Ibid., 20.
35. Ibid., 23–4, 41.
36. Bamford, *Puzzle Palace*, 229–30.
37. Ramasastry, "FISA's Secret Court: An End Run around the 4th Amendment"; Electronic Privacy Information Center, "Foreign Intelligence Surveillance Act Court Orders, 1979–2012"; Colangelo, "The Secret FISA Court: Rubber Stamping on Rights."
38. Bamford, *Puzzle Palace*, 230.
39. Bamford, *Body of Secrets*.
40. Theoharis, *From the Secret Files of J. Edgar Hoover*, 359.
41. Dick, *The Minority Report*; Sutin, *Divine Invasions*.
42. Schneirer & Banisar, *The Electronic Privacy Papers*, 23–54.
43. Cassidy, "Silent Coup in Cyberspace."
44. Ibid.
45. Schneirer & Banisar, *The Electronic Privacy Papers*, 1997, 13.
46. Bamford, *Body of Secrets*.
47. Ibid., Hager, *Secret Power*.
48. Cassidy, "Silent Coup in Cyberspace"; Schneirer & Banisar, *The Electronic Privacy Papers*.
49. Sullivan, "Judges Set Precedent for Workplace Privacy"; Lee, "Watch Your Email!"
50. Scalia in *Kyllo*, June 11, 2001; https://law.onecle.com/ussc/533/533us38.html, accessed March 28, 2022.
51. Brandeis, in Murphy, *Wiretapping on Trial*, 116.
52. Nixon, "U.S. Postal Service Logging All Mail for Law Enforcement."
53. Lee, "The NYPD Wants to Watch You."
54. Dreyfuss, "The Cops Are Watching You."
55. Diamond, *Compromised Campus*; Price, *Threatening Anthropology*.
56. Choudry, *Activists and the Surveillance State*.
57. Davidson, "Buying a Home?"
58. Lee et al., "Taiwan Used Police Surveillance, Government Tracking, and $33,000 Fine to Contain Its Coronavirus Outbreak."
59. Vitak & Zimmer, "More Than Just Privacy."
60. See https://covid19research.ssrc.org/public-health-surveillance-and-human-rights-network/, accessed March 28, 2022.
61. PHSHR 2021, https://covid19research.ssrc.org/public-health-surveillance-and-human-rights-network/report/#ix-conclusion, accessed March 28, 2022.
62. Ibid.
63. See, for example, apps like "Wa Notify" that track individual's proximity to people testing positive for Covid.

64. Barnett, "The Terrorism Trap."
65. Altheide, *Terrorism and the Politics of Fear*, 85.
66. See Johnson, "Agreement Is Reached on Air-Passenger Data."
67. Diamond, *Compromised Campus*, 285.
68. Price, "Outcome-Based Tyranny."
69. DeLillo, *Underworld*, 467.

3. THE NEW SURVEILLANCE NORMAL: GOVERNMENT AND CORPORATE SURVEILLANCE IN THE AGE OF GLOBAL CAPITALISM

1. González, *War Virtually*.
2. Schneier, "Don't Listen to Google and Facebook."
3. Pynchon, *Bleeding Edge*, 420.
4. Swartz, "Consumers Are Souring on Web, Post-NSA, Survey Says."
5. Schneier, Don't Listen to Google and Facebook."
6. Solomon, "If Obama Orders the CIA to Kill a U.S. Citizen, Amazon Will Be a Partner in Assassination."
7. Sanger et al., "As Understanding of Russian Hacking Grows, So Does Alarm."
8. Jones, "US Spies Engaged in Industrial Espionage Will Be Jailed, Says Lawmaker."
9. Chrisafis & Jones, "Snowden Leaks."
10. Glüsing et al., "Fresh Leak on US Spying."
11. Da Globo, "NSA Documents Show United States Spied Brazilian Oil Giant."
12. Ibid.
13. Watts, "NSA Accused of Spying on Brazilian Oil Company Petrobras."
14. Fung, "Darrell Issa: James Clapper Lied to Congress about NSA and Should Be Fired."
15. Watts, "NSA Accused of Spying on Brazilian Oil Company Petrobras."
16. Sanger & Perlroth, "NSA Breached Chinese Servers Seen as Security Threat."
17. Wells, "Serving Oil, Arabs, and the CIA."
18. Price, "The NSA, CIA, and the Promise of Industrial Espionage."
19. Dube, Kaplan, & Naidu, "Coups, Corporations, and Classified Information."
20. Ibid, 1406.
21. Ibid., 1407.
22. Ibid., 1376.
23. Gall & Glanz, "U.S. Promotes Network to Foil Digital Spying."

4. THE DANGERS OF PROMOTING PEACE DURING TIMES OF [COLD] WAR: GENE WELTFISH, THE FBI, AND THE 1949 WALDORF ASTORIA'S CULTURAL AND SCIENTIFIC CONFERENCE FOR WORLD PEACE

1. Caffrey, *Ruth Benedict*, 302.
2. Benedict & Weltfish, *The Races of Mankind.*
3. Caffrey, *Ruth Benedict*, 298.
4. FBI NY100-64734:4, December 7, 1944; cf. Buhle, "Ruth Fulton Benedict."
5. FBI NY100-64734:3, December 7, 1944.
6. FBI 100-2872252-4.
7. FBI 100-2872252-4.
8. FBI 100-1287225-8.
9. Price, *Threatening Anthropology*, 70–8.
10. FBI100-287225-23.
11. Kirchwey, "Battle of the Waldorf," 312.
12. Miller, *Timesbends*, 234.
13. Saunders, *The Cultural Cold War*, 53.
14. Ibid., 45–6.
15. Gillmor, *Speaking of Peace*, 144–7.
16. Kirchwey, "Battle of the Waldorf," 377.
17. Ibid., 377.
18. *Life* magazine, "Red Visitors Cause Rumpus," 43.
19. Gillmor, *Speaking of Peace*, 3.
20. *The New Yorker*, "Talk of the Town," 23–4.
21. Gillmor, *Speaking of Peace*, 3.
22. Mellen, *Hellman and Hammett.*
23. Gillmor, *Speaking of Peace*, 1949, v.
24. O'Connor, "News Tailored to Fit"; *Life* magazine, "Red Visitors Cause Rumpus."
25. Miller, *Timebends*, 235.
26. Saunders, *The Cultural Cold War*, 55.
27. Ibid., 45–56.
28. Ibid., 48–9.
29. Hook, "Dr. Hook Protests."
30. Coleman, "Cat's-paws for Fat Boys," 623.
31. For example, see Marshall, "Notes by the Way," 419.
32. Price, "Subtle Means and Enticing Carrots."
33. The other members of the panel were Colston E. Warne, David Lubbock, Grace F. Marcus, Paul Sweezy, and British anthropologist Raphael Armattoe; see Gillmor, *Speaking of Peace.*
34. Warne, in Gillmor, *Speaking of Peace*, 63.

35. Gaddis, *The United States and the End of the Cold War*; Vidal, *The National Security State*.
36. Gough, "Anthropology and Imperialism"; Asad, *Anthropology and the Colonial Encounter*.
37. Cf. FBI NY100-64734, pp. 20–33.
38. Weltfish, "Racialism, Colonialism and World Peace."
39. FBI NY-100-64734, p. 20.
40. FBI NY-100-64734, pp. 20–5.
41. FBI NY-100-64734, p. 30.
42. FBI NY-100-64734 (emphases in original).
43. FBI100-287225-24.
44. Price, *Threatening Anthropology*, 109–53.
45. Cf. U.S. Senate. "Hearings Before the Permanent Subcommittee on Investigations of the Committee on Government Operations," March 27, April 1 and 2, 1953, 118; Bloom, "The Intellectual in a Time of Crisis."
46. Lanting is the medieval agricultural practice of soaking seeds in stale urine before planting them in order to keep birds from getting the seeds, social lanting refers to stigmatizing an individual or group so that others will not associate with them. See Addy, *A Glossary of Words Used in the Neighborhood of Sheffield*, 27; Price, *Threatening Anthropology*, 369, n3; Price, "Counter-Lineages within the History of Anthropology," 14.
47. Lenin, *Imperialism*.
48. Price, *Threatening Anthropology*, 118–22.
49. Gillmor, *Speaking of Peace*, 82; Saunders, *The Cultural Cold War*, 51.
50. Price, "Academia under Attack: Sketches for a New Blacklist."
51. Stone, "Two Propositions for the Russians," 105.

5. TRIBAL COMMUNISM UNDER FIRE: ARCHIE PHINNEY AND THE FBI

1. Churchill & Wall, *The COINTELPRO Papers*; Matthiessen, *In the Spirit of Crazy Horse*.
2. Churchill & Wall, *The COINTELPRO Papers*.
3. Zigrossi in Churchill & Wall, *The COINTELPRO Papers*, 231.
4. FBI 100-350068-26, p. 10.
5. Phinney, *Nez Percé Texts*.
6. Willard, "American Anthropologists on the Neva."
7. FBI 101-3074.
8. Phinney to Boas August 8, 1933, in Willard, "American Anthropologists on the Neva," 7.
9. Willard, "American Anthropologists on the Neva," 7.
10. FBI 100-350068-3.
11. FBI 100-30068-24.
12. FBI 100-350068-18.

13. FBI 100-350068-24, p. 2.
14. FBI 100-350068-29.
15. FBI 100-350068-29.
16. FBI 100-350068-29.
17. FBI 100-350068.
18. FBI 100-350068.
19. FBI 101-3074, March 31, 1948.
20. FBI 100-350068-3.
21. FBI 100-350068-3, p. 7.
22. FBI 100-350068-28.
23. FBI 100-350068-25.
24. FBI 100-350068-25.
25. FBI BT 100-5025, December 6, 1947.
26. FBI BT 100-5025, December 6, 1947.
27. FBI 100-350068-19.
28. FBI 100-350068-20; FBI 100-350068-V.
29. Price, *Threatening Anthropology*, 181.
30. Littlefield & Knack, *Native Americans and Wage Labor*; Moore, *The Political Economy of North American Indians*.

6. THE FBI'S HISTORY OF UNDERMINING LEGAL DEFENSES: FROM JURY PANEL INVESTIGATIONS TO DEFENSE LAWYER SURVEILLANCE PROGRAMS

1. FBI 62-45014-1, June 24, 1936.
2. Yoder, *Breach of Privilege*, 4.
3. Ibid., 7.
4. Ibid., 10.
5. Ibid., 4.
6. Ibid., 14.
7. Ibid., 16.
8. FBI 100-162180.
9. Risen & Poitras, "Spying by NSA Ally."
10. Yoder, *Breach of Privilege*, 4–5.
11. Haines & Langbart, *Unlocking the Files of the FBI*, 49.
12. Ibid., 49.
13. FBI, Manual of Investigation Operations and Guidelines, Effective January 31, 1978, p. 75.
14. Ibid., 73.
15. Breindel, "A Controversy Renewed."
16. Greenspun had been apprehended engaging in illegal arms shipments to a foreign country.
17. FBI 51-417-7.
18. FBI 122-2557-108.

19. Price, *Weaponizing Anthropology*; Price, "Uninvited Guests."
20. FBI 51-443-1, November 3, 1958.
21. FBI 51-443-1, November 3, 1958, p. 37.
22. FBI 51-443-1, August 11, 1958.
23. FBI 51-443-1.6, November 3, 1958.
24. FBI 51-443-1, 60, November 3, 1958.
25. E.g., FBI 51-443-1, November 3, 1958, p. 8.
26. FBI 51-443-1, November 3, 1958.
27. FBI NY 65-11613, January 14, 1959.
28. FBI 65-58681-445, December 9, 1958.
29. FBI 65-58681-445, December 9, 1958.
30. FBI 65-58681-626.
31. FBI 100-439612-28, March 5, 1970.
32. FBI 100-439612-28, March 5, 1970.
33. FBI 100-439612, November 29, 1973.
34. Rosenbaum, "The Most Hated Lawyer in America."
35. *William Kunstler: Disturbing the Universe*, 49:40.
36. Akhtar, "Pine Ridge Death," 71.
37. The only references to his *Covert Action Information Bulletin* work in his FBI file are inquiries about his involvement with Sheridan Square Publications press of New York, which published some anti-CIA books linked to his *Covert Action Information Bulletin* work (FBI 100-469207, April 17, 1987).
38. FBI 100-469207, December 17, 1971.
39. *New York Times*, "Five Spurn Inquiry into Bank Bombing": 23.
40. FBI 100-469207; NY 100-164391, May 15, 1972.

7. AGENTS OF APARTHEID: RUTH FIRST AND THE FBI'S HISTORICAL ROLE OF ENFORCING INEQUALITY

1. Retired intelligence personnel's memoirs provide useful information on intelligence methods and attitudes prevailing in these agencies. Sometimes the overconfident bragging of careerists' books provide insight into the history of operations (William Sullivan's 1979 *The Bureau: My Thirty Years in Hoover's FBI*), or rationalizations for acts that later become known (as in "Deep Throat," Mark Felt's 1979 memoire *The FBI Pyramid from the Inside*), or even a means for a guilty conscious to come clean on the illegal acts of the agency where they worked (Philip Agee's 1975 *Inside the Company: CIA Diary*, or Wesley Swearingen's 1995 *FBI Secrets: An Agent's Expose*, or Victor Machetti, Fletcher Prouty, and John Stockwell's books). I've read dozens of these intelligence insider memoires, and even the worst ones—lacking any perspective of the ways that the author's career violated the rights and freedom of others, or in

some cases undermined the promise of democracy they believed they were protecting—contain illuminating nuggets. These memoirs often teach us about patterns of surveillance and efforts to discredit, marginalize, or more otherwise silence critical voices from such books—and as starting points for archival research and Freedom of Information Act requests for supporting or exploratory documents, such works are invaluable.

2. Swanepoel, *Really Inside BOSS*, 66.
3. Ibid., 66–7.
4. First, *South West Africa*, 13–14.
5. Ibid., 14.
6. Swanepoel, *Really Inside BOSS*, 67.
7. First, *South West Africa*, 14.
8. Swanepoel, *Really Inside BOSS*.
9. Ibid., 227; Lienhardt et al., "The Oral Tradition."
10. Price, *Threatening Anthropology*, 247.
11. Andrew Cockburn, "A Loophole in U.S. Sanctions Against Pretoria."
12. FBI 105-39635c, April 11, 1955, JEH letter.
13. Weiner, "The Cold War Is Over, But the Blacklist Still Guards U.S."
14. FBI 105-39635-1, August 24, 1955; see Price *Threatening Anthropology*, 154–63.
15. FBI 105-396353-2, August 15, 1955.
16. FBI 105-396353-2, August 24, 1955.
17. 105-396353-2, August 15, 1955.
18. FBI 105-396353-3, December 18, 1970.
19. FBI 105-396353-7, March 4, 1971; FBI 105-396353, March 27, 1974.
20. FBI 105-396353-9, March 9, 1971.
21. FBI 105-396353, March 27, 1974.
22. FBI 105-396353, April 5, 1974, SECRET.
23. FBI 105-396353, May 9, 1975, SECRET.
24. FBI 105-39635, August 20, 1982.
25. Wieder, *Ruth First and Joe Slovo in the War Against Apartheid*, 252.
26. Independent Online 2000.
27. Wieder, *Ruth First and Joe Slovo in the War Against Apartheid*, 253.
28. Hanlon in ibid., 254.

8. HOW THE FBI SPIED ON EDWARD SAID

1. Mariam Said to David Price, November 12, 2005.
2. Cockburn, "The FBI and Edward Said."
3. FBI 105-120604.
4. FBI 105-120604-2.
5. FBI 105-120604.
6. Steve Niva to David Price, November 20, 2005.

7. FBI 105-120604-9.
8. FBI 105-106429-52, December 12, 1972.
9. FBI 105-106429-52, p. 7.
10. FBI 105-106429-62.
11. FBI 105-120604-16.
12. FBI 105-120604-2, May 8, 1974.
13. FBI 105-120604.
14. FBI 105-120604.
15. FBI 105-120604, September 25, 1979.
16. FBI 105-120604.
17. FBI 105-120604.
18. FBI 105-120604-23.
19. FBI 105-120604.
20. FBI 105-120604-23.
21. FBI 105-120604, May 13, 1982.
22. FBI 105-120604, May 20, 1982.
23. FBI 105-120604, July 27, 1982.
24. FBI 105-120604.
25. FBI 105-120604.
26. Kurtz, "Studying Title VI."
27. Kurtz, "Anti-Americanism in the Classroom."
28. Kafka, *The Trial*, 137.

9. SEYMOUR MELMAN AND THE FBI'S PERSECUTION OF THE DEMILITARIZATION MOVEMENT

1. Satisky, "Interview with Seymour Melman," 24:20.
2. FBI 77-0016, January 12, 1956.
3. Noam Chomsky to David Price, May 12, 2009.
4. FBI 105-78087-1-2, June 2, 1959.
5. FBI 105-78987-1-1, June 2, 1959.
6. FBI 105-78987.
7. FBI 105-78987-1-3.
8. FBI 105-78987-8, March 2, 1962.
9. FBI 105-78987, October 8, 1962.
10. FBI 105-78987-A, June 30, 1964.
11. NRDC, "Natural Resources Defense Council Table of US Nuclear Warheads, 1945–2002."
12. FBI 105-78987-12x:2, March 28, 1967.
13. FBI NY 65-24637:3, June 19, 1967.
14. FBI 105-78987, January 19, 1968.
15. FBI NY 105-36247:4, April 28, 1972, SECRET.
16. FBI 105-78987, January 19, 1968.
17. FBI 105-78987; *New York Times* January 6, 1968.

18. FBI NY 105-36247:4, April 28, 1972, SECRET.
19. FBI 105-78987-19, February 6, 1974.
20. FBI NY 105-136620, November 25, 1974, CONFIDENTIAL.
21. Spitzer, "Toward a Marxian Theory of Deviance."

10. TRACES OF FBI EFFORTS TO DEPORT A RADICAL VOICE: ON ALEXANDER COCKBURN'S FBI FILE

1. Cockburn, "Redwood Summer and the Fate of the Panthers"; Cockburn, "How to Not Spot a Terrorist"; Cockburn, "The FBI and Edward Said."
2. Webster, "FBI Destroyed Part of Hunter S. Thompson's File."
3. Haines & Langbart, *Unlocking the Files of the FBI*, 101.
4. FBI 100-HQ-478026, August 15, 1973.
5. FBI 100-HQ-478026-1, August 15, 1973.
6. FBI 100-HQ-478026, August 22, 1973.
7. FBI 100-HQ-478026, August 22, 1973.
8. FBI 100-HQ-478026-2, October 3, 1973.
9. FBI 100-HQ-478026, October 3, 1973, p. 2.
10. FBI 105-233556-35, September 26, 1972.
11. ISA, "International Sociological Association Presidents"; Mitgang, *Dangerous Dossiers*, 142; Weiner, "The Cold War Is Over, But the Blacklist Still Guards U.S."
12. Mitgang, *Dangerous Dossiers*, 146.
13. Weiner, "The Cold War Is Over, But the Blacklist Still Guards U.S."
14. Warren, "US Denies Visa to German Investigative Journalist."
15. Wiener, *Gimmie Some Truth.*
16. FBI 100-478026-4.
17. FBI 100-478026-4, May 18, 1975.
18. FBI 100-478026-3, July 11, 1975.
19. FBI 100-478026-3, July 11, 1975.
20. FBI 100-478026-5, July, 29, 1975.
21. FBI 100-478026-5, August 14, 1975.
22. Andrew Cockburn to David Price, December 14, 2012.
23. Ibid.
24. Ibid.
25. Ramji-Nogales, "A Global Approach to Secret Evidence," n7.
26. Cockburn, "Farewell to Our Greatest President: Adieu, Gerald Ford."
27. Berryhill, "FBI Ordered to Pay UC Berkeley Alumnus $470,000."
28. David Price to DoJ OIP, December 7, 20112.
29. FBI 105-WF-145035-24.
30. FBI 229-NY-3242, February 18, 1989.
31. FBI 229-NY-3242, February 18, 1989, p. 1.
32. FBI 229-NY-3242, February 18, 1989, p. 5.

33. David Price to FBI, September 21, 2014.
34. Cockburn, "The Hunt for the Smoking Gun," 343.

11. *MEDIUM COOL*: DECADES OF THE FBI'S SURVEILLANCE OF HASKELL WEXLER

1. FBI Chicago 100-17425, pp. 3–4.
2. Garcia, "Rebel Citizens and Filmmakers."
3. Wexler, *Tell Them Who You Are*, 12:45.
4. Landau, "The People's Cinematographer—Haskell Wexler."
5. FBI 100-17425 "Chicago File," November 23, 1944, p. 2.
6. FBI 100-17425 "Chicago File," November 23, 1944, p. 2.
7. FBI NY 100-5756, October 20, 1944.
8. FBI 62-55696-9, October 21, 1948.
9. FBI 100-17425, June 7, 1961.
10. FBI Chicago 100-17425, November 23, 1944.
11. Wexler, *Tell Them Who You Are*, 15:40.
12. Landau, "The People's Cinematographer—Haskell Wexler."
13. FBI 100-17425, June 7, 1961.
14. FBI 100-17425, June 7, 1961, p. 10.
15. FBI 61-55676.
16. SAC Los Angeles to Hoover; FBI LA 100-60588, February 23, 1961.
17. SAC Los Angeles to Hoover; FBI LA 100-60588, February 23, 1961, p. 3.
18. FBI LA 100-60588, February 23, 1961, p. 3.
19. SAC LA to JEH; FBI LA 100-60588, February 23, 1961, p. 3.
20. FBI CG 100-17425, June 7, 1961.
21. FBI LA 100-60588, February 23, 1961, SAC Los Angeles to Hoover.
22. FBI 100-60588, June 30, 1961, SAC, LA to Director.
23. FBI 100-60588, June 30, 1961, SAC, LA to Director.
24. FBI 100-60588, LA report, August 2, 1961.
25. FBI 100-60588, LA report, August 2, 1961.
26. FBI 100-60588, LA report, August 2, 1961.
27. FBI 100-60588, LA report, August 2, 1961.
28. FBI 100-60588, LA report, August 2, 1961.
29. FBI LA 100-60588, May 11, 1964, p. 3.
30. FBI 62-55696-27, SAC LA to Hoover, April 12, 1965.
31. FBI 62-55696, April 27, 1972.
32. FBI 62-55696, April 27, 1972.
33. Landau, "The People's Cinematographer—Haskell Wexler."
34. FBI 62-55696-28, April 27, 1972.
35. FBI 62-55696-30, October 30, 1972.
36. FBI 62-55696, April 22, 1974.
37. FBI 62-55696, November 19, 1974, p. 4.
38. FBI 62-55696-32, May 14, 1974.

39. Yates, *Rebel Citizen*.
40. Wexler, *Tell Them Who You Are*, 60:00; cf. Townsend, "Haskell Wexler and the Making of 'One Flew Over the Cuckoo's Nest.'"
41. Tuchman, "The Case of the Pirated Soundtrack," 12.
42. Ibid., 12.
43. Ibid., 12.
44. Ibid., 12–13.
45. Lewis, *Emile de Antonio*, 196.
46. Ibid., 196.
47. Ibid., 198.
48. Ibid., 200.
49. Ibid., 195.
50. Tuchman, "The Case of the Pirated Soundtrack."

12. BLIND WHISTLING PHREAKS AND THE FBI'S HISTORICAL RELIANCE ON PHONE COMPANY CRIMINALITY

1. Rosenbaum. "Secrets of the Little Blue Box."
2. Lapsley, *Exploding the Phone*; Martin, "Joybubbles, 58, Peter Pan of Phone Hackers, Dies."
3. FBI 139-HQ-3481.
4. FBI 139-HQ-3481.
5. FBI 139-HQ-3481.
6. FBI 139-HQ-3481.
7. FBI 139-HQ-3481.
8. FBI 139-HQ-3481.
9. FBI 139-HQ-3481.
10. FBI 139-HQ-3481, August 29, 1969.
11. FBI 139-HQ-3481.
12. FBI 139-HQ-3481.
13. FBI 139-HQ-3481.

13. THE FBI AND CANDY MAN: MONITORING FRED HALEY, A VOICE OF REASON DURING TIMES OF MADNESS

1. Frederick, *Albert F. Canwell: An Oral History*; Scates, "Cold Warrior."
2. FBI SE 105-2638, p. 2; *The People's World* April 7, 1948.
3. "Loyalists Hold American," *New York Times* February 10, 1938: 1.
4. Ibid.
5. FBI 100-381291, September 30, 1960.
6. FBI 100-381291-3.

7. FBI 100-381291, June 22, 1952, pp. 15–16.

8. E.g. letter published in *Tacoma News Tribune* April 18, 1950: 18, col. 4,5,6.

9. FBI 100-381291, June 22, 1951, pp. 15–16.

10. FBI 100-381291, p. 17.

11. FBI 100-381291, p. 81; see Price, *Threatening Anthropology*, 34–49.

12. FBI 100-381291, p. 19.

13. FBI 100-381291, p. 11.

14. FBI 100-381291, p. 11.

15. FBI 100-381291, p. 15.

16. King, "Tacoma's Fred Haley."

17. Alarcon, "Donald N. Wheeler, Communist, Dies at 89."

18. SPL, "Interview with Fred Haley, #2," 31:38.

19. Lynn, "Candy Magnate Championed Civil Rights"; ibid., 34:00.

20. SPL, "Interview with Fred Haley, #2," 37:00.

21. Magden, "The Schuddakopf Case, 1954–1958: Tacoma Public Schools and Anticommunism."

22. *Lewiston Morning Tribune*, December 7, 1956.

23. *The People's World* NW Edition, December 29, 1956: 2, col. 4.

24. FBI 105-2638-3.

25. FBI 105-2638-4, SAC Seattle, September 3, 1957.

26. FBI 105-2638-5.

27. FBI 105-2638-6, June 27, 1960.

28. FBI WFO 105-36385-B, August 8, 1960.

29. FBI 100-318291-7, September 1, 1960.

30. FBI 105-2638-13.

31. FBI 105-2638-7.

32. FBI 105-2638-18.

33. Haley, "Our Schools Can Do What We Want Them to Do," 3.

34. FBI 105-2638-22.

35. FBI 105-2638-22.

36. FBI 105-2638-23.

37. FBI 105-2638-26, March 30, 1962.

38. FBI 105-2638, TNT story September 15, 1962.

39. FBI 105-2638-30.

40. FBI 105-2638-32.

41. SPL, "Interview with Fred Haley, #2," 35:00.

42. Ibid., 36:50.

14. DAVID W. CONDE, LOST CIA CRITIC AND COLD WAR SEER

1. TAF P-28, "Potential Film Program for Japan," CMT to JLS, September 4, 1953.

2. Vonnegut, *God Bless You Mr Rosewater*, 67.
3. NARA Conde Employment File, St. Louis, DWC to Sen Alan Cranston, July 24, 1975.
4. DWC, Article File, "What Are the CIA, Lockheed and Kodama-Kihi Trying to Do?"
5. Ibid.
6. Takemae, *Inside GHQ*.
7. Kurosawa, *Something Like an Autobiography*.
8. NARA, Conde Employment File, St. Louis, DWC to Sen Alan Cranston, July 24, 1975.
9. DWC, Box 33, 1, "What Are the CIA, Lockheed and Kodama-Kishi Trying to Do?"
10. NARA Conde Employment File, St. Louis, DWC to Sen Alan Cranston, July 24, 1975.
11. Ibid.
12. Ibid.
13. Ibid.
14. Ibid.
15. DWC Article File, "What Are the CIA, Lockheed, and Kodama Kihi Trying to Do?"
16. Conde, *CIA—Core of the Cancer*.
17. Ibid., 9.
18. Ibid., 112.
19. Ibid., 12.
20. Ibid., 57.
21. Ibid., 57.
22. DWC Box 32, "Japan Cultural Front," 3.
23. DWC Box 33, Star File 318, pp. 17–18.
24. Mader, *Who's Who in the CIA*.
25. DWC, Box 35, DC to JM, January 29, 1973.

15. E.A. HOOTON AND THE BIOSOCIAL FACTS OF AMERICAN CAPITALISM

1. FBI 62-73410-1, July 27, 1943.
2. FBI 62-73410-1.
3. Rushton, *Evolution and Behavior*; Herrnstein & Murray, *The Bell Curve*; Pinker *Rationality*.
4. See this stunning 2014 letter in the *New York Times* disavowing Wade's work: Coop et al., "Letters: A Troublesome Inheritance."
5. See Nicholas Wade's *A Troublesome Inheritance*; but I'd recommend saving yourself the anguish of reading Wade's now discredited book, especially when you can read this devastating critique in *In These Times* by anthropologist Jonathan Marks: "The Genes Made Us Do It."
6. Vonnegut, *God Bless You, Mr Rosewater*, 264–5.

16. WALT WHITMAN ROSTOW AND FBI ATTACKS ON LIBERAL ANTI-COMMUNISM

1. These old modernization refrains were found in President Obama's September 2010 address to the UN evoking old strains of Rostow's work as he called for a new wave of development projects to combat terrorism. See Obama, "Remarks by the President to the United Nations General Assembly."
2. Blackmer, *The MIT Center for International Studies*.
3. Wells, "A Look inside Hollywood and the Movies."
4. Sahlins, "What Is Anthropological Enlightenment?" 504.
5. Perkins, *Confessions of an Economic Hitman*.
6. Ibid.
7. FBI 161-21-123, October 10, 1967; FBI NH, 161–3.
8. FBI 161-21-134, December 8, 1960.
9. FBI 161-21-134, p. 9.
10. Rostow, "Marx Was a City Boy: or Why Communism May Fail."
11. Ibid., 25.
12. Ibid., 30.
13. Widener 1956:374 appears in FBI 161-21-134.
14. National Review, "Did CIA Take the Senate?"
15. Ibid.; Buckley, "Howard Hunt, R.I.P."
16. FBI 161-21-134, March 23, 1959.
17. Rostow, *Stages of Economic Growth: A Non-Communist Manifesto*.
18. FBI 121-2904-29.
19. FBI 121-2904-29.
20. FBI NY 62-11243.
21. FBI 161-21-15; Rosen to Parsons, December 2, 1960.
22. FBI WFO 77-11633, p. 12.
23. FBI LA 161-2, p. 4.
24. FBI 161-35-3, December, 15, 1960.
25. Tyner & Philo, *War, Violence and Population*, 100.
26. FBI WFO 77-11633.
27. FBI 77-11633, June 3, 1963.
28. FBI 161-21-77, March 29, 1965.
29. FBI 161-21-77, March 29, 1965.
30. FBI 161-21-77, March 29, 1965.
31. FBI 161-21-77, March 2, 1965.
32. FBI 161-21-77, April 30, 1965, p. 2.
33. Appy, *Cold War Constructions*, 141.
34. FBI 161-21-A.
35. FBI WFO 77-11633, February 10, 1966.
36. FBI 161-21-116.
37. *Washington Post*, April 19, 1968.

38. FBI 161-21-A, April 25, 1968.
39. Bernstein, *Loyalties.*
40. Wilford, *The Mighty Wurlitzer.*

17. ANDRÉ GUNDER FRANK, THE FBI, AND THE BUREAUCRATIC EXILE OF A CRITICAL MIND

1. Frank, *Latin America: Underdevelopment or Revolution*; Frank, *On Capitalist Underdevelopment*; Frank, *ReOrient:* Frank, *Global Economy in the Asian Age.*
2. Rostow, *Stages of Economic Development.*
3. Millikan & Rostow, "Notes on Foreign Policy," 8.
4. FBI HQ 100-426013-3, March 2, 1962.
5. FBI HQ 100-426013-1; see also OM 100-6092, April, 26, 1957.
6. FBI OM 100-6092, April 26, 1957.
7. FBI HQ 100-426013.
8. FBI 100-426013, February 12, 1962.
9. FBI 100-426013, February 12, 1962.
10. FBI 100-426013, March 14, 1962.
11. FBI 100-426013-13.
12. Saul Landau wrote me that "Marta was a MIRista, a member of the far left that opposed electoral politics in Chile. Gunder subscribed to that line in so far as he was able to feel comfortable with any line" (Saul Landau to David Price, June 16, 2007).
13. FBI 100-426013, May 1, 1963.
14. André Guner Frank to David Price, July 18, 1996.
15. SM to DHP, May 1, 2007.
16. AGF letter to friends July 1, 1964, copy given to DHP by AGH on July 16, 1996.
17. Ibid.
18. Ibid.
19. Ibid.
20. Ibid.
21. Ibid.
22. Ibid.
23. Ibid.
24. Ibid.
25. Frank, "The Development of Underdevelopment," 25.
26. *Monthly Review*, "Notes from the Editors," 1.
27. FBI 100-426013-5, November 30, 1964.
28. FBI 100-426013-5, November 30, 1964.
29. FBI 100-426013, February 1, 1965.
30. FBI 100-426013-37, January 11, 1965.
31. FBI 100-426013-7, April 26, 1965.

32. FBI 100-426013-8, May 7, 1965.
33. FBI 100-426013-9, May 24, 1965.
34. FBI 100-426013.
35. FBI 100-426013-14, October 27, 1965.
36. FBI 100-426013, March 15, 1966.
37. FBI 100-426013-18.
38. FBI 100-426013-36.
39. FBI 100-426013, December 28, 1970.
40. FBI 100-426013, May 15, 1991.

18. ANGEL PALERM AND THE FBI: MONITORING A VOICE OF INDEPENDENCE AT THE ORGANIZATION OF AMERICAN STATES

1. Wolf, "Angel Palerm Vich, 1917–1980," 613.
2. Puig, *Angel Palerm Vich*.
3. FBI 105-19110-51, November 16, 1961.
4. FBI 105-19110-51, November 16, 1961.
5. López et al., *Palerm en sus propias palabras*; Wolf, "Angel Palerm Vich, 1917–1980."
6. The Pan American Union (PAU) became the Organization of American States (OAS) in 1948.
7. FBI 105-19110-11, February 23, 1954.
8. FBI 105-19110-21, June 8, 1954.
9. Price, *Threatening Anthropology*, 237–54.
10. FBI 105-19110-13, April 14, 1954.
11. FBI 105-19110-17, April 28, 1954.
12. See: FBI 105-19110-18, May 13, 1954. Murra was identified as a fellow Abraham Lincoln Brigade veteran, and as an anthropologist working on a book about Inca Civilization.
13. FBI 105-19110-40, June 1, 1961.
14. FBI 105-19110-47, June 12, 1961.
15. FBI 105-19110-47, June 12, 1961.
16. FBI 105-19110-47, June 12, 1961.
17. FBI 105-19110-47, June 12, 1961.
18. Larsen, *Milestones and Millstones*.
19. FBI 105-19110, October 4, 1961.
20. FBI 105-19110-50, October 17, 1961.
21. FBI 105-19110-58, March 26, 1962.
22. FBI 105-19110, October 17/1961, p. 7.
23. FBI 105-19910-62, May 9, 1962.
24. FBI WFO 105-5516, May 24, 1962, classified SECRET.
25. FBI 105-5516, July 27, 1962.
26. FBI 105-5516.

27. FBI 105-19110-67, September 19, 1962.
28. FBI 105-19110-67, September 19, 1962.
29. FBI 105-5516, September 9, 1962, classified Confidential.
30. FBI 105-5516, September 9, 1962, classified Confidential.
31. FBI 105-5516, September 9, 1962, classified Confidential.
32. FBI 105-19110-68, December 7, 1962, classified Confidential.
33. FBI 105-19110-68, December 7, 1962, classified Confidential.
34. FBI 105-19110-71, May 24, 1963.
35. FBI 105-19110-72, June 13, 1963.
36. FBI 105-19110-72, June 13, 1963.
37. FBI WFO 105-1885, November 1, 1963.
38. Wolf, "Angel Palerm Vich, 1917–1980," 613.
39. FBI 105-19110-76.
40. FBI 105-19110-77, February 10, 1964.
41. FBI 105-19110-78, March 30, 1964.
42. FBI 105-19110-78, March 30, 1964.
43. FBI 105-19110, May 11, 1964.
44. FBI 105-19110, June 12, 1964.
45. FBI 105-19110-88, May 3, 1965.
46. FBI 105-19110-88, May 3, 1965.
47. FBI 105-19110-88, May 3, 1965.
48. FBI 105-19110-88, May 3, 1965.
49. FBI 105-19110-90, May 11, 1965.
50. Wolf, "Angel Palerm Vich, 1917–1980."
51. FBI 105 19110-99.
52. Department of State, Case Control No. 200104029.
53. FBI 105-19110-61, April 18, 1962.
54. FOIA DOS, Case Control No. 200104029, March 1, 1965.
55. Price, *Threatening Anthropology*, 217–20.

19. THE FBI'S PURSUIT OF SAUL LANDAU: PORTRAIT OF THE RADICAL AS A YOUNG MAN

1. The CIA's released files on Landau are limited. I presume these released files are a tincture of the records they hold on him given his decades of work criticizing the CIA, including accusations that the CIA was leading international terror campaigns, and the CIA's role in the Letelier murder. Most of what has been released by the CIA under FOIA on Landau consists of newspaper and magazine clipping on or by Landau clipped from the pages of the *New York Times*, *Los Angeles Times*, *The Nation*, *The Oakland Tribune*. Some of the CIA's released documents show the CIA reading and discussing Landau or his work, for example, one released CIA memo labeled "Extract from the Staff Meeting Minutes of 30 June 1980," states that "The Director called attention to yesterday's *Washington Post* article

'The unresolved Questions in the Leelier Case' by John Dinges and Saul Landau (attached). He asked Bridge to look into it (Action: IG) (AIUO)." There were two sets of CIA staff meeting minutes (from June 30, 1980 and July 18, 1980), both discussing Landau and Dignes' work on the *Assassination on Embassy Row* book (see: www.cia.gov/library/readingroom/docs/CIA-RDP84B00130R000600010203-4.pdf; www.cia.gov/library/readingroom/docs/CIA-RDP84B00130R000600010226-9.pdf; www.cia.gov/library/readingroom/docs/CIA-RDP84B00130R000600010342-0.pdf, all accessed December 7, 2015).
2. FBI 105-4505, March 6, 1956.
3. FBI 105-652, April 4, 1956; SAC Milwaukee to FBI Director.
4. Landau, "From the Labor Youth League to the Cuban Revolution," 108.
5. Ibid., 108.
6. FBI 105-45054-3, May 16, 1956.
7. Stern, "A Short Account of International Student Politics and the Cold War with Particular Reference to the NSA, CIA, etc."
8. FBI 105-45654-24, p. 9.
9. FBI WI 100-13021-8, February 12, 1957.
10. Levin, *Cold War University*, 44.
11. FBI MI 100-13021, June 12, 1959.
12. MI 100-13021, June 21, 1959, pp. 8, 10–11.
13. FBI 105-45054-29, December 27, 1960, p. 2.
14. FBI 105-45054-29, Deccember 27, 1960.
15. FBI 105-45054-31, March 3, 1961.
16. Levin, *Cold War University*, 91.
17. See ibid.; Hayden, "Saul Landau, R.I.P"; Harding, "Remembering Saul Landau."
18. FBI 105-45054-44, June 19, 1961.
19. FBI 105-45054-46, August 14, 1961.
20. Geary, *Radical Ambition.*
21. Landau, "C. Wright Mills: The Last Six Months," 52.
22. FBI 105-45054-48, October 10,1961.
23. Youdovin, "$50 Million Suit Is Filed Against Mills."
24. FBI 105-45054-48-52, January 12, 1962.
25. FBI 105-45054-58, June 15, 1962.
26. FBI 105-45054-65, July 1, 1963.
27. FBI 105-45054-65, p. 4; SF T-2-6/20/62, July 1, 1963.
28. FBI 105-45054, June 11, 1963.
29. FBI 105-45054, May 27, 1963.
30. FBI 105-45054, August 8, 1963.
31. FBI 105-45054-61, September 24, 1963.
32. FBI 105-45054, September 25, 1963.
33. FBI 105-45054, September 25, 1963.
34. FBI 105-45054-68, September 27, 1963.

35. FBI 105-45054-70.
36. FBI 105-45054-71, October 16, 1963.
37. FBI 105-45054-81, December 14, 1965.
38. FBI 105-45054-84, March 16, 1967.
39. FBI 105-45054-93, Ju;y 19, 1967.
40. FBI 105-45054-93, July 19, 1967.
41. FBI 105-45054-96, August 18, 1967.
42. FBI 105-45054-99, September 19, 1967.
43. FBI 105-45054-102, November 30, 1967.
44. FBI 105-45054, December 14, 1967.
45. FBI 105-45054-106, January 15, 1968.
46. See: FBI 105-45054-114, June 5, 1968. Stamps on file pages from summer 1968 say "Copies destroyed 88 JUNE 27, 1972." Other stamps say copy sent to: RAO [NY Regional Administrative Office], SS & CIA" dated August 12, 1969. Also see: FBI 105-45054-116.
47. FBI 105-45054, September 17, 1968.
48. FBI 105-45054-123, June 20, 1969; FBI 105-45054-131, September 26, 1969.
49. FBI 105-45054-132, November 20, 1969.
50. FBI 105-45054, May 29, 1970.
51. FBI 105-45054, May 29, 1970.
52. FBI San Francisco 100-51738.
53. FBI 100-438568.
54. FBI 101-6392.
55. FBI BI 100-495656; NY 100-94428.
56. FBI 100-14416.
57. FBI 105-45054-138, March 22, 1972.
58. FBI 105-45054, August 1, 1973.
59. FBI 105-45054, January 22, 2009.
60. FBI 105-45054, January 22, 2009.
61. FBI 105-45054, January 22, 2009.
62. FBI 105-45054, January 26, 2009.
63. The eight airlines are: Air Canada, Alaska Airlines, American Airlines, Delta Airlines, Hawaiian Airlines, JetBlue Airways, Southwest Airlines, United Airlines. While there has been little study of the ways that ARC has worked with the FBI and other intelligence agencies, during the pre-internet age and present ARC has been used to track the movements of individuals of interest to the Bureau. While primarily existing as a way for the airline industry to work out ticket transaction and refund settlements with travel agencies and airlines, because of the data needed to undertake such tasks, ARC became a vital database for tracking the movements of people in the United States and around the globe. On LinkedIn, ARC describes itself as "the premier driver of air *travel intelli-*

gence and commerce in the travel industry" (emphasis added, see www. linkedin.com/company/arc, accessed February 20, 2021).

64. FBI 105-45054, February 13, 2009.
65. FBI 105-45054, February 13, 2009.
66. FBI 105-45054, April 1, 2009.
67. FBI 105-45054, June 12, 2009.

CONCLUSION: UNBROKEN CHAIN—CONNECTING SEVEN DECADES OF AMERICAN SURVEILLANCE AND HARASSMENT OF PROGRESSIVES ACTIVISTS, VISIONARIES, AND INTELLECTUALS

1. Levin, "Revealed: FBI Investigated Civil Rights Group as 'Terrorism' Threat and Viewed KKK as Victims."
2. Ibid.
3. Ibid.
4. Ibid.
5. Klippenstein & Lichtblau, "FBI Seized Congressional Cellphone Records Related to Capitol Attack."
6. Price, *Threatening Anthropology.*
7. Gitlin. "What the Occupy Wall Street Crackdown Can Teach Us about NSA Spying."
8. PCFJ, "FBI Documents Reveal Secret Nationwide Occupy Monitoring"; Rights and Dissent, "The FBI and Occupy"; Michael & Moynihan, "F.B.I. Counterterrorism Agents Monitored Occupy Movement, Records Show."
9. Gitlin, "What the Occupy Wall Street Movement Can Teach Us about NSA Spying."
10. Isikoff, "Unaware of Tsarnaev Warnings."
11. Rights and Dissent, "The FBI and Occupy."
12. Price, "Extra-Constitutional Proceedings."
13. Gibbons, "Still Spying on Dissent," 1.
14. Ibid., 1.
15. Ibid., 23.
16. Ibid., 24–8.
17. Funk, "How Domestic Spying Tools Undermine Racial Justice Protests"; Morales & Ly, "Released NYPD Emails Show Extensive Surveillance of Black Lives Matter Protesters."
18. ACLU, "Stingray Tracking Devices: Who's Got Them?"
19. Cetnarsky, "Obey."
20. See Price, *Weaponizing Anthropology*; González, *American Counterinsurgency.*
21. Ascherson, "Don't Imagine You're Smarter."

Bibliography

Aberle, David. "Protest Is Not 'Close to Treason.'" *Oregon Daily Emerald* (January 14, 1966): 4.

——"Anthropology: Social Science or Defense Research." *Oregon Daily Emerald* (November 30, 1967): 6.

ACLU (American Civil Liberties Union). "ACLU Letter to the Senate Health, Education, Labor and Pensions Committee Expressing Academic Freedom Concerns re: H.R. 2077, the International Studies in Higher Education Act of 2003." www.aclu.org/FreeSpeech/FreeSpeech.cfm?ID=14952&c=42 2004u (accessed March 10, 2013).

——"Stingray Tracking Devices: Who's Got Them?" November 2018. www.aclu.org/issues/privacy-technology/surveillance-technologies/stingray-tracking-devices-whos-got-them (accessed April 3, 2021).

Addy, Sidney. *A Glossary of Words Used in the Neighborhood of Sheffield.* London: Vaduz, Kraus, 1888 [1965].

Afzal-Khan, F. "Unholy Alliances: Zionism, US Imperialism and Islamic Fundamentalism." *CounterPunch* (December 1, 2003). www.counterpunch.org/khan12012003.html (accessed May 14, 2013).

Agee, Philip. *Inside the Company: CIA Diary.* New York: Farrar, Straus & Giroux, 1975.

Aguilar, Alonso (trans. Asa Zatz). *Pan-Americanism from Monroe to the Present.* New York: Monthly Review Press, 1969.

Akhtar, Zia. "Pine Ridge Death, Mistrials, and FBI Counter Pol Operation." *Criminal Justice Studies* 24 no. 1 (March 2011): 57–82.

ALA. "Code of Ethics of the American Library Association." *American Library Association* (adopted June 28, 1997, amended January 22, 2008). www.ala.org/ala/issuesadvocacy/proethics/codeofethics/codeethics.cfm (accessed March 2, 2011).

Alarcon, Evelina. "Donald N. Wheeler, Communist, Dies at 89." *People's World* (November 22, 2002). www.peoplesworld.org/article/donald-n-wheeler-communist-dies-at-89/?fbclid=IwAR1-cajO9w7U5S3zRJoIXKx DiPuQHCLUN5j4rWPnwq3M7nIQhR8Tka3HCZE (accessed March 22, 2021).

Altheide, David L. *Terrorism and the Politics of Fear.* Walnut Creek, CA: AltaMira Press, 2006.

Appy, Christine. *Cold War Constructions.* Amherst: University of Massachusetts Press, 2000.

Asad, Talal, ed. *Anthropology and the Colonial Encounter.* London: Ithaca Press, 1973.

Ascherson, Neal. "Don't Imagine You're Smarter." *London Review of Books* 40, no. 14 (July 19, 2018): 23–4.

Bamford, James. *Puzzle Palace: Inside the National Security Agency, America's Most Secret Intelligence Agency.* New York: Penguin, 1982.

——*Body of Secrets.* New York: Doubleday, 2001.

Barclay, Harold. *People Without Government: An Anthropology of Anarchy.* London: Kahn & Averill, 1990.

Barnett, Richard J. "The Terrorism Trap." *The Nation* (December 2, 1996): 18–21.

Benedict, Ruth and Gene Weltfish. *The Races of Mankind.* New York: Public Affairs Committee, 1943.

Berner, Richard C. *Seattle in the Twentieth Century. Vol. 2: Seattle 1921–1940: From Boom to Bust.* Seattle: Charles Press, 1991.

Bernstein, Carl. *Loyalties: A Son's Memoire.* New York: Touchstone, 1989.

Berryhill, Alex. "FBI Ordered to Pay UC Berkeley Alumnus $470,000." October 24, 2012. www.dailycal.org/2012/10/24/fbi-ordered-to-pay-uc-berkeley-alumnus-470000/ (accessed January 2, 2021).

Blackmer, Donald M. *The MIT Center for International Studies.* Cambridge, MA: MIT Press, 2002.

Bloom, Samuel W. "The Intellectual in a Time of Crisis: The Case of Bernhard J. Stern, 1894–1956." *Journal of the History of the Behavioral Sciences* 26 (1990): 17–37.

Brace, C. Loring. "Review of The Bell Curve." *Current Anthropology* 37 (S 1996): 156–61.

Breindel, Eric M. "A Controversy Renewed." *The Harvard Crimson* (March 12, 1974). www.thecrimson.com/article/1974/3/12/a-controversy-renewed-pbtbhe-rosenberg-case/?print=1 (accessed January 19, 2020).

Buckley, William F. Jr. "Howard Hunt, R.I.P." *National Review* (January 26, 2007). http://nrd.nationalreview.com/article/?q=MDYzM2MyMDIwMjRiN WZlY2RlZjc3ZDY4YjAxMjBiM2Q (accessed February 13, 2017).

Buhle, Mari Jo. "Ruth Fulton Benedict." In *The American Radical*, edited by Mari Jo Buhle, Paul Buhle and Harvey J. Kaye, 251–63. New York: Routledge, 1994.

Caffrey, Margaret M. *Ruth Benedict: Stranger in This Land.* Austin: University of Texas Press, 1989.

Cassidy, Peter. "Silent Coup in Cyberspace." *Covert Action Quarterly* 52 (1995): 54–60.

Cetnarski, Paul. "Obey. On the Flooding Surveillance in Times of Shrinking Privacy. "An Interview with Anthropologist David H. Price." *Future Urbanism* (Winter 2014): 2014–15. https://futureurbanism.com/interview/obey-on-the-flooding-surveillance-in-times-of-shrinking-privacy/ (accessed March 9, 2021).

Chomsky, Noam. "A Quick Reaction." *CounterPunch* (September 12, 2001). www.counterpunch.org/chomskybomb.html (accessed April 15, 2019).

Choudry, Aziz, ed. *Activists and the Surveillance State: Learning from Repression*. London: Pluto Press, 2019.

Chrisafis, Angelique and Sam Jones. "Snowden Leaks: France Summons US Envoy over NSA Surveillance Claims." *Guardian* (October 21, 2013): A1.

Churchill, Ward, and Jim Vander Wall. *The COINTELPRO Papers*. Boston, MA: South End Press, 1990.

CIRA (Committee on International Relations in Anthropology). *International Directory of Anthropologists*. Washington, DC: CIRA, 1950.

Cockburn, Alexander "Redwood Summer and the Fate of the Panthers." *The Nation* (July 2, 1990).

——"The Hunt for the Smoking Gun." In *End Times: The Death of the Fourth Estate*, edited by Alexander Cockburn and Jeffrey St. Clair, 343–6. Petrolia: CounterPunch Books.

——"Farewell to Our Greatest President: Adieu, Gerald Ford." *CounterPunch* (December 27, 2006). www.counterpunch.org/2006/12/27/farewell-to-our-greatest-president/ (accessed July 12, 2019).

——"How to Not Spot a Terrorist: From Phrenology to Data Mining." *CounterPunch* (February 11–13, 2006). www.counterpunch.org/2006/02/11/how-not-to-spot-a-terrorist/ (accessed November 13, 2019).

——"The FBI and Edward Said." *The Nation* (January 12, 2006): 9.

Colangelo, Philip. "The Secret FISA Court: Rubber Stamping on Rights." *Covert Action Quarterly* 53 (1995): 43–9.

Coleman, McAlister. "Cat's-paws for Fat Boys." *The Nation* 168 (May 28, 1949): 622–5.

Conde, David W. *CIA—Core of the Cancer*. Tokyo: Entente, 1970.

Coop, Graham, Michael B. Eisen, Rasmus Nielsen, et al. "Letters: A Troublesome Inheritance." *New York Times* (August 8, 2014).

Coulter, Ann. *Treason: Liberal Treachery from the Cold War to the War on Terrorism*. New York: Crown Forum, 2003.

D'Souza, Radha. "The Surveillance State: A Composition in Four Movements." In *Activists and the Surveillance State*, 23–52. London: Pluto Press, 2019.

Da Globo. "NSA Documents Show United States Spied Brazilian Oil Giant." *Da Globo* (September 9, 2013). https://g1.globo.com/fantastico/noticia/2013/09/nsa-documents-show-united-states-spied-brazilian-oil-giant.html (accessed March 29, 2022).

Dash, Samuel, Robert Knowlton and Richard Schwartz. 1959. *The Eavesdroppers*. New Brunswick, NJ: Rutgers University Press.

Davidson, Paul. "Buying a Home? Sellers May Use Cameras, Microphones to Spy on House Hunters." *USA Today* (April 30, 2018). www.usatoday.com/story/money/2018/04/30/home-sellers-spying-home-buyers/553818002/ (accessed May 16, 2020).

DeLillo, Don. *Underground*. New York: Simon & Schuster, 1997.

Diamond, Sigmund. *Compromised Campus: The Collaboration of Universities with the Intelligence Community, 1945–1955*. New York: Oxford University Press, 1992.

Dick, Philip K. *The Minority Report*. London: Millennium, 2000.

DoJ (United States Department of Justice). *Sourcebook of Criminal Justice Statistics*. Washington, DC: U.S. Deptartment of Justice, Bureau of Justice Statistics, 1994.

Dreyfuss, Robert. "The Cops Are Watching You." *The Nation* (May 16, 2002).

Dube, Arindrajit, Ethan Kaplan, and Suresh Naidu. "Coups, Corporations, and Classified Information." *Quarterly Journal of Economics* 126, no. 3 (2011): 1375–409.

Edwardson, Mickie. "James Lawrence Fly, the FBI, and Wiretapping." *The Historian* 61, no. 2 (1999): 361–81.

Electronic Privacy Information Center. "Foreign Intelligence Surveillance Act Court Orders, 1979–2012." *Electronic Privacy Information Center Report* (2012). http://epic.org/privacy/wiretap/stats/fisa_stats.html (accessed June 12, 2013).

Elias, Christopher. "A Lavender Reading of J. Edgar Hoover." *Slate* (September 2, 2015). www.slate.com/blogs/outward/2015/09/02/how_collier_s_suggested_j_edgar_hoover_was_gay_back_in_1933.html (accessed September 3, 2015).

Engels, Frederick. *Origins of the Family, Private Property, and the State*. New York: International Publishers, 1884 [1972].

Epstein, Jason. "The CIA and the Intellectuals." *New York Review of Books* (April 20, 1967): 16–21.

Felt, Mark. *The FBI Pyramid from the Inside*. New York: Putnam, 1979.

First, Ruth. *South West Africa*. Baltimore: Penguin Books, 1963.

Fischer, Claude S. *America Calling: A Social History of the Telephone to 1940*. Berkeley: University of California Press, 1992.

Frank, André Gunder. "The Development of Underdevelopment." *Monthly Review* 18 (1966): 17–31.

——*Capitalism and Underdevelopment in Latin America: Historical Studies of Chile and Brazil*. New York: Monthly Review Press, 1967.

——*Latin America: Underdevelopment or Revolution: Essays on the Development of Underdevelopment and the Immediate Enemy*. New York: Monthly Review Press, 1969.

——*On Capitalist Underdevelopment*. New York: Oxford University Press, 1975.

——*ReOrient: Global Economy in the Asian Age*. Berkeley: University of California Press, 1998.

Frederick, Timothy. *Albert F. Canwell: An Oral History*. Olympia, WA: Office of the Secretary of State, 1997.

Funder, Anna. *Stasiland*. London: Granta. 2004.

Fung, Brian. "Darrell Issa: James Clapper Lied to Congress about NSA and Should Be Fired." *Washington Post* blog (January 27, 2014). http://washingtonpost.com/blogs (accessed January 30, 2014).

Funk, Allie. "How Domestic Spying Tools Undermine Racial Justice Protests." *Freedom House* (June 22, 2020). https://freedomhouse.org/article/how-domestic-spying-tools-undermine-racial-justice-protests (accessed March 29, 2022).

Gaddis, John Lewis. *The United States and the End of the Cold War.* New York: Oxford University Press, 1992.

Gall, Carlotta, and James Glanz. "U.S. Promotes Network to Foil Digital Spying." *New York Times* (April 20, 2014).

Garcia, Maria. "Rebel Citizens and Filmmakers: An Interview with Haskell Wexler and Pamela Yates." *Cineaste* (Spring 2016): 24–30.

Geary, Daniel. *Radical Ambition: E. Wright Mills, the Left, and American Social Thought.* Berkeley: University of California Press, 2009.

Gibbons, Chip. "Still Spying on Dissent: The Enduring Problem of FBI First Amendment Abuse." *Rights and Dissent Special Report* (2009). https://rightsanddissent.org/wp-content/uploads/2020/03/Still-Spying-on-Dissent.pdf (accessed February 29, 2021).

Giroux, Henry. "Public Intellectuals Against the Neoliberal University." In *Qualitative Inquiry Outside the Academy*, edited by Norman K. Denzin and Michael D. Gairdina, 35–60. Walnut Creek, CA: Left Coast Press, 2013.

Gentry, Curt. *J. Edgar Hoover: The Man and the Secrets.* New York: Norton, 2001.

Gillmor, Daniel S., ed. *Speaking of Peace: An Edited Report of the Cultural and Scientific Conference for World Peace, New York, March 25, 26 & 27, 1949.* New York: National Council of the Arts, Sciences and Professionals, 1949.

Gitlin, Todd. "What the Occupy Wall Street Crackdown Can Teach Us about NSA Spying." *Mother Jones* (June 27, 2013). www.motherjones.com/politics/2013/06/nsa-spying-occupy-homeland-security/ (accessed 3March 29, 2022).

Glüsing, Jens, Laura Poitras, Marcel Rosenbach, and Holger Stark "Fresh Leak on US Spying: NSA Accessed Mexican President's Email." *Spiegel* (October 20, 2013). http://spiegel.de (accessed December 13, 2013).

González, Roberto. *American Counterinsurgency: Human Science and the Human Terrain.* Chicago: Prickly Paradigm Press, 2009.

——*War Virtually: The Quest to Automate Conflict, Militarize Data, and Predict the Future.* Berkeley: University of California Press, 2022.

Gough, Kathleen. "Anthropology and Imperialism." *Monthly Review* (April 1968): 12–27.

Greenwald, Glen. "NSA Prism Program Taps in to User Data of Apple, Google and Others." *Guardian* (June 6, 2013). www.guardian.co.uk/world/2013/jun/06/us-tech-giants-nsa-data (accessed July 12, 2013).

——2013. "Edward Snowden: The Whistleblower behind the NSA Surveillance Revelations." *Guardian* (June 9, 2013). www.guardian.co.uk/world/2013/jun/09/edward-snowden-nsa-whistleblower-surveillance (accessed July 12, 2013).

Hager, Nicky. *Secret Power: New Zealand's Role in the International Spy Network*. Nelson, NZ: Craig Potton Publishing, 1996.

Haines, Gerald K. and David A. Langbart. *Unlocking the Files of the FBI: A Guide to Its Records and Classification System*. Wilmington, DE: Scholarly Resources Inc., 1993.

Haley, Fred. "Our Schools Can Do What We Want Them to Do." *Washington Education* (April 1961).

Harding, Timothy. "Remembering Saul Landau." *NACLA Report on the Americas* 46.4 (2013): 13–15.

Hayden, Tom. "Saul Landau, R.I.P." (2013). http://tomhayden.com/home/saul-landau-rip.html (accessed September 26, 2014).

Healy, Kieran. "Fuck Nuance." Unpublished manuscript (2015). http://kieranhealy.org/files/papers/fuck-nuance.pdf (accessed September 2, 2015).

Herrnstein, Richard J. and Charles Murray. *The Bell Curve: Intelligence and Class Structure in American Life*. New York: Free Press, 1994.

Hochman, Brian. "Eavesdropping in the Age of *The Evesdroppers*; or, the Bug in the Martini Olive." *Post45* (February 3, 2016). https://post45.org/2016/02/eavesdropping-in-the-age-of-the-eavesdroppers-or-the-bug-in-the-martini-olive/ (accessed June 27, 2021).

Hook, Sidney. "Dr. Hook Protests." *The Nation* 168 (April 30, 1949): 311.

——"What Shall Be Done about Communist Teachers?" *Saturday Evening Post* (September 10, 1949).

Hudson, John. "After Multiple Denials, CIA Admits to Snooping on Noam Chomsky." *Foreign Policy* (August 13, 2013). http://foreignpolicy.com/2013/08/13/exclusive-after-multiple-denials-cia-admits-to-snooping-on-noam-chomsky/ (accessed April 2, 2016).

Independent Online 2000. "Ruth First: Williamson Given Amnesty." *Independent Online* (June 1, 2000). www.iol.co.za/news/south-africa/ruth-first-williamson-given-amnesty-39251 (accessed April 2, 2022).

ISA (International Sociological Association). "International Sociological Association Presidents." (2012). www.isa-sociology.org/about/presidents/isa-president-thomas-bottomore.htm (accessed December 17, 2012).

Isikoff, Michael. "Unaware of Tsarnaev Warnings, Boston Counterterror Unit Tracked Protesters." NBC News (May 9, 2013).

Johnson, David Cay. "Agreement Is Reached on Air-Passenger Data." *New York Times* (January 4, 2004).

Jones, Sam. "US Spies Engaged in Industrial Espionage Will Be Jailed, Says Lawmaker." *Financial Times* (January 31, 2014). www.ft.com/

content/33001728-8a9b-11e3-ba54-00144feab7de (accessed March 29, 2022).

Kafka, Franz. *The Trial*. London: Secker & Warburg, 1945.

Kelley, Clarence, with James K. Davis. *Kelley: The Story of an FBI Director*. Kansas City, MO: Andrews, McMeel & Parker, 1987.

King, Warren. "Tacoma's Fred Haley, Civil Rights Advocate and Candy Maker, Dies." *Seattle Times* (April 17, 2005).

Kirchheimer, Otto. *Political Justice*. Princeton: Princeton University Press, 1961.

Kirchwey, Freda. "Battle of the Waldorf." *The Nation* 168 (April 2, 1949): 377–8.

Klippenstein, Ken and Eric Lichtblau. "FBI Seized Congressional Cellphone Records Related to Capitol Attack." *The Intercept* (February 22, 2021). https://theintercept.com/2021/02/22/capitol-riot-fbi-cellphone-records/?utm_medium=email&utm_source=The%20Intercept%20Newsletter (accessed February 25, 2021).

Kurosawa, Akira. *Something Like an Autobiography*. New York: Vintage, 1983.

Kurtz, Stanley. "Anti-Americanism in the Classroom: The Scandal of Title VI." *National Review Online* (May 16, 2002). www.freerepublic.com/focus/news/684182/posts (accessed March 29, 2022).

——"Studying Title VI." *National Review Online* (June 16, 2003). www.nationalreview.com/articles/207236/studying-title-vi/stanley-kurtz#.

Landau, Saul. "C. Wright Mills: The Last Six Months." *Ramparts* (August 1965): 45–54.

——"From the Labor Youth League to the Cuban Revolution." In *History and the New Left: Madison, Wisconsin, 1950–1970*, edited by Paul Buhle, 107–12. Philadelphia: Temple University Press, 1990.

——"The People's Cinematographer—Haskell Wexler." *The Progressive* (April 1998).

Lapsley, Phil. *Exploding the Phone: The Untold Story of the Teenagers and Outlaws Who Hacked Ma Bell*. New York: Grove Press, 2013.

Larsen, Otto. *Milestones and Millstones: Social Science at the National Science Foundation*. New Brunswick: Transaction Books, 1992.

Lee, Chisun. "The NYPD Wants to Watch You: Nation's Largest Law Enforcement Agency Vies for Total Spying Power." *Village Voice* (December 18–24, 2002).

Lee, Laurie Thomas. "Watch Your Email! Employee E-mail Monitoring and Privacy Law in the Age of the 'Electronic Sweatshop.'" *The John Marshall Law Review* 28 (1994):139–62.

Lee, Wen-Yee, Elizabeth McCauley, and Mark Abadi. "Taiwan Used Police Surveillance, Government Tracking, and $33,000 Fine to Contain Its Coronavirus Outbreak." *Business Insider* (June 4, 2020). www.businessinsider.com/taiwan-coronavirus-surveillance-masks-china-2020-6 (accessed March 29, 2022).

Lenin, Vladimir. *Imperialism, The Highest State of Capitalism*. New York: International Press, 1939.

Levin, Matthew. *Cold War University: Madison and the New Left in the Sixties*. Madison: University of Wisconsin Press, 2013.

Levin, Sam. "Revealed: FBI Investigated Civil Rights Group as 'Terrorism' Threat and Viewed KKK as Victims." *Guardian* (February 1, 2019). www.theguardian.com/us-news/2019/feb/01/sacramento-rally-fbi-kkk-domestic-terrorism-california (accessed July 8, 2020).

Lewis, Randolph. *Emile de Antonio: Radical Filmmaker in Cold War America*. Madison: University of Wisconsin Press, 2000.

Lienhardt, Godfrey, Dennis Duerden, John Nagenda, and Lewis Nkosi. "The Oral Tradition." *New Africa* (July 1966): 124–5.

Life Magazine. "Red Visitors Cause Rumpus." *Life* 26 no. 14 (April 4, 1949): 39–43.

Littlefield, Alice and Martha C. Knack, eds. *Native Americans and Wage Labor: Ethnohistorical Perspectives*. Norman: University of Oklahoma Press, 1996.

López, Ricardo Téllez Girón and Luis Vázquez León, eds. *Palerm en sus propias palabras: las entrevistas al Dr. Ángel Palerm Vich realizadas por Marisol Alonso en 1979*. Puebla: Benemérita Universidad Autónoma de Puebla, 2013.

Lutz, Catherine. "The Military Normal." In *Counter-Counterinsurgency Manual*, edited by The Network of Concerned Anthropologists, 23–37. Chicago: Prickly Paradigm Press, 2009.

Lynn, Adam. "Candy Magnate Championed Civil Rights." *Tacoma News Tribune* (April 6, 2005). www.unknownnews.org/0504120407FredHaley.html (accessed September 13, 2017).

Mader, Julius. *Who's Who in the CIA*. Berlin: W 66 Mauerstrasse 69, 1968.

Magden, Ronald. "The Schuddakopf Case, 1954–1958: Tacoma Public Schools and Anticommunism." *Pacific Northwest Quarterly* 89 no. 1 (1997): 4–11.

Mailer, Norman. *Harlot's Ghost*. New York: Ballantine, 1991.

Marchetti, Victor. *The CIA and the Cult of Intelligence*. New York: Alfred Knopf, 1974.

Marks, Jonathan. "The Genes Made Us Do It: The New Pseudoscience of Racial Difference." *In These Times* (May 12, 2014). http://inthesetimes.com/article/16674/the_genes_made_us_do_it (accessed Feburary 3, 2021).

Marshall, Margaret. "Notes by the Way." *The Nation* 168 (April 9, 1949): 419–20.

Martin, Douglas. "Joybubbles, 58, Peter Pan of Phone Hackers, Dies." *New York Times* (August 20, 2007).

Matthiessen, Peter. *In the Spirit of Crazy Horse*. New York: Viking, 1983.

Mazzetti, Mark and Jonathan Weisman. "Conflict Erupts in Public Rebuke on CIA." *New York Times* (March 11, 2014).

Mellen, Joan. *Hellman and Hammett*. New York: HarperCollins, 1996.

Melman, Seymour. *Inspection for Disarmament*. New York: Columbia University Press, 1958.

——*Our Depleted Society*. New York: Holt, 1967.

——*The Permanent War Economy*. New York: Simon & Schuster, 1974.

Michael, J.G. "Weaponizing Anthropology, the CIA and Publishing, with David Price." *Parallax Views Podcast* (February 1, 2021). https://podcastaddict.com/episode/118568141 (accessed March 29, 2022).

Michael S. Schmidt and Colin Moynihan, "F.B.I. Counterterrorism Agents Monitored Occupy Movement, Records Show." *New York Times* (December 24, 2012).

Miller, Arthur. *Timebends: A Life*. New York: Grove Press, 1987.

Millikan, Max M. and Walt W. Rostow. "Notes on Foreign Policy." In *Universities and Empire*, edited by Christopher Simpson, 39–56. New York: New Press, 1954 [1998].

Mills, Ami Chen. *CIA Off Campus*. Second Edition. Boston, MA: South End Press, 1991.

Mitgang, Herbert. *Dangerous Dossiers: Exposing the Secret War Against America's Greatest Authors*. New York: Random House, 1998.

Monthly Review. "Notes from the Editors." *Monthly Review* 57(2) (2005): 1.

Moore, John H., ed. *The Political Economy of North American Indians*. Norman: University of Oklahoma Press, 1993.

Morales, Mark and Laura Ly. "Released NYPD Emails Show Extensive Surveillance of Black Lives Matter Protesters." CNN (January 18, 2019). www.cnn.com/2019/01/18/us/nypd-black-lives-matter-surveillance (accessed February 14, 2021).

Murphy, Walter. *Wiretapping on Trial: A Case Study in the Judicial Process*. New York: Random House, 1965.

Nader, Laura. "The Vertical Slice: Hierarchies and Children." In *Hierarchy & Society: Anthropological Perspectives on Bureaucracy*, edited by Gerald M. Britan and Ronald Cohen, 31–42. Philadelphia: Institute for the Study of Human Issues, 1980.

New York Times. "Five Spurn Inquiry into Bank Bombing." *New York Times* (June 8, 1971): A23.

National Review. "Did CIA Take the Senate?" *National Review* (February 2, 1957): 103.

New Yorker. "Talk of the Town." *The New Yorker* (April 2, 1949): 23–6.

Nixon, Ron. "U.S. Postal Service Logging All Mail for Law Enforcement." *New York Times* (July 2, 2013).

NRDC. "Natural Resources Defense Council Table of US Nuclear Warheads, 1945–2002." (2010). www.nrdc.org/nuclear/nudb/datab9.asp (accessed November 23, 2010).

O'Connor, Tom. "News Tailored to Fit." *The Nation* 168 (April 16, 1949): 438–40.

Obama, Barack. "Remarks by the President to the United Nations General Assembly." (November 23, 2010). https://obamawhitehouse.archives.gov/the-press-office/2010/09/23/remarks-president-united-nations-general-assembly (assessed April 20, 2021).

Patterson, John. "Haskell Wexler, the Genius Cinematographer Committed to the Left." *Guardian* (December 28, 2015). www.theguardian.com/film/2015/dec/28/haskell-wexler-the-genius-cinematographer-committed-to-the-left (accessed August 14, 2017).

PCFJ (Partnership for Civil Justice Fund). "FBI Documents Reveal Secret Nationwide Occupy Monitoring." (2016). www.justiceonline.org/fbi_files_ows (accessed April 2, 2021).

Peace, William J. *Leslie A. White: Evolution and Revolution in Anthropology.* Lawrence: University of Kansas Press, 2004.

Perkins, John. *Confessions of an Economic Hitman.* San Francisco: Berrett-Koehler, 2004.

Phinney, Archie. *Nez Percé Texts.* New York: Columbia University Press, 1934.

Pinker, Steven. *Rationality.* New York: Penguin, 2021.

Powers, Richard. *Secrecy and Power: The Life of J. Edgar Hoover.* New York: Free Press, 1987.

Price, David H. "Fear and Loathing in the Soviet Union: Roy Barton and the NKVD." *History of Anthropology Newsletter* XXVIII no. 2 (2001): 3–8.

——"Interlopers and Invited Guests: On Anthropology's Witting and Unwitting Links to Intelligence Agencies." *Anthropology Today* 18 no. 2 (2002): 16–21.

——"Subtle Means and Enticing Carrots: The Impact of Funding on American Cold War Anthropology. " *Critique of Anthropology* 23 no. 4 (2003): 373–401.

——"Outcome-Based Tyranny: Teaching Compliance While Testing Like a State." *Anthropological Quarterly* 76 no. 4 (2003): 715–30.

——*Threatening Anthropology: The FBI's Surveillance and Repression of Activist Anthropologists.* Durham, NC: Duke University Press, 2004.

——"Academia under Attack: Sketches for a New Blacklist." In *Anthropologists in the Public Sphere: Speaking Out on War, Peace, and American Power,* edited by Roberto González, 243–6. Austin: University of Texas Press, 2004.

——*Anthropological Intelligence: The Deployment and Neglect of American Anthropology in the Second World War.* Durham, NC: Duke University Press, 2008.

——"Using the Freedom of Information Act as an Anthropological Tool." *Society for Applied Anthropology News* 21 no. 3 (2010): 28–30.

——*Weaponizing Anthropology: Social Science in Service of the Militarized State.* Oakland, CA: AK Press/CounterPunch Books, 2011.

——"Uninvited Guests: A Short History of the CIA on Campus." In *The CIA on Campus: Essays on Academic Freedom and the National Security State*, edited by Philip Zwerling, 33–60. Jefferson, NC: McFarland Publishing, 2011.

——"Extra-Constitutional Proceedings." *Committee Against Political Repression* (August 28, 2012). https://nopoliticalrepression.wordpress.com/2012/08/28/david-price-extra-constitutional-proceedings/ (accessed September 11, 2015).

——"The NSA, CIA, and the Promise of Industrial Espionage." *CounterPunch* (January 28, 2014).

——*Cold War Anthropology: The CIA, the Pentagon, and the Rise of Dual Use Anthropology*. Durham, NC: Duke University Press, 2016.

——"Counter-Lineages within the History of Anthropology: On Disciplinary Ancestors' Activism." *Anthropology Today* 35 no. 1 (2019): 12–16.

——"David W. Conde: Lost CIA Critic and Cold War Seer." *CounterPunch* 26 no. 1 (2019): 21–6.

Price, David H. and William J. Peace. "Un-American Anthropological Thought: The Opler-Meggers Exchange." *Journal of Anthropological Research* 59 no. 2 (2003): 183–203.

Puig, Andrés Fábregas. *Angel Palerm Vich*. El Colegio de Jalisco. 1997.

Pynchon, Thomas. *Bleeding Edge*. New York: Penguin, 2013.

Ramasastry, Anita. "FISA's Secret Court: An End Run around the 4th Amendment." *CounterPunch* (December 4, 2002). www.counterpunch.org/anita1204.html (accessed July 1, 2006).

Ramji-Nogales, Jaya. "A Global Approach to Secret Evidence: How Human Rights Law Can Reform Our Immigration System." *Columbia Human Rights Law Review* 39 (2008): 456–521.

Rights and Dissent. "The FBI and Occupy: The Surveillance and Suppression of Occupy Wall Street." (2007). https://rightsanddissent.org/news/the-fbi-and-occupy-the-surveillance-and-suppression-of-occupy-wall-street/ (accessed February 19, 2021).

Risen, James. "Ex-Spy Alleges Bush White House Sought to Discredit Critic." *New York Times* (June 15, 2011).

Risen, James and Laura Poitras. "Spying by NSA Ally Entangled US Law Firm." *New York Times* (February 15, 2014).

Robins, Nathalie. *Alien Ink: The FBI's War on Freedom of Expression*. New York: William Morrow, 1992.

Rockefeller, Nelson (Chair). *Commission on CIA Activities within the United States*. Washington, DC: Government Printing Office, 1975.

Rosenbaum, Ron. "Secrets of the Little Blue Box." *Esquire* (October 1971): 171–226.

——"The Most Hated Lawyer in America." *Vanity Fair* (March 1992): 68–94.

Rostow, Walt W. "Marx Was a City Boy: or Why Communism May Fail." *Harpers* (February 1955): 25–30.

——*Stages of Economic Growth: A Non-Communist Manifesto*. Cambridge: Cambridge University Press, 1960.

Rushton, Philippe Race, *Evolution and Behavior*. New Brunswick: Transaction Books, 1995.

Russon, Gabrielle. "Despite 9/11, House Lacks Its Own Quick Succession Law." *Chicago Tribune* (November 23, 2007). http://articles.chicagotribune.com/2007-11-23/newSs/0711210732_1_continuity-white-house-terrorist (accessed May 8, 2011).

Sahlins, Marshall. "What Is Anthropological Enlightenment? Some Lessons of the Twentieth Century." In *Culture in Practice: Selected Essays*, 501–26. New York: Zone Books, 2000.

Salisbury, Harrison E. "The Strange Correspondence of Morris Ernst and John Edgar Hoover, 1939-1964." *The Nation* December 1, 1984, 575–89.

Sanger, David E. and Nicole Perlroth. "NSA Breached Chinese Servers Seen as Security Threat," *New York Times* (March 22, 2014).

Sanger, David E., Nicole Perlroth, and Julian E. Barnes. "As Understanding of Russian Hacking Grows, So Does Alarm." *New York Times* (January 2, 2021).

Satisky, Jacques. "Interview with Seymour Melman." (May 17 1989). www.youtube.com/watch?v=V6s1sANWSKU (accessed March 12, 2014).

Saunders, Frances Stoner. *The Cultural Cold War: The CIA and the World of Arts and Letters*. New York: New Press, 2000.

Scates, Shelby. "Cold Warrior: Albert Canwell Is Still Alive, Still Living in Spokane, and Still Hates Commies." *Law and Politics* (February–March 2000): 12–15.

Schneier, Bruce. "Don't Listen to Google and Facebook: The Public-Private Surveillance Partnership Is Still Going Strong," *Atlantic* (March 25, 2014).

Schneier, Bruce and David Banisar, eds. *The Electronic Privacy Papers*. New York: Wiley Computer Publishing, 1997.

Schnell, Jane. "Snapshots at Random." *Studies in Intelligence* 5 (1961): 17–23.

Schrecker, Ellen. *Many Are the Crimes: McCarthyism in America*. New York: Little, Brown, 1998.

Scott, James C. *Seeing Like a State: How Certain Schemes to Improve the Human Condition Have Failed*. New Haven: Yale University Press, 1998.

Sellars, Roy Wood, V.J. McGill, and Marvin Farber, eds. *Philosophy for the Future: The Quest of Modern Materialism*. New York: Macmillan, 1949.

Solomon, Norman. "If Obama Orders the CIA to Kill a U.S. Citizen, Amazon Will Be a Partner in Assassination." *AlterNet* (February 12, 2014). http://alternet.org (accessed March 9, 2014).

Spitzer, Steven. "Toward a Marxian Theory of Deviance." In *Criminal Behavior: Readings in Criminology*, edited by Dellos Kelly, 175–91. New York: Saint Martin's Press, 1980.

SPL (Seattle Public Library). "Interview with Fred Haley, #1." Seattle Public Librar (May 2, 1986). https://archive.org/details/spl_ds_fhaley_01_01 (accessed March 1, 2021).

——"Interview with Fred Haley, #2." (May 2, 1986). https://archive.org/details/spl_ds_fhaley_01_02 (accessed March 1, 2021).

——"Interview with Fred Haley, #3." (May 2, 1986). https://archive.org/details/spl_ds_fhaley_01_03 (accessed March 1, 2021).

SSRC (Social Science Research Council). "Surveillance and the 'New Normal' of Covid-19: Public Health, Data, and Justice." (2021). https://covid19research.ssrc.org/public-health-surveillance-and-human-rights-network/report/ (accessed March 29, 2022).

Stern, Sol. "A Short Account of International Student Politics and the Cold War with Particular Reference to the NSA, CIA, etc." *Ramparts* (March 1967): 29–38.

Stoddard, Theodore. *The Rising Tide of Color Against White*. New York: Scribners, 1920.

Stone, I.F. "Two Propositions for the Russians." In *Speaking of Peace*, edited by Daniel S. Gillmore, 105–6. New York: The National Council of the Arts Sciences and Professors, 1949.

Sullivan, Andrew. "Judges Set Precedent for Workplace Privacy." Reuters. (2000).

Sullivan, William C. *The Bureau: My Thirty Years in Hoover's FBI*. New York: Norton, 1979.

Summers, Anthony. *Official and Confidential: The Secret Life of J. Edgar Hoover*. New York: Putnam, 1993.

Sutin, Lawrence. *Divine Invasions: A Life of Philip K. Dick*. New York: Carol Publishing Group, 1989.

Swanepoel, Petrus Cornelius. *Really inside BOSS: A Tale of South Africa's Late Intelligence Service (And Something about the CIA)*. Derdepoortpark, South Africa: P.C. Swanepoel, 2007.

Swartz, Jon. "Consumers Are Souring on Web, Post-NSA, Survey Says." *USA Today* (April 3, 2014). www.usatoday.com/story/tech/2014/04/02/eset-survey-nsa-consumer-trust-in-the-web/7164519/ (accessed June 18, 2015).

Swearingen, M. Wesley. *FBI Secrets: An Agent's Exposé*. Boston, MA: South End Press, 1995.

Takemae, Eiji. *Inside GHQ: The Allied Occupation of Japan and Ots Legacy*. New York: Continuum, 2002.

Theoharis, Athan."The FBI and the American Legion Contact Program, 1940–1966." *Political Science Quarterly* 100, no. 2 (1985): 271–86.

——*From the Secret Files of J. Edgar Hoover*. Chicago: Ivan R. Dee, 1991.

——*J. Edgar Hoover, Sex and Crime: An Historical Antidote*. Chicago: Ivan R. Dee, 1995.

——"A Brief History of the FBI's Role and Powers." In *The FBI: A Comprehensive Reference Guide*, edited by A. Theoharis, 1–43. Phoenix: Oryx Press, 1999.

Toner, Robin and Janet Elder. "Public Is Wary But Supportive on Rights Curbs." *New York Times* (December 13, 2001).

Townsend, Sylvia. "Haskell Wexler and the Making of 'One Flew Over the Cuckoo's Nest.'" *World Cinema Paradise* (December 19, 2014). http://worldcinemaparadise.com/2014/12/19/haskell-wexler-and-the-making-of-one-flew-over-the-cuckoos-nest/ (accessed January 3, 2015).

Tuchman, Mitch. "The Case of the Pirated Soundtrack." *Los Angeles Times* (September 6, 1981): 11.

Tucker, Eric and Hannah Fingerhut. "American Warier of US Government Surveillance: AP-NORC Poll." *Associated Press* (September 7, 2021). https://apnews.com/article/technology-afghanistan-race-and-ethnicity-racial-injustice-government-surveillance-d365f3a818bb9d096e8e3b5713f9f856 (accessed March 29, 2022).

Tucker, Ray. "Hist! Who's That?" *Collier's Weekly* 15 (August 19, 1933): 49–52.

Tyner, James A. and Chris Philo. *War, Violence and Population: Making the Body Count*. New York: Guilford Press, 2009.

U.S. Senate. "Institute of Pacific Relations Hearings." Senate Subcommittee to investigate the Administration of the Internal Security Act, Committee of the Judiciary. Part 1, July 25–August 5, 1951.

——"Hearings Before the Permanent Subcommittee on Investigations of the Committee on Government Operations." March 27, April 1 and 2, 1953. Washington, DC: Government Printing Office.

Vidal, Gore. "The National Security State." *The Nation* (June 4, 1988).

Vitak, Jessica and Michael Zimmer. "More Than Just Privacy: Using Contextual Integrity to Evaluate the Long-Term Risks from Covid-19 Surveillance Technologies." *Social Media and Society* (July 30, 2020). https://doi.org/10.1177/2056305120948250.

Vonnegut, Kurt. *God Bless You Mr Rosewater*. New York: Holt, Rinehart and Winston, 1965.

Wade, Nicholas. *A Troublesome Inheritance*. New York: Penguin, 2014.

Warren, Michael. "US Denies Visa to German Investigative Journalist." *Seattle Times* (April 12, 2011). http://seattletimes.com/html/nationworld/2014755119_apltargentinausvisadenied.html (accessed September 27, 2020).

Watts, Jonathan. "NSA Accused of Spying on Brazilian Oil Company Petrobras." *Guardian* (September 9, 2013). www.theguardian.com/world/2013/sep/09/nsa-spying-brazil-oil-petrobras (accessed December 7, 2013).

Webster, Stephen C. "FBI Destroyed Part of Hunter S. Thompson's File." *Raw Story* (October 9, 2012). www.rawstory.com/rs/2012/10/09/fbi-destroyed-part-of-hunter-s-thompsons-file/ (accessed November 19, 2020).

Weiner, Amir and Aigi Rahi-Tamm. "Getting to Know You: The Soviet Surveillance System, 1939–57." *Kritika Explorations in Russian and Eurasian History* 13 no. 1 (December 2012): 5–45.

Weiner, Tim. "The Cold War Is Over, But the Blacklist Still Guards U.S." *Philadelphia Inquirer* (June 9, 1991): A1.

Wells, Benjamin. "Serving Oil, Arabs, and the CIA," *New Republic* (July 25, 1975): 10.

Wells, Jeffrey. "A Look inside Hollywood and the Movies: Chicken or the Egg? Zippy or the Coneheads?" *Los Angeles Times* (July 18, 1993). http://articles.latimes.com/1993-07-18/entertainment/ca-14197_1_zippy (accessed November 11, 2015).

Weltfish, Gene. "Racialism, Colonialism and World Peace." In *Speaking of Peace*, edited by Daniel S. Gillmore, 72–7. New York: The National Council of the Arts Sciences and Professors, 1949.

Westin, David. "Our Double Standard of Privacy." *Time* (June 13, 2013). http://ideas.time.com/2013/06/13/our-double-standard-about-privacy/ (accessed February 27, 2014).

Wexler, Mark. *Tell Them Who You Are.* 2004 [Documentary film].

White, Leslie. *The Science of Culture.* New York: Grove Press, 1949.

Wieder, Alan. *Ruth First and Joe Slovo in the War Against Apartheid.* New York: Monthly Review Press, 2013.

Wiener, Jon. *Gimmie Some Truth: The John Lennon FBI Files.* Berkeley: University of California Press, 2000.

Wilford, Hugh. *The Mighty Wurlitzer: How the CIA Played America.* Cambridge, MA: Harvard University Press, 2008.

Willard, William. "American Anthropologists on the Neva: 1930–1940" *History of Anthropology Newsletter* 20 no. 1 (2000): 3–9.

William Kunstler: Disturbing the Universe [film]. Distributed by Arthouse Films. 2009.

Willing, Richard. "Poll: 4 in 10 Americans Don't Trust FBI." *USA Today* (June 20, 2001): A3.

Wolf, Eric B. "Angel Palerm Vich, 1917–1980." *American Anthropologist* 83 (1981): 612–15.

Woodward, Bob. *The Secret Man.* New York: Simon and Schuster, 2004.

Wright, Peter and Paul Greenglass. *Spycatcher.* New York: Penguin Viking, 1987.

Yates, Pamela. *Rebel Citizen.* New Day Films. 2015.

Yoder, Traci. *Breach of Privilege: Spying on Lawyers in the United States.* National Lawyers Guild Report, 2014.

Youdovin, Ira S. "$50 Million Suit Is Filed Against Mills." *Columbia Daily Spectator* 105, no. 63 (February 13, 1961): 1.

ARCHIVAL SOURCES

DWC   David W. Conde Papers, Special Collections, University of British Columbia.

DWCR David W. Conde Records, National Archives and Records Administration, St.Louis, Missouri.

MM   Margaret Mead Papers. Manuscript Division, Library of Congress, Washington, DC.

TAF   Papers of The Asia Foundation, The Hoover Institution, Stanford University.

Index

SAVAK, 3
Scalia, Antonin, 45
Schaap, William, 111–12, 315 n37
Schlesinger, Arthur, 75
Schoenman, Ralph, 157
Schrader, Paul, 175
Shostakovich, Dmitri, 75
Schuddakopf, Margaret Jean, 189–91
Schumer, Charles, 44
Seale, Bobby, 24
Second World War, 1, 38, 64, 71,
    107–8, 123, 140, 166, 184–92,
    202, 206, 212, 231
September 11, 2001, viii, 7, 8, 11, 27,
    30–2, 45–7, 50–1, 53, 83, 138,
    149, 151, 153, 158, 202, 252, 304
Shahn, Ben, 73
Shanghai Chinese People's Liberation
    Army's Unit 61398, 58
Shipley, Ruth, 20, 121
Slovo, Joe, 116
Smith, William French, 41–2
Snowden, Edward, 5, 12, 29–30, 35,
    46, 53, 56–9, 62, 63, 101, 302,
    303, 305
Soble, Jack, 108–9
Socialism, 18, 26, 63, 82, 96, 106, 115,
    126, 140, 150, 151, 153, 154, 190,
    226, 228, 233, 235, 237, 240, 243,
    248, 250, 251, 253, 269, 273, 275,
    276, 286, 293–4, 296
Socialist Workers Party, 151–2, 250
Solar Winds hack, 58
South Africa, 115–26
South Korea, 48–9
Soviet Union 4, 7, 17, 23, 39, 40, 63,
    74–6, 82, 85–7, 91, 94–5, 105,
    107, 117, 141–7, 162, 170, 186,
    193–4, 196, 203, 227–8, 234,
    240–1, 243, 255, 272–4, 278–9
Spanish Civil War, 167, 185–7, 253–5,
    260, 264, 269–71, 325 n12
    see also Abraham Lincoln Brigade
Spartacus, 73
Spitzer, Steven, 148
Spock, Benjamin, 143–4, 146

Stages of Economic Growth, 225, 229,
    232
Stalin, Joseph, 76, 166, 211, 228, 275
Stasi, 1, 3, 4, 8, 32, 63
Steinbeck, John, 153
Stern, Alfred, 170
Stern, Bernhard, 73, 81
Stern, Isaac, 73
Stewart, Lynne, 100
Stigma viii, 198, 313
Stingrays, 301
Stockwell, John, 161
Stone, I. F., 83
Students for a Democratic Society,
    111, 143, 172
Studies on the Left, 277
Styron, William 161
Sullivan, William, 21–4, 38, 233, 315
    n1
Sutherland, Donald, 171
Swanepoel, Petrus, 116–20
Swearingen, M. Wesley, 22, 174, 275,
    315 n1.
Sweezy, Paul, 77, 284–5

The Lives of Others, 1–2
Tacoma School Board, 189–92, 194–5
Taiwan, 48–9, 205
Taylor, Maxwell, 234–5
Terkel, Studs, 73, 166
Theoharis, Athan, 20, 22, 24
Thompson, Hunter S., 150
Thompson, Roger, 232
Tolson, Clyde, 22–4, 28, 99, 218
Total Information Awareness, 46
Trotskyites, 105, 151–2, 279
Trout, Kilgore, 200–1, 222–3
Trudeau, Arthur S. 228–9
Truman, Harry, 153, 189, 236, 270
Trump, Donald, 2, 46, 48–9, 295

Unit 8200, 58
United Nations, 80, 122, 241, 250,
    323 n1
University of California, Berkeley, 160,
    166, 284
University of Chicago, 240, 244–5

Thanks to our Patreon subscribers:

Andrew Perry
Ciaran Kane

Who have shown generosity and comradeship in support of our publishing.